Turning Defenders into Defendants

This book documents the mobilisation of law to retaliate against, intimidate, and even punish environmental defenders in Southeast Asia. It draws on case studies from Indonesia, Thailand, and the Philippines, which have taken measures to provide legal protection to environmental defenders by adopting anti-SLAPP provisions. Despite these provisions, attacks utilising legal means against environmental defenders have persisted. Environmental activists and local communities defending their livelihoods and the environment against the encroachment of extractive industries and state-backed development projects are turned into defendants before the courts. The book explains (1) the nature of legal attacks on environmental defenders in Southeast Asia, (2) the consequences of these attacks on environmental movements in those countries, and (3) the responses of environmental movements in navigating the existing politico-legal structures to resist these attacks and their strategies to strengthen the protection of environmental defenders in the region.

Agung Wardana is an associate professor at Universitas Gadjah Mada, Indonesia. He was awarded an Alexander von Humboldt Fellowship to undertake research at the Max Planck Institute for Comparative Public Law and International Law, Germany (2021–2024). He is the author of *Contemporary Bali: Contested Space and Governance* (Palgrave Macmillan, 2019).

Transnational Environmental Law

TEL

Transnational Environmental Law (TEL) is a series of books for the study of environmental law and governance beyond the state. It approaches legal and regulatory developments with an interest in the contribution of non-state actors and an awareness of the multi-level governance context in which contemporary environmental law unfolds. TEL has a broad disciplinary focus open to scholarly contributions covering a wide range of environmental issues and the evolving dynamics between environmental law and other legal disciplines. TEL strives for a new generation of environmental scholarship that will bridge geographical boundaries, scholarly styles and generations.

BOOKS IN THE SERIES

Roger Merino, *Governing International Commons: From Polycentric to Plurinational Governance in the Amazon*

Annika Frosch, *Navigating the Souring Seas: The Global Experimentalist Governance of Ocean Acidification*

Agung Wardana, *Turning Defenders into Defendants: The Use of Lawfare against Environmental Activists in Southeast Asia*

Turning Defenders into Defendants

The Use of Lawfare against Environmental Activists in Southeast Asia

Agung Wardana

Universitas Gadjah Mada

CAMBRIDGE
UNIVERSITY PRESS

CAMBRIDGE
UNIVERSITY PRESS

Shaftesbury Road, Cambridge CB2 8EA, United Kingdom

One Liberty Plaza, 20th Floor, New York, NY 10006, USA

477 Williamstown Road, Port Melbourne, VIC 3207, Australia

314–321, 3rd Floor, Plot 3, Splendor Forum, Jasola District Centre, New Delhi – 110025, India

103 Penang Road, #05–06/07, Visioncrest Commercial, Singapore 238467

Cambridge University Press is part of Cambridge University Press & Assessment, a department of the University of Cambridge.

We share the University's mission to contribute to society through the pursuit of education, learning and research at the highest international levels of excellence.

www.cambridge.org
Information on this title: www.cambridge.org/9781009676649

DOI: 10.1017/9781009676670

When citing this work, please include a reference to the DOI 10.1017/9781009676670

First published 2026

A catalogue record for this publication is available from the British Library

A Cataloging-in-Publication data record for this book is available from the Library of Congress

ISBN 978-1-009-67664-9 Hardback

CONTENTS

FIGURES

TABLES

SERIES EDITORS' PREFACE

Fifteen years ago, the journal *Transnational Environmental Law* (*TEL*) was launched. Over the past decade and a half, the field of transnational environmental law, together with the journal *TEL*, has developed from an emerging and somewhat unknown quantity into a conceptually diverse and dynamically developing scholarly community. The rapid evolution of this field has sadly been mirrored by profound environmental and political changes during this time. *TEL* was created with a sense of cautious optimism, ambition for innovation, and hope for new and improved climate change governance. New governance actors and regulatory instruments were being championed, and there was growing public awareness of the climate crisis and broader environmental challenges, such as biodiversity, fostering political will to address these pressing concerns. TEL scholarship underlines the crucial role of governance beyond the state and the parallel importance of environmental multilateral leadership.

The creation of the *Transnational Environmental Law Book Series* builds on the success of the journal *TEL* in supporting this field of research and its contributors. As the journal, the *TEL Book Series* will cover important developments related to the regulation of environmental impacts beyond the state. It recognises the increasing roles of non-state and sub-state actors in contemporary environmental law, as well as their continued interaction with state actors and international organisations. While (transnational) environmental law is at the core of these developments, other areas of law (e.g., international trade, finance, investment, human rights, labour, taxation, and commercial law) are increasingly implicated in the regulation of environmental impacts due to the growing awareness, and urgency, of the need to include environmental considerations in all areas of legal scholarship and practice. The series will therefore be open to a wide range of legal disciplines and will welcome innovative and interdisciplinary methods in problem definition and analysis.

The launch of the *TEL Book Series*, in many ways, continues the mission of the journal, seeking to provide a platform for pathbreaking conceptual innovation in environmental law and governance, and aiming to be specifically inclusive of the voices of traditionally underrepresented actors. However, while from a scholarly and editorial perspective, the past fifteen years may be considered a success – with the field of TEL growing into increasing maturity and breadth, and *TEL* having become a leading environmental law journal worldwide – the environmental realities on the ground provide a stark contrast with these achievements. The continuation of *TEL*'s mission thus comes from a place of continuous resolve rather than cautious optimism: resolve to ensure that the regulatory innovations piloted and critiqued by TEL scholarship will result in tangible environmental improvements, and to continue to inventory the causes and effects of the critical ecological tipping points at which we find ourselves.

Against this backdrop, we are especially proud to present the first volume in the *TEL Book Series*. Agung Wardana's contribution provides compelling and rare insights into environmentalism in Southeast Asia, a region that is home to incredible environmental riches whose management comes at great (personal) cost to environmental defenders. Understandably, the physical attacks that these environmental defenders have been subject to, which in some cases have culminated in murder, have received broad attention in scholarship and media. Less attention has been given to the increasing examples of the law being used as a deterrent by silencing, intimidating, or even criminalising environmental defenders, for example through the use of Strategic Lawsuits Against Public Participation (SLAPP). Wardana coins the concept of 'hegemonic environmental lawfare' as the framework against which to analyse such strategies of mobilising law (both civil and criminal) by the powerful actors (both private and public) to maintain the status quo and to turn environmental defenders into legal defendants.

The precarious legal position of environmental defenders is a topic that falls squarely within TEL's scope, even if in this case the geographical focus of the book is limited to three countries – Indonesia, Thailand, and the Philippines. Agung Wardana is in a strong, if not unique, position to comment on this situation, both theoretically and empirically. The findings of these Southeast Asian case studies provide lessons learned that hold relevance for TEL at a global scale. We are delighted to inaugurate the *TEL Book Series* with this important contribution.

Thijs Etty
Josephine van Zeben
Series Editors,
Transnational Environmental Law Book Series

GLOSSARY

ABRI	Angkatan Bersenjata Republik Indonesia/Indonesian Military Forces
AIEL	Asian Institute for Environmental Law
APNED	Asia Pacific Network of Environmental Defenders
ASEAN	Association of Southeast Asian Nations
CARP	Comprehensive Agrarian Reform Program
CIFOR	Center for International Forestry Research
CPP-NPA	Communist Party of the Philippines – New People's Army
RSPO	Roundtable Sustainable Palm Oil
MP3EI	Master Plan for Acceleration and Expansion of Indonesia's Economic Development
TEMCO	Thailand Exploration and Mining Corporation
MNRE	Ministry of Natural Resources and Environment – Thailand
EIA	Environmental Impact Assessment
CSR	Corporate Social Responsibility
DENR	Department of Environment and Natural Resources
ECNEQ	Enhancement and Conservation of National Environmental Quality
EHRD	Environmental Human Rights Defenders
EPM	Environmental Protection and Management
FPIC	Free Prior Informed Consent
KKCRN	Khao Khuha Community Rights Network
KRBKG	Khon Rak Ban Kerd Group
NCPO	National Council for Peace and Order
OHCHR	Office of the United Nations High Commissioner of Human Rights
PNNI	Palawan NGO Network, Inc
SLAPP	Strategic Lawsuit against Public Participation
UNECE	United Nations Economic Commission for Europe
WALHI	Wahana Lingkungan Hidup Indonesia/Friends of the Earth Indonesia

ACKNOWLEDGEMENTS

This book is derived from my postdoctoral fellowship entitled 'The Risk in Protecting the Environment: A Southeast Asian Perspective', which was generously funded by the Alexander von Humboldt Foundation at the Max Planck Institute for Comparative Public Law and International Law (MPIL), Heidelberg, Germany (August 2021–July 2024). As a Global South scholar, I was privileged to have the opportunity to spend three years conducting research at one of the world's best research institutes for legal studies situated in Germany's most beautiful city. For this, I would like to express my greatest gratitude to the Alexander von Humboldt Foundation. Thanks to Judith Köster, who has been very helpful in bridging communication between the foundation and me. References from Carol Warren and the late Keebet von Benda-Beckmann were essential to make my fellowship application successful. At the institute, I thank Anne Peters as academic mentor, Team Peters (among others: Tom Spark, Julia Emsteva, Angelo Jr Golia, Shio Min, and Christian Schulteiss), and a highly professional service from the MPIL's administrative and library staff.

This book would not have existed without the kind support of many people across the region. I am also especially indebted to Chenny Wongkar as research assistant and Sutharee Wannasiri and Asia Wy for helping me with the data collection in Thailand and the Philippines, respectively. In Indonesia, I thank the Faculty of Law, Universitas Gadjah Mada, especially the Dean and Vice Deans, for permitting me to extend my fellowship and finish the book manuscript. Colleagues at the Faculty of Law have been very supportive and encouraging. During my fieldwork, I received support from Parid Ridwanuddin (WALHI/Friends of the Earth Indonesia), Venan (Sunspirit East Nusa Tenggara), Rynaldo Sembiring and Grita Anindarini (Indonesian Center for Environmental Law), Justice Nani Indrawati (Indonesian Supreme Court), and the Pari Island community (Bang Boby, Bang Eddy, Teh Aas, Bang Arif, and Bang Tono). Thanks also to Sekar Aji Banjaran, Haris Prabowo, and Afif Saputra (Greenpeace Indonesia) for the conversation and generosity in permitting me to use their photo as the cover for this book. In Thailand, I thank Puttanee Kangkun (Fortify Rights), Atty. Sor Rattanamane, and Thanaporn Nithiprit. In the Philippines, I would like to thank Dante Gatmaytan (University of the Philippines), Lia Mia Torres (Asia Pacific Network of Environmental Defenders), Rocky Guzman (Asian Research Institute for Environmental Law), and Atty. Grizelda Mayo-Anda and Atty. Bobby Chan. In Germany, I was very delighted to receive a warm welcome from Alethea and Bayu, teh Lulu and family (Frank and Jacob), Francis and family (Katia and Rafal), Gupta's family (Ayan, Aisya, and Atul), Michiko's family, Aghnia and Joscha as well as Annette Hornbacher and William Sach (Heidelberg University).

The generous comments and feedback I have received have been instrumental in improving the presentation and arguments of this book. I am deeply grateful to Carol Warren and Jim Warren (Murdoch University), Kaniska Jayasuriya (Murdoch University), Jely Galang (University of the Philippines Diliman), Chad Patrick Osorio (University of the Philippines Diliman), and Bencharat Chua (Mahidol University). The earlier draft of this book was presented on several occasions, such as at the Humboldt Network Meeting (Mainz University), the ASEAS UK Conference 2023, and the 2024 Summer School of Indonesian Environmental History (History Department, Universitas Gadjah Mada). I was particularly pleased to receive valuable inputs from Adriaan Bedner, Jacqueline Vel, Tody Sasmitha, and other researchers at the Van Vollenhoven Institute (VVI), Leiden University. I also want to extend my heartfelt thanks to my reading group: Dzaki, Nivia, Elang, Alfatani, Keke, Deka, and Rio for their insightful discussions and comments on the draft. Thanks to Oktaria Asmarani for reviewing the book proposal and Rebecca Meckelburg for working very hard in copy-editing the earlier draft of this book. The encouragement and professional support from Tobias Ginsberg, Matt Gallaway, and Gemma Smith, the editorial team of Cambridge University Press, and peer-reviewers have significantly improved the quality of my work. However, any remaining weaknesses in this book are solely mine.

Finally, I dedicate this book to my beloved family: Yogi, Kana, Bhanu, and Bumi. I am grateful for their love, happiness, spirit, and patience. They are a refuge for my soul to get through difficult times.

Introduction

Environmental movements have been playing an essential role in defending the environment and in the development of environmental law. In the US, Lazarus notes that the emergence of modern environmental movements in the 1960s contributed to the adoption of the 1969 National Environmental Policy Act, the 1970 Clean Air Act, and the 1972 Clean Water Act, as well as the establishment of the Environmental Protection Agency.[1] Across the Atlantic, in the UK, despite a hostile legal opportunity structure in the country, environmental movements have persistently resorted to the court to highlight the weaknesses of the existing legal system in protecting the environment and to improve access to justice within the system.[2] In Southeast Asian countries, innovations carried out by environmental lawyers and activists have pushed the normative boundaries of the legal framework to be responsive to the demands of environmental justice.[3] In Indonesia, for instance, a notable example of this is the recognition of legal standing for environmental NGOs in 1989 after the Indonesian Forum for the Environment (WALHI) brought a lawsuit on behalf of the environment against the government and the Inti Indorayon company.[4] In the Philippines, environmental and Indigenous peoples' rights organisations have played an instrumental role in crafting and defending the rights of Indigenous communities, notably in their relations to environmental and natural resources, through landmark legislation on the Indigenous Peoples' Act of

[1] Richard J. Lazarus, *The Making of Environmental Law* (University Chicago Press, 2004).

[2] Lisa Vanhala, 'Legal Opportunity Structures and the Paradox of Legal Mobilisation by the Environmental Movement in the UK', (2012) 46 (3) *Law and Society Review* 523.

[3] Agung Wardana, 'A Quest for Agency in the Anthropocene: Law and Environmental Movements in Southeast Asia', (2023) 32 (1) *Review of European, Comparative & International Environmental Law* 57.

[4] David Nicholson, *Environmental Dispute in Indonesia* (KITLV Press, 2009).

1997.[5] Thailand has demonstrated how massive anti-eucalyptus movements can shape national politics and forest governance.[6]

The centrality of environmental movements in environmental advocacy, however, has made them targets for parties whose interests are in conflict with this advocacy. Due to their work, environmental movement activists face diverse threats. The UN Special Rapporteur on the Situation of Human Rights Defenders states that globally, during 2015–16 alone, there were 450 attacks on human rights defenders working on environmental and land issues.[7] In 2015, for instance, Berta Caceres and Nelson Garcia from the Civic Council of Popular and Indigenous Organizations of Honduras were killed for protesting against dam development in the Gaulcarque River, a sacred river for Indigenous communities.[8] In Indonesia, the same year, Salim Kancil, a farmer who fought against sand mining in his village, was found dead on the street.[9] In 2017 alone, forty-eight Philippine environmental defenders died across the archipelago, including eight members of the Indigenous Taboli-manubo peoples, defending their rights against agribusiness at Lake Sabu.[10] Indeed, Global Witness reported that 2017 was 'the deadliest year on record' as 207 land and environmental defenders across the globe were murdered.[11]

Besides killings, environmental activists face increasing physical assaults, intimidation, and criminalisation. In 2019, María Alis Ramírez, a Colombian anti-extractive activist, left her country to take refuge in New Zealand due to various threats to her life and family.[12] In Cambodia, Doem Kundy and Hun Vannak, members of Mother Nature Cambodia, were sentenced to a year in prison for filming a boat suspected of conducting illegal sand dredging and exporting.[13] Three other activists of Mother Nature Cambodia – Sun Ratha, Ly Chandaravuth, and Yim Leanghy – were sentenced to five to ten years in jail for 'conspiracy and insulting the monarchy' after documenting a polluted river close to the Royal

[5] Wolfram Dressler, 'A Window into the "Everyday" Struggles of Environmental Defenders in Palawan Island, the Philippines', (2021) 22 (1) *Policy Matters* 17.

[6] Sophie Lewis and Janette Bulkan, 'The Political Logics of EU-FLEGT in Thailand's Multistakeholder Negotiation: Hegemony and Resistance', (2022) 29 *Journal of Political Ecology* 384.

[7] UN General Assembly, 'Report of the Special Rapporteur on the Situation of Human Rights Defenders A/72/150' (2017) <http://undocs.org/en/A/72/170> accessed on 23 March 2018.

[8] ibid.

[9] Global Witness, *On Dangerous Ground: 2015's Deadly Environment: The Killing and Criminalization of Land and Environmental Defenders Worldwide* (Global Witness, 2015).

[10] Global Witness, *Their Faces: Defenders on the Frontline* (Global Witness, 2019) <www.globalwitness.org/en/campaigns/environmental-activists/their-faces-defenders-frontline/?accessible=true#> accessed 19 July 2019.

[11] Global Witness, *At What Cost? Irresponsible Business and the Murder of Land and Environmental Defenders in 2017* (Global Witness, 2018) 8.

[12] Laila Vergara, 'Alis Ramírez: A Defender of the Colombian Amazon Now Living as Refugee in New Zealand', *Mongabay* (8 April 2024) <https://news.mongabay.com/2024/04/alis-ramirez-the-defender-of-the-colombian-amazon-now-living-as-a-refugee-in-new-zealand/> accessed 12 April 2024.

[13] Syme de Leon, *Defending in Numbers: Resistance in the Face of Repression* (Asian Forum for Human Rights and Development/FORUM-ASIA, 2019).

Palace.[14] In Vietnam, Hoang Thi Minh Hong, a prominent environmental activist from the Center of Hands-on Action and Networking for Growth and Environment (CHANGE), was convicted of tax evasion and sentenced to three years in prison. The CHANGE had campaigned against the wildlife trade before it was shut down in 2022 following the government's increased pressure on environmental organisations.[15] Previously, in the same year, Nguy Thi Khanh, a Vietnamese environmental advocate and winner of the internationally prestigious Goldman Prize for environmental activists, had been found guilty of tax evasion and imprisoned for two years.[16] Despite denying that the tax evasion case was related to her anti-coal activism, the government has weaponised this vague tax law to silence her and four other environmental activists who were considered 'threats to authority'.[17]

Indeed, this phenomenon of legal attacks on environmental activists is not an exclusive feature of the Global South. In the Global North, environmental activists are increasingly under pressure from governments and companies, making it a transnational phenomenon. In the UK, Stephen Gingell, a climate activist of Just Stop Oil, was imprisoned for six months after being accused of 'interference with key national infrastructure' during a slow march protest in London.[18] He was the first protester charged by the newly enacted Public Order Act 2023, which 'brings in criminal offences and proper penalties for selfish, guerrilla protest tactics'.[19] Human Rights Watch reported that in Australia, new anti-protest laws have been enacted in Victoria and Tasmania to 'invoke harsh penalties for non-violent protest', which has led to 'disproportionately punishing climate protesters in violation of their basic rights to peaceful protest'.[20] Similarly, in the US, 21 states have enacted 'critical infrastructure' protection acts to impose criminal sanctions aimed at preventing environmental activists from staging protests by trespassing or

[14] Carolyn Cowan, 'Rights Groups Demand End to Cambodia's Persecution of Green Activists', *Mongabay* (23 June 2021) <https://news.mongabay.com/2021/06/rights-groups-demand-end-to-cambodias-persecution-of-green-activists/> accessed 12 April 2024.

[15] Isabel Esterman, 'Vietnamese Environmentalist Sentenced to 3 Years in Prison for Tax Evasion', *Mongabay* (28 September 2023). <https://news.mongabay.com/2023/09/vietnamese-environmentalist-sentenced-to-3-years-in-prison-for-tax-evasion/> accessed 12 April 2023.

[16] Isabel Esterman, 'Worries and Whispers in Vietnam's NGO Community after Activist's Sentencing', *Mongabay* (19 July 2022) <https://news.mongabay.com/2022/07/worries-and-whispers-in-vietnams-ngo-community-after-activists-sentencing/> accessed 12 April 2024.

[17] ibid.; Esterman (n 15).

[18] Damien Gayle, 'Just Stop Oil Activist Jailed for Six Months for Taking Part in Slow March', *The Guardian* (15 December 2023). <www.theguardian.com/environment/2023/dec/15/just-stop-oil-activist-is-first-to-be-jailed-under-new-uk-protest-law> accessed 12 April 2024.

[19] Nina Lakhani, Damien Gayle, and Matthew Taylor, 'How Criminalisation Is Being Used to Silence Climate Activists Across the World', *The Guardian* (12 October 2023) <www.theguardian.com/environment/2023/oct/12/how-criminalisation-is-being-used-to-silence-climate-activists-across-the-world> accessed 12 April 2024.

[20] Human Rights Watch, 'Australia Climate Protesters' Rights Violated: Disproportionate Punishments, Excessive Bail Conditions', *Human Rights Watch* (22 June 2022) <www.hrw.org/news/2022/06/22/australia-climate-protesters-rights-violated> accessed 12 April 2024.

entering 'critical infrastructure' facilities, which include natural gas stations and storage, petroleum refineries, and pipelines.[21] Gordon notes that 'these laws both target environmental activists and further tether corporate fossil fuel interests as "critical" or compulsory to the functioning of the nation state'.[22] Meanwhile, Germany declared *Letzte Generation* to be a criminal organisation and launched an investigation against the organisation.

While the vulnerability of environmental activists to physical threat has been a serious concern, the use of law to intimidate environmental defenders has been more widespread and its impacts should not be underestimated. Many countries have taken necessary steps to protect environmental defenders from legal intimidation. The Council of Europe, for instance, issued Recommendation CM/Rec (2024) 2 of the Committee of Ministers to Member States on Countering the Use of Strategic Lawsuits against Public Participation (SLAPPs). The recommendation urges its member states to ensure that 'their national legal systems and their implementation provide a comprehensive legal framework and coherent set of structural and procedural safeguards to prevent and minimise the harmful effects of SLAPPs, as well as a full set of remedies and support measures for the harms caused by SLAPPs'.[23]

In Southeast Asia, three countries have taken legal measures to date (Table I.1). In the Philippines, anti-SLAPP provisions have been inserted in several environment-related legislations, including the Clean Water Act and the Ecological Solid Waste Management Act. In addition, the Philippines Supreme Court has enacted Rules of Procedure for Environmental Cases to incorporate anti-SLAPP provisions within the legal system. Meanwhile, in Indonesia, after a long debate, an anti-SLAPP provision was finally adopted in Article 66 of the 2009 Environmental Protection and Management (EPM) Act. This was followed by the issuance of the Indonesian Supreme Court's Chief Justice Directive No. 36 of 2013 concerning Guidance for the Handling of Environmental Cases, which explicitly includes guidance for judges on dealing with SLAPP cases. In Thailand, Section 21 of the Public Prosecution Institution and Public Prosecutors Act, B.E. 2553 (A.D., 2010) was amended to provide authority for the public prosecutor to drop cases which lacked public interest. This was then followed by the revision of the Criminal Procedure Code in Thailand to prevent human rights defenders from SLAPP action by enacting Articles 161/1 and 165/2.[24]

[21] Nina Lakhani (n 19).

[22] Constance Gordon, 'Criminalising Care: Environmental Justice under Political and Police Repression', (2024) 18 (1–2) *Environmental Communication* 138, 140.

[23] Council of Europe, Recommendation CM/Rec (2024) 2 of the Committee of Ministers to Member States on Countering the Use of Strategic Lawsuits against Public Participation (SLAPPs), 6.

[24] Article 161/1 of the Criminal Code states that '[i]n the case of a private complainant if it appears to the court – or through examination of evidence called at trial – that the complainant has filed the lawsuit in bad faith or distorted facts in order to harass or take undue advantage of a defendant, or to procure any advantage to which the complainant is not rightfully entitled, the court shall order dismissal and forbid the complainant to refile such case again'.

Table I.1 Anti-SLAPP provisions in Indonesia, Thailand, and the Philippines

Indonesia	Thailand	The Philippines
The 2009 Environmental Protection and Management Act Article 66: '[a]ny person who fights for the rights to a good and healthy environment should not be charged through criminal proceedings or sued through civil proceedings'. Elucidation of Article 66: '[t]he provision is intended to protect victims and/or the reporting parties adopting legal means for environmental pollution and/or damage. The protection is intended to prevent acts of retaliation from the reported parties through criminal and/or civil offences in accordance with the independence of the judiciary body'.	In the context of criminal defamation, Sections 161/1 and 165/2 of the Criminal Procedure Code state: 'The prosecution in bad faith under paragraph one shall include the intentional action of the plaintiff.' Section 21 of the Public Prosecution Institution and Public Prosecutors Act, B.E. 2553 (A.D., 2010): 'Should a public prosecutor find that the institution of a criminal case would not be in the interest of the public and would have an effect on the safety and security of the Nation or an important benefit of the Country, he shall submit the matter to the Attorney General, and the Attorney General shall have the power to order that the institution of the case be withheld.'	The 2010 Rules of Procedure for Environmental Cases, Rule 6: (SLAPP), defines '[a] legal action filed to harass, vex, exert undue pressure or stifle any legal recourse that any person, institution or the government has taken or may take in the enforcement of environmental laws, protection of the environment or assertion of environmental rights shall be treated as a SLAPP and shall be governed by these Rules'. It shall be dismissed.

Chapter 3 examines in detail how the adoption of anti-SLAPP provisions in these countries should not be understood as a conscious policy to protect the exercise of civil and political rights. In fact, the adoption of these provisions has been the outcome of contestation in law-making processes involving civil society organisations and pressures from international organisations, especially the UN, human rights organisations, and mass media. From the government viewpoint, the adoption of such provisions might secure a certain measure of legitimacy by being seen to be responsive to public demands and international recommendations. However, as a resource-extractive economy remains central to national development and existing political regime structures, attacks on environmental defenders remain an alarming threat to environmental advocacy in those countries – despite the adoption of anti-SLAPP provisions.[25]

[25] In the Philippines, nine members of the Didipio Earth Savers Multipurpose Association (DESAMA) were accused of illegal forest occupation, although the court finally dismissed the case. In Thailand, sixteen

At the time of writing (2024), Daniel Tangkilisan, an Indonesian environmental activist, was sentenced to seven months in prison by the District Court of Jepara for making an online speech that 'caused unrest' as he protested against illegal shrimp farms that polluted Karimunjawa Marine Park.[26] A couple of months previously, Jonila Castro and Jhed Tamano, two Philipino youth environmental activists who were assisting local communities in resisting the reclamation of Manila Bay, were 'abducted' by military forces who accused them of being communist community organisers.[27] This persistent phenomenon demonstrates the disturbingly minimal effect of the anti-SLAPP provisions in these countries. These laws do not prevent attacks on environmental defenders, nor do they protect defenders in the legal process when they are turned into defendants.

This book examines the phenomenon in Southeast Asia of environmental defenders facing criminal or civil cases brought against them. It analyses who are legally intimidated, in what contexts, and the implications for environmental movements in the region. The book documents the mobilisation of law to silence, intimidate, and even punish environmental defenders in Southeast Asia. It draws on the experiences of the three countries (Indonesia, Thailand, and the Philippines) in the region that have taken measures to provide legal protection to environmental defenders by adopting anti-SLAPP provisions. Despite these provisions, legal actions against environmental defenders have persisted. In these countries, environmental activists and local communities defending their livelihoods and the environment against the encroachment of extractive industries and state-backed development projects are turned into defendants before the courts. The book explains (1) the nature of legal attacks on environmental defenders in Southeast Asia, by focusing on Indonesia, Thailand, and the Philippines; (2) the consequences of these attacks on environmental movements in those countries; and (3) the responses of environmental defenders and movements in navigating the existing politico-legal structures to resist these attacks utilising legal means and their strategies to strengthen the protection of environmental defenders.

members of the Thepa Anti-Coal Community were convicted for participating in a demonstration against constructing a coal power plant in Songkhla Province. In Indonesia, Budi Pego, a community organiser for protesting gold mining in Tumpang Pitu Mountain of East Java, was convicted for spreading communism when he led a demonstration in which a communist symbol appeared in one of the rally's banners. Under Indonesian law, spreading communism is considered a severe crime, and Budi Pego then was sentenced to four years in prison by the Supreme Court. See Legal Rights and Natural Resources Center, 'SLAPP Suit against Ifugaos in Didipio Dismissed', (2011) <http://cpcabrisbane.org/Kasama/2011/V25n3and4/Didipio.htm> accessed 19 July 2019; Della Syahni, 'Ada UU Menjamin, Mengapa Pejuang Lingkungan Tetap Dijerat Hukum?' *Mongabay Indonesia* (17 September 2018) <www.mongabay.co.id/2018/09/17/ada-uu-menjamin-mengapa-pejuang-lingkungan-tetap-terjerat-hukum/> accessed 21 May 2019.

[26] Basten Gokkon, 'Indonesian Court Jails Environmentalist for Flagging Illegal Farms in Marine Park', *Mongabay* (5 April 2024) <https://news-mongabay-com.cdn.ampproject.org/c/s/news.mongabay.com/2024/04/daniel-tangkilisan-karimunjawa-marin-national-park-indonesia-environmental-activist-jailed/amp/> accessed 12 April 2024.

[27] Gaea K. Cabico, 'Green Activists Say They Were Abducted by Military, Deny Surrender', *Philstar* (Manila, 19 September 2023) <www.philstar.com/headlines/2023/09/19/2297469/green-activists-say-there-were-abducted-military-deny-surrender> accessed 18 April 2024.

Methodological Matters

Methodologically, the book can be situated within the emerging literature on transnational environmental law, which 'embodies an *approach* to legal studies and practice' to understand how 'environmental law responds to the global nature of most of today's environmental problems'.[28] As this approach opens possibilities to reveal the role of actors, state and non-state actors, in generating legal norms, rules, and legal practices across national borders, this book pays particular attention to conflicts involving different actors in accessing and controlling the environment and its associated resources by mobilising law and legal institutions to advance their interests. In doing so, legal attacks on environmental defenders are seen as a transnational phenomenon for at least two reasons. First, it is a transnational legal practice exercised strategically by powerful business actors aiming at retaliating environmental defenders whose activism has managed to disrupt business-as-usual practices. It originated in the US under a strategic lawsuit against public participation (SLAPP) and has spread across jurisdictions, including in the Global South. Second, it is transnational in terms of how this phenomenon is conceived and responded to by social actors, including through the adoption of the US-inspired anti-SLAPP provisions within domestic legal systems and regional instruments once the domestic legal system appears to be inadequate to prevent those attacks increasingly involving transnational actors, such as transnational and multinational corporations, for example the Escazu Convention.

As suggested by Morgera, Parks, and Schroeder, a transnational environmental law phenomenon needs to be examined using a combination of three methodologies to expose its complexities and provide a more comprehensive understanding. These methodologies are comparative legal research, empirical legal research, and interdisciplinarity.[29] Accordingly, this book undertakes a comparative study between three Southeast Asian countries – Indonesia, Thailand, and the Philippines – to analyse anti-SLAPP provisions in environmental law and court decisions concerning SLAPP cases in those countries. In the latter context, it combines qualitative and quantitative analyses, enabling readers to understand the phenomenon, uncover the meaning and significance of human behaviour and experience, and explore the contexts where law and legal institutions are mobilised as a resource in environmental conflicts. It critically reviews the literature (scholarly studies, newspaper articles, archival collections, legal documents, and departmental reports) more broadly concerning environmental law, SLAPP, and environmental politics. Semi-structured interviews were conducted to gather data from key

[28] Veerle Heyvaert and Thijs Etty, 'Introducing Transnational Environmental Law', (2012) 1 (1) *Transnational Environmental Law* 1, 2–3.

[29] Elisa Morgera, Louisa Parks, and Mika Schroeder, 'Methodological Challenges of Transnational Environmental Law', in V. Heyvaert & L. Duvic-Paoli (eds.), *Research Handbook on Transnational Environmental Law* (Edward Elgar, 2020), 48–65.

informants representing the victims of legal intimidation and environmental and human rights organisations. Here, empirical findings were analysed from courts' case directories, NGOs' databases, news outlets, and reports from non-governmental and international organisations. Quantitatively, the book analyses 178 cases of attacks made against environmental defenders in these three countries during 2010–22. These attacks targeted 792 environmental defenders (13 per cent were women) with various backgrounds, including residents of affected communities, Indigenous peoples, environmental NGO activists, journalists, and expert witnesses. Although these case numbers are far from exhaustive, as many legal attacks are undetected due to the lack of available data, they are sufficient to expose the anatomy of legal attacks by the state and corporations against environmental defenders in the region concerning its geographies, sectors, modes of legal actions, and outcomes. As a transdisciplinary study, this book situates the phenomenon of legal attacks on environmental defenders within the broader structural contexts by borrowing theory and concepts from social sciences, especially political economy, criminology, and political ecology.

Legal Attacks on Environmental Defenders

The Liberal Stream and the Critical Stream

In the current literature, scholars have understood attacks on environmental defenders through legal means differently. In legal scholarship, especially on environmental law, Pring and Canan term this phenomenon SLAPP, developed from the US experience. The SLAPP is regarded as a threat to exercising the right to petition as guaranteed by the Petition Clause of the US Constitution.[30] In her comparative work on the US, Canada, and the UK, another legal scholar, Fiona Donson, prefers to use 'legal intimidation' to widen the basis of legal attacks to include the rights to freedom of expression.[31] Despite using different conceptual frameworks, Pring and Canan and Donson share an important feature in common in terms of the legal means mobilised to retaliate against environmental defenders in which they limit the means within the scope of civil procedures. Meanwhile, non-legal scholars tend to overemphasise 'criminalisation' or 'penalisation', in which they focus primarily on how powerful actors mobilise the criminal justice system to silence environmental movements and dissent.[32]

Categorised conceptually, this book identifies two different streams these studies fall within: the liberal stream and the critical stream. The liberal stream sees

[30] George W. Pring and Penelope Canan, *SLAPPs: Getting Sued for Speaking Out* (Temple University Press, 1996).

[31] Fiona Donson, *Legal Intimidation* (Free Association Press, 2000).

[32] Valeria Veigh Weis, *Criminalization of Activism: Historical, Present, and Future Perspectives* (Routledge, 2022); Anna Di Ronco, *Policing Environmental Protest: Power and Resistance in Pandemic*

environmental activism as the exercise of civil rights, such as the right to petition, the right to free speech, and the right to peaceful assembly. The exercise of these rights should not be prevented as everyone has equal opportunity to participate in responding to environmental issues; hence, when individuals are attacked or retaliated against for exercising their rights, such attacks should be considered a violation of rights. The terms 'SLAPP' and 'legal intimidation' exemplify the liberal stream because the understanding of retaliation through legal means against environmental defenders is built within the civil rights framework. The problems of this stream in capturing a diverse range of legal attacks, especially in the Global South, are threefold. First, it confines legal attacks involving two private actors: companies and defenders. The state is assumed to be a neutral institution in which such attacks should be addressed and resolved. This understanding contains a rights paradox. On the one hand, companies or private actors who claim to suffer reputation damage or economic losses justify their lawsuits against wrongdoers (including environmental activists) as an exercise of the right to remedy. On the other hand, environmental activists who campaign for the protection of the environment claim that they are exercising the right to petition or the right to freedom of expression, which should not be retaliated against by any means, including through strategic lawsuits. In this context of rights claims, following Marx, the postulate applies that when equal rights collide, power decides.[33] According to the liberal rule of law, the power to decide which right should prevail is the authority of the judiciary. If SLAPP lawsuits are perceived as a conflict of rights (the right to remedy and the right to freedom of expression), those lawsuits should be resolved by the court based on a 'proportionality test' or balancing test. Consequently, as SLAPP lawsuits are not aimed to win a case but to give chilling effects on environmental defenders,[34] the court's examination of the lawsuits will serve exactly the purpose to prolong and deepen those effects.

Second, the liberal stream reduces environmental struggles to a procedural matter of 'participating' in environmental matters. It ignores the fact that environmental struggles in the Global South are very often characterised as 'environmentalism of the poor',[35] a self-defence mechanism against the encroachment on resources on which livelihoods depend (see Chapter 2). Thus, the struggles of local communities to defend their sacred forests cannot be reduced to a case of exercising their rights to public participation once the government plans to convert the forest to plantation or mining activities. Rather, their struggles pose the question of their material and cultural existence that is signified by the forest. Respecting the rights to participate,

Times (Bristol University Press, 2023); Mary Menton and Philippe Billon, *Environmental Defenders: Deadly Struggles for Life and Territory* (Earthscan. 2021).

[33] Karl Marx, *Capital Volume I* (Penguin, 1976) 344.

[34] Pring and Canan (n 28); Byron Sheldrick, *Blocking Public Participation: The Use of Strategic Litigation to Silence Political Expression* (Wilfrid Laurier University Press, 2014).

[35] Joan Martinez-Alier, *The Environmentalism of the Poor: A Study of Ecological Conflicts and Valuation* (Edward Elgar, 2002).

petition, or freedom of expression by providing spaces for local communities to enjoy the forest or access decision-making processes does not equate to veto rights to stop the government or companies from converting the forest. It is often the case that mechanisms for public participation are designed in tokenistic ways to make resource appropriation by the state or corporations look legitimate and democratic.

Third, the liberal stream overlooks the underlying capitalist economic model in which continuous expansion and appropriation of resources for profit accumulation are essential to it, leading inevitably to environmental-related social conflicts. Under this model, the state is not a neutral institution, but it is the terrain through which power struggles to access or defend resources by different social actors and groups takes place. When dominant groups resort to law and legal institutions, due to structural asymmetries of power the legal battle is likely to serve the interest of the dominant group better, regardless of the outcome of the court decision. At the very least, the chilling effect on environmental defenders and their families should not be underestimated, as shown in Chapter 5.

In contrast to the liberal stream, the critical stream investigates empirically the structural context from which the use of law in environmental conflicts has emerged. Informed by critical criminology, non-legal scholars characterise the legal attacks on environmental defenders through the criminal justice system as 'criminalisation'. This criminalisation occurs at the primary level (categorising conducts that pose threats to the capitalist economic model as crimes in the criminal code) and at the secondary level (selective enforcement of the law by 'over'-criminalising dissent while 'under'-criminalising activities that potentially cause environmental harm).[36] Here, the critical stream does not assume the state and its legal embodiment, especially criminal law, as neutral institutions but as part of the machinery to maintain existing power structures in society.[37] Despite its important contribution to understanding of legal retaliation in environmental conflicts, current perspectives within the critical stream tend to be dominated by a narrow focus on the use of the criminal justice system to silence environmental defenders. Thus, they overlook the use of other legal procedures, including administrative law and civil procedures, that are used to attack environmental defenders, the chilling effects of which are no less harmful than those of criminal procedures although they appear more subtle. Incorporating civil and administrative procedures to the analysis is important in understanding the attack on environmental defenders comprehensively because those '[l]egal procedures', as Hirsch and Lazarus-Black put it, comparably 'contribute to the making of hegemony'.[38]

[36] Valeria Veigh Weis (ed.), *Criminalization of Activism: Historical, Present, and Future Perspectives* (Routledge, 2022).

[37] Richard Quinney, *Critique of Legal Order: Crime Control in Capitalist Society* (Routledge, 1974).

[38] Susan F. Hirsch and Mindie Lazarus-Black, 'Introduction/Performance and Paradox: Exploring Law's Role in Hegemony and Resistance', in M. Lazarus-Black & S. Hirsch (eds.), *Contested States: Law, Hegemony and Resistance* (Routledge, 2012) 10.

Hegemonic Environmental Lawfare

Maintaining the critical stream's essential elements to reveal the structural contexts through which legal attacks on environmental defenders are exercised while widening its scope to comprehensively capture a diverse range of legal procedures mobilised by the dominant groups against environmental defenders is also vital. This is the gap that this book aims to fill using a socio-legal study. For this purpose, it applies the social conflict approach of the Murdoch School, which embraces the view that institutions, including the state, are not autonomous and neutral entities insulated from society. Because 'they distribute power and resources, they are always fought over ... by social groups, seeking to entrench their preferences as policy, to empower themselves and/or their allies, and to direct resources towards favoured entities'.[39] Instead, institutions are contingent outcomes of 'struggles between socio-political forces, especially social classes and class fractions, and ethnic, religious, gendered and state-based groupings'.[40] In these struggles, those forces 'have different social, economic and political positions, resources and agendas' and form 'coalitions to advance and defend their interests'.[41]

In this understanding of the state, the law as the legal embodiment of the state should also be seen as neither an autonomous system of rules nor an instrument of the ruling elite but as an outcome of and terrain through which social conflicts are fought. In this regard, law plays a role in social conflicts by mobilising its coercive elements (imposing rules for the opponent group to comply with and punishing them when they fail to comply) and its hegemonic element (creating public consent in reproducing the necessary social conditions for capitalist production). In other words, the law in social conflicts should be understood as a form of 'lawfare' – a form of power struggles within the domain of the legal sphere. Indeed, traditionally, 'lawfare' is mainly used in relation to war and armed conflicts. However, in this book, I apply the conception of 'lawfare' through the anthropological lens introduced by Comaroff and Comaroff as 'the resort to legal instruments, to the violence inherent in the law, to commit acts of political coercion'.[42] In this regard, there are two forms of lawfare: (1) insurgency lawfare, which is the use of law to protect or defend rights and livelihoods (legal mobilisation by the powerless), and (2) hegemonic lawfare, referring to the use of law to maintain the hegemony of the powerholders (legal mobilisation by the powerful).

In the literature, Comaroff and Comaroff's conceptual framework of 'lawfare' has been used by several scholars. Zanin et al., for instance, analyse the mobilisation of law and legal institutions by the Bolsanaro regime to silence Lula da Silva in Brazil

[39] Shahar Hameiri and Lee Jones, 'Theorising Political Economy in Southeast Asia', T. Carroll, S. Hamieri, and L. Jones (eds.), *The Political Economy of Southeast Asia* (Palgrave Macmillan, 2020) 15.

[40] ibid. [41] ibid.

[42] John L. Comaroff and Jean Comaroff, 'Law and Disorder in the Postcolony: An Introduction', in J. Comaroff and J. L. Comaroff (eds.), *Law and Disorder* (University of Chicago Press, 2006) 30.

once it was in power.[43] Others, such as Zaffaroni et al. and Weis, examine the use of the criminal justice system to intimidate political opposition in the Global South.[44] This book follows the path of using 'lawfare' in a non-traditional sense, but innovates by applying 'lawfare' to the study of environmental conflicts involving actors with asymmetrical power relations: the state and corporations against environmental defenders. Through this framework, I demonstrate the strategic objectives of mobilising the law by powerful actors to maintain the status quo. In the context of legal attacks against environmental defenders, the concept of hegemonic environmental lawfare (HEL) is used to refer to the forms of legal recourse used by powerholders to maintain hegemony related to the environment, including resource extraction. Here, HEL is pursued through various legal mechanisms, including the civil and administrative law, and criminal procedures.

When the criminal justice system is mobilised by powerholders, there are three categories of events in which HEL may be exercised. The first category is principled criminal offences in which environmental defenders undertake a principled action which involves them committing a criminal conduct. In this case, the state through law enforcement agencies criminally prosecutes environmental defenders for intentionally breaking the criminal law as an act of disobedience. These actions may include committing eco-sabotage, an illegal act including trespassing, dismantling, or damaging targeted companies' or other parties' equipment, properties, or facilities while staging protests. The second category concerns trumped-up criminal charges when environmental defenders are criminally charged through the use of fabricated offences to justify their prosecution. For example, the defenders are accused of unlawfully possessing weapons, terrorism, insulting the monarchy, desecrating national symbols, or committing tax evasion. The third category is that HEL can result from an act of self-defence, where environmental defenders commit unlawful acts out of necessity (no other means), and their actions are proportionate (the harm caused by such behaviour should not be disproportionate to the social and environmental harm they struggle to avoid). An example of this is the Taryani and others case in West Java, Indonesia, in which environmental defenders were accused of assaulting a company's security guard in order to release a woman protester whom the guard strangled.[45] They were then charged with committing physical assault against the guard.

[43] Cristiano Zanin, Valeska Martins, and Rafael Valim, *Lawfare: Waging War through Law* (Routledge, 2022).

[44] Eugenio Zaffroni, Cristina Caamaño, and Valeria Vegh Weis, *Lawfare: The Criminalization of Democratic Politics in the Global South* (Brill, 2023); Valeria Vegh Weis, 'What Does Lawfare Mean in Latin America? A New Framework for Understanding for Criminalization of Progress Political Leaders', (2022) *Punishment & Society*. https://doi.org/10.11771/1462474521116348.

[45] Rahmawati, 'Mereka Yang Dipidana Karena Menolak PLTU Indramayu (1)', *Kompas* (Jakarta, 9 February 2020) <https://pemilu.kompas.com/read/2020/06/08/07370001/mereka-yang-dipidana-karena-menolak-pltu-indramayu-1> accessed 9 February 2022.

From Governance to Lawfare

This book is based on several simple propositions. In Southeast Asia, where the locus of power has been concentrated in few politico-business elites, the state–business relationship appears to be intimate, marked by historical junctures where capitalist classes emerged through the state's role as handmaiden to operate primarily in extractive industries, such as mining, logging, or plantations.[46] These classes have maintained their power and access to resources either by sponsoring politicians or running for public office themselves, making them relatively resilient to institutional changes. Extractive industries from which these classes derive their wealth operate on the basis of state concessions, licences, or contracts, and they also need to access the state's power to mobilise coercive and ideological apparatuses in maintaining a conducive climate for capital accumulation. Meanwhile, the state needs industries to collect state revenues, provide jobs, and pursue economic growth, from which its budgets for public services are derived and its legitimacy is underpinned. Thus, there is an inherent bias of the state towards these industries continuously expanding and accelerating their operations.[47] As a result, the quest for new spaces for resource extraction and state-backed development projects has routinely caused environmental conflicts involving the state, corporations, affected communities, and civil society organisations.

In their attempt to contain environmental conflicts, the state and corporations and their associated agents, collectively or individually, use diverse means to tame, co-opt, silence, intimidate, or retaliate against opponent groups. These means may take a wide range of forms from the most blatant strategy, such as murder or disappearance, to the most subtle, including participatory mechanisms such as corporate social responsibility (CSR), as demonstrated by Sinclair in the context of the mining industry.[48] The most blatant strategy may have immediate intimidating effects on the opponent groups in creating an atmosphere of fear. However, in the age of democracy, human rights, and the rule of law, resorting to this violent strategy as a long-term strategy may lead to a crisis of legitimacy both for corporations and the state. Meanwhile, employing more subtle means for containing environmental conflicts may pose less risk to the companies' legitimacy. However, those means may have fewer chilling effects to prevent opponent groups from continuing their struggles, because not all opponents are willing to submit themselves to a company's designated mechanisms to channel grievances.

Between the most blatant and the most subtle strategies lie laws and legal institutions that strategically may serve both coercive and hegemonic objectives

[46] Richard Higgott and Richard Robison (eds.), *Southeast Asia: Essays in the Political Economy of Structural Change* (Routledge, 1985); Richard Robison, *Indonesia: The Rise of Capital* (Equinox, 1986).

[47] Hameiri and Jones (n 39) 15.

[48] Lian Sinclair, *Undermining Resistance: The Governance of Participation by Multinational Mining Corporations* (Manchester University Press, 2024).

for the powerful classes. Here, laws and legal institutions, following Poulantzas's analysis of the state and its institutions,[49] should be seen as the outcome and the terrain where conflicts over power and resources are fought by the dominant class, class fractions, and oppressed groups. Laws and legal institutions can provide an empowering dimension as evidenced by 'legal mobilisation by the powerless' in which subaltern groups challenge dominant groups and the state utilising legal means.[50] In the context of legal retaliation, dominant groups may also resort to law, including the criminal justice system, to charge environmental defenders, claiming that their choice to resort to the law in resolving conflicts demonstrates their respect for the rule of law. Hence, resorting to lawfare is preferable if direct violence is no longer tolerable because this strategy lies somewhere between the most blatant means and the most subtle means encompassing two dimensions: the coercive element (creating the chilling effect) and the hegemonic element (creating consent to the status quo). In other words, once lawfare is pursued, it does not only intimidate environmental defenders but it also works to create conducive conditions to reproduce social relations for production and maintain the existing structures of power.

Through the HEL framework, arguments advanced in this book can be situated in both conceptual and empirical contexts. At the conceptual level, the book develops a new framework termed HEL for explaining legal actions against environmental defenders as a strategic means to contain environmental conflicts in society. Resorting to HEL should be seen as an attempt of powerholders to seek a more subtle means for controlling and restraining environmental movements with little risk of losing their legitimacy. The dominant view argues that legal actions against defenders, including SLAPP and criminalisation, misuse the legal procedure that occurs within an unreliable condition of the rule of law. In contrast to this view, these actions should be seen as a consequence of the neoliberal domination of the rule of law. Under this model, law and legal institutions are paradoxically depicted as independent – where judicial decision-making is based on due process and legal technocracy in the pursuit of logical coherency, but at the same time are instrumentalised to facilitate the market economy to flourish. Horwitz writes that the rule of law promotes 'procedural justice' that 'enables the shrewd, the calculating, and the wealthy to manipulate its forms to their own advantage'.[51] In other words, it provides a myth of equality before the law, which assumes an equal chance for both parties to win a legal battle. As will be demonstrated in the book, in countries where there is evidence of structural asymmetries of power, such as unequal relations of power and access to resources and uneven access to justice among social actors, the rule of law becomes an ideological underpinning for the state and powerful elites to

[49] Nicos Poulantzas, *State, Power, Socialism* (Verso, 2000).

[50] Michael McCann, 'Litigation and Legal Mobilisation', in K. Whittington, R. Kelemen, & G. Caldeira (eds.), *The Oxford Handbook of Law and Politics* (Oxford University Press, 2008) 534.

[51] Morton Horwitz, 'The Rule of Law: An Unqualifies Human Goods?' (1977) 86 *Yale Law Journal* 561, 566.

resort to the courts in order to retaliate against environmental struggles. As the trial will be facilitated by a perceived-to-be 'independent judiciary', by taking this strategy, they appear to restrain their power to some degree avoiding risks to their legitimacy further when resorting to coercion.

At the empirical level, the book contradicts the dominant analysis that emphasises the role of private actors as the agents who launch legal actions against environmental defenders. The experiences of Indonesia, Thailand, and the Philippines demonstrate the active role of the state in retaliating against environmental defenders. This is evidenced by the weaponisation of the criminal justice system to intimidate, silence, and even convict environmental defenders, mobilising crimes against public order or against state ideologies and symbols, as demonstrated in Chapter 4. In those crimes, the state has a monopoly on the interpretation on what constitutes threats to 'public order' and 'state ideology'. Accusing environmental defenders of committing these crimes can be understood as mobilising HEL to practise the politics of 'othering' activists as criminals, communists, or terrorists, which in turn aims at delegitimising environmental movements and undercutting popular support so that repression against them looks justifiable. This finding on the dominant role of the state in attacking environmental defenders through legal means is consistent with UNESCO's report concerning the safety of environmental journalists. The report found that most attacks on environmental journalists globally were conducted by state actors, such as the police, military forces, or local authorities, in which '[f]or every ten attacks in the data, state actors committed at least five'.[52] Specifically in Asia and the Pacific, it found that in 60 per cent of these attacks legal sanctions involved imprisonment.[53]

An Emerging Theme on Environmental Defenders

This book enriches emerging debates about environmental defenders that cuts across disciplinary boundaries, including environmental law, law and society, criminology, and political ecology literatures. In the contemporary literature on environmental law, few studies concern the use of law to silence environmental activists or defenders. As discussed in Chapter 1 the most cited text on the subject has been George W. Pring and Penelope Canan's *SLAPPs: Getting Sued for Speaking Out.*[54] Fiona Donson's work on this topic, entitled *Legal Intimidation*,[55] and a more recent book by Byron Sheldrick, *Blocking Public Participation: The Use of Strategic Litigation to Silence Political Expression*, extend on contemporary concerns within these debates.[56] Comparing the three books, however, it is evident that they conceive legal actions against defenders within the framework of rights – as an

[52] UNESCO, *Press and Planet in Danger: Safety for Environmental Journalists: Trends, Challenges and Recommendations* (UNESCO, 2024) 5.

[53] ibid., 11. [54] Pring and Canan (n 28). [55] Donson (n 29). [56] Sheldrick (n 32).

attack on an exercise of rights, especially the right to petition[57] and the right to freedom of assembly, association, and expression.[58] Hence, they tend to overlook the structural context in which the increasingly common strategy of powerholders resorting to courts to control environmental movements has emerged. Moreover, they exclusively focus on the experience of legal actions in the Global North.

Beyond legal scholarship, there are other studies that contribute different perspectives in their explorations of the issue. From a critical criminology perspective, Valeria Vegh Weis in her edited book entitled *Criminalisation of Activism: Historical, Present, and Future Perspectives* looks at the mobilisation of the criminal justice system against activists.[59] While several chapters include cases from the Global South,[60] the scope of the book itself deals with activism in general, rather than an exclusive focus on environmental activism. Mary Menton and Philippe Le Billon's edited book entitled *Environmental Defenders: Deadly Struggles for Life and Territory* focuses on environmental defenders, where modes of attack are predominantly through direct violence, such as murder and physical assault.[61] Di Ronco's *Policing Environmental Protest: Power and Resistance in Pandemic Times* limits its scope geographically and temporally to the policing of environmental resistance in Italy during the Covid-19 pandemic.[62] These studies focus their analysis on the mobilisation of the criminal justice system to attacks on environmental defenders, thus are not well-equipped to capture the use of other legal mechanisms, such as civil procedures that have been the focus of environmental law scholars in the Global North and administrative law procedures that are increasingly used by governments in the Global South.

In the literature on law and society, legal mobilisation has been one of the central themes. Legal mobilisation is understood to be 'the process by which individuals make claims about their legal rights and pursue lawsuits to defend or develop those rights'.[63] Studies on law and social movement have been dominated by studies of how law and legal institutions are mobilised by social forces, including environmental movements, to achieve progressive outcomes.[64] Luz Munoz and David

[57] Pring and Canan (n 28) [58] Donson (n 29); Sheldrick (n 32). [59] Valeria Vegh Weis (n 34).

[60] For examples: Gabriela Gusis and Rodrigo Videla, 'Social Protest and Punitive Treatment in Argentina: An Analysis from Latin America Critical Criminology', in V. Vegh Weis (ed.), *Criminalisation of Activism: Historical, Present, and Future Perspectives* (Routledge, 2022) 161–169; Paula Lacerda and Igor Rolemberg, 'Violence and Violations of Rights against Leaderships in the Brazilian Amazon', V. Vegh Weis (ed.), *Criminalisation of Activism: Historical, Present, and Future Perspectives* (Routledge, 2022) 170–179; Israel Toledo, Roxana Cavalcanti and Grace Souze, 'An Analysis of the Criminalisation of Socio-Environmental Activism and Resistance in Contemporary Latin America', V. Vegh Weis (ed.), *Criminalisation of Activism: Historical, Present, and Future Perspectives* (Routledge, 2022) 180–190.

[61] Mary Menton and Philippe Le Billon, *Environmental Defenders: Deadly Struggles for Life and Territory* (Earthscan, 2021).

[62] Anna Di Ronco, *Policing Environmental Protest: Power and Resistance in Pandemic Times* (Bristol University Press, 2023).

[63] Charles Epp, *The Rights Revolution: Lawyers, Activists, and Supreme Courts in Comparative Perspective* (University of Chicago Press, 1998) 18.

[64] Vanhala (n 2); Lisa Vanhala, 'Legal Mobilisation under Neo-Corporatist Governance: Environmental NGOs before the Conseil d'Etat in France, 1975-2010' (2016) 4 (1) *Journal of Law and Courts* 103–130; Rachel Cichowski, *The European Court and Civil Society: Litigation, Mobilisation and Governance*

Moya take the example of Spanish environmental organisations and examine how 'subnational courts have become important venues for legal mobilisations by NGOs, in parallel with the development of multilevel systems of governance and policy decentralisation'.[65] These studies tend to look at the concept of legal mobilisation from an optimistic viewpoint through which powerless individuals or groups pursue liberal or progressive social agendas. However, '[l]egal mobilisation by the powerful', as Michael McCann observed, 'has gone unstudied by legal mobilisation scholars'.[66] This is the invitation that this book aims to accept. This book goes beyond the existing literature by taking legal mobilisation by the powerful in the context of environmental conflicts as its focus. The book examines how powerful elites have mobilised laws and other legal mechanisms and how such mobilisations should be understood as a form of 'lawfare' that aims to manage social conflict between different social groups or classes in society.

The Book Structure

The book is structured into several parts. Besides the Introduction and Conclusion, there are three substantive parts that explain the theoretical framework used throughout the book, the context of the phenomenon being examined, and the strategic dimensions of attacks on environmental defenders utilising legal means in Southeast Asia. Part 1 is devoted to reviewing previous studies to demonstrate the book's scholarly contribution to the literature and developing the conceptual framework that is used in the remainder of the book. Chapter 1 explores Lawfare in Environmental Conflicts, looking at the link between environmental disputes, movements, and defenders and the use of the law to target environmental defenders. It explains and clarifies how environmental conflict and the concept of 'defenders' are conceived and employed throughout the book. The chapter introduces the conceptual framework – HEL – to examine attacks against environmental defenders through legal means. Furthermore, the chapter elaborates on the strategic dimensions of HEL: geographies, weaponry, externalities, and resistance. It argues that HEL in Southeast Asia should be placed in a wider structural context by scrutinising the functions of law and legal institutions in capitalist development in the region. In contrast to the widely held view that legal actions against environmentalists are an 'abuse of legal procedures' or due to the 'absence of the rule of law', it is argued that the narrative of the rule of law underpins the choice to resort to legal machineries in

(Cambridge University Press, 2007); Luz Munoz and David Moya, 'Creating Space for Supranational Law: Environmental Legal Mobilization and Spanish NGOs', in S. Sterett & L. Walker (eds.), *Research Handbook on Law and Courts* (Edward Elgar, 2019) 320–334.

[65] Luz Munoz and David Moya, 'Creating Space for Supranational Law: Environmental Legal Mobilization and Spanish NGOs', in S. Sterett & L. Walker (eds.), *Research Handbook on Law and Courts* (Edward Elgar, 2009) 320.

[66] Michael McCann (n 50) 534.

addressing environmental conflicts. From this perspective, HEL is a response and reaction to the question of legitimacy in relation to the political and economic status quo.

Part 2 provides the background contexts of the countries under study: Indonesia, Thailand, and the Philippines. This part is divided into two chapters: Chapter 2 entitled Environmental Politics and Defenders' Struggles traces the historical junctures that have shaped the political-economic trajectories in those countries. It explains the structural contexts through which environmental movements have emerged as responses to political and economic transformation. The chapter demonstrates how the political-economic structure of the country where they operate has shaped the diverse characteristics of environmental movements in terms of their organisational structures, strategies, and modalities.[67] Chapter 3 elaborates on environmental law and anti-SLAPP provisions in those countries. It explains how environmental law in these countries has evolved from an instrumental-based and piecemeal approach to an integrative and comprehensive one influenced by the development of international environmental law and cross-fertilisation from different countries. Beyond that, environmental concerns have also been understood as a human right issue, which has led to the incorporation of environmental rights in the constitution and relevant legislation and policies. In addition, environmental law provides legal frameworks on how public participation in environmental matters should be governed, facilitated, or constrained, which in turn influence how environmental movements conduct their struggles and how state and non-state actors implicated in their struggle respond to them. These legal frameworks are important elements that have shaped the ways in which public engagement on environmental issues is controlled, advanced, or restricted and how environmental movements navigate and mobilise those frameworks to make their claims.

Part 3 analyses four strategic dimensions of HEL. This part is divided into three chapters. Chapter 4 compares HEL in Indonesia, Thailand, and the Philippines while interrogating the two strategic dimensions of geographies and weaponry. The geographical dimension encompasses three forms of jurisdiction: (1) subject-matter jurisdictions, that is, the legal procedures mobilised to silence, intimidate, or attack environmental defenders (criminal, civil, and administrative law); (2) territorial jurisdictions (legal institutions' geographical scope of competence); and (3) sectoral jurisdictions (economic sectors where HEL is exercised). The weaponry dimension explains the legal provisions, including criminal offences, mobilised by state and private attackers to intimidate and punish environmental defenders. It reveals how environmental defenders in three countries are harassed through legal means, mainly the criminal justice system in resource-rich or industrialised regions. In contrast to Pring and Canan's finding that private players exclusively initiate SLAPP

[67] Hein-Anton van der Heijden, 'Political Opportunity Structure and the Institutionalisation of the Environmental Movement', (1997) 6 *Environmental Politics* 25, 26.

actions, the experiences in Indonesia, Thailand, and the Philippines demonstrate that HEL is predominantly carried out by the state. The mobilisation of the criminal justice procedure is preferable for corporations because the legal proceeding is operated by the state agencies, namely the police department or the public prosecutor office, and the cost of proceedings is borne by the state. In contrast to using the civil procedure where the plaintiff should pay for proceedings fees and hire legal attorneys, the criminal proceeding provides a more cost-efficient strategy for corporations with relatively effective outcomes, including avoiding direct legal battles against environmental defenders under the cloak of enforcing criminal law.

Chapter 5 explains the third strategic dimension of lawfare: externalities. As a form of strategic legal action, hegemonic environmental lawfare aims to create projective externalities, referring to the consequences that seek to be borne by environmental movements beyond the actual legal cases. The chapter is divided into two sections: (a) leadership decapitation, which discusses the outcomes of hegemonic environmental lawfare targeting those who are regarded as the central figures or leaders of environmental struggles, and (b) creating externalities, which elaborates on the impacts of lawfare beyond lawsuits concerning environmental movements in the countries. Here, as a strategic legal action, HEL aims not only to assault targeted environmental defenders but also to create projected externalities for maintaining social order suitable for capital accumulation and economic growth. Through the courts, deviant labels for environmental movements (such as communist, anti-development, anti-monarch radicals) are given a formal rubber stamp so that public support for the movements is prevented.

Chapter 6, titled Resistance against Lawfare, examines how environmental movements challenge, halt, or prevent HEL. The first section deals with rights-based legal mobilisation. It examines the mobilisation of human rights to build arguments in challenging lawfare in litigation and legal reform at the domestic, regional, or international levels. The second section problematises the rights-based mobilisations in Southeast Asia, demonstrating its problem in the region. Inspired by the 'duty-turn' in resistance studies, the third section proposes duty-based legal mobilisation by conceptualising the obligation to defend the environment as a justificatory defence in resisting lawfare. Finally, the book concludes by emphasising that HEL emerges as a reaction and response of powerholders to address challenges to their pursuit of economic growth and capital accumulation posed by environmental defenders without risking their social and political legitimacy. Rights-based legal mobilisation appears insufficient to resist HEL effectively if the existing political and economic structure remains intact. The book's conclusion closes by providing insights for future research agenda on HEL.

PART ONE

Conceiving Law as Weapon

CHAPTER 1

Lawfare in Environmental Conflicts

This chapter explores the emergence and consolidation of 'lawfare' as a strategy used by states and powerful elites for managing environmental conflicts. It focuses on the use of legal means to retaliate against and constrain the actions of environmental defenders in Southeast Asia, which have been increasingly frequent in the last decade. This phenomenon should be seen as a consequence of the failure of the neoliberal mode of environmental governance to contain environmental conflicts through conventional means, including participatory mechanisms, such as corporate social responsibility (CSR) and public consultation. It marks a shift from neoliberal environmental governance towards a form of 'authoritarian statism' where the state aims to regulate civil society by containing political dissent through the mobilisation of the legal system and to create challenging conditions for coalition building between civil society groups.[1]

The underlying question addressed in this chapter is how the dynamics of legal retaliation against environmental defenders should be understood. This chapter sets out the discussion of this within the literature, outlines its limitations, and moves to discuss an alternative framework to make sense of attacks on environmental defenders through legal means. The first section discusses the concept of environmental conflicts and environmental defenders. The book employs the term 'environmental defenders' as one among many other terms commonly used in the literature to demonstrate its connectedness to 'environmentalism' as a mode of opposition to resource extraction and exploitation following the decline of traditional left politics in the Southeast Asian region. The second section surveys concepts that scholars employ in understanding legal attacks on environmental defenders, including 'strategic lawsuit/litigation against public participation

[1] Kanishka Jayasuriya, 'Authoritarian Statism and the New Right in Asia's Conservative Democracies', (2018) 48 (4) *Journal of Contemporary Asia* 584, 586.

(SLAPP)', 'legal intimidation', and 'criminalisation/penalisation'. Here, they are analysed within two main streams – the liberal and critical streams – based on their basic propositions in how they view society, the state, and the role of law in society. Despite the differences between these streams, they provide inadequate frameworks to give a comprehensive and critical explanation of legal actions against environmental defenders in the Southeast Asian context. Instead, this book puts forward the concept of 'hegemonic environmental lawfare' (HEL), which can be situated in the critical stream, to capture the phenomenon more comprehensively, including understanding its modalities, structural contexts, and consequences.

Environmental Conflicts and Defenders

Environmental Conflicts

Since the early 2000s attacks on environmental defenders have been increasingly common in environmental conflicts. Those who struggle to defend the environment and their means of livelihoods are retaliated against through diverse means by states whose development policies rely on resource extraction to drive GDP growth and companies that invest heavily in resource extraction. Here, 'environmental conflict' is understood broadly as 'a social conflict relating to the environment'.[2] Political ecology scholars examine environmental conflicts from different perspectives, including structural analyses, governance and power relations, discourses and ideologies, and collective action or resistance.[3] Peluso and Watts, for instance, challenge a neo-Malthusian causal-effect relation between resource scarcity and violence by conceptualising violence 'as a site-specific phenomenon rooted in local histories and social relations yet connected to a larger processes of material transformation and power relations'.[4] Other scholars examining environmental conflicts see those conflicts as not only primarily concerned with competition over environmental resources but also that conflicts can be derived from responses to social and environmental externalities referring to 'costs external to the project or economic activity . . . that are borne by individuals and communities other than those reaping the benefits'[5] due to structural asymmetries based on gender, class, and race relations. These scholars demonstrate that 'environmental conflicts' are 'part of larger gendered, class, and race-based struggles and *vice versa*'.[6]

[2] Philippe Le Billon, 'Environmental Conflict', in T. Perreault, G. Bridge, & J. McCarthy, *The Routledge Handbook of Political Ecology* (Routledge, 2015) 560.

[3] Paul Robbins, *Policy Ecology: A Critical Introduction*, 2nd Ed., (Wiley-Blackwell, 2012) 24.

[4] Nancy Peluso and Michael Watts, 'Violent Environments', in N. Peluso & M. Watts (eds.), *Violent Environments* (Cornell University Press, 2001) 5.

[5] Philip Hirsch and Carol Warren, 'Introduction: Through the Environmental Looking Glass', in P. Hirsch & C. Warren (eds.), *The Politics of Environment in Southeast Asia: Resources and Resistance* (Routledge, 1998) 12.

[6] Robbins (n 3) 22.

Legal scholars also examine environmental conflicts by scrutinising the role of law in these conflicts. However, they focus on different dimensions of these conflicts, such as legal frameworks and regulation,[7] dispute resolution mechanisms,[8] and public participation and access to justice.[9] Here, environmental conflicts tend to be framed as environmental disputes, a particular episode in an environmental conflict when actors resort to legal rights or provisions to justify their interests or positions.[10] Nicholson, for instance, proposes that environmental disputes can be resolved in three ways.[11] The first approach is interest-based, which addresses environmental problems or disputes using alternative dispute resolution methods such as mediation or negotiation. The second is the power-based approach, where environmental disputes are addressed through more direct power struggles, such as demonstrations, boycotts, and other forms of direct action. The third approach is rights-based, which is conducted within adjudication procedures such as courts and tribunals.

Empirically, environmental movements may resort to one or may combine approaches depending on the nature of the environmental conflicts they are involved in. The rights-based approach tends to embrace the notion of law through what Turk terms a 'moral functional perspective', in which law is seen as a mechanism to resolve conflicts or disputes.[12] In fact, in the Global South, where the legal system is far from neutral or politically independent from the other arms of the state, environmental activists are generally sceptical about the use of law in resolving environmental conflicts, particularly in settling issues through the courts, because the judiciary is viewed as another oppressive state institution.[13] Laws may become a resource in environmental conflict that is mobilised by social actors to ground their interests at the expense of other interests. The conflict may have a legal dimension in the process, either as the source of conflict or as a resource to resolve conflict. As a source of conflict, legal provisions may be crafted by particular social groups to govern a geographical space, people, and resources within it at the expense of other social groups. As a resource, law may be mobilised by some groups to challenge their rival's interests while advancing their own interests.

Actors in Environmental Conflicts

Environmental conflicts demonstrate the often-conflicting interests involved in constructing, representing, claiming, and contesting the use (or abuse) of the

[7] Zou Keyuan, 'Legal Control of Environmental Disputes in East Asia', (2010) 13 (1) *Journal of International Wildlife Law & Policy* 63.

[8] David Nicholson, *Environmental Dispute Resolution in Indonesia* (Brill, 2010).

[9] Engobo Emeseh, 'Environmental Victims, Access to Justice and the Sustainable Development Goals', in C. Eboe-Osuji and E. Emeseh (eds.), *Nigerian Yearbook of International Law* (Spring, 2017) 291–315.

[10] Nicholson (n 8). [11] ibid.

[12] Austin Turk, '*Law as Weapon in Social Conflict*' (1976) 23 (3) *Social Problems* 276, 277.

[13] Paul Jobin, Ming-sho Ho and Hsin-Huang Michael. Hsiao, 'Environmental Movements and Politics of the Asian Anthropocene: An Introduction', in P Jobin, M. Ho & H. M. Hsiao (eds.), *Environmental Movements and Politics of the Asian Anthropocene* (ISEAS Publishing, 2021) 20.

environment and natural resources in particular circumstances.[14] In general, conflicts may involve three main actors: the state, capital (corporations), and civil society (affected communities and/or environmental organisations). In the context of legal retaliation against environmental defenders, it is necessary to examine the relationships between actors in environmental conflicts that lead to the use of law to manage such conflicts. Mentioning only these three main actors is not to ignore a range of other actors involved in environmental conflicts, such as local customary or religious leaders, lawyers, militias, vigilante groups, or hitmen. However, their role in these conflicts tends to be a supporting one in the sense that their interests are associated with the interests of aforementioned three main actors and are mobilised primarily to advance the interests of the main actors. In certain cases, for example, companies that face resistance from local communities hire criminal gangs or hitmen to intimidate, physically assault, or even kill leading figures in the resistance.[15] In Argentina, Nicaragua, and Spain, Conde et al. demonstrate how lawyers may play an important role in slowing justice for environmental victims who fight through litigation.[16]

In this book, the relationship between state, capital, and society is understood from the social conflict theory or the Murdoch School approach. The school of thought, '[i]nspired by Marxist understandings of capitalist social relations and development', foregrounds '*social conflict*, primarily between class forces, as central to explaining political and economic life'.[17] It argues that the main drivers of political outcomes are struggles between sociopolitical forces with opposing social, economic, and political positions, resources, and goals, who compete for power and control of resources and form coalitions to assert and defend their interests.[18] The Murdoch School rejects the assumption that the state is an 'intrinsically interest-neutral and … potentially benign agent of development and modernisation'.[19] Instead, following Poulantzas and Jessop, this approach asserts that institutions are never neutral. As states allocate resources and power, they are constantly challenged by different social groups attempting to cement their

[14] Nemer E. Narchi, 'Introduction: Environmental Violence in Mexico: A Conceptual Introduction', (2015) 42 (5) *Latin American Perspectives* 5, 13.

[15] Philippe Le Billon and Päivi Lujala, 'Environmental Defenders: Kilings, Perpetrators, and Drivers of Violence', in M. Menton & P. Billon (eds.), *Environmental Defenders: Deadly Struggles for Life and Territory* (Earthscan, 2021) 64–75; Arnim Scheidel, Daniela Del Bene, Juan Liu, et al., 'Environmental Conflicts and Defenders: A Global Overview', (2020) 63 *Global Environmental Change* 1; Global Witness, *On Dangerous Ground: 2015's Deadly Environment: The Killing and Criminalization of Land and Environmental Defenders Worldwide* (Global Witness, 2016).

[16] Marta Conde, Mariana Walter, Lucrecia Wagner and Grettel Navas, 'Slow Justice and Other Unexpected Consequences of Litigation in Environmental Conflicts', (2023) 83 *Global Environmental Change* 1.

[17] Toby Carroll, Shahar Hameiri and Lee Jones, 'Preface', T. Carroll, S. Hameiri and L. Jones (eds.), *The Political Economy of Southeast Asia* (Palgrave Macmillan, 2020) vi.

[18] Shahar Hameiri and Lee Jones, 'Theorising Political Economy in Southeast Asia', in T. Carroll, S. Heimiri and L. Jones (eds.), *The Political Economy of Southeast Asia* (Palgrave Macmillan, 2020) 15.

[19] Vedi R. Hadiz, *Localising Power in Post-Authoritarian Indonesia: A Southeast Asia Perspective* (Stanford University Press, 2010) 49.

preferences in policy, empower themselves and/or their networks, and to funnel resources to preferred groups or entities. In other words, institutions, particularly state institutions, should be viewed as 'a contingent outcome' of struggles over power.[20] To put it simply, the state and other institutions are 'both the outcomes of and terrain for political and social conflicts between groups over resources and power'.[21] In the state–market relation, the state tends to be biased towards business actors. Hameiri and Jones argue that

> the economy strongly influences political conflict and decision-making. At the most basic level, states survive because they tax economic activity. If the economy falters, the state itself is in trouble. That could precipitate cuts in expenditure, which might provoke social unrest or shifts in perceptions of political legitimacy. To avoid this, in a very general sense, political leaders must adopt policies that promote growth. Even setting aside the much-theorised relationship between the state and capital and changes in the balance of forces over time, it should not be surprising that, under capitalism, states exhibit a systemic bias towards the interests of business.[22]

Here the Murdoch School's understanding of the state–market relation can contribute to scholarly explanations for the increasingly common phenomenon of repression and intimidation of environmental movements and environmental defenders by the state and powerful groups in Southeast Asia. In countries like Indonesia, Thailand, and the Philippines, where economic power is concentrated around politico-business elites, these elites have become 'political actors in their own right' and are 'capable of dominating the state despite a change of political leadership'.[23] Moreover, the network between the state and politico-business elites has been sustained by the state's insistence on expanding and accelerating investment in extractive industries and state-sponsored projects from which contracts, concessions, and other preferences are distributed by the dominant faction of the state to its alliances. In other words, the narrative of 'economic growth . . . is an important political basis for sustaining this power network'.[24] Under this structural condition, the state tends to be biased towards those politico-business interests, and, consequently, other interests that potentially pose a threat to disrupt state agendas are likely to be contained and neutralised by any means necessary. Environmental movements are no exception. As Lakhani, Gayle, and Taylor put it, 'criminalisation required lawmakers, prosecutors, police and courts to be involved – the same people

[20] Hameiri and Jones (n 18) 15.

[21] Lian Sinclair, 'The Power of Mining MNCs: Global Governance and Social Conflict', in J. Mikler and K. Ronit (eds.), *MNC in Global Politics: Pathways of Influence* (Edward Elgar, 2020) 141.

[22] Hameiri and Jones (n 18) 4–5.

[23] Toby Carroll, 'The Political Economy of Southeast Asia's Development from Independence to Hyperglobalisation' in T. Carroll, S. Hameiri and L. Jones (eds.), *The Political Economy of Southeast Asia* (Palgrave Macmillan, 2020) 53; see also Richard Robison and Vedi Hadiz, *Organizing Power in Indonesia: The Politics of Oligarchy in an Age of Markets* (RoutledgeCurzon, 2004).

[24] Carroll (n 23) 54.

and agencies we need to tackle the climate crisis and biodiversity loss'.[25] Thus, attacks on environmental defenders utilising legal means reveal the essential role of the state in the operation of the legal system to intimidate environmental defenders.

Environmental Movements and Defenders

The next important clarification is to understand the connection between environmental movements and environmental defenders. Here, environmental movements are conceived broadly as 'networks of individuals and groups of actors who engage in collective action and share similar concerns regarding not only the physical environment but also the built environment and cultural environment'.[26] They are collective social forces that advocate for the protection of the environment against destructive encroachments by corporations and the state. Indeed, these movements are far from monolithic as they have different characteristics due to variables within their respective domestic spheres, such as the nature of political cleavages, the institutional structure of the state, the strategies of politico-business elites, and power relations within the party system.[27] Additionally, the formal institutional structure of the state and the informal strategies of political elites vis-à-vis environmental activists play a role in shaping the characteristics of environmental movements. These variables affect how movements operate and interact with the state and civil society actors, such as academic or religious institutions, leading to diverse organisational arrangements,[28] strategies,[29] and impacts, which may include advancing environmental laws and regulations, increasing state and corporate accountability in environmental matters, and halting or at least slowing the pace of environmentally destructive development projects.

[25] Nina Lakhani, Damien Gayle, and Matthew Taylor, 'How Criminalisation Is Being Used to Silence Climate Activists across the World', *The Guardian* (12 October 2023) <www.theguardian.com/environment/2023/oct/12/how-criminalisation-is-being-used-to-silence-climate-activists-across-the-world> accessed 12 April 2024.

[26] James K. Wong and Alvin Y. So, 'Environmental Movements in Post-Handover Hong Kong: Between Managerialism and Radicalism', in P. Jobin, M. Ho, H. Michael Hsiao (eds.), *Environmental Movements and Politics of the Asian Anthropocene* (ISEAS Publishing, 2021) 84.

[27] Hirsch and Warren (n 5) 1; Jobin, Ho, and Hsiao (n 13) 1; Arne Kalland and Gerard Persoon, 'An Anthropological Perspective on Environmental Movements', in A. Kalland and G. Persoon (eds.), *Environmental Movements in Asia* (Routledge, 2013) 1.

[28] In Southeast Asia, in terms of organisations, environmental movements may include (1) non-governmental organisations like the Palawan NGO Network, Inc. (PNNI) in the Philippines, the Project of Ecological Recovery in Thailand, the Mother Nature Cambodia in Cambodia, the Indonesian Forum for the Environment (WALHI) in Indonesia, and *Sahabat Alam Malaysia* (SAM) in Malaysia; (2) religious groups like Buddhist monks in Cambodia and the Catholic Church in the Philippines; (3) grassroots-led movements like the Stop Lynas Coalition in Malaysia and communities against the Formosa in Vietnam; (4) professional-led organisations like the Environmental Jurists Association in Taiwan; or (5) and combinations of these. They may use different strategies such as direct actions, litigations, technocratic, or cooperation, and mobilise different collective identities, including indigeneity (*Masyarakat Adat* in Indonesia or *Orang Asli/Orang Asal* in Malaysia), farmers, youths, fishermen, and consumers.

[29] Environmental movements in Southeast Asia employ strategic litigation, policy advocacy, and mobilisation of different collective identities to address environmental issues and influence policy changes.

In Southeast Asia, the emergence of environmental movements has been influenced by internal and external forces.[30] Domestic factors include the relationships between state–environmental movements, state–business actors, and institutional structures within the state. Recognition of environmental rights in state constitutions, access to justice mechanisms, and state–business interests shape the legal-political opportunity structure for environmental movements. Externally, international factors, such as international donors and NGOs, may either advance or moderate environmental activism. Environmental movements in Southeast Asia are relatively distinct from those in the Global North. In the Global North, they often express urban middle-class concerns about quality of life;[31] in contrast, Southeast Asian environmental movements emerge primarily as 'a response to threats on livelihood, notably those of the poor'[32] due to the failure of states to protect the environment against big business interests.[33] Tsing observes that environmental movements in Southeast Asia are closer to those in Latin American countries, especially in the nexus between environmental movements and Indigenous or economically vulnerable communities.[34]

In the literature on environmental conflicts, environmental movements and environmental defenders tend to be ontologically juxtaposed. Verweijn et al., for instance, warn of the effects of singling out specific figures in environmental movements as 'environmental defenders', which may create a sense of martyrdom or heroic individuals who obscure the collective character of the movements.[35] They argue that '[t]he notion of "environmental defenders" … directs attention to particular individuals, who are singled out for their activism, rather than seeing this activism as a product of collectives as a whole'.[36] In this book, instead of seeing 'environmental defenders' as having a personalising effect on environmental movements, the relation between the two is seen as a continuum: environmental movements are collective actions encompassing individuals or groups with shared interests and common goals, whereas environmental defenders are referred to when individuals within the movements become victims of attacks by any means. In other words, the term 'environmental defenders' is an attempt to put human faces on an environmental movement whose participants experience harm due to their involvement in these movements. Through their faces, the struggles and sufferings of environmental movement activists are made visible to the public's

[30] Agung Wardana, 'A Quest for Agency in the Anthropocene: Law and Environmental Movements in Southeast Asia', (2023) 32 (1) *Review of European, Comparative, and International Environmental Law* 57.

[31] See H. van Der-Heijden, 'Political Opportunity Structure and the Institutionalisation of the Environmental Movement', (1997) 6 *Environmental Politics* 25, 26.

[32] Hirsch and Warren (n 5) 10.

[33] Wardana (n 30).

[34] See Anna Tsing, 'Indigenous Voice', in M. de la Cadena and O. Starn (eds.), *Indigenous Experience Today* (Berg, 2007) 50.

[35] Judith Verweijn, Fran Lambrick, Philippe Le Billon, et al., '"Environmental Defenders": The Power/Disempower of a Loaded Term', in M. Menton & P. Billon (eds.), *Environmental Defenders: Deadly Struggles for Life and Territory* (Earthscan, 2021) 44.

[36] ibid., 38–39.

eyes and in turn may widen the support for their causes. Even in cases where the public is divided over how they see environmental causes, people who do not support an environmental cause may have a sympathy towards individuals in the movement who suffer from morally and legally unacceptable treatment, such as intimidation, physical assaults, or even murdered for defending their cause. In brief, the term 'environmental movement' here is used to stress the collective actions exercised to defend the environment or local livelihoods, while the term 'environmental defender' is used to personalise the experience of harm suffered by individuals due to their involvement in the movement, which are part of the retaliation strategies carried out by the state or corporations, or their hitmen.

Several conceptual terms are used both by scholars and different state and international institutions when referring to persons who suffer harm from these retaliation strategies. These are 'land and environmental defenders', 'environmental human rights defenders', 'environmental defenders', 'eco-defenders', and 'eco-justice activists'. In the Global North, the use of the term 'environmental defenders' is less common than in the Global South. In the Global North, the term 'activists', such as 'environmental activists' and 'eco-justice activists', is used to identify individuals who advocate for the protection of the environment.[37] In the context of the Global South, scholars such as Le Billon and Lujala prefer the term 'environmental and land defenders' as the best concept for describing 'people trying together [to defend their] community, territory, environmental protection, and livelihoods'.[38] Verweijen et al. suggest that the term 'environmental defenders' is closely associated with the Western dichotomy between 'nature' and 'culture', in which 'environment' is perceived to lay within 'the natural' or outside cultural domains.[39] Accordingly, the term 'environmental defender' falls within the scope of protecting the natural environment, whereas 'land defenders' refers to those active in safeguarding land rights and territories from harmful activities which fall within the domain of culture. For these scholars, it is necessary to add 'land' into 'environmental defenders' to encompass their work within both natural and cultural domains.

More recently, UN bodies concerned with human rights have framed environmental defenders as 'environmental human rights defenders'. This is because 'environmental defenders' are 'considered a subset of human rights defenders working on economic, social, and cultural rights'.[40] Due to the absence of special regimes on environmental defenders, this designation has been an attempt to integrate them under existing human rights regimes to ensure similar applications

[37] ibid., 9.

[38] Philippe Le Billon and Päivi Lujala, 'Environmental Defenders: Killings, Perpetrators, and Drivers of Violence', in M. Menton & P. Billon (eds.), *Environmental Defenders: Deadly Struggles for Life and Territory* (Earthscan, 2021), 66.

[39] Verweijen et al. (n 35) 39.

[40] ibid., 37. See John Knox, *Environmental Human Rights Defenders: A Global Crisis* (Universal Rights Group, 2017).

of standards, rules, and mechanisms. With this integration, the 1999 declaration on human rights defenders also applies to environmental defenders.[41] Since the late 1990s, the term environmental human rights defenders and issues concerning them have been picked up by international organisations, among others, through the adoption of the UN Human Rights Council's Resolution 40/11 concerning Recognising the Contribution of Environmental Human Rights Defenders to the Enjoyment of Human Rights, Environmental Protection and Sustainable Development.[42] Within the designation of 'environmental human rights defenders' as an official term, however, is attached 'the logic and language of human rights', such as 'liberal individualism' and 'Eurocentrism'.[43] The term expresses an anthropocentric notion which obscures diverse motives for environmental defenders' actions that may lay beyond nature's instrumental value, including the right of nature.

This book, however, retains the term 'environmental defender' for at least two reasons. Conceptually, unlike in the Western mind, where the term 'environment' reflects the 'nature-culture' dichotomy, this is not necessarily the case in Southeast Asia. As pointed out by Hirsch and Warren, even though the definition of 'environment' appears to be ambiguous, the substance of environmental conflicts 'is more concrete and reflects basic questions of allocation of, competition for, and conflict over natural resources or the uses to which they are put'.[44] Working in Indonesia's context, Warren observes that 'the Indonesian term for environment, *lingkungan*, has always had a primarily social connotation in the Indonesian language'.[45] In Thailand, 'nature' is perceived as an organised or law-like process of which humans are a part, with a relationship based on interdependence and utilitarian values. The 'environment' (*sing waed lorm*) is 'a subset of nature or human's habitat'.[46] Moreover, in the Philippines, Davide Jr. points out that 'the word "environment" is inseparable from the concept of nature . . . (*kalikasan*)', which is regarded as 'the life sources that enable all life to survive and thrive'.[47] Based on these understandings,

[41] UN General Assembly Resolution No. 53/44 concerning the Declaration on the Right and Responsibility of Individuals, Groups and Organs of Society to Promote and Protect Universally Recognised Human Rights and Fundamental Freedoms.

[42] The resolution, among others, urges 'all State to take all measures necessary to ensure the rights, protection and safety of all persons, including environmental human rights defenders'. See Para 2 of the 2019 UNHRC Resolution No. 40/11 concerning Recognising the Contribution of Environmental Human Rights Defenders to the Enjoyment of Human Rights, Environmental Protection and Sustainable Development, adopted on 21 March 2019.

[43] Verweijen et al. (n 35) 38.

[44] Hirsch and Warren (n 5) 1.

[45] Carol Warren, 'Tanah Lot: The Cultural and Environmental Politics of Resort Development in Bali', P. Hirsch & C. Warren (eds.), *The Politics of Environment in Southeast Asia: Resources and Resistance* (Routledge, 1998) 229; see also Robert Cribb, 'The Politics of Pollution Control in Indonesia', (1990) 30 (12) *Asian Survey* 1123, 1126–1127.

[46] Opart Panya and Solot Sirisai, 'Environmental Consciousness in Thailand: Contesting Maps of Eco-Conscious Minds', (2003) 41 (1) *Southeast Asian Studies* 59, 65. In the Thai legal context, the 1992 Enhancement and Conservation of National Environmental Quality Act (B.E. 2535), defines 'environment' as 'natural things, which form the physical and biological surrounding man and man-made things'.

[47] Hilaro G. Davide Jr., 'The Environment as Life Sources and the Writ of *Kalikasan* in the Philippines', (2012) 29 *Pace Environmental Law Review* 592, 593.

land, waters, forests, and other resources as the source of life are inseparable from the environment; thus, defending the environment may include defending natural resources, territory, environmental rights, and even the rights of nature. Accordingly, the concept 'environmental defenders' in this context includes within it the terms 'land defenders' and 'environmental human rights defenders'.

Historically, 'environment' has served as 'a legitimised arena of resistance'.[48] Hirsch and Warren observe that due to 'the decline of traditional left politics of opposition in most non-communist Southeast Asian countries ... environment has been used as the basis for articulating claims over resources on the part of marginal groups where previous claims had been ignored or painted as subversive'.[49] Hall, Hirsch, and Li also point out that 'environmentalism had served from the early 1980s as a convenient proxy for the opposition at a time when land-based mobilisation was still labelled Communist and hence subversive'.[50] Similarly, Warren notes: '[i]n Indonesia, environmental issues have become highly politicised, not only because the environment became for a time a surrogate for the expression of dissent on broader issues, but also because they are ultimately connected with questions of cultural identity and social security'.[51] This is comparable in the context of Thailand and the Philippines, where environmental conflicts that are 'fundamentally about land' are cloaked in 'the mantle' of environmentalism (Chapter 2).[52] This was an attempt to escape from being tagged by the regimes as a communist movement and motivated by the need to scale up local struggles as well as build allies beyond the local scale. In the latter context, the narrative of environmentalism appears to be 'legitimising discourse appeals to national and transnational constituencies' that help the movement to 'draw connections between local events and global problems'.[53]

Therefore, while carrying the baggage of the term 'environmentalism', the term 'environmental defender' should also be seen as a legitimising discourse to connect people's struggles beyond their own localities. As already discussed, 'environmental defender' is a term used with a strategic motive: to shine a spotlight on members of communities, individuals involved in environmental movements, and environmental activists who are victims of retaliation by powerful social groups through SLAPP, criminalisation, intimidation, assaults, or even murder. The harm they suffer from retaliation actions must be acknowledged and personalised to create emphatic responses and mobilise public support. In this regard, Le Billon and Lujala refer to five categories of environmental defenders with their respective motives: (a) Indigenous communities (protecting their territorial, cultural, and

[48] Hirsch and Warren (n 5) 2. [49] ibid., 1

[50] Derek Hall, Philip Hirsch and Tania Li, *Powers of Exclusion: Land Dilemmas in Southeast Asia* (Hawai'i University Press, 2011) 187.

[51] Warren (n 45) 229.

[52] Philip Hirsch, 'The Political Economy of Land and Agrarian Relations in Southeast Asia', in T. Carroll, S. Hameiri and L. Jones (eds.), *The Political Economy of Southeast Asia* (Palgrave Macmillan, 2020) 357; see also Larry Lohmann, 'Peasants, Plantation and Pulp: The Politics of Eucalyptus in Thailand', (1991) 24 (4) *Bulletin of Concerned Asian Scholars* 3–7.

[53] Hall, Hirsch and Li (n 50) 185.

ecological integrity); (b) rural communities, such as farmworkers and peasants (defending their right to 'access and sustain land livelihoods'); (c) environmental activists, including artists and intellectuals (preventing ecologically harmful activities and demanding justice); (d) professionals, such as lawyers and journalists (reporting on and defending the rights of Indigenous peoples or economically vulnerable communities); and (e) public officials, such as conservation and forestry personnel (enforcing environment-related law and regulations).[54]

Framing Legal Retaliation against Defenders

In the scholarly context, attacks on environmental movements and defenders utilising legal means have been conceptualised differently. Those conceptualisations can be seen using diverse terms in capturing such phenomenon, among others: 'green backlash',[55] 'criminalisation',[56] 'SLAPP',[57] and 'legal intimidation'. Indeed, each concept encapsulates a different scope of attacks, actors involved in the attacks, attack modalities, as well as the constitutional basis upon which environmental movements exercise their work (Table 1.1). The concept of 'green backlash', for instance, was introduced by Rowell, referring to attacks on environmental defenders, which may take many forms, such as killing, kidnaps, threats, as well as the use of legal means for silencing environmental defenders.[58] In this regard, the backlash represents reactionary or defence mechanisms from those whose interests are negatively implicated by environmental struggles. As a broad concept, 'green backlash' is unable to explain sufficiently the different nature and consequences of attacks utilising legal means compared to the use of direct forms violence.

From diverse concepts commonly used in the literature as shown in Table 1.1, they can be categorised into two wider streams. They are the liberal stream and the critical stream. In this section, these streams are discussed to elucidate their contributions to as well as their weaknesses in explaining why legal actions against environmental defenders in Southeast Asia take place. Furthermore, building on the

[54] Le Billon and Lujala (n 38) 65.

[55] Andrew Rowell, *Green Backlash: Global Subversion of the Environmental Movement* (Routledge, 1996).

[56] Valeria Veigh Weis, *Criminalization of Activism: Historical, Present, and Future Perspectives* (Routledge, 2022); Mary Menton and Philippe Le Billon, *Environmental Defenders: Deadly Struggles for Life and Territory* (Earthscan, 2021) 42; Anna Di Ronco, *Policing Environmental Protest: Power and Resistance in Pandemic Times* (Bristol University Press, 2023) 9.

[57] George W. Pring and Penelope Canan, *SLAPPs: Getting Sued for Speaking Out* (Temple University Press, 1996); Chad Settle and Jason Shogren, 'Environmental Conflict with SLAPP Reputations', (2001) 4 *Environmental Economics and Policy Studies* 129–139; Thalia Anthony, 'Quantum of Strategic Litigation – Quashing Public Participation', (2009) 14 (2) *Australian Journal of Human Rights* 1, 20; Byron Sheldrick, *Blocking Public Participation: The Use of Strategic Litigation to Silence Political Expression* (Wilfrid Laurier University Press, 2014); Nikhil Dutta, *SLAPPs in the Global South: Features and Policy Responses* (International Centre for Not Profit Law, 2020).

[58] Rowell (n 55).

Table 1.1 Frameworks in capturing legal retaliation against environmental defenders

Terminology	Authors	Right Contexts	Legal Means	Mobilising Actors	Geography
Strategic Lawsuit/ Litigation against Public Participation (SLAPP)	Pring & Canan (1996)	The Petition Clause	Civil Lawsuit	Private actors	Global North (the US)
	Settle & Shogren (2001)	The Petition Clause	Civil Lawsuit	Private actors	Global North (the US)
	Anthony (2019)	The right to freedom of expression	Civil Lawsuit	Private actors	Global North (Australia)
	Dutta (2020)	The right to freedom of expression	Civil Lawsuit and Criminal Defamation	Private actors (including state officials)	Global North and Global South
	Byron Sheldrick (2014)	The right to association, assembly, and expression	Civil Lawsuit	Private actors (including state officials)	Global North (Canada)
Legal intimidation	Donson (2000)	The right to freedom of expression	Civil Lawsuit (libel/ defamation)	Private (non-state) actors	Global North (Canada and the UK)
Criminalisation	Vegh Weis (2022); Menton & Le Billon (2021); Di Ronco (2023; 2022; 2021); Gordon (2024)	The right to freedom of expression, including the right to protest, and livelihood rights	Criminal Law	Private and state actors	Global North and Global South
Judicialisation	Angela Lindt (2023)	The right to political participation, assembly, and expression	Criminal Law	State actors	Global South (Peru)

critical stream, a new conceptual framework, HEL, will be developed in the following section to more adequately account for the exercise of law in attacking environmental defenders in the region.

The Liberal Stream

The liberal stream holds several main propositions in common. First, it embraces the concept that society consists of individuals and groups that coexist and contribute different roles and shared interests to achieve collective goods. Second, the state as a product of social contract is a neutral agent that balances diverse interests in society. Thirdly, the law as the state's legal embodiment is the most rational form of authority from which the legitimacy of the state is derived and through which disputes among citizens are resolved. Accordingly, the rule of law is regarded as 'the core value' of a modern society and 'that all other values depend on this rule'.[59] In the context of environmental conflicts, the liberal stream is represented by legal and non-legal scholars who frame environmental struggles in relation to citizen's civil and political rights, be they the right to petition, the right to freedom of expression, or the right to peaceful assembly. The exercise of those rights should be respected based on the assumption that every citizen has an equal opportunity to participate in issues of environmental concern. However, if citizens in exercising those rights are attacked or retaliated against, such attacks or retaliation should be condemned as a violation of rights. Paradoxically, from the liberal stream viewpoint, resorting to courts to demand remedy is also an exercise of the right to an effective remedy for those who suffer damage or losses caused by other citizen's conduct. Thus, it is the role of the court to strike a balance between the right to public participation and the right to an effective remedy in cases brought before it. In addition, for preventing legal attacks, the liberal stream encourages the state to strengthen and respect the right to public participation in environmental matters.

The most notable example of the liberal stream is represented by SLAPP. The term SLAPP was coined and popularised by George W. Pring and Penelope Canan in their seminal book entitled *SLAPPs: Getting Sued for Speaking Out*. Conceptually, in Pring and Canan's understanding, SLAPP does not exclusively occur within environmental conflicts. They identify different sectors in which SLAPPs have been commonly used, one of which is in environmental matters known as eco-SLAPP.[60] Even though they do not define the term clearly, they do provide two basic features on for identifying a SLAPP lawsuit. The first one is the nature of activities carried out by activists leading to retaliation actions utilising legal means. Here, they situate SLAPP as an attack on those who exercise the right to petition as guaranteed by the Petition Clause of the US Constitution. The second feature is related to legal procedures through which SLAPP is brought to prevent or silence or challenge eco-defenders in exercising their activism.[61] In this regard, they confine SLAPP to taking place within the

[59] Richard Quinney, *Critique of Legal Order: Crime Control in Capitalist Society* (Routledge, 1974) 20–21.
[60] Pring and Canan (n 57). [61] ibid.

civil procedure, which can be interpreted as involving two private actors resorting to the court to resolve their conflict.

Following on from Pring and Canan's book, the concept of SLAPP has become attractive to other jurisdictions given that the common phenomenon is also observable beyond the US. In Europe, the Council of Europe has issued a recommendation to address SLAPPs in the region. In the recommendation, SLAPP is defined as 'legal actions that are threatened, initiated or pursued as a means of harassing or intimidating their target, and which seek to prevent, inhabit, restrict or penalise free expression on matters of public interest and the exercise of rights associated with public participation'.[62] In the absence of the Petition Clause, the constitutional basis to identify SLAPP has been expanded to incorporate the right to freedom of expression (the UK, Australia), the right to association, assembly, and expression (Canada), and other procedural rights closely related to the right to public participation. Byron Sheldrick uses the 'SLAPP' framework in examining legal attacks on activists, stressing that they are not only a strategic attempt to block public participation but also pose threats to democratic principles and values.[63] From a cost–benefit analysis, Settle and Shogren examine how SLAPP when used as a company's strategy to silence opposition may have an impact on its reputation.[64]

In the jurisprudential context, several landmark cases in Global North countries have also developed through the lens of SLAPP and resulted in the need to undertake measures to prevent it at the domestic level. In Australia, for instance, learning from the *Australian Wool Innovation Ltd* v. *Newkirk* Case (1995) and the *Gunns Ltd* v. *Marr & Ors* Case (2005), Anthony proposes the need for a legislative measure to provide protection for environmental activists.[65] In the UK, Fiona Donson demonstrates that the McLibel case is regarded as a landmark case which has managed to mobilise the general public to scrutinise the behaviour of big corporations.[66] Byron Sheldrick examines several notable SLAPP cases in Canada, which include *MacMillan Bloedel* v. *Galiano Island Trust Committee* (1995), *Mainstream Canada* v. *Staniford* (2012), and *Barrick Gold and Banro* v. *Éditions Ecosociété* (2008).[67] The Canadian Court also considers SLAPP cases, and it provides a characterisation of SLAPP as follows:

> A SLAPP suit is a claim for monetary damages against individuals who have dealt with a government body on an issue of public interest or concern. It is a meritless action filed by a plaintiff whose primary goal is not to win the case but rather to silence or intimidate citizens who have participated in public policy or decision-making proceedings … I find, therefore, that this action not only contains an

[62] Council of Europe, Recommendation CM/Rec (2024)2 of the Committee of Ministers to Member States on Countering the Use of Strategic Lawsuits against Public Participation (SLAPPs), 4.
[63] Sheldrick (n 57). [64] Settle and Shogren (n 57). [65] Anthony (n 57) 20.
[66] Donson (n 57). [67] Sheldrick (n 57).

> unreasonable claim, is meritless and devoid of any factual foundation, but also has been used as an attempt to stifle the democratic activities of the defendants, the neighbourhood residents. I find the plaintiff's conduct reprehensible and deserving of censure by an award of special costs. (*Fraser* v. *Saanich* (District) [1999], paragraph 49, 52)

Furthermore, in her comparative work on the US, Canada, and the UK, Fiona Donson prefers to use 'legal intimidation' rather than SLAPP. This is part of her attempt to widen the basis of SLAPP, which Pring and Canan put on the foundation of the Petition Clause, a specific clause in the US Constitution articulating the country's history. Meanwhile, other countries, Canada and the UK being her focus, do not have a Petition Clause; hence, the constitutional basis for SLAPP should be widened to freedom of expression.[68] Accordingly, the term 'legal intimidation' has a wider constitutional basis than the original concept of SLAPP. Even though they have different constitutional bases in conceiving what rights are being prevented by legal attacks on environmental defenders, both Pring and Canan and Donson share at least two similar features in common. First, their frameworks situate the legal means mobilised by SLAPP filers within the framework of the civil procedures. Hence, they do not pay attention to the mobilisation of the criminal courts in silencing environmental defenders.

Second, their conceptual frameworks are developed out of the phenomenon of legal attacks on environmental defenders in the Global North countries, namely the US, Canada, and the UK. Consequently, the concepts of SLAPP and 'legal intimidation' need to be treated cautiously when considering the experience of the Global South. This is because in the Global South attacks utilising legal means cannot be reduced to a legal battle involving two private actors (company versus environmental defenders) utilising civil procedures. Although the use of civil procedures to retaliate against environmental defenders also occurs, the primary legal weapon for retaliating against environmental defenders takes place through the criminal justice system. In the Global South, defamation, as the most common weapon used to retaliate against defenders, for instance, is not only designated as a civil wrongdoing but also as criminal conduct resulting in a criminal sanction if found guilty. In India and Indonesia, the crime of defamation is the legacy of the colonial criminal code. Accusing defenders of committing defamation, a company, individual, or government official may have an option either to resort to the civil procedure or to the criminal court system. Given this empirical case, Nikhil Dutta expands on the original concept of SLAPP to incorporate criminal proceedings in order to analyse the phenomenon in several Global South countries, such as India, Indonesia, Malaysia, and South Africa.[69] Focusing specifically on criminal defamation, Dutta attempts to maintain a boundary between the

[68] Donson (n 57). [69] Dutta (n 57).

original concept of SLAPP and SLAPP as a form of backlash carried out by both private actors and through state repression instituted by government agencies.[70] Despite being widened to incorporate the use of criminal proceedings, Dutta's concept of SLAPP shares a similar feature with Pring and Canan's original concept of SLAPP. They all limit their analysis to the attack exercised by private actors, be they individuals or corporations; hence, obscuring the role of the state in the phenomenon from the picture.

There are several flaws in the liberal stream analysis. First, retaliation against environmental defenders through legal actions is understood in this perspective within the narrative of rights, especially within the civil and political rights framework. Chapter 6 explains how the liberal rights-based framework for conceiving attacks on environmental defenders through legal means is problematic conceptually and practically in Southeast Asia. In the liberal rights-based framework, civil and political rights are understood as a foundational element for liberal democracy relying on an individualistic notion of rights. However, this may risk 'individualising' environmental concerns and grievances as a personal matter instead of as a collective interest pursued through environmental struggles. Due to their nature as negative rights, civil and political rights require minimal state intervention to protect those who exercise such rights. Limitations on those rights are made possible by law and through court decisions. Thus, those who claim their rights are violated should resort to the court to seek remedies. The court will examine the conflicting rights between the injured party (claiming to exercise the right to an effective remedy) and the activists (claiming to exercise the rights to freedom of expression) based on 'the proportionality test'[71] to rule which rights should prevail.

Second and more important, the liberal stream also confines its analysis on the consequences of legal actions against environmental defenders to participation in environmental matters. The perspective regards participation as paramount within a pluralistic society where every citizen should have equal access to participate in public decision-making. Accordingly, SLAPP or legal intimidation is seen as a strategy to prevent citizens from exercising their rights to influence public decision-making processes. Consequently, decisions are made based on bias towards one particular interest at the expense of the other interests because the latter was improperly represented during the process. Thus, the liberal perspective overlooks the underlying capitalist economic model, which dispossesses local communities from their sources of livelihood under the name of economic growth. This model has inevitably created a concentration of wealth in the hands of a small group of elites, which in turn has shaped the state's decisions

[70] ibid., 17.

[71] In the proportionality test, conflicting rights are decided based four stages of examination: (1) legitimate aim; (2) suitability; (3) necessity; and (4) proportionality *stricto sensu*. See Fransciso Urbina, 'A Critique of Proportionality', (2012) 57 *The American Journal of Jurisprudence* 49.

in defending the wealth of this small group. Given this reality, enjoying the rights to petition, protest, freedom of expression, and public participation in an unequal society does not necessarily mean that the environment and people's livelihoods will be better protected. This is because the state may use its authority to facilitate the exploitation of the environment and expropriate the means of people's livelihoods under the banner of the public interest. In Southeast Asia and the Global South 'public interest' tends to be understood in developmental terms and limited to issues of economic growth and often empty rhetoric about job creation.

The Critical Stream

In contrast to the liberal stream, which conceives of legal attacks on environmental defenders within the framework of rights, the critical stream explains these attacks by interrogating the underlying political economic structures of the society. With this purpose, the stream builds its understanding based on the proposition that society, especially capitalist society, is marked by social conflicts over access to power and resources. The state is not neutral in these conflicts, and law, especially criminal law, plays an important mechanism in supressing the status quo's opponents. Shin Imai observes that

> [t]here is [a] very clear and international pattern to criminalise communities in which the nexus between corporations and governments is very important ... mining and fossil fuel companies need the [host] state to criminalise defenders, and also often rely on their own government to use diplomatic influence to pressure the host state to deploy troops, pass laws, arrest activists and deny bail.[72]

Accordingly, legal attacks on environmental defenders should be situated within this broader structural context. This is to understand the contexts within which powerful groups mobilise law to intimidate, silence and punish environmental defenders.

Within the literature on environmental politics, the critical stream can be identified in scholarly works that address the mobilisation of the criminal justice system to overcriminalise environmental defenders. Here, attacks utilising legal means are often characterised as 'criminalisation' or 'penalisation'. Scholars refer to it as the use of criminal law to attack environmental defenders, which may include different types of crimes.[73] Mireanu, for instance, argues that '[t]he criminalisation of

[72] Nina Lakhani, Damien Gayle, and Matthew Taylor, 'How Criminalisation Is Being Used to Silence Climate Activists across the World', *The Guardian* (12 October 2023) <www.theguardian.com/environment/2023/oct/12/how-criminalisation-is-being-used-to-silence-climate-activists-across-the-world> accessed 12 April 2024.

[73] Mary Menton and Philippe Le Billon, *Environmental Defenders: Deadly Struggles for Life and Territory* (Earthscan, 2021); Constance Gordon, 'Criminalising Care: Environmental Justice Under Political and Police Repression', (2024) 18 (1–2) *Environmental Communication* 138–145; Manuel Mireanu, 'The Criminalisation of Environmental Activism in Europe', (2014) LIX (2) *Studia UBB Sociologia* 87–103; Anna Di Ronco, *Policing Environmental Protest: Power and Resistance in Pandemic Times* (Bristol

environmental dissent functions as a mechanism of governance that seeks to survey, control, tame and punish the population'[74] and it very often 'has little to do with the acts that one has committed. . . . Suspects are being criminalised for what the state imagines they might cause in the future, rather than for actual deeds.'[75] However, not all scholars who use the term 'criminalisation' are influenced by the critical criminology literature. Lindt, for instance, perceives the criminalisation of activists as an 'abuse of criminal law' or 'misuse of criminal law'.[76] This characterisation is based on the moral-functionalist assumption of criminal law that it is essentially good for society, but it opens an opportunity to be abused or misused from its noble objectives. As a result, this perspective exposes the reality of criminal law as an instrument for punishing those regarded as 'deviant' in a given society.

Meanwhile, for critical criminology scholars, criminal law in capitalist societies is a technology of power that sustains capitalism's mode of production and perpetuates the ruling classes' hegemony through criminalisation. This process can be carried out through two stages: 'primary criminalisation' (an act categorised as a crime through criminal legislation) and 'secondary criminalisation' (selective enforcement of criminal acts).[77] In the context of environmental conflicts, primary criminalisation against environmental defenders has been observed in many countries. In Indonesia, for instance, the inclusion of Article 162 of the 2004 Mining Law is a perfect example of primary criminalisation when activities that are considered disruptive to the mining industry are criminalised.[78] In the Global North, a similar trend has also been observed. Di Ronco, for instance, notes that Italy and the UK have enacted draconian regulations as a response to environmental resistance. She argues:

> [d]evelopment in Italy and the U.K. both point at the creeping and dangerous ways in which some governments are clamping down on the right to protest. That these regulations mostly target environmental protesters is no surprise: public awareness has grown substantially over the past years, and more and more people are being mobilised. Attempts to constrain such mobilisation should be resisted as they are unnecessary, disproportionate and ultimately inconsistent with efforts to tackle global climate change.[79]

University Press, 2023); Ekin Kurtiç, 'Criminalizing Environmental Activism in Turkey', (2022) 147 *Middle East Brief, Crown Center for Middle East Studies, Brandeis University* 1.

[74] Mireanu (n 73) 89. [75] ibid., 89.

[76] Angela Lindt, 'The Dark Side of Judicialization: Criminalizing Mining Protests in Peru', (2023) 58 *Latin America Research Review* 368, 373.

[77] Valeria Veigh Weis, 'Introduction', in V. Veigh Weis (ed.), *Criminalization of Activism: Historical, Present, and Future Perspectives* (Routledge, 2022) 3.

[78] Article 162 of the 2004 Mining Law stipulates that 'any person who obstructs or interferes with the mining activities . . . shall be punished with a maximum imprisonment of 1 (one) year or a maximum fine of Rp 100,000,000.00 (one hundred million rupiah)'.

[79] Anna Di Ronco, 'What Happened When Italy Criminalised Environmental Protest', *The Conversation* (12 May 2021) <https://theconversation.com/what-happened-when-italy-criminalised-environmental-protest-158014> accessed 25 December 2023.

Secondary criminalisation is evidenced when environmental defenders are targeted for selective enforcement of the criminal law. In Turkey, for instance, Ekin Kurtiç demonstrates the relationship between the state's self-proclamation as 'green' and an increase in criminalisation of environmental activists. She argues that a self-proclaimed green government has drawn boundaries between legitimate forms of environmentalism that are state-sponsored and apolitical environmentalism, on the one hand, and illegitimate environmentalism that operates outside the state-sponsored framework, on the other. The latter is regarded by the state as a political movement that may pose 'a threat to democratic security, which provides a pretext to oppress activists with the full weight of Turkey's criminal justice system'.[80]

Veigh Weis develops further the 'primary' and 'secondary' criminalisation frameworks through the dialectics of over-criminalisation and under-criminalisation.[81] Over-criminalisation is the state's move to categorise as many crimes as possible that are considered to disrupt the workings of the capitalist mode of production and hinder the process of hegemony. However, activities that may cause social and environmental harm are under-criminalised because they are considered essential to the functioning of the capitalist mode of production.[82] In the context of extractivism, for instance, under-criminalisation is evidenced by how '[e]conomic and powerful actors are not perceived as offenders because social and environmental harms are seen as the result of "normal" business activities'; consequently, victims from such harms tend to be overlooked and normalised as a side effect of economic activities.[83] Based on this perspective, the critical stream understands legal attacks on environmental defenders as a form of over-criminalisation of environmental dissent at the primary and secondary levels because such struggles may pose threats to the capitalist mode of production.

However, these critical streams, especially the criminalisation approach, suffer limitations in their ability to comparatively examine legal attacks on environmental defenders. While the liberal stream pays less attention to the mobilisation of the criminal justice system to attack environmental defenders, the critical stream's criminalisation framework overlooks the resort to civil procedures to attack environmental defenders. As will be discussed in Chapter 4, the chilling effects of utilising civil procedures on defenders may be no less harmful than criminal procedures, including demanding excessive compensation that leads to impoverishment of defenders. Moreover, taking criminalisation, SLAPP, and legal intimidation together, they tend to stress most predominantly the effects suffered by individual defenders who are directly targeted using the law. This book takes the analysis further, arguing that attacks on environmental defenders utilising legal

[80] Kurtiç (n 73) 6.

[81] Valeria Veigh Weis, *Criminalization of Activism: Historical, Present, and Future Perspectives* (Routledge, 2022).

[82] Valeria Vegh Weis, *Marxism and Criminology: A History of Criminal Selectivity* (Brill, 2017).

[83] Maria Laura Böhm, *The Crime of Maldevelopment: Economic Deregulation and Violence in the Global South* (Routledge, 2019) 2.

means can be seen as a proxy for containing socio-environmental conflicts with less risk to the legitimacy of the attacker than direct violence. There is a need to fill this gap in the literature by developing a more comprehensive framework without losing important insights on the structural conditions from which these attacks emerged and the unequal relations of power between actors involved as well as the wider societal impacts of these attacks. To this purpose, this book responds to this opportunity to investigate and explain both the legal and social dimensions of legal actions directed towards environmental defenders.

HEL as a Conflict Management Strategy

Since 1990s, the concept of 'environmental governance' has emerged as 'both the social organisation of decision making with respect to the environment, and the production of social order via the administration of nature'.[84] A rapid acceptance of this concept is contributed by its reflection of 'a broader institutional turn in which greater attention is paid to the relationships between institutional capacities, the coordination and coherence of economic processes, and social action'.[85] In this understanding, environmental governance should be regarded as a particular mode of environmental conflict regulation managed through institutional-legal means in which environmental problems are understood through the lens of procedural rights, such as partnership, inclusion, and participation, instead of justice and distribution. Although environmental governance opens new spaces of political contestations beyond the formal arena of representative democracy and encourages new actors in environmental politics, such as environmental NGOs, private firms, and other non-state actors, it may 'stabilise extractive regimes' by using participatory mechanisms to maintain their legitimacy.[86] However, in a time of global environmental crises, including the climate crisis, where many people question the legitimacy of extractive regimes and at the same time pose challenges to existing neoliberal environmental governance, politico-business elites have attempted to find ways to secure their legitimacy to address these challenges. Their inability to secure legitimacy and mobilise consent (hegemony) has led increasingly to the use of authoritarian measures to buttress the state's support for economic growth-led development and capital accumulation for politico-business elites, including the use of lawfare against environmental defenders.[87]

This phenomenon marks a shift from neoliberal environmental governance to increasing 'authoritarian statism' where legal mobilisation becomes central to the

[84] Gavin Bridge and Tom Peerault, 'Environmental Governance', in N. Castree et al. (eds.), *A Companion to Environmental Geography* (Blackwell, 2009) 477.

[85] ibid., 475. [86] ibid., 482.

[87] Kanishka Jayasuriya, 'Authoritarian Statism and the New Right in Asia's Conservative Democracies', (2018) 48 (4) *Journal of Contemporary Asia* 584, 592.

disciplining and criminalisation of environmental dissent.[88] Here, authoritarianism can be observed not only through 'the exercise of brute coercive force' but also through 'the reconfiguring of state and institutional power in an attempt to insulate certain policies and institutional practices from social and political dissent'.[89] Authoritarian statism links the regulation and management of conflict much more directly to the political economy of lawfare, where 'policing' and securitising environmental governance seems to be increasingly common in the era of global socio-ecological crises. It may reveal how law plays a dual role in environmental conflicts, both as a means of coercion and as a platform for creating consent. In contrast to the 'moral functionalist' conception of law, which embraces law as a dispute settlement mechanism, the law should be seen as a technology of social power which both generates and exacerbates social conflicts.[90] In other words, from a social conflict perspective, laws and legal institutions are both the outcome and the future terrain where social conflicts over power and access to resources are fought. As the terrain of current and future struggles, the juridical system is a field where lawfare is exercised with the intention to halt the 'capacity to resist' of identified 'enemies'.[91]

Indeed, lawfare has been used previously in several different contexts, especially in war and security studies. In this book, the concept is not conceptualised within the context of military strategies[92] nor is it a form of 'drop-by-drop coup' executed through the criminalisation of populist leaders.[93] Instead, this book follows the concept used by Comaroff and Comaroff. They provide two different definitions of lawfare. The first one is that lawfare is understood as 'the use of force to conquer and control indigenous populations through coercive use of legal means'.[94] This definition fits better in the context of colonialism, in which 'alien' forces impose their power on a native population. However, it can be problematic to use in a conflict where insider/outsider forces find it difficult to draw boundaries neatly. In *Law and Disorder in the Postcolony*, Comaroff and Comaroff develop the concept of lawfare further, as 'the resort to legal instruments, to the violence inherent in the law, to commit acts of political coercion'.[95] There are two forms of

[88] Nicos Poulantzas, *State, Power, Socialism* (Verso, 2000) 239.

[89] Ian Bruff, 'The Rise of Authoritarian Neoliberalism', (2014) 26 (1) *Rethinking Marxism* 113, 115.

[90] Austin Turk, 'Law as Weapon in Social Conflict', (1976) 23 (3) *Social Problems* 276.

[91] Howard Caygill, *On Resistance: A Philosophy of Defiance* (Bloomsbury, 2013).

[92] Charles Dunlap, 'Lawfare: A Decisive Element of 21st-Century Conflicts?' (2009) 54 Joint Force Quarterly 34; Craig Jones, 'Lawfare and the Juridification of the Late Modern War', (2016) 40 (2) *Progress in Human Geography* 221.

[93] Valeria Vegh Weis, 'What Does Lawfare Mean in Latin America? A New Framework for Understanding for Criminalization of Progress Political Leaders', (2022) *Punishment & Society* https://doi.org/10.11771/1462474521116348; Vegh Weis (n 77) 10; Cristiano Zanin, Valeska Martins, and Rafael Valim, *Lawfare: Waging War through Law* (Routledge, 2022).

[94] John L. Comaroff, 'Colonialism, Culture, and the Law: A Foreword', (2021) 26 *Law and Social Inquiry* 306.

[95] John L Comaroff and Jean Comaroff, 'Law and Disorder in the Postcolony: An Introduction', in J. Comaroff & J. L. Comaroff (eds.), *Law and Disorder* (University of Chicago Press, 2006) 30.

lawfare: 'insurgency lawfare' and 'hegemonic lawfare'.[96] 'Insurgency lawfare', what McCann terms 'legal mobilisation by the powerless'[97] or Lindt calls 'judicialisation from below',[98] refers to using law to protect or defend rights and livelihoods from violations committed by the state or corporations. Meanwhile, 'hegemonic lawfare', also known as 'legal mobilisation by the powerful' by McCann or 'judicialisation from above' by Lindt, concerns the use of law to maintain the hegemony of the powerholders. In this mode of lawfare, law and legal institutions 'serve as hegemonic instruments of elites to consolidate their power'.[99] This understanding demonstrates a different face of law: apart from being 'a means of resistance', it is also 'a marker of hegemony'.[100]

Attacks on environmental defenders should be regarded as HEL. It is hegemonic because 'it induces people to comply with a dominant set of practices and institutions without the threat of physical force and that this hegemony is overarching because it encompasses people of diverse races, classes, and genders'.[101] To borrow Mary Lawlor's words, the UN Special Rapporteur on Human Rights Defenders, HEL '[a]t its core it's about maintaining the power structures in place'.[102] In this regard, natural resource extraction and exploitation conducted under the banner of development and growth, through which the existing political-economic structure is underpinned, has been disrupted by environmental struggles exercised by affected communities and environmental activists. As these communities and activists do not agree with the dominant discourse on development and economic growth, they do not provide consent to the state and corporations to expropriate their means of livelihoods and exploit the environment. Therefore, HEL was launched by powerful groups to discipline those dissenting groups that were involved in environmental struggles and educate the public on the risk of not submitting to the status quo. HEL is more comprehensive than SLAPP, where legal procedures mobilised by the powerholders to retaliate against defenders is undertaken using legal actions that encompass civil procedures, the criminal courts system, and administrative law procedures. Moreover, actors who launch HEL are not predominantly private actors, namely corporations or their agents, but more significantly, the dominant elements of the state through its apparatuses or officials.

[96] John Comaroff, 'Foreword', in Martins Zanin & Valim(eds.), *Lawfare: Waging War through Law* (Routledge, 2022), vii–xi.

[97] Michael McCann, 'Litigation and Legal Mobilisation', in K. Whittington, R. Kelemen, & G. Caldeira (eds.), *The Oxford Handbook of Law and Politics* (Oxford University Press, 2008) 534.

[98] Lindt (n 76). [99] ibid., 369.

[100] Susan F. Hirsch and Mindie Lazarus-Black, 'Introduction/Performance and Paradox: Exploring Law's Role in Hegemony and Resistance', in M. Lazarus-Black & S. Hirsch (eds.), *Contested States: Law, Hegemony and Resistance* (Routledge, 2012) 9.

[101] Douglas Litowitz, 'Gramsci, Hegemony, and the State', (2000) 5 *BYU Law Review* 515, 517.

[102] Nina Lakhani, Damien Gayle, and Matthew Taylor, 'How Criminalisation Is Being Used to Silence Climate Activists across the World', *The Guardian* (12 October 2023) <www.theguardian.com/environment/2023/oct/12/how-criminalisation-is-being-used-to-silence-climate-activists-across-the-world> accessed 12 April 2024.

HEL's Dual Functions

Obedience to the state in capitalist society cannot solely depend on 'power and material force' (domination) but may also be built upon consent (hegemony).[103] Lovett, echoing Hegel, argues that 'domination will tend to be self-defeating' because it is 'maintained through legitimation beliefs'[104] and this legitimacy may come into question when the exercise of direct coercion is excessive. In the context of Southeast Asia, Aspinall, for instance, observes that '[r]egimes that rely on little else but repression to maintain themselves often end up radicalizing society and creating powerful revolutionary oppositions'.[105] Indeed, '[v]iolence is a very effective medium for enforcing the unequal distribution of life-chances ... in the short term, but is costly to maintain and often in contradiction to the "modern" institutions of legitimation'.[106] This is why the use of direct force or violence is masked by various subtle mechanisms of pacification, including the mobilisation of law and its legal institutions in order to maintain the status quo.

In characterising HEL as a strategy employed by the state and powerholders to achieve obedience, at first we need to demonstrate the connection between law and hegemony. Genovese argues that 'the law acts hegemonically to assure that their particular consciences can be subordinated ... to the collective judgment of society'.[107] Gramsci writes:

> If every state tends to create and maintain a certain type of civilisation and citizen (and hence of collective life and of individual relations), and to eliminate certain customs and attitudes and to disseminate others, then the Law will be its instrument for this purpose. ... It must be developed so that it is suitable for such purpose – so that it is maximally effective and productive of positive results.[108]

In this understanding, the law should be seen as playing a vital role in bridging force and consent. This is because law is both an instrument of force due to its inherent violence element,[109] but also a means of mobilising consent due to its 'educative function' to serve 'the political and cultural hegemony of the ruling classes'.[110] The

[103] Antonio Gramsci, *Selections from the Prison Notebooks*, edited and translated by Quintin Hoare & Geoffrey N. Smith (International Publishers, 1987) 57; see also Anne Showtack Sasson, 'Hegemony, War of Position and Political Intervention', in A. S. Sassoon (ed.), *Approaches to Gramsci* (Writers and Readers, 1982) 101.

[104] Frank Lovett, *A General Theory of Domination and Justice* (Oxford University Press, 2010), 11.

[105] Edward Aspinall, *Opposing Suharto: Compromise, Resistance, and Regime Change in Indonesia* (Stanford University Press, 2005) 2.

[106] Daniel Miller, Michael Rowlands, and Christopher Tilley, 'Introduction', in D. Miller, M. Rowlands & C. Tilley (eds.), *Domination and Resistance* (Routledge, 1989) 5–6.

[107] Eugene Genovese, *Roll, Jordan, Roll: The World the Slaves Made* (Vintage, 1976) 27.

[108] Gramsci (n 103) 246.

[109] Marx, for instance, states: '[c]ruelty is a characteristic feature of laws'. See Karl Marx, 1842, 'Proceedings of the Sixth Rhine Province Assembly. Third Article. Debates on the Law on Thefts of Wood', *Marxist*. <https://marxists.architexturez.net/archive/marx/works/1842/10/25.htm#p1> accessed 17 December 2023.

[110] Gramsci (n 103) 258.

relationship between force and consent cannot be seen as existing 'side by side like two calculable homogeneous magnitudes, related in such a way that more consent corresponds to less violence'.[111] In this context, consent and force are interdependent in the sense that governing a society in the modern time requires consent from the society being governed, and the use of coercive methods in such governance is also 'conditioned by this consent'.[112] Both consent and coercion are exercised within the framework of the legal system, revealing the dual functions of the system as a form of direct force (domination) and simultaneously intellectual-moral leadership (hegemony).

Following the dual faces of law, this book conceptualises HEL as having dual functions in maintaining favourable conditions for capitalist development. They are (1) the coercive function (as a direct form of domination) and (2) indirect intellectual and moral leadership (hegemony). The first function is derived from the common characterisation of the role of law in society as expressed through its violent element. Benjamin explains the relationship between violence and law, arguing that '[a]ll violence as a means is either law-positing or law-preserving. If it lays claim to neither of these predicates, then it forfeits all validity. From this, however, it follows that every violence as a means ... itself participates in the problematic character of law as such.'[113] In a similar tone, Comaroff and Comaroff note that '[l]aw originates in violence and lives by violent means, the notion, in other words, that the legal and the lethal animate and inhabit one another'.[114] Hence, violence is an inherent element of law. In colonial history, law was 'a nonviolent means of committing great violence' through which land was appropriated, and labour was extracted; but its 'language of legality' was also 'the lingua franca' through which peace and the terms of coloniser–colonised relations were negotiated.[115]

Criminal law demonstrates the close connection between law and violence. Here, the state classifies behaviours according to a code of legality and illegality and punishes illegal behaviours as a form of revenge or retaliation permissible by various moral justifications.[116] Criminal law and violence should be seen as mutually reinforcing, in which violence constitutes the law, and the law needs violence for its effective implementation. Marx once wrote how criminal law defines the very foundation of the (capitalist) state that cannot be transferred to private entities because '[e]very right of the state in relation to the criminal is at the same time a right of the criminal in relation to the state'.[117] Accordingly, HEL utilising

[111] Poulantzas (n 88) 81. [112] Sasson (n 103) 94–95.

[113] Walter Benjamin, *Toward the Critique of Violence: A Critical Edition* (Stanford University Press, 2021), 48.

[114] Comaroff and Comaroff (n 95) 31.

[115] John L. Comaroff, 'Foreword', in M. Lazarus-Black and S. Hirsch (eds.), *Contested States: Law, Hegemony and Resistance* (Routledge, 1994) xii.

[116] See David Boonin, *The Problem of Punishment* (Cambridge University Press, 2008) 2.

[117] Karl Marx (n 109).

criminal law should be seen as the exercise of power by the state in relation to environmental defenders. With all its apparatuses, including the judiciary, the state is crucial in shaping notions of 'legality' and 'violence'.[118] However, HEL should not be reduced merely to a form of what Galtung conceptualises as 'physical violence'.[119] HEL, in all its forms, including criminalisation, serves as technology of the power to reproduce the 'atmosphere of violence', which encompasses the physical violence that directly targets environmental defenders, structural violence experienced by those involved in environmental movements, and cultural violence experienced by the general population when it legitimises the physical and structural violence against environmental defenders and movements.

Besides as a means of coercion, HEL should also be understood as a platform for creating consent. This hegemonic objective takes place within two different fields of application: 'the domain of institutionalized political structures' (within the state) and 'the domain of the political practices of the dominant classes' (within civil society).[120] In the former, HEL aims to create bureaucratic discipline by consolidating and maintaining logical coherence within the state structure on what constitutes the state's general interest and, at the same time, how constraints to achieve it should be overcome. In the latter, HEL plays a hegemonic function where it is projected on the society to provide 'the general direction imposed on social life' and to legally enforce discipline on those 'who do not "consent" either actively or passively'.[121] This hegemonic function of HEL within the sphere of civil society becomes more effective if the legal mobilisation by the state and the powerholders presents itself as a legitimate exercise of power and rights that contributes to the achievement of the public interest. Thus, law and adjudication through which HEL is played out relies on an apolitical self-image that, as Rajagopal put it, 'provides an ideological cover for the pursuit of private, partisan ends which are often dressed up as public interest'.[122]

Addressing a Legitimacy Deficit

In a globalised capitalist world, given that scales for political and social conflicts are widely open, ranging from local to international, the outcomes of the struggles are contingent. Hence, in conditions of social conflict, elites and their opponents must continuously rework their positions and strategies. In his book *Participation*

[118] Anna Zalik, 'Protest-as-Violence in Oil Fields: The Contested Representation of Profiteering in Two Extractive Sites', in S. Feldman, C. Geisler, and G. Menon (eds.), *Accumulating Insecurity: Violence and Dispossession in the Making of Everyday Life* (University of Georgia Press, 2011) 262.

[119] Böhm (n 83) 154.

[120] Nicos Poulantzas, *The Poulantzas Reader: Marxism, Law and the State*, edited by James Martin (Verso, 2008) 88.

[121] Gramsci (n 103) 12.

[122] Balakrishnan Rajagopal, 'The Role of Law in Counter-Hegemonic Globalization and Global Legal Pluralism: Lessons from the Narmada Valley Struggle in India', (2005) 18 *Leiden Journal of International Law* 345, 352.

without Democracy, Rodan explains how 'the development of market capitalism with its deepening inequalities and its disruption of established patterns of social power and interest generates new political challenges for both entrenched elites and those at the political margins'.[123] This has led to the designation of 'political instruments to enforce and consolidate deepening concentrations of power and wealth and to domesticate opposition' under what he calls 'the mode of participation' (MOP).[124] As a response, different participatory mechanisms beyond existing institutional structures have been developed to contain social conflicts. They are assumed to benefit both the powerholders (as political tools 'to enforce and consolidate deepening concentrations of power and wealth and to domesticate opposition') and their opponent groups (as political instruments for dismantling those concentrations).[125]

Specifically in extractive industries, the expansion and acceleration of capital in the age of globalisation has consequences for the local environment and livelihoods, leading to resistance and conflicts. In Southeast Asia, Sinclair demonstrates how conflicts involving the mining industry against affected communities and civil society organisations mobilising their international alliances have created a crisis of legitimacy for the industry. Thus, the industry addresses the crisis of legitimacy through dual scalar strategies: (1) globalising self-governance to prevent binding legal frameworks restricting mining activities and (2) localising conflicts through company-sponsored participatory mechanisms, such as CSR, to contain resistance from affected communities and NGOs.[126] A similar approach has also taken place in the plantation industries through the non-binding Roundtable Sustainable Palm Oil and other community engagement programs, which have contributed to the reproduction of hegemony and enhanced the industry's legitimacy.[127]

Indeed, these authors contribute to a deep and critical understanding of how powerful elites design their strategies to respond, react, contain, and depoliticise struggles from opponents through different modes of participation, including CSR, participatory budgeting, or community-driven development projects. However, it should not be assumed that all opponent groups are willing to participate in these distinct modes. In the context of the Philippines, for instance, progressive social forces refuse to participate in the state's organisation to pursue a development agenda.[128] In their work, Rodan and Sinclair leave the question of how powerholders and the state respond to local communities' struggles that operate outside the state- or corporate-sponsored participatory mechanisms open for further

[123] Gary Rodan, *Participation without Democracy: Containing Conflict in Southeast Asia* (Cornell University Press, 2018) 1.

[124] ibid. [125] ibid.

[126] Lian Sinclair, 'The Power of Mining MNCs: Global Governance and Social Conflict', in J. Mikler & K. Ronit (eds.), *MNC in Global Politics: Pathways of Influence* (Edward Elgar, 2020) 139–158.

[127] Izabela Delabre and Chukwumerije Okereke, 'Palm Oil, Power, and Participation: The Political Ecology of Social Impact Assessment', (2019) 3 (3) *Environment and Planning E: Nature and Space* 1.

[128] Toby Carroll, *Delusions of Development: The World Bank and the Post-Washington Consensus in Southeast Asia* (Palgrave Macmillan, 2010).

elaboration. It is clear that these mechanisms do not replace conventional strategies of resorting to violent means and existing state's institutional structures for handling social conflicts evidenced by the fact that extrajudicial killings in mining and plantation conflicts remain alarming.[129] This demonstrates how violence has been continuously used by those whose profit accumulation agendas are disrupted by environmental struggles.

However, as mentioned earlier, the excessive use of direct violence in domesticating environmental struggles may put the legitimacy of the extractive industries and the state at risk. As Bonanno correctly observes:

> The capitalist system has always required the maintenance of adequate levels of legitimation and social stability to allow capital accumulation. This means that, while the working and subordinate classes are exploited along with natural resources, the capitalist class must make sure that this exploitation does not reach unsustainable levels. ... Once the contradiction between the maintenance of an adequate level of legitimation and the exploitation of labour and natural resources could not be managed, crises emerged.[130]

The increasingly common use of law to silence dissent should be seen as an attempt by powerholders to find different means to react or respond to their legitimacy deficit. In Honduras, for instance, 'in response to anti-mining mobilisations, confrontations at the extractive frontier have hardened: when the mining industry fails to obtain consent from communities, it resorts to the criminalisation of dissent and intimidation of activists'.[131] In the context of authoritarian regimes, it has been noted that those regimes 'switch to the rule of law as a legitimatizing narrative only after the failure of their initial policy objectives or after popular support for the regime has faded'.[132]

A similar tendency also occurs in seemingly democratic regimes where legal mobilisation against environmental defenders is justified under the rule of law narrative. In Thailand, Thongchai Winichakul, a prominent Thai historian, points out that how people who are deemed as threats to national security, narrowly understood as a political stability of the monarchy, are prosecuted by the state

[129] UN General Assembly, 'Report of the Special Rapporteur on the Situation of Human Rights Defenders A/72/150' (2017) <http://undocs.org/en/A/72/170> accessed 23 March 2018; Global Witness, *On Dangerous Ground: 2015's Deadly Environment: The Killing and Criminalization of Land and Environmental Defenders Worldwide* (Global Witness, 2016); Global Witness, '*Their Faces: Defenders on the Frontline*' (2019) <www.globalwitness.org/en/campaigns/environmental-activists/their-faces-defenders-frontline/?accessible=true#> accessed 19 July 2019; Global Witness, *At What Cost? Irresponsible Business and the Murder of Land and Environmental Defenders in 2017* (Global Witness, 2008) 8.

[130] Alessandro Bonanno, *The Legitimation Crisis of Neoliberalism: The State, Will-Formation, and Resistance* (Palgrave Macmillan, 2017) 245.

[131] Nick Middeldrop, Carlos Morales, and Gemma van der Haar, 'Social Mobilisation and Violence at the Mining Frontier: The Case of Honduras', (2016) 3 (4) *The Extractive Industries and Society* 930.

[132] Tamir Moustafa and Tom Ginsburg, 'Introduction: The Functions of Court in Authoritarian Politics', in T. Ginsburg and T. Moustafa (eds.), *Rule by Law: The Politics of Court in Authoritarian Regimes* (Cambridge University Press, 2008) 6.

apparatus is what he terms as the 'royalist rule of law.[133] In this context, the courts may not be directly controlled in every case by the status quo, but as national security is the ultimate goal of the state, they are compelled to take this goal into consideration in judicial decision-making.[134] In Indonesia, the narrative of the rule of law is used to engage in legal battles. A legal attorney for Luhut Pandjaitan, coordinating minister for maritime and investment (2014–24), brought defamation charges against Haris Azhar and Fatia Maulidiyanti, two NGO activists, after they exposed the minister's connection to mining activities in Papua. The attorney justified the legal action stating that 'our country is a state based on the rule of law, so we should not take refuge in democracy in order to commit slander and defamation. Because democracy must be based on the law.'[135] For him, the dispute should be resolved through legal means because based on the due process of law, the legal system provides rights for disputing parties to present evidence in challenging the allegation or proving otherwise.

Based on this assumption, HEL provides a more secure means to contain environmental conflicts because the law and legal institutions provide a myth of fair play based on pre-existing rules of the game. In this regard, 'the judiciary is an *actor*, whose task it is to guarantee that the government and citizens obey the limitations set by their exercise of power'.[136] Moreover, if a dispute occurs over whether the government or citizens have overstepped the limitations, the judiciary becomes the reference on which parties should depend. The act of resorting to the law to resolve conflicts may create a positive public perception towards power-holders and the state, assuming that 'the more that the powerful appeal to the law as the self-sufficient justification for their power, the more they have to respect it themselves for their legitimacy to be sustained'.[137] Legal institutions provide a framework for resolving disputes perceived by the public as fair and reasonable. Legal channels increase the legitimacy of state action while reducing the possibility of widespread backlash or accusations of authoritarianism. By adhering to legal procedures, states and strong actors can maintain public trust and support, which is crucial for long-term stability and governance.

However, it should be noted that the rule of law narrative contains a double-edged sword. The more the regime's legitimacy relies on the narrative, the wider the legal and opportunity structure opens for the regime's opponents to mobilise to challenge the regime. This is because, to maintain legitimacy through the law, the regime has to concede a considerable degree of autonomy to the judiciary and legal

[133] Prachatai, 'Thongchai Winichakul: We Live under "Royalist Rule of Law"', *Prachatai English* (Bangkok, 7 Juni 2024) <https://prachataienglish.com/node/10970> accessed 10 June 2024.

[134] ibid.

[135] Dwi Bowo Raharjo, 'Disebut Kriminalisasi Aktivis, Tim Hukum Moeldoko: Tidak Berdasar, Hanya Pengalihan Isu', *Suara* (30 July 2021). <www.suara.com/news/2021/07/30/230500/disebut-kriminalisasi-aktivis-tim-hukum-moeldoko-tak-berdasar-hanya-pengalihan-isu> accessed 31 March 2024.

[136] Adriaan Bedner, 'An Elementary Approach to the Rule of Law', (2010) 2 *Hague Journal on the Rule of Law* 48, 68.

[137] David Beetham, *The Legitimation of Power* (Palgrave Macmillan, 1991) 68.

institutions in order to be trusted by society. Hence, for opponent groups, resorting to the law may open an opportunity to transform HEL into forms of strategic litigation to expose the root causes of environmental conflicts and educate the public on the causes. As judicial independence is a central feature of the liberal notion of the rule of law,[138] overt intervention by the judiciary should be avoided. Thus, the corporatist relationship between the judiciary and the executive power is pursued more subtly, without dictating individual cases, but simultaneously ensuring that the macro-political and economic interests of the executive power are secured. This can be pursued through indirect intellectual and moral leadership, where executive power is the presentation of the nation's general will; hence, its policies as an embodiment of the public interest are enacted in the pursuit of general welfare. Cases brought before them should be heard routinely through the application of its principles of 'general, abstract, formal, and strictly codified',[139] which, in the last instance, according to Poulantzas, will serve the interests of the status quo.[140]

In the context of Indonesia, for instance, indirect leadership from the executive body to the judiciary is exemplified by President Jokowi's repetitive statement that '[i]nvestment is an important instrument to drive our economic growth'.[141] It is expected that all state structures and apparatuses will internalise this paramount state interest. Hatta Ali, the Chief Justice of the Supreme Court of Indonesia, in the 2019 Supreme Court's annual report, embraces the law and development proposition by stating that 'law is one of the most important factors in economic growth. To create spaces for economic growth, the Supreme Court has taken a role in resolving many legal barriers for pursuing people's welfare,'[142] including by settling disputes concerning land acquisition for development projects in the public interest which are largely in favour of the government's interest. Hence, when the paramount goal of economic growth has become a shared platform of the *trias politica*, any attempt to interfere or disrupt the national interest in the pursuit of economic growth should be contained. Environmental struggles are not an exception.

[138] Kanishka Jayasuriya, 'Introduction: A Framework for the Analysis of Legal Institutions in East Asia', in K. Jayasuriya (ed.), *Law, Capitalism and Power in Asia: The Rule of Law and Legal Institutions* (Routledge, 1999) 16.

[139] From Poulantzas's original words, this is understood as: '(a) *general*, contrary in this respect to individual dispositions that only concern a specific case or person; (b) *abstract*, constructed using concepts that are autonomous from concrete reality; (c) *formal*, stripped of concrete, "material" content; and (d) *strictly codified*: by this we mean the specific structuration whose goal is to preserve the existence – and thus also guarantee the predictability – of a normative order, by allowing for its "complete reversibility"' Poulantzas (n 120) 36.

[140] ibid.

[141] Rangga Pandu and Resinta, 'Jokowi Urges National Police to Guard, Secure Investment' *Antara News* (Jakarta, 3 December 2021) <https://en.antaranews.com/news/202617/jokowi-urges-national-police-to-guard-secure-investment> accessed 02 February 2022.

[142] Supreme Court of Indonesia, 'Mahkamah Agung Berperan Dalam Pertumbuhan Ekonomi Negara' (Mahkamah Agung, 7 Februari 2020) <www.mahkamahagung.go.id/id/berita/4026/mahkamah-agung-> accessed 02 February 2022.

Prosecutions or suppressions of environmental struggles are publicly justifiable because they have hindered the achievement of this public interest, and the lack of public condemnation to this prosecution or suppression is seen as a measure of de facto 'legitimacy' to the state action.

For powerful elites, the resort to law in containing environmental conflicts can be beneficial for other purposes. This includes maintaining the social order by relying on the political and educational dimension of open trial procedures through which the public can observe and learn from cases being heard by the court. As critical criminologists point out, the practice of criminalising people in large numbers is a consistent element of the state's ability to actively build or create social order. Criminalisation techniques allow capitalist states to oscillate between overt repression and gaining public consent for the state's repressive goals.[143] As Poulantzas puts it: '[l]aw is always present from the beginning in the social order' because it organises the field of repression in order to prevent legally prohibited actions and to prescribe conducts to be protected.[144] In a similar tone, Comaroff and Comaroff state that '"[t]he law" . . . has become the medium in which politics are played out, in which conflicts are dealt with across otherwise incommensurable axes of difference, in which the workings of the "free" market are assured, in which social order is ostensibly erected and the substance of citizenship made manifest'.[145] In this light, resorting to the courts to contain environmental conflicts is aimed at assuring the market, maintaining social order, and reconstructing the subjectivities of environmental defenders.

Through HEL, legal decisions and precedents set by the courts can have far-reaching consequences for developing a culture of legalities on how conflicts should be resolved. This culture is marked by the migration of politics to the courts when '[c]onflicts once joined in parliaments, by means of street protests, mass demonstrations, and media campaigns, through labour strikes, boycotts, blockades, and other instruments of assertion, tend more and more . . . to find their way to the judiciary'.[146] If the state that is capable of using 'legitimate' coercion to pursue its conceived public interest resorts to engagement in a legal battle to resolve conflicts with its opponent groups, this path should be seen as developing a standardised model of conflict resolution mechanism that should also be taken by the groups in defending their interests or expressing their dissent and grievances. Once this 'culture of legalities' is developed, it may define the boundaries between the 'civilised' and 'uncivilised' forms of environmental struggles. To be called 'civilised', actors involved in environmental conflicts should utilise existing institutional structures designated for resolving conflicts through the standardised model. For those who exercise their struggles outside the standardised model, they will be

[143] Ignas Bernant and David Whyte, 'Criminalization as Strategy of Power: The Case of Catalunya 2017–2020', in V. Vegh Weis (ed.), *Criminalization of Activism: Historical, Present, and Future Perspectives* (Routledge, 2022) 141.

[144] Poulantzas (n 88). [145] Comaroff and Comaroff (n 95) 22. [146] ibid., 26–27.

stigmatised as 'uncivilised' struggles, a label by which the use of repressive measures, including direct coercion, will be justified.

Strategic Dimensions of HEL

As a conceptual framework, HEL can assist scholars in understanding its strategic dimension more completely. Following Comaroff, Zanin et al. propose that lawfare has three strategic dimensions: geographies, weaponry, and externalities.[147] This book proposes another strategic dimension that should be considered in analysing HEL: resistance. Borrowing from Stanley and McColloch in the context of state crimes, the failure to engage with resistance in lawfare scholarship 'may lead to feelings of despair, disinterest or impotence' and 'states of mind that facilitate passivity' towards the exercise of hegemonic lawfare.[148] Moreover, it overlooks the history of struggles that, according to Poulantzas, 'are always at the foundation of power'.[149] In other words, the exercise of power by the powerful groups upon society never occurs without being questioned and challenged, which may take an 'everyday form of resistance'[150] or open struggles. Therefore, in this section, four dimensions of HEL are unpacked before they are operationalised to reveal the anatomy of HEL in Southeast Asia.

Geographies

Geographies refer to the jurisdictions within which legal battles occur. In Zanin et al.'s words, geographies are conceived of as 'a jurisdictional, administrative or political body which is responsible for applying the law'[151] which encompasses two forms: the subject-matter jurisdiction and the territorial jurisdiction. The subject-matter jurisdiction is the legal fields within which HEL is brought and exercised, and those legal fields are civil law, criminal law, and administrative law, in which each of these fields of law has its distinct proceedings and implications in the practice of HEL. Meanwhile, territorial jurisdiction refers to the legal institutions with the geographical scope of competence to administer HEL brought before them. As political geography scholars have commonly argued, geographical scales are not an empty container within which social conflicts occur. They may also be a resource

[147] Cristiano Zanin, Valeska Martins, and Rafael Valim, *Lawfare: Waging War through Law* (Routledge, 2022).

[148] Elizabeth Stanley and Jude McColloch, 'Resistance to State Crime', in E. Stanley & J. McCulloch (eds.), *State Crime and Resistance* (Routledge, 2013) 2.

[149] Poulantzas (n 88) 9.

[150] James C. Scott, *Weapons of the Weak: Everyday Forms of Peasant Resistance* (Yale University Press, 1985).

[151] Zanin, Martins, and Valim (n 146) 44.

that may shape the outcome of those conflicts.[152] This is because a particular configuration of power is embedded in a specific geographical scale, which in turn may facilitate a social group's mobilisation of available resources and the building of alliances within a given scale while at the same time constraining the ability of the other group involved in the conflict to do the same. In the context of HEL, in Thailand for instance, a company may resort to a court that is far away from the targeted environmental defenders' place of residence. This spatial strategy aims at intensifying the cost of attending the trial, thus maximising chilling effects suffered by the defenders.

In addition to these two jurisdictions, HEL also requires another jurisdiction to be scrutinised. As already discussed, environmental conflicts may occur in various economic sectors, including mining, plantation, coastal, and marine. Thus, when analysing HEL we need to pay particular attention to the sectors in which HEL is commonly exercised. As shown by Middeldrop, Morales, and van der Haar, in Honduras, the mining sector relies on criminalisation and violence to expand its mining frontier.[153] Chapter 4 reveals how, in Southeast Asia, the mining and plantation sectors are the two most dangerous sectors within which HEL is predominantly exercised by the dominant group to attack environmental defenders. This is not only because of the nature of these sectors, which is extractive, in that they continuously seek new frontiers and require large expanses of land to ensure profitability, but also because these sectors underpin the existing political-economic structure from which the material wealth of politico-business elites is derived. This aligns with Peluso and Watts's observation that 'extensive and destructive violence is likely when the resources are either in great abundance or have great economic or strategic value'.[154] Hence, it is also safe to say that the bigger a sector's contribution in underpinning the political and economic status quo, the more likely it is to resort to HEL in managing the environmental conflicts it causes.

Weaponry

Weaponry encompasses legal provisions, articles, or rules mobilised as the basis for taking legal actions against environmental defenders.[155] As the subject-matter jurisdiction may include civil, criminal, and administrative law, HEL's weaponry dimension can also be found in those legal fields. The vaguer a legal provision is, the easier it may be stretched to retaliate against defenders. In civil law, for instance, the tort law provision is commonly used by those whose interest in accumulating profits is disrupted by environmental movements. Within the field of administrative law,

[152] Shahar Hameiri, Caroline Hughes, and Fabio Scarpello, *International Intervention and Local Politics* (Cambridge University Press, 2017).

[153] Middeldrop, Morales, and van der Haar (n 131) 937.

[154] Nancy Peluso and Michael Watts, 'Violent Environments', in N. Peluso & M. Watts (eds.), *Violent Environments* (Cornell University Press, 2001) 34.

[155] Zanin, Martins, and Valim (n 146) 16.

provisions related to compulsory registration for civil society organisations are also prone to being weaponised to retaliate against environmental organisations whose activities and advocacy are considered barriers for the state or corporations in their pursuit of economic growth and capital accumulation.

Meanwhile, the use of the criminal justice system in HEL may be derived from three forms: principled crimes of disobedience, trumped-up crimes, and conducts of self-defence. Each form of crime employs a different set of legal weaponry. Offences related to public orders, trespassing, and property damage have become a standard weapon in uncivil disobedience. During the Covid-19 pandemic, governments in many countries undertook strict health measures, including prohibiting public gatherings; hence, spaces for mobilising public protests also shrank. Environmental activists who refuse to submit under the designated mechanisms in expressing their dissent were likely to be prosecuted.[156] As Di Ronco observed in Italy, charges against activists exercising civil disobedience are very often 'ill-substantiated or unnecessarily exaggerated'.[157] This is also the case in crimes related to property damage, in which law enforcement officers focus on establishing proof that someone's right of ownership is being infringed upon by the defendant regardless of the value of the property.[158] In some cases, environmental defenders who broke a company's glass window, priced at less than US$500, during a mass protest were convicted and sentenced to several months in prison. This demonstrates how the sanctity of private property is valued more highly by the existing criminal justice system than human lives spent in jail for defending the environment and local livelihoods. This would seem to confirm Hay's characterisation of criminal law's history that it 'is as much concerned with the authority as it is with property'.[159]

Moreover, trumped-up criminal cases may use different criminal offences. They include criminal defamation (offline or online) as a weapon for corporations or government officials who accuse environmental defenders of having defamed their reputations. As a 'discursive crime', defamation provides a perfect means for intimidating defenders because the offence does not aim to prove whether a statement expressed by the defendant is accurate; instead, it seeks to establish evidence of the defendant's motive or intent to defame someone's reputation.[160] As demonstrated in Chapter 4, criminal offences that provide a more considerable authority for law enforcement officials to interpret their elements are instrumental in exercising HEL. In Southeast Asia, crimes against a state's ideology or symbols are crafted as trumped-up criminal cases because what constitutes disruptions to public orders or conduct against a state's ideology and symbols is within the

[156] Di Ronco (n 73) 2. [157] Di Ronco (n 79). [158] Sheldrick (n 57) 19.

[159] Douglas Hay, 'Property, Authority, and the Criminal Law', in D. Hay, P. Linebaugh, J. Rule, E. P. Thompson and C. Winslow, *Albion's Fatal Tree: Crime and Society in Eighteenth-Century England* (Pantheon Books, 1975) 25.

[160] David Streckfuss, *Truth on Trial in Thailand: Defamation, Treason, and Lese-Majeste* (Routledge, 2011) 51.

domain of law enforcement officials' interpretation. Furthermore, conducts of self-defence are crafted as a criminal offence by law enforcement officials in cases where protesters resort to physical violence to protect other fellow protesters (mainly women or elderly) from repression during clashes in demonstrations. In addition, crimes like theft are also weaponised when defenders confiscate equipment that companies use to cut down trees within Indigenous territories.

Externalities

HEL, as a strategic legal action directed towards environmental defenders, is not aimed at resolving environmental conflicts but is exercised to deflect them into the legal sphere. In this regard, it not only intimidates targeted defenders individually but also creates externalities for environmental struggles in general. Here, externalities refer to consequences intended to be borne by groups involved in environmental resistance in general. For this purpose, HEL employs two tactical methods: leadership decapitation and projecting tactics. The former is a method often used in counter-insurgency or counterterrorism operations in which leaders or key individuals within insurgent or terrorist groups are arrested or killed to create a leaderless condition.[161] In environmental struggles that heavily depend on charismatic leadership to provide the direction and moral bonding needed for collective action, the leadership decapitation method can be very effective in weakening the struggles or creating conflicts over leadership within the movement. Here, the legal actions directed towards individual defenders who are regarded as the leading or central figures in environmental struggles should be seen as an exercise of this method.[162] As will be discussed in Chapter 5, the outcomes of the leadership decapitation tactics in Southeast Asia are somewhat mixed. Some of them are convicted and sent to prison, whereas others are acquitted or discharged from criminal charges for many reasons, including the lack of evidence, especially in trumped-up cases. Meanwhile, others are still carrying the status of being a defendant because their legal proceedings have been put on hold or pending; thus, this condition prolongs the chilling effect and becomes a means to control them in halting their involvement in the struggles, or their case will be opened at any time needed.

The projecting tactic is a method of governing civil society to maintain the existing social order based on property rights, social hierarchy, and resource extraction.[163] Adding to Pring and Canan,[164] HEL is essential to deflect socio-environmental

[161] Patrick Johnson, 'Does Decapitation Work? Assessing the Effectiveness of Leadership Targeting in Counter-insurgency Campaigns', (2012) 36 (4) *International Security* 47.

[162] Andrea Brock and Nathan Stephens-Griffin, 'Policing Environmental Justice', (2021) *IDS Bulletin, Online* First, https://doi.org/10.19088/1968-2021.130 <https://opendocs.ids.ac.uk/opendocs/handle/20.500.12413/16915> accessed 24 April 2023.

[163] Andrea Brock and Nathan Stephens-Griffin, 'Policing Environmental Justice', (2021) *IDS Bulletin*, Online First, https://doi.org/10.19088/1968-2021.130 <https://opendocs.ids.ac.uk/opendocs/handle/20.500.12413/16915> accessed 24 April 2023, 3.

[164] Pring and Canan (n 57).

conflicts by transforming their conflict, forum, issues, and subjectivities. In conflict transformation, HEL aims to turn socio-environmental conflicts triggered by environmental and ecological injustices into a language game involving interpretation of law and facts. Forum transformation is a motive of HEL to move the forum or spaces for voicing environmental concerns from the public sphere, within which every person can participate and express their dissents, to an exclusively designated courtroom in which only licensed parties are allowed to speak. Transforming issues means translating the community's problems and concerns regarding livelihoods into a legal issue such as libel or slander.

Most notable in governing civil society is the subjectivity transformation, in which, through HEL, environmental defenders' identity is reconstructed as deviant before the public's eyes. Labelling environmental activists is a contextualised tactic by the state officials and business actors made in accordance with a generalised threat in the country. As Mirenau puts it, this mode, by attaching a 'demonised' category such as criminals, terrorists, communists, anti-development, or foreign agents, is essential for making a boundary between 'good us' versus 'dangerous them', which in turn may justify the need for repression in order to maintain public order and security.[165] In the European context, 'the "terrorist" label functions as the most important alarm that justifies a host of heavy repressive measures against environmental activists'.[166] As will be seen in Chapter 5, in Indonesia, Thailand, and the Philippines, where the impacts of the Cold War never entirely disappeared from the public's sense of fear, the state has used the communist label or red-tagging. This red-tagging has also been effective in delegitimising environmental movements and keeping them distant from popular support.

Resistance

Resistance is a dimension that tends to be ignored by hegemonic lawfare scholars.[167] The concept and material action of resistance should be integrated into HEL in order to understand that environmental defenders being legally attacked should not be perceived as a passive and powerless target. Despite the structural constraints and lack of resources, environmental defenders and their supporting groups keep resisting HEL. Following Delmas, resistance here is defined as 'a multidimensional continuum of dissenting acts and practices, which includes lawful and unlawful acts (or "principled disobedience"), and expresses, broadly, an opposition and refusal to conform to established institutions and norms, including cultural values, social practices, and laws'.[168] In the context of HEL, analysis of resistance poses questions concerning how HEL is contested, prevented, challenged, or stopped by environmental defenders and

[165] Mireanu (n 73) 89. [166] ibid., 88. [167] Zanin, Martins, and Valim (n 146).
[168] Candice Delmas, *A Duty to Resist: When Disobedience Should be Uncivil* (Oxford University Press, 2018), 10.

movements whose struggles to defend livelihoods and the environment are retaliated against.

An act or event should meet four criteria to be called resistance: opposition, intention, communication, and transformation. Opposition is 'a central element of resistance' because it demonstrates a striking stance against 'a regime, an economic system, or particular practices, cultures, laws or events that are perceived as unjust, harmful, or damaging'.[169] Intention is 'another central part of resistance' since an act of resistance should contain 'social, moral or political intent' or 'requires some level of consciousness or human agency. . . . Thus, intention reframes mere opposition into morally and politically meaningful acts.'[170] In terms of communication, it should be noted that resistance 'is a form of communication'.[171] Here, an objective of resistance is 'to communicate condemnation of a wrong'.[172] Finally, resistance involves transformation because it aims to change an existing condition and pursue a better condition. Hence, resistance 'is bound up with the ways in which people understand their capacity to make or oppose changes. . . . For resistance to occur, people must have some (even small) sense of agency or hope that things could be different.'[173] Delmas writes that '[i]n the case of structural oppression, for instance, injustice hides within the normal working of the system. Resistance to it should aim in part to educate the public.'[174]

Legal action against environmental defenders is predominantly conceived of from the liberal perspective in which it is framed within the notion of rights. This has consequences for the framing of resistance, which means resisting those legal actions tends to fall within rights. This claim may be mobilised as a defence in legal cases indicating retaliation against environmental defenders, or in policy advocacy to adopt or strengthen anti-SLAPP provisions taking place at the domestic, regional, or international levels. Chapter 6 shows that rights-based legal mobilisation is the most common form of resistance to HEL exercised by environmental movements in Southeast Asia in litigation as well as legal reform at the regional organisational level (ASEAN), despite the problematic nature of rights in the region. Rights-based legal mobilisation to resist HEL in the Southeast Asian region is often ineffective, thus another mode of legal resistance is necessary. In response to this need, the concept of duty-based legal mobilisation is used, drawing on Delmas's argument[175] that resistance is no longer a right but a duty in the face of structural injustice. Instead of presenting legal arguments based on procedural rights as the basis for environmental struggles, duty-based legal mobilisation relies on an 'eco-defence' argument. This argument embraces the idea that any conduct by defenders in their struggles to protect their livelihood and the environment should be seen as a form of collective defence.

[169] Elizabeth Stanley and Jude McColloch, 'Resistance to State Crime', in E. Stanley & J. McCulloch (eds.), *State Crime and Resistance* (Routledge, 2013) 5.
[170] ibid., 5. [171] ibid. [172] Delmas (n 168) 128. [173] Stanley and McColloch (n 169) 6.
[174] Delmas (n 168). [175] Delmas (n 168) 182.

The argument is built on two basic propositions. First, the environment provides a means of survival for local communities and supports diverse ecosystems by fulfilling their basic needs. Second, in a society where the politico-business interests are dominantly articulated in the public policy, the state-backed development projects that appropriate local communities' means of livelihoods and ecosystems should be seen as a form of environmental invasion. Therefore, it should be argued that those communities acquire a moral and legal duty to take action to defend their means of livelihoods and ecosystems from the invasions that potentially take over or destroy their ecosystems and livelihoods. The struggles for this purpose should be seen as a defence against invaders. If this is agreed upon, eco-defence can be used as a legal defence in defending HEL cases utilising the criminal justice system. It should be noted, however, that introducing the eco-defence argument is not meant to be a panacea to resolve HEL because it is an inherent consequence of existing power structures which are reliant on resource extractions thus shaping the contemporary politics of the environment. It means that persistent and organised political struggles to dismantle the structures that contributed to the use of HEL in the first place are still paramount.

PART TWO
Country Studies in Contexts

CHAPTER 2

Environmental Politics and Defenders' Struggles

This chapter traces the critical junctures that have shaped the political-economy trajectories of Indonesia, Thailand, and the Philippines. Explaining these structural contexts is essential to understanding how environmental problems in these countries are causally connected to development models pursued from colonialism to the postcolonial period, industrialisation endeavours, and the contemporary period of neoliberal globalisation.[1] These histories of pre- and postcolonial developments have given rise to the emergence of environmental movements as a response to capitalist development where environmental degradation has been its inherent consequence. As the state-sponsored development agenda progresses, it also tells us under what circumstances environmental defenders, as part of these environmental movements, find themselves the subjects of attacks, including through legal means in those countries. In this chapter, environmental movements are characterised as networks of individuals and groups of actors that operate collaboratively and have shared concerns about the physical, built, and/or cultural environments.[2] Those movements occur within the sphere of civil society as a site of struggle over power.[3] The chapter demonstrates how their emergence has been a product of 'the transformative and conflictual nature of capitalist development',[4] which in those countries is marked by resource extraction and exploitation, especially for mining,

[1] Paul K. Gellert, 'The Political Economy of Environmental Degradation and Climate Disaster in Southeast Asia', in T. Carroll, S. Hameiri and L. Jones (eds.), *The Political Economy of Southeast Asia* (Palgrave Macmillan, 2020) 367–387.

[2] James K. Wong and Alvin Y. So, 'Environmental Movements in Post-Handover Hong Kong: between Managerialism and Radicalism', in P. Jobin, M. Ho & H. M. Hsiao (eds.), *Environmental Movements and Politics of the Asian Anthropocene* (ISEAS Publishing, 2021) 84; H. van der Heijden, 'Political Opportunity Structure and the Institutionalisation of the Environmental Movement', (1997) 6 *Environmental Politics* 25, 26.

[3] Garry Rodan, *Civil Society in Southeast Asia* (Cambridge University Press, 2022) 12.

[4] ibid., 13.

timber, and plantations, leading to dispossession and destruction of local communities' means of livelihoods.

Indonesia

Indonesia provides a problematic example in the politics of the environment. On the one hand, the country is geographically vulnerable to the impacts of global environmental changes in the Earth's systems, significantly rising sea levels due to its archipelagic condition consisting of 17,000 islands with coastlines of 99,093 km.[5] Ecologically, Indonesia is regarded as a mega-biodiversity country because it is the home of 12 per cent of the global mammal species, 16 per cent of global species of reptiles, 17 per cent of bird species,[6] and 25 per cent of the world's fresh- and salt-water species.[7] On the other hand, Indonesia is highly dependent on a natural resource-based economy. In the past twenty years, around 40 per cent of its total exports has been dominated by resource commodities, including those with minimal processing.[8] Indonesia has been an important player in the global mining industry, producing copper, coal, gold, bauxite, nickel, and tin. Covering ninety-three million hectares, mining industry concessions contribute up to 5 per cent of the national economy and its products represent 16 per cent of total exports.[9] Moreover, Indonesia is the biggest palm oil producer globally, with plantations covering around fourteen million hectares of terrestrial areas.[10] The palm oil industry alone contributes up to 17 per cent of Indonesia's agricultural gross domestic product.[11] Consequently, this overriding extractive economic model has caused significant environmental issues, such as deforestation, forest fires, biodiversity loss, environmental degradation, and pollution. Thus, environmental issues in the country should be understood as a consequence of the existing political and economic structure, especially how environmental and natural resources are governed and their associated (positive and negative) impacts are distributed along societal lines.

[5] Government of Indonesia, *Indonesia Biodiversity Strategy and Action Plan 2015–2020* (Kementerian Perencanaan Pembangunan Nasional/BAPPENAS, 2016) 23.

[6] 'Indonesia Main Details: Biodiversity Facts' The Secretariat of the Convention on Biological Diversity' (CBD, nd.) <www.cbd.int/countries/profile/?country=id> accessed 4 April 2020.

[7] Ministry of Forestry, *Indonesian Forestry* (Ministry of Forestry & GIZ/Forclim, 2011) 3.

[8] Gellert, (n 1) 374.

[9] Price Waterhouse Coopers (PWC) Indonesia, 'Mining in Indonesia: Investment and Taxation Guide' (PWC, 2019) 25–26 <www.pwc.com/id/en/energy-utilities-mining/assets/mining/mining-guide-2019.pdf> accessed 20 October 2020; Anugrah Perkasa, 'Konversi Lahan: Ini Perbedaan Luas Area Tambang dan Pertanian', *Bisnis.com*, (Jakarta, 27 May 2018) <https://ekonomi.bisnis.com/read/20160527/44/551949/konversi-lahan-ini-perbedaan-luas-area-tambang-dan-pertanian> accessed 20 October 2020.

[10] Muhammad Idris, 'Deretan Daerah dengan Lahan Sawit Terluas', *Kompas* (Jakarta, 01 February 2020) <https://money.kompas.com/read/2020/02/01/164000226/deretan-daerah-dengan-lahan-sawit-terluas-siapa-juaranya-?page=all> accessed 20 October 2020.

[11] Herry Purnomo et al., 'Reconciling Oil Palm Economic Development and Environmental Conservation in Indonesia: A Value Chain Dynamic Approach' (2020) 111 *Forest Policy and Economics* 1.

The Structure of Power

Indonesia's contemporary political-economic structures have been profoundly shaped by colonialism. Politically, the Dutch colonial administration disrupted the decentralised political structures that existed in pre-colonial Indonesia, leading to the consolidation of power in the hands of the Dutch colonial authorities, the marginalisation of local rulers and elites, and the creation of a centralised administrative system that continues to influence modern-day politics in Indonesia.[12] Economically, colonialism transformed a primarily agrarian-based economy into one geared towards extracting and exporting natural resources such as oil, rubber, and timber. This led to the development of large plantations and labour exploitation, which shaped the subsequent development of Indonesia's economy.[13] This was pursued by enacting the 1870 Agrarian Law, which declared a doctrine of *domain verklaring* (free state domain). This doctrine stated that any land without European private ownership status was designated to be the property of the colonial state. It served as a means of dispossession by the colonial state enabling 'legal' transfer to commercial plantation enterprises.[14] For example, in Java, these colonial enterprises led to heavy forest cutting to 'build sugar factories, coffee warehouses, tobacco-drying sheds, and housing compounds . . . Forests also provided fuel for industrial sugarcane processing, roasting coffee, and drying tobacco from the extensive government plantations.'[15]

In many colonised countries, the experience of colonialism also gave rise to nationalist movements challenging colonial rule. These movements responded to use of the draconian colonial criminal code targeting leaders of opposition movements. In the Philippines, for instance, under Spanish rule, the use of lawfare was exercised in the notable case of Jose Rizal, who was executed after being falsely convicted of insurrection, sedition, and conspiracy for his resistance to the colonial system.[16] Similarly, in Indonesia, Sukarno was charged by the colonial court for inciting riot, violence, and insurrection against colonial rule. In his defence, known as *Indonesia Menggugat* (Indonesia Accuses), Sukarno states that his trial is 'terror with the law in hand' [*Het is de terreur met de wet in de hand*].[17] The Soekarno case was an example of the lawfare exercised by the colonial Dutch, who used the colonial criminal justice system to silence nationalist figures in the Netherlands Indies. Ironically, the colonial criminal code has been incorporated into the national

[12] Adrian Vickers, *A History of Modern Indonesia* (Cambridge University Press, 2005).

[13] See Richard Robison, *Indonesia: The Rise of Capital* (Equinox Publishing, 1986).

[14] A Sutedi, *Implementasi Prinsip Kepentingan Umum di Dalam Pengadaan Tanah untuk Pembangunan, Revised Ed.* (Sinar Grafika 2020).

[15] Nancy L. Peluso, 'The History of State Forest Management in Colonial Java', (1991) 35 (2) *Forest & Conservation History* 65, 68.

[16] See Miguel Bernard, 'The Trial of Rizal', (1998) 46 *Philippine Studies* 46.

[17] Sukarno, *Indonesia Menggugat: Pidato Pembelaan di Depan Pengadilan Kolonial Bandung* (Inti Idayu Press, 1983 [1930]) 11.

legal system by the postcolonial government, in which draconian provisions have also been mobilised to silence critical voices, including environmental defenders.

In the postcolonial era, under the leadership of President Sukarno (1945–67), Indonesia's political and economic structures were shaped by his 'Guided Democracy' model, which aimed to combine elements of nationalism, Islamism, and communism (Nasakom) with an emphasis on independence from foreign domination. It highlighted the state's role as the principal development agent and aimed to strike a balance between opposing social groupings' interests. The president wielded enormous political power, with significant control over the legislative body, judiciary, and military. Sukarno promoted an economic nationalism programme to boost native industry and lessen the country's reliance on international imports. To foster the development of Indigenous businesses, the government nationalised essential industries such as oil and gas and enacted import substitution programmes. A land reform initiative was also launched to redistribute land from significant landowners to small farmers and landless peasants. This programme attempted to redress the unequal land distribution that marked the colonial period. However, it was put to an end after Sukarno was forcibly removed from power by General Suharto in the aftermath of the 1965–66 mass killings.

In this traumatic event, it is estimated that 500,000 people, including Indonesian Communist Party members, leftist intellectuals, and Sukarno supporters, were killed.[18] General Suharto installed himself as the president (1967–98) to consolidate power, launched more market-oriented economic policies, and moved away from the socialist and nationalist policies of the Sukarno era. Suharto's government pursued a policy of *developmentalism*, focusing on economic growth and modernisation. This involved attracting foreign investment and implementing industrialisation programmes to promote domestic entrepreneurship and industrial development. Suharto's New Order regime was characterised by a system of crony capitalism in which the president's personal cronies and family members were given preferential treatment, including access to resources and business opportunities.[19] This crony capitalism was transformed into 'a capitalist oligarchy that fused public authority and private interest, epitomised in the rise of such families as the Soehartos'.[20] In this authoritarian era, extractive industries, such as forestry, gas, oil, and mining, had been the 'material basis of the oligarchy's power and wealth'[21] that has continuously shaped the country's political and economic trajectories to date.

[18] Edward Aspinall, *Opposing Suharto: Compromise, Resistance, and Regime Change in Indonesia* (Stanford University Press, 2005), 5; For a lengthy discussion on this, see John Roosa, *Pretext for Mass Murder: The September 30th Movement and Suharto's Coup d'Etat in Indonesia* (University of Wisconsin Press, 2006).

[19] Robison (n 13).

[20] Richard Robison and Vedi Hadiz, *Reorganising Power in Indonesia: The Politics of Oligarchy in an Age of Markets* (Routledge Curzon, 2004) 43.

[21] Paul Gellert, 'Oligarchy in the Timber Markets of Indonesia: From APKINDO to IBRA to the Future of the Forests', in B. Resosudarmo (ed.), *The Politics and Economics of Indonesia's Natural Resources* (ISEAS, 2005) 146.

To maintain its power, the regime relied on 'three pillars of control'.[22] The first pillar was the extension, formalisation, and consolidation of military domination over the socio-political life of the society through the doctrine of *dwi fungsi ABRI* (dual security-developmental function of the Indonesian Military Forces). In the economic sphere, the military was also involved in natural resource extractions, for instance by providing security for logging or mining companies amidst conflicts with local communities. Gellert pointed out that the military forces backed 51 per cent of illegal sawmills operating close to Bukit Tigapuluh National Park.[23] The second pillar was restructuring the major political and civil society institutions. The inherited architecture of political parties, legislatures, and elections was preserved, but a combination of interference, manipulation, and harsh coercion modified it. The government also controlled associational life, including workers' and farmers' organisations, which were either abolished or trapped into a single corporatist organisation. The third pillar was constructing 'a comprehensive ideological justification for authoritarian rule' through 'a revived Pancasila ideology' stressing 'social harmony and the organic unity between state and society'.[24] In this regard, '[a]ll forms of division, and political opposition in particular, were labelled inimical to the Indonesian national character'.[25]

The Persistence of Resources-Based Economy

Suharto's authoritarian regime was marked by tremendous economic expansion, heavily relying on extractive industries, such as oil, gas, mining, and forestry. In achieving this, the regime, in the first year, enacted three critical pieces of legislation to facilitate large-scale resource extraction: (1) the 1967 Foreign Investment Act to attract foreign companies with a set of incentives, including tax relaxation; (2) the 1967 Forestry Act to designate all forests within the state domain, essentially an extension of the Dutch colonial *domain verklaring*, to make it available for granting logging concessions; and (3) the 1967 Mining Act to open possibility of mining exploration on all terrestrial areas of the country.[26] As a result, multinational corporations entered Indonesia to extract its natural resources, especially the mining sectors, which contributed significantly to state revenue. In the 1970s–80s, more than 60 per cent of the state's annual revenues came from the oil and gas sector.[27] As Resosudarmo observed, in the 1990s, Indonesia's major export commodities were oil and gas (30 per cent of the total export) and mineral and related products (19 per cent).[28]

[22] Aspinall (n 18) 22–23. [23] Gellert (n 21) 158. [24] Aspinall (n 18) 22–23. [25] ibid.

[26] Budy Resosudarmo, 'Introduction', in B. Resosudarmo (ed.), *The Politics and Economics of Indonesia's Natural Resources* (ISEAS, 2005) 2–3.

[27] Francisia Seda, 'Petrolium Paradox: The Politics of Oil and Gas', in B. Resosudarmo (ed.), *The Politics and Economics of Indonesia's Natural Resources* (ISEAS, 2005) 183.

[28] Resosudarmo (n 26) 3.

Moreover, the authoritarian regime also relied on the forestry sector as one of its economic backbones. In 1967, the regime granted a forest concession system to provide the right for companies or individuals to exploit forest products supposedly through a 'selective cutting' system to provide sufficient time for trees to rejuvenate. Under the system, forests were allocated to Suharto's cronies, disregarding its ecological impacts and the fact that millions of people lived in and around the forests.[29] As a result, in the 1970s, there was a boom in log exports and this was followed by an export boom in plywood (1980s–90s) and recently by exports of pulp and paper, contributing to 15 per cent of total exports at its peak in 1989.[30] In the 1990s, forest products contributed 10 per cent of Indonesia's total exports.[31] As a consequence, the rate of deforestation was alarming, as reported by Azis and Salim, 'from approximately 1.6 million hectares per annum in 1985–97 to 3.8 million hectares per annum in 1997–2000. It is estimated that around 65 per cent of Indonesia's wood supply has come from illegal logging.'[32] Specifically in Kalimantan, from 1973 to 2020, the decline of Kalimantan's forest was mainly caused by logging industries, palm oil plantations, and mining concessions,[33] and, according to CIFOR, 92 per cent of the 6.04 million hectares of deforestation in Kalimantan from 2000 to 2017 were converted into palm oil plantations.[34]

The monetary crisis in the late 1990s gave momentum to the opposition's demand for the resignation of Suharto after more than three decades in power. However, in the post-authoritarian era, this resource-based economy has been retained by successive presidents, including B. J. Habibie (1998–99), Abdurrahman Wahid (1999–2001), Megawati Sukarnoputri (2001–04), Susilo Bambang Yudhoyono (2004–14), and Joko Widodo (2014–24). During those periods, extractive industries were given favourable policy parameters by enacting business-friendly resource laws and regulations concerning mining, forestry plantations, spatial planning, and taxation. The presidency of Megawati, for instance, enacted Government Regulation in Lieu of Law No. 1 of 2004 concerning the revision of Forestry Law No. 41 of 1999 to permit the mining industry to undertake mining operations within a forest-protected area. This regulation was supplemented under President Yudhoyono by enacting Government Regulation No. 2 of 2008 concerning types and tariffs of non-tax state revenues to allow the use of forests for developmental purposes, including mining and plantations, provided that the user pay 1.8–3 million

[29] Iwan Azis and Emil Salim, 'Development Performance and Future Scenarios in the Context of Sustainable Utilisation of Natural Resources', in B. Resosudarmo (ed.), *The Politics and Economics of Indonesia's Natural Resources* (ISEAS, 2005) 127.

[30] Gellert (n 21) 147. [31] Budy Resosudarmo (n 26) 3. [32] Azis and Salim (n 29) 128.

[33] Rhett A. Butler, '30% of Borneo's Rainforests Destroyed Since 1973', *Mongabay* (16 July 2014) <news.mongabay.com/2014/07/30-of-borneos-rainforests-destroyed-since-1973> accessed 20 October 2020.

[34] Barbara Fraser, 'Is Deforestation in Borneo Slowing Down?' *Forest News* (15 January 2019) <forestsnews.cifor.org/59378/has-borneos-deforestation-slowed-down?fnl=en> accessed 20 October 2020.

rupiah (US$120–200) per hectare as a non-tax state revenue.[35] In 2006, the Yudhoyono administration was put to the test in the Lapindo mudflow case where the Lapindo Brantas, a mining company owned by Aburizal Bakrie, the coordinating minister for people's welfare and a powerful conglomerate and politician, flooded seven villages in Sidoarjo (East Java) permanently due to uncontrolled mudflow from the company's drilling operation. However, the administration did not hold the company accountable; instead, it allocated funds from the state budget to compensate affected communities whose homes and livelihoods were destroyed. This case demonstrated the authoritarian legacy of 'cronyism and rent-seeking, which continue to shape Indonesian politics' in the post-authoritarian era.[36]

Moreover, infrastructure has also been a priority in the country's development to stimulate economic growth. President Yudhoyono also launched an ambitious infrastructure development programme known as the Master Plan for Acceleration and Expansion of Indonesia's Economic Development (MP3EI) by designating economic corridors for each region in the archipelago as a competitive advantage, making it attractive for investors. Under the presidency of Joko Widodo (Jokowi), a set of economic development strategies left by his predecessors has also been incorporated into his development plan. Under the slogan 'Work, Work, Work', he focused on undertaking massive infrastructure projects because the lack of infrastructure has been regarded as one of the main issues that make Indonesia unattractive to foreign investors. For this purpose, Jokowi's administration has also transformed Yudhoyono's MP3EI projects under the banner of national strategic projects. Even more ambitiously, he launched a project to relocate the capital city from Jakarta to East Kalimantan that many observers have criticised as causing 'a major biodiversity catastrophe in modern times'.[37] Consequently, the projects have not only inherited agrarian conflicts caused by MP3EI projects' land dispossession but have also created new conflicts to pursue new projects, including conflicts with Indigenous communities where the new capital city is to be built. To secure his ambition of economic development, Jokowi instructed the National Police Chief that '[i]f there is a disturbance to investment at the regional level, [the police should] guard and assist it so that every investment can be realised' and warned 'the National Police Chief to replace the Regional Police Chief if he cannot oversee and guard the investment'.[38]

More recently, during the Covid-19 pandemic, the Jokowi administration has undertaken major legal reforms through the enactment of controversial legislation,

[35] Siti Maimunah, 'Megawati, SBY & Komodifikasi Hutan', *Indoprogress* (8 April 2013) <https://indoprogress.com/2013/04/megawati-sby-komodifikasi-hutan/> accessed 16 June 2023.

[36] Jim Schiller, Anton Lucas and Priyambudi Sulistiyanto, 'Learning from the East Java Mudflow: Disaster Politics in Indonesia', (2008) 85 *Indonesia* 51, 59.

[37] Paige Van de Vuurst and Luis E Escobar, 'Perspective: Climate Change and the Relocation of Indonesia's Capital to Borneo', (2020) 8 *Frontiers in Earth Science* 1, 4.

[38] Rangga Pandu and Resinta, 'Jokowi Urges National Police to Guard, Secure Investment' *Antara News* (Jakarta, 3 December 2021) <https://en.antaranews.com/news/202617/jokowi-urges-national-police-to-guard-secure-investment> accessed 02 February 2022.

an Omnibus Law concerning job creation to attract foreign investors. The law changes, revises, and replaces seventy-nine economic-related laws that were regarded as constraints to investments, including the relaxation of labour standards and environmental safeguards.[39] For instance, in the context of environmental policies, the Omnibus Law removes the requirement of having at least 30 per cent forest cover for each region. With this removal, Papua, a remaining natural forested region in which forests cover 70 per cent of its terrestrial areas, is targeted for conversion into palm oil plantations and mining operations. Prior to the enactment of the Omnibus Law, still during the pandemic, the government enacted a new legislation – Mineral and Coal Mining Law No. 3 of 2020 – to revise the 2009 Mineral and Coal Mining Law. This new piece of legislation aims to stimulate mining industries in the country due to the slowdown of the economy caused by the pandemic. With a strict health measure or 'lockdown' in place, massive public demonstrations against two controversial laws were prevented effectively.[40] As resistance moved online through social media, activists were threatened with prosecution for utilising the Information and Electronic Transaction Law to commit online defamation. Taken together, enactment of all these pro-business laws will exacerbate socio-environmental conflicts caused by massive expansion of investments to extract natural resources and develop infrastructure. Consequently, attacks against environmental defenders have increased following the escalation of socio-environmental conflicts in the country due to the expansion of extractive industries facilitated by state law.

Environmental Struggles

The colonial declaration of *domain verklaring* has been maintained by the postcolonial state of Indonesia to justify access to resources. However, this has become a source of conflicts between governments and Indigenous communities whose territories are designated as state-backed development projects. Even under the authoritarian New Order regime, resource extraction was not absent from conflicts. The regime granted concessions to individuals or corporations close to Suharto by disregarding sustainability and local interests.[41] As a result, conflicts between local communities and extractive industries grew and deepened as it became clear that although local resources were exploited, the communities received little or no benefit from these operations.[42] In the forestry sector, conflicts and social unrest have been caused by the transformation of forest landscapes that had been the basis of local livelihoods into the corporates' profit accumulation activities.[43] In turn,

[39] Agung Wardana, 'The Indonesian Paradox in the Anthropocene' (2021) 24 *Asia Pacific Journal of Environmental Law* 230.

[40] Raymond Grenfell and Agung Wardana, 'Impact of Platform Capitalism on Community Activism in Indonesia', (2021) 3 *Southeast Asian Media Studies Journal* 53, 61.

[41] Resosudarmo, (n 26) 3. [42] ibid., 4. [43] Gellert, (n 21) 150.

critical voices against resource extraction and state-backed projects grew, as did suppression by military forces.

The authoritarian regime both engaged with environmental organisations and suppressed environmental activism to contain resistance and environmental conflicts. This dual strategy was adopted because the regime also needed to collaborate with environmental organisations in accessing international aid.[44] In 1980, the Ministry of Development Supervision and the Environment facilitated the establishment of the Indonesian Forum for the Environment (WALHI) as a government collaborator.[45] However, in the late 1980s, the intimate relationship between the authoritarian regime and WALHI started to fall apart. The 'defining moment' was the construction of the Kedung Ombo Dam, a World Bank-financed project in Central Java. In this project, an extended tract of land was appropriated, and local farmers were displaced.[46] After two decades of silence following the 1965–66 mass killings,[47] peasant movements collaborating with students and non-governmental movements also reemerged under the banner of environmental justice. Their struggles were accused of being 'communist', leading to arrest and detention. Similarly, this also occurred in Bali, where local farmers and student activists opposed the development of resort complexes, such as the Bakrie Nirwana Resort owned by Aburizal Bakrie, a powerful conglomerate close to Suharto. To navigate the accusation of being communist, the opponent groups framed their resistance under the banner of cultural integrity because the project was constructed near the Tanah Lot Temple, one of the most sacred temples for Balinese Hindus; hence, it might 'pollute' the sanctity of the temple.[48] In the outer islands of Indonesia, especially Sumatera, Sulawesi, and Kalimantan, environmental justice movements converged with local communities defending forests and other local resources, which later evolved into Indigenous peoples' movements.[49]

Besides popular forms of resistance, such as demonstrations that were easily suppressed by the military forces, opponent groups also resorted to the courts to engage in legal battles. WALHI filed a lawsuit against Inti Indorayon, a pulp and

[44] F Sinanu, 'Coming of Age' (Inside Indonesia, 15 July 2006) <www.insideindonesia.org/coming-of-age>.

[45] ibid.

[46] George Aditjondro, 'Large Dam Victims and Their Defenders: The Emergence of an Anti-Dam Movement in Indonesia', in P. Hirsch and C. Warren (eds.), *The Politics of Environment in Southeast Asia: Resource and Resistance* (Routledge, 1998); Nancy Peluso, Suraya Afiff, and Noer Rachman, 'Claiming the Grounds for Reforms: Agrarian and Environmental Movements in Indonesia', (2008) 8 *Journal of Agrarian Change* 377, 385.

[47] During the massacres, many members of the communist-affiliated Indonesian Peasants' Front (BTI) were killed, and in the aftermath, the organisation was also prohibited.

[48] Caron Warren, 'Tanah Lot: The Cultural and Environmental Politics of Resort Development in Bali', in P. Hirsch and C. Warren (eds.), *The Politics of Environment in Southeast Asia: Resource and Resistance* (Routledge, 1998); Agung Wardana, 'Legal Engineering in a Contest over Space in Bali', (2018) 19 *Australian Journal of Asian Law* 1.

[49] Tania Li, 'Articulating Indigenous Identity in Indonesia: Resource Politics and the Tribal Slot', (2000) *Comparative Studies in Society and History* 149.

paper company in North Sumatera, for polluting the environment. Even though the decision was a landmark because it recognised environmental organisations' legal standing for the first time, it failed in its substantive merits.[50] This proved how challenging such legal battles were because the law was viewed instrumentally as a crucial tool for carrying out the regime's social engineering methods to aid economic development, as underpinned by Kusumaatmadja's doctrine of *Hukum dan Pembangunan* (Law and Development).[51] In terms of administering justice, the authoritarian system incorporated the judiciary under the Ministry of Justice as an institutional mechanism for applying executive influence over judicial decision-making processes.[52] This 'corporatist' model is marked by 'concertation or collaboration between the judiciary and the executive'[53] that limited the outcomes in the legal battles against government-backed projects and industrial activities that served elite economic interests. The Kedung Ombo Case, mentioned earlier, was one notable case that demonstrated a solid executive influence over the judiciary power during this period. The court ruled in favour of the plaintiffs' allegations and ordered compensation seven times the amount requested. However, due to political pressure from President Suharto, who asked the court to reconsider the ruling, the Supreme Court eventually reversed it.[54]

In the post-authoritarian era of Indonesia since 1998, it is apparent that the country has moved towards two seemingly paradoxical junctures. On the one hand, the fall of the authoritarian regime opens up political opportunity structures to move towards 'inclusive growth' aiming at widening public participation and poverty alleviation. This was pursued by transforming the centralised state structure to a decentralised (regional autonomy) model through which significant authorities, including those granting investment permits, were transferred from the central government to the district government. Ostensibly, this would hasten the investment process and bring the decision-making closer to local communities, leading to better decisions.[55] In the same mode, the notions of human rights and public participation (once a suspicious concept under the authoritarian regime) have become popular discourse in the country. As a result, a constitutional engineering strategy was undertaken by amending the 1945 Indonesian Constitution to enhance

[50] *WALHI v the Inti Indorayon* [1989]. See David Nicholson, *Environmental Dispute Resolution in Indonesia* (KITLV Press, 2009).

[51] See Mochtar Kusumaatmadja, *Hukum Masyarakat dan Pembinaan Hukum Nasional* (Binacipta, 1995).

[52] David Nicholson, *Environmental Dispute Resolution in Indonesia* (KITLV Press, 2009) 261.

[53] Kanishka Jayasuriya, 'Corporatism and Judicial Independence within Statist Legal Institutions in East Asia', in K. Jayasuriya (ed.), *Law, Capitalism and Power in Asia: The Rule of Law and Legal Institutions* (Routledge, 1999) 147.

[54] David Bourchier, 'Magic Memos, Collusion and Judges with Attitude', in K. Jayasuriya (ed.), *Law, Capitalism and Power in Asia: The Rule of Law and Legal Institutions* (Routledge, 1999) 209–210.

[55] Carol Warren and John McCarthy, *Community, Environment and Local Governance in Indonesia: Locating the Commonweal* (Routledge, 2009); Agung Wardana, *Contemporary Bali: Contested Space and Governance* (Palgrave Macmillan, 2019).

the separation of powers,[56] to limit the presidential term in office,[57] as well as to incorporate human rights provisions.

On the other hand, despite the rapid change of the state structure and legal institutions embracing democratic and human rights values, the established political-economic structure remained intact. As Robison and Hadiz observe, the politico-business elites who were incubated under the authoritarian regime have managed to reorganise themselves by 'hijacking' the new institutional arrangement.[58] Hence, instead of making meaningful public participation at the local level, the marginalisation of the local communities has been perpetuated by the new institutional arrangement. Massive investments at the local level have been confronted by local communities and environmental activists' resistance. Unlike the authoritarian regime, where environmental movements against development projects were suppressed by utilising direct forms of coercion such as forced convictions, disappearance, and even murder, in the reform era, the use of law as an instrument of intimidation has become more apparent. Echoing Jones in the case of Bahrain, in post-authoritarian Indonesia, an increased use of law to repress dissenting voices 'represents a qualitative change in the evolution of control methods'.[59] Although direct coercion does not entirely disappear from the public eye, at least discursively, when it does occur, the state appears to condemn it as a violation of the newly embraced values (democracy, human rights, and the rule of law). This is not to mention the impacts of the expansion of extractive industries in perpetuating environmental conflicts. According to WALHI, in 2016–17, there were 302 conflicts over natural resources across the archipelago, leading to lawfare to win those conflicts.[60]

Thailand

Geographically, Thailand consists of six regions. They are Eastern Thailand, Western Thailand, Northern Thailand, Northeast Thailand, Southern Thailand, and Central Thailand, with Bangkok as the capital city. It is situated in the mainland of Southeast Asia, within the bordering countries of Laos, Myanmar, Cambodia, and Malaysia. Even though it was never formally colonised by a European power, in the late nineteenth and early twentieth centuries, Thailand (Siam) was a cosmopolitan place reflecting its position as 'increasingly part of the colonial economy but not a colonial subject dominated by a single master'.[61] It was subjected

[56] Under the authoritarian regime, the Judiciary Body was under the Ministry of Justice.

[57] Before the amendment, there was no limit to the presidential term in office.

[58] Robison and Hadiz (n 20).

[59] Marc Owen Jones, *Political Repression in Bahrain* (Cambridge University Press, 2020), 204.

[60] Della Syahni, 'Ada UU Menjamin, Mengapa Pejuang Lingkungan Tetap Dijerat Hukum?' *Mongabay Indonesia* (Jakarta, 17 September 2018) <www.mongabay.co.id/2018/09/17/ada-uu-menjamin-mengapa-pejuang-lingkungan-tetap-terjerat-hukum/> accessed 21 May 2019.

[61] Chris Baker and Pasuk Phongpaichit, *A History of Thailand, 3rd Ed.* (Cambridge University Press, 2014) 89–90.

to significant pressure from European colonial powers and was compelled to make several concessions to prevent direct colonisation. The pressures included territorial threats from European nations, unequal treaties, and economic constraints. In this regard, Thailand is very often referred to as a 'semicolonial',[62] 'crypto colonial',[63] or 'postcolonial' country.[64] Baker and Phongpaichit argue that the geographical and temporal context contributed to the ability of Thailand to avoid colonial rule. It was geographically 'a buffer between French and British ambitions as the era of colonial land-grabbing came to an end', and due to 'the Ayutthayan-era practice of absorbing foreigners into the government', it managed to adapt colonial ideas of progress and features such as technologies, legal codes, and military conscription 'into a semi-colonial compromise'.[65]

Like Indonesia, natural resources have played an instrumental role in Thailand's economic, social, and legal transformations. Thailand's forestry sectors, for instance, have contributed to transforming the feudalistic mode of production towards market capitalism.[66] In the pre-world war period, Thailand's teak was a forest commodity that had attracted timber companies to operate in Northern Thailand; hence, forest governance was changed to suit their interests.[67] By the end of the 1880s, following the 1855 Bowring Treaty,[68] Thailand's teak industry, which Chinese and Burmese companies had dominated, was taken over by European companies, especially from the British Empire,[69] marking what Lohman calls the 'forest colonisation' in the country.[70] As a result, exports of Thailand's teak skyrocketed and peaked in the early 1890s, making Thailand among the biggest teak-producing countries in the world.[71] As the timber companies gained more wealth and power, they required a secure and stable environment for long-term

[62] Peter Jackson, 'The Ambiguities of Semicolonial Power in Thailand', in P. Jackson and R. Harrisons (ed.), *The Ambiguities Allure of the West: Traces of the Colonial in Thailand* (Hong Kong University Press, 2010).

[63] Michael Herzfeld, 'The Absent Pressure: Discourses of Crypto-Colonialism', (2002) 101 *South Atlantic Quarterly* 899.

[64] McCargo defines colonialism, following Sukarno's speech during the 1955 Bandung Conference, as a 'form of economic control, actual physical control by a small but alien community within a nation'. For him, in Thailand, 'the real "aliens" are the people running the country [royal, military and bureaucracy], not those being sought to control'. Partha Chatterjee cited in Duncan McCargo, 'Things Fall Apart? Thailand's Post-Colonial Politics', (2017) 9 *Suvannabhumi* 85, 86–87.

[65] Baker and Phongpaichit (n 61) 77–79.

[66] Oliver Pye, 'Forest Policy and Strategic Groups in Thailand', (2005) 36 *Internationales Asienforum* 311, 315.

[67] ibid.

[68] A treaty between the British Empire and Siam (Thailand) on commercial and political relationships between the two countries. It 'stabilised import and export duties, preserved the Siamese court's monopoly on domestic opium sales, gave British traders the right to deal directly with Siamese merchants, and upheld the legal protection of extraterritoriality that the British had enjoyed before Bowring's arrival'. Richard Ruth, *A Brief History of Thailand* (Tuttle Publishing, 2021) 49.

[69] Pye (n 66) 316.

[70] Larry Lohman, 'Land, Power and Forest Colonization in Thailand', (1999) 3 *Global Ecology and Biogeography Letters* 180.

[71] Pye (n 66) 317.

investments and safeguarding teak resources from competing interests.[72] However, the economic depression of the late 1920s gave momentum to criticise the monarchy for managing the national economy. This condition, in turn, led to the 1932 revolution, which brought the absolute monarchy to an end.[73] In the following years of the post-absolutist era, the emergence of nationalism under the leadership of Phibun led not only to the transformation of Siam into Thailand to better represent a nation-state based on Thai-ness but also to economic nationalism in which domestic and state-owned enterprises dismantled foreign domination.[74] As a result, commoner politics emerged that 'cautiously linked hands' with the Sino-Thai (*lukjin*) enterprises.[75]

The Cold War era was also an important historical juncture that has continued to shape Thai domestic politics. During this period, Thailand was under the influence of the US as its 'new foreign patron', which was even 'more intrusive than anything Siam had experienced in the colonial era'.[76] In 1952, to prevent the spread of communism, a new Anti-Communist Activities Act, replacing the 1933 Anti-Communist Act, was enacted to include any activities 'to overthrow the democratic system headed by the monarch', 'to change the economic system of the nation based on private ownership', and 'to engage in activities likely to cause agitation among the people and confusion in the social order'.[77] Another strategy to keep communism at bay was economic modernisation, 'through private capitalism', under which Sarit Thanarat's government, supported by US economic aid, aimed to develop the economy by expanding agricultural and fishing industries, transforming the hinterlands for mining extractions, and constructing energy infrastructure.[78] With the US government's support 'in safeguarding its interests in the region against communist threats', the military took the opportunity 'to deepen its roots in politics'.[79] As Baker and Phongpaichit put it, '[d]ollars consolidated Thailand's militarized state'.[80] As a result, this consolidation has 'contributed to the military's *modus operandi* for its authoritarianism and later its political interventions' to overthrow elected governments repeatedly ever since.[81] Due to the military's suppression of peasants' or labour's political organisations, the parliament was dominated by business actors. As a result, business practices received lenient legal barriers and even operated in

[72] ibid., 318. [73] Baker and Phongpaichit, (n 61) 117. [74] Pye (n 66) 323.

[75] Baker and Phongpaichit (n 61) 130. [76] ibid., 139.

[77] Toru Yano, 'Some Characteristics of Political Leadership in Thailand: Sarit Thanarat's "Revolutionary Party Edicts"', (1972) 10 (3) *The Developing Economies* 233, 241.

[78] Michael K. Connors, 'The Two Faces of Democracy', in P. Chachavalpongpun (ed.), *Routledge Handbook of Contemporary Thailand* (Routledge, 2020), 60; Baker and Phongpaichit, (n 61) 139; Eli Elinof and Vanessa Lamb, 'Environmental Politics in Thailand: Pasts, Presents, and Futures', in P. Chachavalpongpun (ed.), *Routledge Handbook of Contemporary Thailand* (Routledge, 2020) 381.

[79] Pavin Chachavalpongpun, 'Introduction: A Timeless Thailand', in P. Chachavalpongpun (ed.), *Routledge Handbook of Contemporary Thailand* (Routledge, 2020) 5.

[80] Baker and Phongpaichit (n 61) 148.

[81] Kevin Hewison, 'Black Site: The Cold War and the Shaping of Thailand's Politics', (2020) 50 *Journal of Contemporary Asia* 551, 556.

connection with state officials, which allowed them to access 'the semi-official armed forces that enforced the military government's policies of control'.[82]

Thus, new elites emerged in the country. They consisted of leading military generals, senior state officials, and new business conglomerates in which, weaponising the narrative of development and without democratic control, natural resources were extracted on an unprecedented scale as the basis of their wealth and power.[83] At this moment, forests also received considerable attention. The forest product was one of the pillars of the Thai economy. For illustration, during World War II, two-thirds of Thai terrestrial territories were covered by forest, but due to economic expansion, only one-third remained forest over the next three decades.[84] Besides providing business opportunities for forest products, forested mountains, particularly in the Northeast Thai Region, became the operational base for the communist forces, which the government targeted with counter-insurgency strategies.[85] For this purpose, in the mid-1960s, the government cleared the forest further 'to deny cover to the rebels' by building 'military roads into the forests and shepherded pioneer settlements along them' and granting logging concessions to favourable companies.[86] In 1964, the government conducted a forest mapping project 'to preserve 40 per cent of the country's forest' and to sterilise it from human settlement. Consequently, by 1974, approximately five to six million people who lived within the state forest were regarded as 'squatters', and in the 1990s, the number had increased to ten to twelve million.[87]

This has created chronic conflict in Thailand between the state and forest communities that have been considered illegal forest settlers. In the early 1990s, for instance, Suchinda led the Internal Security Operations Command to set up a Khor Jor Kor project to reorganise land use in Thai National Forest Reserves, which evicted more than 2,000 families who were regarded as 'forest squatters'.[88] Affected communities, with the assistance of NGOs, organised demonstrations to bring together other victims of development projects.[89] Finally, the project was halted. Nonetheless, as will be demonstrated in Chapter 5, conflicts over forests have also resorted to lawfare where members of local communities, especially Indigenous peoples, were silenced by the state in their struggle to defend forests as their livelihoods.

The Emergence of Environmental Concerns

Due to the impacts of the rapid economic transformation, environmental concerns had become a nationwide political issue in the early 1970s.[90] These concerns led to the emergence of environmentalism in the country, which was contributed to by

[82] Baker and Phongpaichit (n 61) 243–244. [83] ibid., 139. [84] ibid., 217.
[85] Pye (n 66) 326. [86] Baker and Phongpaichit (n 61) 217. [87] ibid., 158.
[88] Pye (n 66) 330. [89] Elinof and Lamb (n 78) 383–384.
[90] Phillip Hirsch and Larry Lohmann, 'Contemporary Politics of Environment in Thailand', (1989) 29 *Asian Survey* 439, 442.

several notable cases. The first was a political scandal in April 1973 when a military helicopter crashed in Kanchanaburi Province. It carried powerful figures and military officials who wanted to conduct an illegal hunting expedition using state-owned equipment in a forest area that was later designated as the Thung Yai Naresuan Wildlife Sanctuary (Western Thailand).[91] The scandal that the government concealed through a fabricated story became a complete showcase of Thanom Kittikachorn's corrupt, cruel, and brazen regime.[92] This scandal, in turn, had increased the public interest in nature and wildlife conservation and 'the surge of public feeling that resulted in the October 1973 democratic revolt'[93] led by students, which ended Thanom's anti-communist military dictatorship.[94] The second important milestone was the Thailand Exploration and Mining Corporation (TEMCO) case, which was 'the most sustained environmentally-oriented political battle' in Thailand during 1974–75.[95] The case related to a favourable mining concession granted by Prime Minister Seni Pramoj in Southern Thailand to TEMCO, a company dominated by the US-based Union Carbide.[96] A student-led movement against the concession, fusing its narrative of anti-imperialism with the general public's underlying Thai nationalism, had managed to force the government to withdraw the concession.[97]

Violent attacks against Thammasat University student activists in October 1976 by the military and right-wing groups (Village Scouts, Krating Daeng, and Nawapon) led many student activists to seek refuge in the jungle and join the Communist Party of Thailand.[98] The traumatic event of the Thammasat massacre, as well as public outrage at the state's violence,[99] pushed the monarchy and the military to reconsider their positions and to appoint Thanin Kraivichien as the new prime minister.[100] Against the communist insurgencies, Thanin employed new methods by constructing roads to open isolated forests where the communist guerrillas used them as a sanctuary and, at the same time, to allow logging companies that were closely associated with military elites to transport their heavy equipment and employees to cut down previously inaccessible forests.[101] Hence, forests became a site of dissent against the authoritarian regime, where struggles over the environment were also articulated.[102] An important legacy of these struggles in the context of Thai environmental movements has been the establishment of the Peasant Federation of Thailand, 'whose organisational structure and membership became the backbone of several environmental groups in the 1980s and 1990s that linked environmental struggles to issues of livelihood'.[103]

[91] ibid. [92] Ruth (n 68) 224. [93] Hirsch and Lohmann (n 90) 442.

[94] Michael K. Connors, 'The Two Faces of Democracy', in P. Chachavalpongpun (ed.), *Routledge Handbook of Contemporary Thailand* (Routledge, 2020) 60.

[95] Hirsch and Lohmann (n 90) 442–443. [96] ibid. [97] ibid. [98] Ruth (n 68) 221.

[99] Chachavalpongpun (n 79) 5.

[100] Michael K. Connors, 'The Two Faces of Democracy', in P. Chachavalpongpun (ed.), *Routledge Handbook of Contemporary Thailand* (Routledge, 2020) 60.

[101] Ruth (n 68) 245–246. [102] Hirsch and Lohmann (n 90) 443; Elinof and Lamb (n 78) 381.

[103] Elinof and Lamb (n 78) 381.

In the 1980s, the government policy towards economic liberalisation resulted in resource conflicts across the country.[104] In the mining sector, based on this policy, private mining companies were allowed to undertake large exploration and exploitation of gold mining by bidding on potential areas.[105] The Tungkum company won the bid in Loei Province (Northeast Region). It then started mining operations, which caused social and environmental impacts on local villagers and turned them into anti-mining communities.[106] In the following decades, mainly in the 2000s–10s, the company filed several SLAPP lawsuits against members of these communities in order to punish and intimidate dissenting voices against the company.[107]

In the forestry and plantation sector, forested areas were logged and converted into agricultural areas for cash crop commodities.[108] As natural forests declined, the future of Thailand's forestry industry became uncertain, and in the early 1980s, revenues from exporting logs and sawn wood were continuously dropping.[109] To address this resource crisis, the industry proposed using degraded forest areas to grow fast-growing tree species, especially eucalyptus.[110] In 1987, a Green Isaan project was introduced under the leadership of Thai Military General Chavalit Yongchaiyudh, whose ambition was to be prime minister; to gain political support, he pledged 'to make the northeast "green" within five years by improving water resources and raising the percentage of forest areas'.[111] However, the project was protested by forest-dependent communities that regarded eucalyptus as 'selfish' trees because they did not allow intercropping and degraded the soil and water supply.[112] This anti-eucalyptus movement was violently repressed by the military's Internal Security Operations Command, and its leaders, including monks, were attacked, detained, and arrested.[113] In early 1989, Thai environmental movements gained momentum to protest deforestation after a major landslide hit Southern Thailand, which caused hundreds of villagers to die; as a result, the government revoked logging concessions and declared a ban on logging.[114]

[104] Thawilwadee Bureekul, 'Access to Environmental Justice and Public Participation in Thailand', in A. Harding (ed.), *Access to Environmental Justice: A Comparative Study* (Koninklijke Brill, 2007) 271.

[105] Wichean Anpraser, 'SLAPPs as a Form of Exclusion in Resource Governance: The Case of an Anti-Gold Mine Campaign in Loei Province, Thailand', (2021) 42 *Kasertsart Journal of Social Sciences* 746.

[106] ibid.

[107] Liberty Asia, 'Making the Case for Abolishing Criminal Defamation Laws', (2018). http://freedom.collaborative.prod.s3.amazonaws.com/uploads/20180628_Liberty%20Asia_Defamation%20Paper_final.pdf, 4.

[108] Pye (n 66) 327. [109] ibid. [110] ibid.

[111] Francois Molle, Philippe Floch, Buapun Promphakping and David Blake, 'The "Greening of Isaan" in Politics, Ideology, and Irrigation Development in the Northeast of Thailand', in F. Molle, T. Foran, & M. Kaekoenen (eds.), *Contested Waterscapes in the Mekong Region: Hydropower, Livelihoods and Governance* (Earthscan, 2009) 259–268.

[112] Larry Lohmann, 'Peasants, Plantations, and Pulp: The Politics of Eucalyptus in Thailand', (1991) 23 Bulletin of Concerned Asian Scholars3.

[113] ibid., 17.

[114] Sophie Lewis and Janette Bulkan, 'The Political Logics of EU-FLEGT in Thailand's Multistakeholder Negotiation: Hegemony and Resistance', (2022) 29 *Journal of Political Ecology* 384–404.

Continuous Political Turbulence

From the late 1980s to the mid-1990s, Thailand experienced rapid economic growth. However, its politics were far from stable. In 1988, Chitichai Choonhavan, who replaced Prem Tinsulanonda, continued to pursue a business-friendly administration. However, his administration did not last long. In 1991, Chitichai Choonhavan was overthrown by General Suchinda Keprayon. In early 1992, Suchinda appointed himself prime minister and announced a new constitution that provoked mass demonstrations against 'despotic' constitutional provisions. Around 200,000 protesters joined the demonstrations in Bangkok in May 1992. However, Suchinda's military junta responded to them violently, which resulted in at least fifty-two dead and many protesters injured and disappeared, known as the Black May tragedy.[115] After forty-seven days in power, Suchinda resigned, opening a path towards a democratic political system and a decline of the military's role in politics through the mid-1990s.[116] Thailand undertook a constitutional reform by enacting the 1997 Constitution, which included constitutional provisions for citizens' rights to monitor the exercise of power by the government.[117] Responding to the demand for better environmental management due to the negative impacts of rapid economic development, the Constitution also opened public participation in public affairs, including environmental protection and management.[118] As a result, affected communities, as well as environmental NGOs, became actively involved in advocacy to defend their livelihoods and the environment. By the late 1990s, they had become important actors in political struggles at the national level.[119] However, state agencies and corporations whose development projects and capital accumulation processes were implicated saw these struggles as a constraint; hence, attacks on public participation through legal means became another instrument to silence environmental defenders in their work.[120]

Indeed, promulgating the 1997 Constitution opened the political space and facilitated competition between political parties.[121] However, progressive developments were soon hit by the 1997 financial crisis, which devastated Thailand's economy. Akin to the Indonesian case, the crisis in Thailand was also worsened by 'crony capitalism' resulting from the liberalisation of the banking system, in which political and economic elites borrowed large sums of money from financial institutions without adequate collateral in the event that they could not pay their loans.[122] The enactment of the 1997 Constitution and the financial crisis paved the

[115] Chachavalpongpun (n 79), 6; Baker and Phongpaichit (n 61) 249–251. [116] Ruth (n 68) 255.

[117] Jakkrit Sangkhamanee, 'State, NGOs, and Villagers: How the Thai Environmental Movement Fell Silent', in P. Jobin, M. Ho and H. M. Hsiao (eds.), *Environmental Movements and Politics of the Asian Anthropocene* (ISEAS, 2021) 231.

[118] ibid. [119] Elinof and Lamb (n 78) 381.

[120] Human Rights Lawyers Association, *Recommendations on the Protection of Those Who Exercise Their Rights and Freedom from Strategic Lawsuits against Public Participation* (Human Rights Lawyers Association, 2019), 10.

[121] Sangkhamanee (n 117) 231. [122] Ruth (n 68) 259.

way for Thaksin Shinawatra, a telecommunication tycoon, to enter the national political arena.[123] When the existing government relied on the International Monetary Fund's (IMF) loans and prescriptions to address the crisis, Thaksin presented himself as a defender of Thai business against Western imperialism represented by the IMF.[124] In early 2001, he won the general election with substantial support from rural populations and civil society, including environmental NGOs. As Jakkrit Sangkhamanee puts it, Thaksin shifted environmental politics from street occupation to electoral mobilisation through populist policy and elections. He not only altered the way resources were allocated and dispersed but he also 'created a wider economic desire and political aspiration among the rural populace'.[125] Consequently, this populist model enabled new formations in environmental politics. The alliance between rural communities and NGOs established a decade earlier for challenging the government's development projects and policies was weakened by rural communities shifting their alliance to Thaksin's government.[126]

Thaksin's administration was regarded as 'an authoritarian wolf dressed in democratic sheep's clothing'.[127] Once his power had become consolidated, he ran the state like the CEO of his corporation. In resource governance, for instance, he established the Ministry of Natural Resources and Environment to enable a corporate model of natural resources management under a centralised agency.[128] Like his predecessors, those resources were utilised to facilitate economic growth, which brought his administration under scrutiny from previously supportive environmental groups. However, using intimidation tactics, Thaksin's government managed to muffle dissenting voices emerging from those groups and communities who were affected by state-initiated development projects.[129] Despite the lack of meaningful participation in public affairs and his administration's lack of transparency, Thaksin won a second term in 2005, making his first term in office the first full four-year term served by a prime minister.[130] However, his second term was more challenging because he faced a mass anti-Thaksin movement (later known as the Yellow Shirts) that accused him of corruption.[131] As a result, the military staged a coup in September 2006 to topple Thaksin's government, but this in turn was challenged by a mass mobilisation of Thaksin's supporters (the Red Shirts). Chachavalpongpun explains that the emergence of the Yellow Shirt movement versus the Red Shirt movement indicates a further division of Thai society 'not only along ideological lines but also along different classes, regions and economic status'.[132] As the result of the coup, the Thai polity was back in the hands of the military force under the leadership of General Surayud Chulanont. In the aftermath, environmental groups that opposed Thaksin found it even more difficult to voice

[123] Chachavalpongpun (n 79) 7.
[124] Ruth (n 68) 264–265.
[125] Sangkhamanee (n 117) 228–229.
[126] ibid.
[127] Ruth (n 68) 22.
[128] Sangkhamanee (n 117) 234.
[129] Ruth, (n 68), 268, Sangkhamanee (n 117) 234.
[130] Chachavalpongpun (n 79) 8.
[131] ibid., 8.
[132] ibid., 9.

their environmental concerns under the military government. Sangkhamanee observed that 'during the period of the junta and military-backed civilian governments (2006–11), the vital critical work of the environmental movement almost disappeared'.[133] This was partly also contributed to by a serious break between the activist movement and the rural population supporting Thaksin.

In mid-2011, Yingluck Shinawatra, Thaksin's sister, took power as prime minister after winning the general election. Similar to Thaksin, her relationship to environmental movements was an uneasy one because she 'followed[ed] in her brother's footsteps in capitalizing on natural resources and the environment for economic development'.[134] This could be observed in the Mae Wong Dam case, a 400-million-dollar dam within the Mae Wong National Park project initiated in the late 1980s. In 2012, once her administration approved the budget, the implementation of the project led to a mass anti-dam resistance organised by the Seub Nakhasathien Foundation, which was concerned about its impacts on natural forests and wildlife.[135] Responding to the public protest, Yingluck finally suspended the Mae Wong Dam project. However, her term in office was not long. She resigned and called for a new election after mass demonstrations organised by the People's Democratic Reform Committee, which occupied Bangkok's financial district for months and demanded her resignation.[136]

In May 2014, the military coup was initiated by the National Council for Peace and Order (NCPO), led by General Prayut Chan-o-cha, who then took the power to control the country under a military government. Following the coup, Thai economic growth had fallen behind its other neighbouring countries[137] and the military junta launched a long-term vision of 'Thailand 4.0' to lift the country out of the middle-income trap. To pursue the vision, massive infrastructure development projects were announced to boost economic growth. As mentioned by Somkid Jatuspripitak, the deputy prime minister of Thailand, under the leadership of General Prayut, 'Thailand has announced a number of mega-investment projects for transport and logistics infrastructure including construction of roads, expressways, mass rapid transit systems, high speed rail networks as well as construction and development of new airports, seaports, and logistics hubs over the next five years.'[138] One of the most ambitious projects was the development of the Eastern Economic Corridor, which has been regarded as 'a centrepiece of the junta's policy to boost growth in Thailand and targets investment into hi-tech industries, as it

[133] Sangkhamanee (n 117) 239. [134] ibid., 240.

[135] Bhanubhatra Jittiang, 'Frames, Blunders, Vulnerabilities, Polarization, and Facebook: The Struggle of the Anti-Mae Wong Dam Movement in Thailand' (MA thesis, George Washington University 2015) <https://scholarspace.library.gwu.edu/downloads/0k225b199?locale=en> accessed on 9 February 2023.

[136] Chachavalpongpun (n 79) 11.

[137] Panu Wongcha-um and Patphicha Tanakasempipat, 'Thai Junta's Key Economic Project Draws $9 billion investment', *Reuters* (Bangkok, 12 January 2018) <www.reuters.com/article/us-thailand-economy-eec-idUSKBN1F110G> accessed 19 June 2023.

[138] Somkid Jatusripitak, 'Preparing for Thailand 4.0' First Forum (n.d). <https://firstforum.org/wp-content/uploads/2021/05/Report_13729.pdf> accessed 19 June 2023, 12.

transitions from those reliant on cheap labor'.[139] In addition, the designation of Special Economic Zones in ten provinces situated on the border with neighbouring countries aims to serve the government's economic and security interests.[140] To accelerate those projects, under the 2014 interim Constitution, the military government of the NCPO weakened environmental safeguards by allowing project proponents to start their projects while simultaneously preparing for the environmental impact assessment (EIA). Hence, whatever the outcome from the EIA process, the projects would be undertaken.[141] The military government resumed the Mae Wong Dam, which Yingluck had suspended, and environmental movements against the project were repressed.[142]

Following Lorsch, it can be argued that the massive development of infrastructure projects in pursuing Thailand 4.0 should be seen as a tool of Prayut's administration to 'legitimize their regime to the Thai people, and strengthen foreign policy while unifying the political elites'.[143] Because the administration lacked 'procedural legitimacy' in taking over power from the previous government, it attempted to seek political legitimacy through its performance in maintaining or even increasing the rate of economic growth.[144] As the junta's long-term visions would require political stability to be pursued, it needed strict control of civil society. This was prepared by enacting a new interim Constitution in 2014, which granted more power to the NCPO to appoint the members of the National Legislative Assembly[145] to cement the military's political position.[146] Section 44 of the 2014 interim Constitution gave the state absolute authority to suspend civil liberties, including freedom of expression.[147] In addition, the NCPO also enacted several new laws to support its

[139] Wongcha-um and Tanakasempipat (n 137).

[140] Kanokwan Manorom, 'NGOs and Civil Society in Thailand' in P. Chachavalpongpun (ed.), *Routledge Handbook of Contemporary Thailand* (Routledge, 2020) 375.

[141] Sangkhamanee (n 117) 243. [142] ibid., 251.

[143] Beck Lorsch, 'The Two Railroads: Prayut's Search for Unity, Growth, and Modernity', *Modern Southeast Asia* (18 January 2022) <https://seasia.yale.edu/two-railroads-prayuts-search-unity-growth-and-modernity> accessed 19 June 2023.

[144] ibid.

[145] Section 6 of the 2014 Interim Constitution stipulates: 'There shall be a National Legislative Assembly consisting of not more than two hundred and twenty members appointed by the King, upon the advice of the National Council for Peace and Order, from persons of Thai nationality by birth and being not less than forty years of age.'

[146] Chachavalpongpun (n 79) 12.

[147] Section 44 of the 2014 interim constitution stipulates: 'In the case where the Head of the National Council for Peace and Order deems necessary for the purpose of reforms in various fields, for the enhancement of unity and harmony among people in the country, or for the prevention, restraint, or suppression of any act which undermines public order or national security, the Monarchy, the national economy, or State affairs, irrespective of whether such act occurred inside or outside of the Kingdom, the Head of the National Council for Peace and Order, with the approval of the National Council for Peace and Order, shall have power to order, restrain, or perform any act, whether such act has legislative, executive, or judicial force; the orders and the acts, including the performance in compliance with such orders, shall be deemed lawful and constitutional under this Constitution, and shall be final. When those have been carried out, a report shall be submitted to the President of the National Assembly and the Prime Minister for acknowledgement without delay.'

economic agenda. One of them was the 2016 Mineral Act, which enabled private businesses to begin mining operations considerably more quickly and easily, with fewer constraints on detrimental consequences for local residents, forestland ecosystems, and water basins.[148] Disrupting these processes to achieve the purported public interest should be considered an act of dissent and sanctioned. To criminalise dissent, including by environmental defenders, the NCPO passed new criminal provisions, including reviving the 1914 Martial Law Act, the prohibition on assembly of more than five people, and using existing draconian criminal provisions. Consequently, as recorded by Streckfuss, during 2016–20, there were 198 cases involving *lese-majeste*, sedition, prohibited assembly, causing public disorder, and other politically motivated criminal charges.[149]

The Philippines

Like Indonesia, the Philippines is an archipelagic country. It comprises more than 7,000 islands, which are grouped into three island groups: Luzon, Visayas, and Mindanao. Similar to Indonesia, the Philippines has also been regarded as one of the mega-biodiversity countries in the world, with a considerable number of flora and fauna species, especially mammals, birds, amphibians, and vascular plants. As Weng Cahiles puts it, the Philippines is home to 52,177 species, more than half of which are found nowhere else on the planet.[150] It is home to 5 per cent of the world's flora, with very high species endemicity, as well as at least twenty-five plant genera and 39 per cent of terrestrial animal species. It is also located within the Coral Triangle, regarded as the global epicentre of marine biodiversity. Philippine waters contain the highest concentration of species per unit of surface area on the planet.[151] However, the Philippines' rich environment and biodiversity have been compromised by its political and economic structure, which relies heavily on natural resource extraction. Consequently, the country has been facing rapid depletion of natural resources due to mining and logging, resulting in destruction of the environment and a rapid loss of biodiversity.[152] As an archipelago, the Philippines has also been one of the most vulnerable countries to the impacts of climate change, especially typhoons. Due to inequalities, those impacts hit powerless communities hardest.[153]

[148] Sangkhamanee (n 117) 244.

[149] David Streckfuss, 'Lese-Majeste Within Thailand's Regime of Intimidation', in P. Chachavalpongpun (ed.), *Routledge Handbook of Contemporary Thailand* (Routledge, 2020) 140.

[150] Weng Cahiles, 'Grim Regime: Unceasing Killings Despite the Pandemic', in T. Lopez (ed.), *Reclaiming the Narrative: The Struggles of Environment Defenders in Five Countries in Southeast Asia* (APNED & CEC 2021) 70.

[151] ibid. [152] ibid., 71.

[153] Maria Christina Mundin, 'Access to Environmental Justice: A Closer Look at the Rules of Procedure for Environmental Cases', (2011) 55 *Ateneo Law Journal* 1066, 1067.

Resources in the Colonial and Postcolonial Periods

The Philippines has experienced a complex history of colonisation, with several foreign powers exerting control over the islands in different periods. Spain (1565–1898) was the first to colonise the Philippines and implemented centralised colonial administration. Specifically in land governance, the Spanish colonial administration imposed the Regalian Doctrine, declaring that the colonial state owned all land and natural resources that lacked private title based on the European model. This made it possible for the Spanish colonial administration to introduce the hacienda land system, in which vast landholdings were controlled by Spanish elites and religious institutions, resulting in a concentration of land in the hands of a few, creating social inequality and limiting opportunities for Indigenous peoples. The nineteenth century witnessed the development of a cash crop economy in searching for new sources of income to the colony following the abolishment of the galleon trade (the Manila-Acapulco Trading System) in 1815. This led to an export-oriented, agriculture-based economy by opening resource frontiers. With the introduction of crops such as maize, tobacco, coffee, and sugarcane, Spanish influence also altered agricultural methods in the country towards a large-scale plantation model.[154] Consequently, this model led to significant ecological changes, including deforestation, alteration of landscapes, biodiversity loss, and soil degradation.

The second was American colonisation (1898–1946). Under the control of the US colonial power, as observed by Bowie and Unger, the Philippines 'built on the Spanish legacy of an entrenched oligarchy, but a weak state'.[155] The colonial government retained the Regalian Doctrine in resource management since this colonial construct has 'justified the appropriation of land and natural resources and regulation of land ownership' in the country.[156] In addition, the American colonial government enacted policies to modernise and strengthen the Philippine economy, such as encouraging industrialisation and introducing new agricultural practices 'through wage labour in agriculture' and 'exploitative semi-feudal land control arrangements'.[157] In 1934, the Tydings–McDuffie Act was enacted by the US to prepare the country for independence,[158] marking the Philippine Commonwealth period (1935–46). Governed under the 1935 Constitution, natural resource management was pursued through resource nationalism in which its extraction was permitted only for Filipino citizens or companies owned by its citizens. Despite the institutional changes in this period, 'the advent of democracy did not prevent the entrenchment of oligarchic rule'.[159] Considering those Spanish

[154] James Warren, 'Typhoons and the Inequalities of Philippine Society and History', (2016) 64 *Philippine Studies: Historical & Ethnographic Viewpoints* 455.

[155] Alasdair Bowie and Danny Unger, *The Politics of Open Economies: Indonesia, Malaysia, the Philippines, and Thailand* (Cambridge University Press, 1997) 102.

[156] Antonio La Viña, 'After More Than 100 Years of Environmental Law, What's Next for the Philippines?' (2014) 88 *Philippines Law Journal* 195, 226.

[157] Rodan (n 3) 44. [158] Bowie and Unger (n 115) 102. [159] ibid.

and American colonial experiences together, Sidel argues that 'the peculiar institutional legacies of colonial rule facilitated the emergence and entrenchment of small-town bosses, provincial "war-lords", and authoritarian presidents by providing mechanisms for private monopolization of resources and prerogatives of the state'.[160]

The early postcolonial Philippines was marked by changes in political leadership and their respective challenges in nation-building, economic development, and social issues. For instance, Manuel Roxas (president from 1946 to 1948) focused on rehabilitating the post–World War II economy by rebuilding infrastructure, reviving industries, and attracting foreign investment to stimulate economic growth.[161] Agrarian matters were also a policy strategy to address the concentration of landownership and promote equitable distribution of agricultural land among the populace. However, its implementation was limited under his administration. Agrarian reform then became a priority of Ramon Magsaysay (1953–57) to distribute agricultural land to peasants in order to address rural poverty and land inequality, as well as to promote cooperatives and to provide support for rural development.[162] Moreover, because of the fear of communism following the communist revolution in China, the Philippines turned to the US to build a 'mutual security treaty', and this US assistance was tied to the adoption of a bilateral trade agreement to provide access for the US economic interest in the country, including duty-free access for US goods and 'parity rights' (a non-discriminatory treatment) granted to US citizens akin to Filipino citizens in accessing natural resources and public services.[163] Furthermore, in 1957, Carlos P. Garcia (1957–61) took power and advocated for the 'Filipino First' policy, which aimed to prioritise the interests of Filipino businesses and promote economic nationalism to limit the influence of foreign capital.[164] The enactment of the 1950 Import Control Act, the 1954 Retail Trade Nationalisation Act, and the Rice and Corn Nationalisation Act curtailed the Chinese role in the economic sector.[165] This policy led to the emergence of strong Indigenous entrepreneurs in the national economy, marking a relatively distinct feature compared to Indonesia and Thailand, where Chinese capital appears dominant.

Another important conjuncture that shaped the trajectory of the country's political economy is the authoritarian regime of Ferdinand E. Marcos (1965–86). He was

[160] John Sidel, Capital, Coercion and Crime: Bossism in the Philippines (Stanford University Press, 1999), 19.

[161] Emmanuel Albela, 'The Economic Programs of Philippine Third Republic (1946–1972)', (2018) 1 *Tala Kasaysayan: An Online Journal of History* 8; see also Miguel Jimenez, 'Views on the Philippine Economy through the Nationalist Lens: 1945-1992', (2018) 1 *Tala Kasaysayan: An Online Journal of History* 39.

[162] Eric Portera and Antonio Hila, 'Liberating Farmers from Tenancy Bondage: The Land and Agrarian Reform Programs of President Ramon Magsaysay (1954–1957)' (2020) 3 *Philippine Social Science Journal* 142.

[163] Bowie and Unger (n 155) 105–106.

[164] Miguel Jimenez, 'Views on the Philippine Economy through the Nationalist Lens. 1945-1992' (2018) 1 *Tala Kasaysayan: An Online Journal of History* 39.

[165] Bowie and Unger (n 115) 104.

elected in late 1965 with a strong preference for accommodating the interests of the US, and followed an export-oriented economic model under the guidance of technocrats from the US/World Bank.[166] To this end, he needed to create a friendly and apolitical climate for foreign business enterprises by suppressing opposition forces and resistance, especially from the Maoist New People's Army, through the enactment of martial law in 1972.[167] In the early years of martial law, the Marcos administration undertook structural changes to make the country more attractive to foreign capital, including 'opening the Philippines to a flood of bilateral and international aid to promote infrastructure projects, accepting successive waves of "development" experts in every field from public administration to population control ... opening up the economy to greater penetration by foreign banks'.[168] Writing in 1977, David Wurfel argued that martial law served as a means of ensuring regime survival by guaranteeing political stability and claims to legitimacy. This is because political stability was 'a crucial prerequisite of economic growth' and economic growth was the basis for the regime's legitimacy before the populace.[169]

Like their Indonesian counterparts, Philippine natural resources under the Marcos regime were extracted through 'systems of patronage and clientelism', in which President Marcos awarded licences or concessions to his families and cronies as a strategy for maintaining loyalty and regime survival.[170] Although experiencing a considerable rate of economic growth, the rate of poverty had increased from 41 per cent before his presidency to 60 per cent under his administration, creating public discontent that ultimately led to the popular resistance forcing him to step down in 1986.[171] As Yong puts it: 'the people's oppositional movements in the Philippines were also induced by the economic crisis, which opened an opportunity for regime change'.[172] Despite his regime coming to an end, the political legacy remains. Parallel to the case of Indonesia, as observed by Robison,[173] the rise of new 'oligarchs' in the Philippines in the 1970s was also deeply 'tied to the operations of transnational capital' under the repressive martial law which facilitated the integration of Marcos's cronies with the global capitalist economy.[174]

In the post-Marcos era of the Philippines, natural resource extraction remained essential for development policies to pursue a sustained economic growth rate.

[166] Robert Stauffer, 'The Philippine Political Economy: (Dependent) State Capitalism in the Corporatist Mode', in R. Higgott & R. Robison (eds.), *Southeast Asia: Essays in the Political Economy of Structural Change* (Routledge, 1985) 249.

[167] David Wurfel, 'Martial Law in the Philippines: The Methods of Regime Survival', (1977) 50 *Pacific Affairs* 5, 6.

[168] Stauffer (n 166) 255.

[169] Wurfel (n 167) '8; See also Mark Thompson, *The Philippines: From 'People Power' to Democratic Backsliding* (Cambridge University Press, 2023) 10.

[170] Sokphea Young, *Strategies of Authoritarian Survival and Dissensus in Southeast Asia: Weak Men Versus Strongman* (Palgrave Macmillan, 2021) 21.

[171] Ronald Mendoza, Oscar Bulaong, and Gabrielle Mendoza, 'Oligarchy and Governance in the Philippines: 1970s vs 2020s' (2022) <https://ssrn.com/abstract=4032259 or http://dx.doi.org/10.2139/ssrn.4032259> accessed 13 May 2022, 8.

[172] Young (n 170) 222. [173] Robison (n 13). [174] Stauffer (n 166) 257.

President Corazon Cojuangco Aquino, for instance, established the initial foundations of the neoliberal political economy model by emphasizing the role of foreign companies in national recovery, as expressed in the Medium-Term Philippine Development Plan of the National Economic and Development Authority.[175] Under her presidency, the Philippine government enacted the 1987 Administrative Code as 'a blueprint for the exploitation of resources'.[176] In the context of land administration, the Republic Act 6657 concerning the Comprehensive Agrarian Reform Program (CARP) was passed by Congress to undertake a land distribution programme. However, in its implementation, 'each presidential administration had its exemptions to maintain the patron-client governmentality in the Philippines'.[177] A notable example of this is the exemption of 358.22 hectares in Hacienda Luisita, controlled by the Aquino family and then registered to the Cojuangcos' Tarlac Development Corp. (Tadeco) from being an object of land distribution under the CARP. Subsequently, the contested status of Tadeco's sugar plantation in relation to the CARP created a severe conflict between Aquino's family business and plantation workers with landless farmers. This led to the Hacienda Luisita massacre in November 2004, where seven people were shot, and the police and soldiers injured hundreds in a mass protest demanding land distribution.[178] This case demonstrates how plantations, historically linked to wealthy and powerful political elites, thanks to the Spanish colonial administration, have been an economic sector within which struggles for livelihood and state repression have been routine.

In mining, the post-authoritarian periods were marked by an increasing role of non-state actors. Unlike under the Marcos regime (1965–86), when the state took the lead in developing and exploiting minerals while simultaneously preventing foreign corporations from entering the sector,[179] post-Marcos governments have been characterised by neoliberal economic policies aiming at opening markets and deregulating industries, including extractive industries.[180] The Fidel Ramos administration (1992–98), for instance, enacted the Philippine Mining Act 1995 (RA 7942) to establish 'a neoliberal mining framework for the sector',[181] which has three main features of resource governance: (1) a state preference for foreign companies with vast financial resources to become the engine of mineral exploration and extraction, to the point where small-scale mining was widely (and incorrectly) perceived as

[175] Jewellord Singh and Alvin Camba, 'Neoliberalism, Resource Governance and the Everyday Politics of Protests in the Philippines', in J. Elias & L. Rethel (eds.), *The Everyday Political Economy of Southeast Asia* (Cambridge University Press, 2016) 52.

[176] Dante Gatmaytan-Magno, 'Artificial Judicial Environmental Activism: *Oposa V. Factoran* as Aberration', (2007) 17 (1) *Indiana International & Comparative Law Review* 5.

[177] Aliya Paleo, 'The Case of Agrarian Reforms in the Philippine-USA Relations: A Biopolitical Perspective', in F. A. Cruz & N. M. Adiong (eds.), *International Studies in the Philippines: Mapping New Frontiers in Theory and Practice* (Routledge, 2020) 136.

[178] Dax Simbol, '12 Years On, Still No Justice for Hacienda Luisita Massacre Victims', *Rappler* (Manila, 16 November 2016) <www.rappler.com/moveph/152595 hacienda-luisita-12-years-justice/> accessed 25 May 2022.

[179] Singh and Camba (n 175) 52. [180] ibid. [181] ibid.

unsafe and environmentally disastrous in comparison to large-scale mineral extraction; (2) to promote a 'socio-environmental model' in which international financial institutions, most notably the World Bank group, sought to contain the social and ecological consequences of natural resource extraction without jeopardising the role of private investment in financing the expansion of extractive industries; and (3) 'to contain social conflicts through hollow participatory, consultative mechanisms'.[182] In order to revive the mining industry, President Gloria Macapagal Arroyo (2001–10) in 2003 issued an Executive Order 270 (EO 270) and the Mineral Action Plan[183] emphasising that 'the exploration, development and utilization of the country's mineral resources should be pursued within the framework of sustainable development and must therefore contribute to economic growth, environmental protection, and social equity and development'.[184] When President Benigno Aquino III (2010–16) took office, persistent anti-mining campaigns increased public awareness of the socio-ecological impacts of large-scale mining. Utilising the discourse on 'sustainable mining', his administration undertook a moratorium on new mineral exploration to facilitate reviews of the compliance of the existing mining operations with the standards stipulated by EO 270.[185] Nonetheless, the mining industry has profited from its reliance on 'both expansive land appropriations and cheap labour exploitation' in this period as well.[186]

In the post-authoritarian era, despite changing leaders, external shocks, and domestic political upheavals accompanying these political transformations, the core tenets of neoliberal development strategies in economic planning have been preserved.[187] Having been implemented for three decades by different presidents, from Corazon Aquino to Benigno Aquino III, those strategies failed to lift Filipinos out of poverty.[188] As a result, the failures, as Ramos argued, provided fertile ground for Duterte's rise to power (2016–22).[189] Starting his political career in the mid-1980s as mayor of Davao City, 'one of the most violent cities in the Philippines' involving power struggles between communist rebels, anti-communist vigilantes, and the military as well as warlord politicians, Duterte managed to triangulate those forces effectively through political violence.[190] In his presidency, Duterte was 'keen on assuring capital that despite his forceful promise for change, it's business as usual for business', indicating 'a preservation of neoliberal logic consistent with development strategies of the last 30 years'.[191] In Duterte's development plan, raising domestic and foreign direct investment was seen as the most crucial strategy for growth in the industrial and service sectors. The administration committed to

[182] ibid., 52–53. [183] ibid., 53.

[184] Minerals Development Council, *Investor's Prospectus on Philippine Mining* (Republic of the Philippines, 2007) 12.

[185] Singh and Camba (n 175) 67. [186] Gellert (n 1) 374.

[187] Charmaine Ramos, 'The Return of Strongman Rule in the Philippines: Neoliberal Roots and Developmental Implications', (2021) *Geofourm* <https://doi.org/10.1016/j.geoforum.2021.04.001> accessed 15 June 2023, 4.

[188] ibid., 4–6. [189] ibid. [190] Thompson (n 169) 7. [191] Ramos (n 187) 6–7.

creating the infrastructure necessary for lowering the cost of trade and production to supplement the state's regulatory powers. As its centrepiece economic policy, Duterte's government casts the 'Build, Build, Build' campaign, an ambitious infrastructure development programme involving '75 flagship projects, including six airports, nine railways, three bus rapid transit systems, 32 roads and bridges, four seaports, four energy generation facilities, ten water resource projects, and five flood control facilities'.[192]

In the context of resource and environmental management, in his first term in office, President Duterte appointed the late Regina Lopez, a well-known environmentalist, as the Environmental Secretary to prove his promise during the presidential campaign to protect the environment. As Secretary, in her first year in office, Regina Lopez focused on conducting an audit of the mining industry; the audit in 2017 led to closing twenty-three and suspending five large-scale mining operations.[193] Due to her brave order, the mining industry fought back through the Commission of Appointments, whose vice chairman was Ronaldo B. Zamora, the brother of Manuel Zamora, the owner of Nickel Asia Corporation, the largest nickel mining company in the country.[194] The Commission removed her from the position, and she was replaced by Roy Cimatu, a former military officer, as the Environmental Secretary. Cimatu eventually revoked Lopez's closure and suspension order.[195]

A similar experience was faced by Rafael Mariano, whom President Duterte appointed as the Agrarian Reform Secretary. As a farmer activist, in 2017 he moved to support peasants by instituting a two-year moratorium on land conversion to conduct a comprehensive review of the agrarian policy. This included freezing all Agriculture Venture Arrangement applications, a policy instrument created in 1999 to permit 'agribusiness corporations to control lands that are supposedly exclusive to agrarian reform beneficiaries and other land tenure owners through joint ventures, lease contracts and other arrangements'.[196] Economist Calixto V. Chikiamco argues the appointment of Rafael Mariano as Agrarian Reform Secretary was a mistake because 'with his leftist oriented policies, he scared possible investors in agriculture. For example, he tried extending coverage of a failed land reform programme and tried to undo even successful joint venture

[192] ibid., 7.

[193] Jose Leon A. Dulce, Clemente G. Bautista Jr., Gianina Camille E. Glarino and Karl Daniel A. Begnotea, 'A War of Plunder against Environmental Defenders in the Philippines' (2021) 22 *Policy Matters* 28, 30.

[194] Jee Y. Geronimo, 'Lopez Urges CA: "Make Decision for Common Good"', *Rappler* (Manila, 28 February 2017). <www.rappler.com/nation/162797-gina-lopez-commission-on-appointments/> accessed 25 May 2022.

[195] Keith Schneider, 'The Rise and Fall of Regina Lopez, the Philippines' Maverick Environmental Minister' *Mongabay* (Manila, 9 May 2017). <https://news.mongabay.com/2017/05/the-rise-and-fall-of-regina-lopez-the-philippines-maverick-environment-minister/> accessed 25 May 2022; Jose Leon A. Dulce et al. (n 193) 30.

[196] Dulce et al. (n 193) 30.

programs.'[197] The extension of land reform would also include the sugar plantation of Tadeco, owned by former president Benigno Aquino III's Cojuangco family in Hacienda Luisita, Tarlac Province, as the object of land distribution.[198] Hence, Mariano's reputation and newly enacted policies became the target of delegitimation strategies by accusing him of being directly involved in the attack initiated by the Communist Party of the Philippines – New People's Army (CPP-NPA) in Davao in April 2017.[199] Eventually, the Commission Appointments removed him from his position, and his successor lifted the moratorium and agrarian reform policies.[200]

Regina Lopez's and Rafael Mariano's experiences demonstrate how crony capitalism and politico-business elites have continued to shape the country's political and economic landscape, even in the post-Marcos era.[201] Institutional reform programmes have been undertaken in the aftermath in order to liberalise the economy, but this has had little effect on dismantling the concentration of power within the hands of a few political clans. In turn, this concentration of power, combined with the state's security policy against communist insurgency as well as the 'War on Drugs', has contributed to massive attacks against environmental defenders in the contemporary Philippines. As Rodan puts it, '[s]hared interests between dominant capitalists and political elites have been so deep and systematic that forces in civil society have been routinely thwarted in attempts to reform state power'.[202]

Environmental Movements

In the context of evolving social movements, the Philippines has been represented as the benchmark of social movement developments in the region. According to Jorge V. Tigno, the emergence and proliferation of vibrant civil society movements in the country have been shaped by several historical conjunctions. They were rooted in the *cofradias*, philanthropic civil associations that 'were allowed by the Spanish colonial authorities to be established at the local levels'.[203] Bankoff's historical account demonstrated that these associations were not merely religious congregations but were also established to provide mutual support among their

[197] Calixto V. Chikiamco, 'The Economic Mistakes of the Duterte Administration' *Business World Online* (Manila, 17 October 2021)<www.bworldonline.com/opinion/2021/10/17/404078/the-economic-mistakes-of-the-duterte-administration/> accessed 25 May 2022.

[198] Aliya Paleo, 'The Case of Agrarian Reforms in the Philippine-USA Relations: A Biopolitical Perspective', in F. A. Cruz & N. M. Adiong (eds.), *International Studies in the Philippines: Mapping New Frontiers in Theory and Practice* (Routledge, 2020).

[199] Julliane Love De Jesus, 'CA Rejects Mariano's Appointment at DAR', *Inquirer* (Manila, 6 September 2017). <https://newsinfo.inquirer.net/926664/ca-rejects-marianos-appointment-at-dar> accessed 25 May 2022.

[200] Geronimo (n 194); Jose Leon A. Dulce et al. (n 193) 30.

[201] Mendoza, Bulaong, and Mendoza (n 171) 21. [202] Rodan (n 3) 42.

[203] Jorge V. Tigno, 'The Philippines', in A. Ogawa (ed.), *Routledge Handbook of Civil Society in Asia* (Routledge, Oxon, 2018) 113.

members.[204] Civil society organisations became more radicalised in the 1960s and 1970s. However, they were severely restricted under Marcos's martial law, which prohibited them from advocating 'the anti-dictatorship cause' while 'encouraging them to support the regime'.[205] In 1974, the authoritarian regime planned to construct a World Bank-funded mega dam project along the Chico River in the Cordilleras, Northern Luzon, which would displace more than 100,000 Indigenous peoples. The state violently repressed resistance by the Indigenous groups, and the military force murdered the resistance leader, Macli-ing Dulag. Eventually, the World Bank withdrew its funding, and the regime cancelled the project.

Despite the repressive conditions under martial law, the 1980s witnessed a proliferation of civil society organisations with a political orientation, especially following the assassination of Benigno Aquino, a prominent leader of the Anti-Marcos movement, in 1983.[206] They became a service provider for desperate communities as the state did not provide basic supports due to corruption and inefficiencies.[207] As a result, their political mobilisation, known as 'People's Power' movement in the 1980s, which managed to topple Ferdinand Marcos's authoritarian regime, has inspired social movements against authoritarianism across the region.[208] In the aftermath, thanks to the flocks of foreign aid to 'fund reconstruction and to stabilize democratic institutions',[209] in the post-dictatorial era, civil society organisations in the form of non-governmental organisations (NGOs) and people's organisations (POs) continued to grow significantly, up to threefold, during the 1984–95 period.[210]

Today, many NGOs and POs in the Philippines focus on environmental and natural resources management. Environmental movements in the country have played an instrumental role in opposing the expansion of extractive industries through campaigns and legal actions, contributing to the progressive development of environmental law.[211] Due to the heavy dependency on extractive industries as the engine of economic growth, the opposition of environmental movements is characterised as a constraint to development and business enterprises. In turn, those actors whose interests are confronted by the work of environmental movements take measures to impede the movements by coercive means if necessary. Hence, conflicts over natural resources and the environment present a persistent picture of how the capitalist development model counters environmental defenders whose livelihoods and environment are appropriated and compromised under the banner of economic growth.

Consequently, those conflicts have made the Philippines one of the most dangerous countries for environmental defenders. Wolfram Dressler calls it 'a deeply

[204] Greg Bankoff, 'Dangers to Going It Alone: Social Capital and the Origins of Community Resilience in the Philippines', (2007) 22 *Continuity and Change* 327, 331

[205] Jorge V. Tigno (n 203) 114. [206] ibid., 115. [207] ibid., 114. [208] ibid., 110.

[209] Greg Bankoff (n 204) 327. [210] Jorge V. Tigno (n 203) 115.

[211] Agung Wardana, 'A Quest for Agency in the Anthropocene: Law and Environmental Movements in Southeast Asia', (2023) 32 *Review of European, Comparative, and International Environmental Law* 57.

violent space for environmental defenders'.[212] According to the Kalikasan PNE, a national environmental organisation, there were at least 272 defenders killed in the Philippines in the eight years between 2001 and 2019, the majority of them being peasants and Indigenous peoples.[213] In 2015 alone, 90 per cent of thirty-one human rights defenders killed across the archipelago were environmental defenders.[214] The 'atmosphere of violence' has escalated since Duterte became president in 2016 by reworking 'his initial populist mandate of returning public order to the country to unleash his own authoritarian populist agenda of violence, political control and neoliberalism that differs little from previous administrations'.[215] Killings related to environmental conflicts during the administration of Duterte increased by 8.2 and 3.2 times compared to the Arroyo administration (2001–10) and the Aquino administration (2010–16), respectively.[216]

Under the Duterte regime, attacks on environmental defenders escalated. During 2016–19, at least 157 environmental defenders were murdered, and this figure continues to grow, not to mention the thousands of other extra-judicial killings under the administration in the name of the 'War on Drugs'.[217] The Center for Environmental Concerns – Philippines (CEC), an environmental national organisation based in Manila, estimated that more than 19,000 environmental defenders 'were subjected to a wide range of human rights abuses', including murders, threats and intimidation, 'red-tagging' and 'terror-tagging', as well as strategic lawsuits against public participation.[218] Even during the global pandemic of Covid-19 and the imposed national-scale lockdown, the attacks on environmental defenders were far from declining. As in Indonesia, where the restrictive health policy was used to prevent environmental defenders from exercising their struggles,[219] the CEC reported up to 558 victims, which included '295 forced evacuations, 142 illegal arrests and detention, 58 SLAPP, 53 threat and intimidation, 51 political detentions, 25 assaults, 12 surveillance, 4 extrajudicial killing (EJK), and 1 enforced disappearance victims'.[220]

May 2022 was expected to be a defining moment for environmental defenders, especially Indigenous communities in the Philippines. Many environmental activists tried to intervene in the election by endorsing Leni Robredo, the former vice president, as the friendliest presidential candidate for the environment and environmental defenders. For them, the general election would change the country's

[212] Wolfram Dressler, 'A Window into the "Everyday" Struggles of Environmental Defenders in Palawan Island, the Philippines', (2021) 22 *Policy Matters* 17, 18.

[213] Kalikasan PNE, 2020, Submission to the OHCHR for HRC Report 41/2 by the Kalikasan People's Network for the Environment in the Philippines (online) <https://app.box.com/s/ertqfy2miuhdatq07e5wqzvnhvz7zrtf> accessed 30 March 2022.

[214] Frontline Defenders, *Annual Report 2016: Stop Killing Human Rights Defenders* (International Foundation for the Protection of Human Rights Defenders, 2016), 14.

[215] Wolfram Dressler (n 212) 18.

[216] Dulce et al. (n 193) 29.

[217] Dressler (n 212) 18.

[218] Jordan Fronda, Marian Grafil and Leon Dulce, *Environmental Defenders in the Time of COVID-19* (Center for Environmental Concerns Philippines, 2020) 5.

[219] Grenfell and Wardana (n 40) 53.

[220] Fronda, Grafil and Dulce (n 218) 11.

violent landscape if the favourable presidential candidate won the vote. However, Ferdinand 'Bong-bong' Marcos and Sara Duterte won the presidential and vice presidential positions easily by 'assuring continuity with "Dutertismo" and invoking nostalgia for Marcos, Sr.'s authoritarian rule'.[221] This win was contributed to partly by the use of social media to rebrand the old Marcos era as 'a golden age of crime-free prosperity' despite its horrendous human rights abuses, corruption, and near-economic failure.[222] Observers have pointed out that the election result shows the swing of the young urban middle class to escape uncertainty and economic discontent by romanticising a strong state represented by the Marcos regime. Hayton, for instance, observes that '[t]he failure of the political system to improve the economic position of most of the population has caused general disillusion with the state of Philippine politics'.[223] This conjuring of nostalgia, however, has been paid for by environmental defenders, whose concerns for protection of environmental values and natural resources put them in direct conflict with capital's voracious demand for growth.

In brief, the chapter has demonstrated how neoliberal policies and the political interests of elites in the three countries have implicated the environment and local communities' livelihoods. In turn, environmental conflicts have become increasingly common across those countries due to the elites' interests at the expense of the ecological and affected communities' interests. In this regard, the states in Indonesia, Thailand, and the Philippines have had an ambivalent position in relation to the environment and the affected communities. On the one hand, the existence of those states relied on extractive activities from which their source of revenues is derived, and the existing structure of power was underpinned. Thus, their policies tend to be biased towards the extractive industries under the banner of economic development. On the other hand, the states are also terrain through which struggles against environmental injustices as consequences of the increasingly powerful extractive capital in the countries are fought for. Responding to these struggles, the states have utilised environmental governance as a particular mode of conflict regulation through legal means, a theme that brings us to the next chapter.

221 Thompson (n 169) 5–6.

222 Jonathan Head, 'What Marcos' Presidency Means for Filipinos', *The Asean Post*, 11 May 2022. <https://theaseanpost.com/geopolitics/2022/may/11/what-marcos-presidency-means-filipinos> accessed 11 May 2022.

223 Bill Hayton, 2022, 'Why Business as Usual Will Prevail in the Philippines', *Chathamhouse*, 3 May 2022 <www.chathamhouse.org/2022/05/why-business-usual-will-prevail-philippines> accessed 11 May 2022.

CHAPTER 3

Anti-SLAPP in Environmental Law

This chapter traces the evolution of modern environmental law in Indonesia, Thailand, and the Philippines. Following Heyvaert and Etty, environmental law should be seen as 'the product of a rich combination of local, regional and transboundary communications and pressures'.[1] The chapter reveals how environmental law is shaped by environmental conflicts between social forces with competing interests over the environment and natural resources in these countries and, in turn, shapes how those conflicts are contained and struggles over resources are fought for by these different social forces. The first part of this chapter explains how the structural conditions elaborated on in the previous chapter shape domestic environmental law as a bureaucratic means to intervene in the market economy under the rubric of environmental protection and, at the same time, a platform to navigate environmental concerns caused by the consequence of rapid industrialisation. Due to the persistent struggles of environmental movements to achieve legal reform and engage in strategic litigation strategies, environmental law has evolved to be a specific body of law concerning the protection of the environment and the recognition of environmental rights, making it a resource to be mobilised by environmental movements in political claim-making.

As institutions of power in three countries are underpinned by resource extraction, power struggles have continuously taken place, including in the legal sphere. They involved how environmental issues should be defined and regulated and whose interests should be protected at the expense of others' interests in the environmental law regime. Due to asymmetrical access to legal resources, people who struggle to defend their environmental rights become more vulnerable to being attacked and intimidated through legal means by powerful actors whose interests in

[1] Veerle Heyvaert and Thijs Etty, 'Introducing Transnational Environmental Law', (2012) 1 (1) *Transnational Environmental Law* 1, 4.

resource extraction are affected by the struggles. This strategy to intimidate environmental defenders, conceptually known as SLAPP, has its roots in US legal culture and has been duplicated in Southeast Asia. In Indonesia, for instance, it is no coincidence that the two first SLAPP cases were filed by two subsidiary companies of the US-based Newmont Gold Company, indicating the transnational nature of SLAPP as an increasingly common legal practice in dealing with environmental conflicts. In response, these countries have developed legal frameworks of anti-SLAPP to protect environmental defenders and to ensure they can participate in environmental matters without fear of retaliation. Therefore, the second part of this chapter discusses the enactment of anti-SLAPP provisions in the three countries in response to the increasing number of SLAPP cases. It shows how the provisions were formulated differently by Indonesia, Thailand, and the Philippines, informed by a specific context from which lawfare against environmental defenders in those countries is exercised.

Modernising Environmental Law

Indonesia

Over the past few decades, environmental law in Indonesia has evolved dramatically, reflecting a rising demand for the significance of conserving natural resources and biodiversity. This trend can be traced back to the colonial period. According to Robert Cribb, in the Dutch Colonial era, environmental policy was dominated by conservation aspects that focused on three models.[2] The first is a species-based protection model motivated by the pressure on animals due to hunting.[3] This partial animal conservation is expressed in ordinances specifically to protect certain animals, for example the Bird Protection Ordinance (1905) and the Pearl and Fisheries Protection Ordinance (1916), which stipulated that within three nautical miles, there should be no taking of pearls and sponges to guarantee stocks for future exploitation; the Animal Protection and Ordinance (1931) mainly for elephants and rhinos; and the Hunting Ordinance (1931), which aimed to maintain game stocks so that the hunting hobby of the colonial nobility could continue.[4] The second model of colonial conservation policy was based on natural monuments (*natuurmonumenten*). Lobbying from Dutch nature conservation groups motivated the enactment of the Nature Reserve and Wildlife Sanctuary Ordinance (1932), which extended protection to natural sites that were natural habitats for protected animals.[5] The third conservation model was protected areas significant for scientific

[2] Robert Cribb, 'The Politics of Environmental Protection in Indonesia', (1988) *Working Paper No. 48, Centre of Southeast Asian Studies, Monash University*, 2–3.
[3] ibid.
[4] Koesnadi Hardjasoemantri, *Hukum Tata Lingkungan, 8th Ed.* (Gadjah Mada University Press, 2018).
[5] Cribb (n 1) 2–3.

research, especially in the context of biodiversity.[6] Influenced by European Romanticism, the colonial conservation approach reinforced the experience of oppression of natives because they were prohibited from hunting, collecting wood, and utilising forest products for their needs in order to maintain the aesthetic value of nature.[7]

In the early years of Indonesia's independence, under Sukarno's administration (1945–67), environmental concerns were largely absent from national policy and law-making. Paradoxically, it heavily relied on the Dutch colonial leftover ordinances governing the environment. During the 1950s–60s, there was tremendous pressure on protected areas for agriculture and firewood. People entered the forest area and cut it down to make fields and firewood. Forestry came under the purview of the agriculture department, as forests were not considered to have an ecological function or to protect ecosystems; instead, they were considered to have a production function. Environmental law enforcement is weak because the bureaucracy and government do not see the benefits of preserving the environment. In 1964, the Forestry Department was formed separately from the Department of Agriculture, and a division in charge of nature and animal conservation management was also established under it.

Modern environmental law in the country has evolved following the 1972 Stockholm Conference on Human Environment. Due to the agenda to pursue economic development initiated by the authoritarian regime of Suharto (1967–98), by the 1970s, increasing pollution levels and environmental degradation had become a significant issue. With pressure from the international community following the 1972 adoption of the Stockholm Declaration and the 1980 Montevideo Expert Meeting, increasing environmental issues at the domestic level had led to the enactment of the 1982 Environmental Management Law as the country's first environmental legislation which provided a legal framework for environmental management and protection albeit the provisions were too vague and general. Since then, Indonesia has enacted various laws and regulations to protect the environment, promote sustainable development, and replace colonial ordinances.[8] The authoritarian regime used environmental management as a tool to respond to public concerns about environmental problems to avoid political disorder and, simultaneously, to consolidate 'bureaucratic control' over the economy in the name of protecting the environment.[9]

The economic crisis in the late 1990s that brought the regime from power has opened opportunities for democratisation, known as the era of *Reformasi*. Following the fall of Suharto's authoritarian regime in May 1998, B. J. Habibie, the vice president, took over the administration. Habibie pursued economic

[6] ibid., 2–5. [7] ibid., 6.

[8] Among others, the 1920 Fisheries Ordinance, which had been in effect for sixty years, was replaced by Law No. 9 of 1985. The Nature Conservation Ordinance of 1932, which had been in force for fifty-eight years, was finally revoked by Law No. 5 of 1990 on the Conservation of Natural Resources and Ecosystems.

[9] Cribb (n 1) 25.

liberalisation under his presidency (1998–99), aiming at recovering the post-crisis economy under the reform package of the World Bank and the International Monetary Fund (IMF). The package included dismantling monopolies and opening various sectors to free competition to attract foreign investment and stimulate economic growth. A constitutional engineering strategy was also undertaken to signal foreign investors that the country was firmly committed to the rule of law and economic liberalisation.[10] This also has brought politico-legal opportunities to pursue better environmental and natural resource governance, which include the enactment of People's Consultative Assembly Decree (TAP MPR) No. IX of 2001 concerning Agrarian and Natural Resources Management Reform that sets up environmental and natural resource management principles under the justice and social welfare framework. Human rights provisions were incorporated during the amendment of the 1945 Constitution, including Article 28 H(1), which proclaims that '[e]very person shall have the right to live in physical and spiritual prosperity, to have a home and enjoy a good and healthy environment, and shall have the right to obtain medical care'. With this constitutional provision, Indonesia has become one of the countries explicitly expressing their constitutional environmental rights.

One of the most ambitious institutional reform agendas was decentralisation. It was seen as a solution to accelerate the investment process by transferring authorities to grant permits to district/municipal governments. In environmental and resource governance, the Letter of Intent (LoI) between the Government of Indonesia and the IMF in the early 2000s also directed natural resource utilisation to be more competitive in the global market. As a result, several pro-market legislations were enacted, including the 1999 Forestry Act, the 2001 Oil and Gas Act, and the 2009 Mineral and Coal Mining Act. Reformist intellectuals also celebrated decentralised resource governance based on the assumption that it would bring the decision-making process closer to communities affected by the decision, thus resulting in better decisions on resource allocations. However, this expectation has not materialised. As Gellert observes, district governments were authorised through the decentralisation policy to grant timber utilisation and timber extraction permits; consequently, there 'was a boom in permit allocation'.[11] Instead of preventing conflicts that frequently occurred during the centralistic era of the authoritarian regime, decentralisation has exacerbated conflicts over natural resources across the archipelago even further.

Following this institutional change, there was a solid demand to reform the existing environmental law regime and adopt a decentralised model of the environment. The Government of Indonesia pledged to undertake this reform in LoI with the IMF on 20 January 2000. It justified that

[10] Daniel A. Farber, 'Rights as Signals', (2002) 31 *Journal of Legal Studies* 83.

[11] Paul Gellert, 'Oligarchy in the Timber Markets of Indonesia: From APKINDO to IBRA to the Future of the Forests', in B. Resosudarmo (eds.), *The Politics and Economics of Indonesia's Natural Resources* (ISEAS, 2005) 154.

> Indonesia's natural environment has continued to deteriorate during the crisis. Weak policy implementation and weak market institutions have combined to undermine Indonesia's base of natural resources. . . . Our policy and institutional framework for natural resource management will focus on three key objectives. First, we will include greater consultation and stakeholder participation in decisions affecting our natural resources, particularly in the formulation of new policies, and the location and selection of public investments. To ensure that these decisions are based on good information, we propose to expand and improve environmental monitoring of Indonesia's air, water, forests, and marine resources. Second, we will move towards a pricing structure for natural resources that better reflects their true value. And third, we will pay special attention to improving forest management and ensuring a sustainable production of goods and services from our forest resources.[12]

In this light, the 2009 Environmental Protection and Management (EPM) Act was enacted based on a combined approach between command-and-control and market-based strategies to environmental management.[13] Nevertheless, due to the involvement of civil society organisations, especially environmental NGOs in the law-making process, the 2009 EPM Act also incorporates several relatively progressive provisions, including a strong recognition of the right to a good and healthy environment as a human right, the strict liability provisions, the recognition of class action and legal standing for environmental NGOs, and the use of a 'toolbox' approach in law enforcement where criminal sanctions can be applied simultaneously with civil and administrative instruments.[14] More importantly in the context of environmental defenders is the adoption of an anti-SLAPP provision in Article 66 of the 2009 EPM Act, as discussed in *Adopting Anti-SLAPP Provisions.*

Thailand

As discussed in the previous chapter, contemporary Thailand has been marked by political instability. It has experienced thirteen successful coups and twenty constitutional changes, only two of which (the 1932 Constitution and the 1978 Constitution) lasted more than a decade. Connors observes: '[o]f the 11 permanent constitutions, nine were abrogated after a coup d'etat. The predominant political pattern is a "vicious cycle": the perennial return of the coup after a new constitution is promulgated and an election occurs.'[15] The most recent constitution is the 2017 Constitution, a draft sponsored by the National Council for Peace and Order (NCPO) and approved through the 2016 constitutional referendum. McCargo and others argue that misinformation, military intimidation, and repression against

[12] See 'The Letter of Intent of the Government of Indonesia' (International Monetary and Fund, 20 January 2000) <www.imf.org/external/np/loi/2000/idn/01/> accessed 2 February 2022.

[13] Agung Wardana, *Contemporary Bali: Contested Space and Governance* (Palgrave Macmillan, 2019).

[14] For a discussion on criminal environmental law, see Michael Faure, 'The Revolution in Environmental Criminal Law in Europe', (2017) 35 (2) *Virginia Environmental Law* 321.

[15] Michael K. Connors, 'The Two Faces of Democracy', in P. Chachavalpongpun (ed.), *Routledge Handbook of Contemporary Thailand* (Routledge, 2020), 56.

draft opponents made such approval possible.[16] The 2017 Constitution has been heavily criticised on two grounds. First, it led to a dysfunctional bicameral legislative body because members of the House of Representatives were affected by a restrictive electoral system. In contrast, the 250 members of the Senate were appointed for the first time by the NCPO, with six seats dedicated to military commanders. A joint vote to appoint a prime minister between the members of the Senate and the House of Representatives has made it possible for General Prayut to turn his position from the leader of the military junta into an elected prime minister.[17] The second reason is that the legitimacy of the 2017 Constitution is questionable because it has been a product of a military coup imposed upon the people without meaningful participation in the drafting process.[18] Hence, dissenting voices have demanded an amendment to the constitution.

Flux in the constitution as the fundamental law in the country has also affected how the environment and natural resources are governed, and public participation in environmental matters is facilitated or constrained. In this context, two constitutions have been relevant to developing environmental law in the country, namely the 1997 and 2007 constitutions. Harding and Leyland have argued that both constitutions 'have encouraged participation in national and local government by placing a duty on the State through directive principles to promote public participation in laying down policies, decision-making, and formulation of economic and social development'.[19] The 1997 Constitution was promulgated in response to public demands for democratic reform and participation in public affairs, including monitoring the state's exercise of power.[20] It set out the duty of the state to 'promote and encourage public participation in the preservation, maintenance, and balanced exploitation of natural resources and biological diversity and the promotion, maintenance, and protection of the quality of the environment in accordance with the persistent development principle as well as the control and elimination of pollution affecting public health, sanitary conditions, welfare and quality of life'.[21]

The 1997 Constitution also guaranteed the right of association and the role of environmental groups, scholars, and local communities in environmental management. Section 45 stipulated:

> [a] person shall enjoy the liberty to unite and form an association, a union, league, co-operative, farmer group, private organization or any other group. The restriction

[16] Duncan McCargo, Saowanee Alexander and Petra Desatova, 'Ordering Peace: Thailand's 2016 Constitutional Referendum', (2017) 39 (1) *Contemporary Southeast Asia* 65.

[17] Khemthong Tonsakulrungruang, 'Undoing Authoritarianism: Thailand's Campaign to Amend the 2017 Constitution', *I-Connect* (8 January 2020) <www.iconnectblog.com/undoing-authoritarianism-thailands-campaign-to-amend-the-2017-constitution/> accessed on 27 January 2023.

[18] Ibid.

[19] Andrew Harding and Peter Leyland, *The Constitutional System of Thailand: A Contextual Analysis* (Hart, 2011) 135–236.

[20] Thawilwadee Bureekul, 'Access to Environmental Justice and Public Participation in Thailand', in A. Harding (ed.), *Access to Environmental Justice: A Comparative Study* (Koninklijke Brill, 2007), 275.

[21] Section 79 of the 1997 Thai Constitution.

> of such liberty under paragraph one shall not be imposed except by virtue of the law specifically enacted for promoting the common interest of the public, maintaining public order or good morals or preventing economic monopoly.

Section 56 consists of three paragraphs that spell out the right to public participation in environmental matters,[22] the preventive measures,[23] and the right to petition.[24] In the context of environmental advocacy, Section 46 was instrumental because it recognised the right of local communities in environmental and resource management, stating:

> Persons so assembling as to be a traditional community shall have the right to conserve or restore their customs, local knowledge, arts or good culture of their community and of the nation and participate in the management, maintenance, preservation and exploitation of natural resources and the environment in a balanced fashion and persistently as provided by law.

Similarly, the 2007 Constitution also encouraged public participation. This was a product of the public pressure demanding a more expansive space for participation, considering environmental problems had been a persistent national issue. By 2000, in the forestry sector, for instance, Thai forests only remained 15 per cent of the terrestrial areas.[25] Akin to Section 58 of the 1997 Constitution, the 2007 Constitution guaranteed the right to receive information and participate in the decision-making process in environmental matters in Sections 56 and 57. Section 56 of the 1997 Constitution concerning the right of citizens to present a petition against the government was also retained in the 2007 Constitution. Section 59 of the 2007 Constitution stipulated that '[a] person shall have the right to present a petition and to be informed of the result of its consideration within the appropriate time'. Moreover, Section 60 of the 2007 Constitution stipulated that '[a] person shall have the right to sue a government agency, State agency, State enterprise, local government organisation or other State authority which is a juristic person to be liable for an act or omission was done by its government official, official or employee'. Sections 66 and 67 of the 2007 Constitution granted community rights

[22] The first paragraph stipulates that '[t]he right of a person to give to the State and communities participation in the preservation and exploitation of natural resources and biological diversity and in the protection, promotion and preservation of the quality of the environment for usual and consistent survival in the environment which is not hazardous to his or health and sanitary condition, welfare or quality of life, shall be protected, as provided by law'.

[23] It states that '[a]ny project or activity which may seriously affect the quality of the environment shall not be permitted unless its impacts on the quality of the environment have been studied and evaluated and opinions of an independent organisation, consisting of representatives from private environmental organisations and higher education institutions providing studies in the environmental field, have been obtained prior to the operation of such project or activity, as provided by law'.

[24] The last paragraph guarantees that '[t]he right of a person to sue a State agency, State enterprise, local government organisation or other State authority to perform the duties as provided by law under paragraph one and paragraph two shall be protected'.

[25] Chris Baker and Pasuk Phongpaichit, 'Thailand in the Longue Duree', in P. Chachavalpongpun (ed.), *Routledge Handbook of Contemporary Thailand* (Routledge, 2020) 16.

in environmental and resource management similar to Section 46 of the 1997 Constitution. Wichean Anpraser observes that those constitutional rights had 'formed the basics of participatory resource governance'.[26] However, the 2007 Constitution was replaced by the military junta's 2014 interim Constitution, followed by the 2017 Constitution, which has shrunk spaces of civic engagements.

Below the constitution, environmental policy has been translated into legislation, government regulations, and other operative legal instruments. Before the 1972 Stockholm Conference, laws and regulations related to the environment in Thailand had been rather sectoral and piecemeal. The 1913 Forest Protection Act, for instance, focused on the forestry sector, which extended state protection of forested areas beyond teak forested areas due to 'excessive extraction and conflicts', and it was followed by the 1938 Forest Protection and Conservation Act, which defined and classified particular forests to be preserved permanently.[27] Other legislations included were the 1941 Forestry Act, the 1961 National Park Act, the 1964 National Forest Act, and the 1947 Fishery Act, whose main objective was not protecting the environment but instrumentalising natural resources.[28] Through the 1964 National Forest Act, for instance, 40 per cent of Thai terrestrial areas were classified as National Forest Reserves; accordingly, communities living within the reserves were regarded as illegal forest occupiers, thus perpetuating conflicts between the state and forest communities.[29] More recently, following the 2014 military coup, these conflicts have been exacerbated further by the NCPO's rulings No. 64/2557 and No. 66/2557 to fight forest encroachment. As a result, Indigenous peoples and economically vulnerable communities were forcibly evicted from their livelihoods and many of them were also criminalised and sued by legal actions taken by the government.[30]

Comprehensive environmental management and protection legislation was not enacted until 1975. It was influenced by international pressure to establish domestic environmental law and the experience of major pollution of the Mekong River in 1972 when the water was contaminated by industrial discharge from factories along the river.[31] During this period, the government enacted the 1975 Enhancement and Conservation of National Environmental Quality Act (ECNEQ), marking the

[26] Wichean Anpraser, 'SLAPPs as a Form of Exclusion in Resource Governance: The Case of an Anti-Gold Mine Campaign in Loei Province, Thailand', (2021) 42 *Kasertsart Journal of Social Sciences* 747.

[27] Jim Sato, 'Development of Official Community Forests in Thailand', (1998) *Japan: Institute for Global Environmental Strategies*. <www.iges.or.jp/en/publication_documents/pub/researchreport/en/740/ir98-3-12.pdf> accessed 7 July 2023.

[28] Winai Ruangsri, Senior Research Justice of the Supreme Court of Thailand, 'Environmental Law in the Thai Supreme Court Green Bench', (2011), addressed at the *Roundtable ASEAN Chief Justice and Senior Judiciary on Environmental Law and Enforcement*, in Jakarta, 5–7 December, 3.

[29] Lotte Isager and Søren Ivarsson, 'Contesting Landscapes in Thailand: Tree Ordination as Counter-Territorialization', (2002) 34 *Critical Asian Studies* 395, 399.

[30] Lionel Blackman, *Government of Thailand & Chaiwat Limlikhitaksorn v. Wuth Boonlert & Samak Donnapee* (Columbia Law School, 2020) 7.

[31] Chantra Tongcumpou and Nick Harvey, 'Implications of Recent EIA Changes in Thailand', (1994) 14 *Environmental Impact Assessment Review* 271, 272.

modernisation of environmental law in the country. This act employed a comprehensive approach and established three principles in environmental management: the protection of the environment and natural resources, the remedy of affected areas, and the polluter pays principle.[32] In terms of institutional arrangements, the 1975 ECNEQ granted three government agencies the responsibility to implement the act: the Office of Natural Resources and Environmental Policy and Planning, the Pollution Control Department, and the Department of Environmental Quality Promotion.[33] In 1978, the 1975 ECNEQ was revised to incorporate assessment (EIA) for the first time as a preventive mechanism for protecting the environment from pollution and degradation.[34]

Following the 1992 Rio Conference, the concept of sustainable development, which was articulated and given political weight at the international level in the conference through its Rio Declaration, was adopted by Thailand in the 1992 Enhancement and Conservation National Environmental Quality Act/ECNEQ (B. E. 2535).[35] The enactment of the 1992 ECNEQ was also a response of the Thai government in addressing environmental degradations resulting from rapid economic development in the 1980s and several environment-related conflicts, namely movements against dams, eucalyptuses, tourism development, and destruction of local livelihood.[36] Through this enactment, the government aimed at 'getting the market signals right, internalising externalities and finding the right level of compromise where there are unavoidable conflicts of interests between environmental and developmental objectives'.[37] Substantially, the act grants citizens the right to public participation in enhancing and conserving national environmental quality. Section 6 of the 1992 ECNEQ explicitly stipulates that

> [f]or the benefit of contribution to the enhancement and conservation of national environmental quality, any individual may have the following rights and duties: (1) obtaining information . . . and news from the government in matters related to the enhancement and conservation of environmental quality, except the information or news that the government considers to be secrets pertaining to the protection of national security or secrets regarding the right to privacy, rights in property, or the rights in trade and business of a person which are duly protected by law; (2) receiving damages or compensation from the State in the case of loss or harm suffered as a result of dispersion of pollutants or pollution, which is caused by an affairs or a project initiated, supported, or undertaken by a government agency or a state enterprise; (3) making a complaint to government officials accusing an offender . . . in the case of witnessing an act committed in infringement or violation of the laws relating to pollution control or conservation of natural resources; (4) providing cooperation and assistance to government officials in carrying out the

[32] Ruangsri (n 27) 3. [33] ibid. [34] Tongcumpou and Harvey (n 30) 272.
[35] Bureekul (n 19) 272.
[36] Philip Hirsch, 'The Politics of Environment: Opposition and Legitimacy', in K. Hewison (ed.), *Political Change in Thailand: Democracy and Participation* (Routledge, 1997) 180.
[37] ibid., 188.

functions relating to the enhancement and conservation of environmental quality; (5) implementing this Act or other laws that relate to the enchantment and conservation of environmental quality.

Despite this explicit provision, citizens' rights should be exercised through environmental NGOs registered in the Ministry of Science, Technology, and Environment.[38] Besides the fact that NGOs do not have much power according to the law, Bureekul argues that this model has not worked well empirically. This is because there is a possibility of distortion in communicating and delivering the interests of affected communities during a decision-making process by the NGOs whose interests may differ from those of the communities.[39] Regardless of its weaknesses and several changes in constitutions (in 1997, 2006, 2007, 2014, and 2017), the 1992 ECNEQ has remained in place regarding environmental matters in Thailand.

The Philippines

Comparable to Indonesia, modern environmental law in the Philippines has been developed since the 1972 Stockholm Conference on Human Environment. Before that, environmental law relied heavily on regulations and provisions inherited from the Spanish and US colonial administrations. During Spanish colonial rule, the 1866 Water Law was enacted to authorise 'the Spanish Governor General to suspend industrial operations if it caused contamination of water resources injurious to public health'.[40] Institutionally, *Inspeccion General de Minas* (Mining Bureau) and *Inspeccion General de Montes* (Forestry Bureau) were established in 1837 and 1863 to develop mining and forestry industries in the archipelago.[41] Under American colonial rule, both bureaus were retained and followed by enacting a legal framework dealing with forestry (the 1904 Forestry Act) and mining (the 1936 Mining Act) which focused on instrumentalising Philippine natural resources

[38] Section 7 of the 1992 ECNEQ stipulates:

> In order to encourage public participation in the enhancement and conservation of environmental quality, non-governmental organisations (NGOs) that have the status of judicial persons under Thai law or foreign law and whose activities relate directly to the environmental protection or the conservation of natural resources and who do not pursue political purposes nor aim to make profits from the engagement in such activities, shall be entitled to apply to the Ministry of Natural Resources and the Environment for registration as NGOs for environmental enhancement and conservation natural resources in accordance with the criteria . . . procedures, and conditions as prescribed in the ministerial regulations related thereto.

[39] Bureekul (n 19) 274.

[40] Merlin Magallona and Ben Malayang III, 'Environmental Governance in the Philippines', (2000) *Proceedings of the International Symposium on Environmental Governance in Asia, Tokyo, Sophia University.* <http://site.iugaza.edu.ps/tissa/files/2010/02/Environmental_Governance_in_the_Philippines.pdf> accessed 7 July 2023.

[41] Jely A. Galang, 'Chinese Laborers on Mining Frontier: The Case of Copper Miners in Northern Luzon, 1856-98' (2021) 10 *Southeast Asian Studies* 3, 10; Antonio La Viña, 'After More Than 100 Years of Environmental Law, What Is Next for the Philippines?' (2014) 88 *Philippines Law Journal* 195, 196.

for the benefit of the colonial administration. This was despite a strong nationalistic provision of the 1935 Constitution, especially Article XIII, Section 1, which stipulated that

> [a]ll agricultural timber, mineral lands of public domain . . . belong to the State, and their disposition, exploitation, development, or utilization shall be limited to citizens of the Philippines or to corporations or associations at least sixty per centum of which is owned by such citizens, subject to any existing right, grant, lease, or concession at the time of inauguration of the Government established under this Constitution.[42]

Following the Stockholm Conference, the Philippines, under the administration of President Ferdinand Marcos, laid the basic environmental law framework containing principles in environmental and natural resources management.[43] He also took several policy measures in environmental matters, including enacting the 1977 Philippine Environmental Policy (Presidential Decree No. 1157),[44] which, according to Magallona and Malayang III, departed from a 'piecemeal approach' to environmental protection towards an integrative approach to cover 'the entire spectrum of the environment'.[45] This was followed by enacting the 1978 Presidential Decree No. 1586 to establish an environmental impact assessment system, promulgating the 1975 Revised Forestry Code and the 1976 Pollution Control Decree.[46]

The fall of the Marcos regime, followed by a constitutional engineering strategy to undertake institutional reform, has brought a fresh perspective to environmental law. A new constitution (the 1987 Philippine Constitution) has been established, which takes a human rights-based approach to environmental matters by stating that '[t]he State shall protect and advance the right of the people to a balanced and healthful ecology in accord with the rhythm and harmony of nature'.[47] With this formulation, the Philippines has been considered the first country in the Southeast Asian region to recognise environmental rights explicitly in the constitution. Indonesia, for instance, just took an environmental constitutionalism measure by including the right to a good and healthy environment in the amendment of the 1945 Constitution following the fall of the Suharto authoritarian regime in the late 1990s. To ensure popular participation in development, the newly adopted

[42] Karl F. K. Poblador, 'The Transformation of Property Rights in the Philippine Timber and Gold Mining Industries during the American Colonial Period', (2014) 29 (1) *Kasarinlan: Philippine Journal of Third World Studies* 11, 18.

[43] Dante Gatmaytan-Magno, 'Artificial Judicial Environmental Activism: *Oposa V. Factoran* as Aberration', (2007) 17 *Indiana International & Comparative Law Review* 1, 5.

[44] The Presidential Decree No. 1151 (1977) dictated the Philippine Environmental Policy to (a) create, develop, maintain, and improve conditions under which man and nature can thrive in productive and enjoyable harmony with each other; (b) to fulfil the social, economic, and other requirements of present and future generations of Filipino; and (c) to ensure the attainment of an environmental quality that is conducive to a life of dignity and well-being.

[45] Magallona and Malayang III (n 39) 2.

[46] Gatmaytan-Magno (n 42) 5.

[47] Section 16 of Article II of the 1987 Constitution of the Philippines.

constitution, the 1987 Constitution of the Republic of the Philippines, especially Article 6, Section 5, establishes a 'party-list' system to allow 'representatives from marginalized groups and sectors . . . to be elected as party-list representatives in the House of Representatives'.[48] Utilising the Modes of Participation Framework, Rodan argues that this system is a form of a 'particularist ideology' that contributes to increasing the fragmentation of the progressive forces in the Philippines as the politics become more 'issue-oriented'.[49]

As a result of environmental constitutionalism, which sets the state's duty to undertake necessary measures to protect and advance environmental rights, the Philippine environmental law has proliferated in the post-authoritarian period. In terms of institutional arrangement, the Aquino administration restructured Marcos's Ministry of Natural Resources into the Department of Environment and Natural Resources with a mandate to implement government policies in natural resources within the framework of 'a sound ecological balance and protecting and enhancing the quality of the environment'.[50] Congress has also enacted legislation, including the 1990 Toxic Substances and Hazardous and Nuclear Wastes Control Act, the 1992 National Integrated Protected Areas System Act, the 1997 Indigenou Peoples Right Act, and the 1998 Animal Welfare Act.[51] Despite such proliferation, Dante Gatmaytan-Magno observes that '[e]vidently, there is no single framework that binds the environmental concerns in a comprehensive manner in the Philippines. Instead, there are an abundance of laws and regulations which address separate environmental issues.'[52] However, many would agree that Philippine environmental law is among the region's most progressive environmental legal frameworks compared to other countries.[53]

As suggested by La Viña, despite being progressive on paper, Philippine environmental law has failed to materialise in reality. In the context of the 1997 Indigenous Peoples Rights Act, for instance, the act requires the application of free, prior, and informed consent (FPIC) before utilising Indigenous communities' domains or territories. However, the mining sector tends to ignore the application of the FPIC and other provisions in the act. Indeed, there have been many difficulties and anomalies in exercising FPIC,[54] which in turn has exacerbated conflicts between Indigenous communities and mining companies in many parts of the region. Furthermore, in the early 2010s, President Benigno Aquino III issued executive orders (E.O.) to address environmental concerns caused by both sectors. They were E.O. No. 23 (2011) to 'impose a moratorium on the cutting and

[48] Jorge V. Tigno, 'The Philippines', in A. Ogawa (ed.), *Routledge Handbook of Civil Society in Asia* (Routledge, 2018) 117.

[49] Garry Rodan, *Participation without Democracy: Containing Conflict in Southeast Asia* (Cornell University Press, 2018), 56. See also Garry Rodan, *Civil Society in Southeast Asia* (Cambridge University Press, 2022).

[50] La Viña (n 40) 198. [51] Gatmaytan-Magno (n 42) 7. [52] ibid.

[53] Ibid. See also, for instance, Alan Tan, *Preliminary Assessment of Philippine's Environmental Law* (APCEL, 2016).

[54] La Viña (n 40) 202.

harvesting of timber in natural and residual forests' and E.O. No. 79 (2012) to lay out a 'roadmap for mining sector reforms, including guidelines on environmental protection and responsible mining' and to provide 'additional areas closed to mining operations ("no-go" areas)' as well as to set 'initial steps for exercising stringent control on utilization of mineral resources'.[55] However, those orders were considered too late and inadequate to address problems that have been increasingly complex and deeply rooted in the existing political-economic structure.[56] As a result, deforestation and destructive mining operations persist, causing significant environmental problems and socio-environmental conflicts, which in turn have been attempted to be tackled by using law as a means of intimidation.

Progressing Environmental Law through the Courts

Litigation has been a significant component of environmental movements in Southeast Asian countries. Several landmark decisions have been made. The *Map Ta Phut* Case (2009) in Thailand highlights how environmental groups used the administrative court to block the construction of chemical enterprises within a 'pollution control zone' of Map Ta Phut, shocking the Thai business community.[57] In Indonesia, the courts are not only a place of resistance but also a place to articulate a new perspective of society's connection with the environment. It can be seen in a pollution case concerning *Indonesian Forum for the Environment* (*WALHI* v. *the Inti Indorayon* (1989)) in Lake Toba, North Sumatra. Although the court dismissed the case's substantive merits, it approved WALHI's legal standing as an environmental NGO to launch a lawsuit based on the concept of 'guardianship'.[58] In 2003, the Mandalawangi case occurred concerning a group of 275 victims of land erosion filing a lawsuit against the local and national governments and a state-owned company managing production forests which caused the erosion.[59] In this case, class action was recognised in Indonesia for the first time. As a result of environmental activism, the recognition of both NGO legal standing and class action procedures has increased access to justice for citizens in environmental matters. More recently, environmental movements have utilised the citizen lawsuit (*actio popularis*)[60] to expose the failure of the state as a duty bearer to protect the

[55] ibid., 203–204. [56] ibid., 204.

[57] Hurights Osaka, 'Map Ta Phut: Thailand's Minamita?' (June 2012) <www.hurights.or.jp/archives/focus/section2/2012/06/map-ta-phut-thailands-minamata.html> accessed 18 October 2024.

[58] See Christopher Stone, *Should Trees Have Standing? Law, Morality and the Environment* (3rd ed., Oxford University Press, 2010).

[59] Decision of Badung District Court No. 49/Pdt.G/2003/PN.BDG (*Dedi and others* v. *Perhutani and others*).

[60] Under the Indonesian civil law procedure, the citizen lawsuit is differentiated from the NGO lawsuit (NGO legal standing in Indonesia) regarding their plaintiffs. The citizen lawsuit provides standing to sue filed to citizens (as natural persons) exercising their rights to demand the state as a duty-bearer to undertake necessary measures or actions to comply with its obligation, including protecting and fulfilling the citizen's

right to a clean and healthy environment, as in the *Forest Fires of Palangkaraya* case (2016) concerning forest fires in Central Kalimantan.[61]

A similar trend in the use of litigation has also been demonstrated in the Philippines. The *Minors Oposan* v. *Factoran* case (1993) is a significant example. In this case, a group of children claiming to represent the future generation sued the Secretary of the Department of Environmental and Natural Resources for providing logging permits that resulted in the loss of tropical forests in the Philippines. The legal basis for this action was Section 16 of Article II of the Philippines' 1987 Constitution concerning 'the right of the people to a balanced and healthful ecology in accordance with the rhythm and harmony of nature'.[62] The Supreme Court of the Philippines issued a groundbreaking decision on intergenerational justice, recognising children's legal standing to defend the right to a clean environment for their generations and future generations. The recognition of the legal standing on behalf of future generations in the case has received international attention as a landmark decision. The United Nations Development Programme characterised this decision as 'the first time globally that future generations were recognized as having standing to bring claims and the first time that environmental rights of future generations had been considered and upheld by a country's apex court'.[63] According to Hassan, the case is a crucial contribution of judicial activism in the Global South to developing international environmental law.[64] Furthermore, to enhance its reputation as a model for judicial environmental activism, the Supreme Court of the Philippines took an important innovative measure in 2010 by adopting the Rules of Procedures for Environmental Cases.[65]

Indeed, the stance taken by the courts in those cases appears to be progressive, in which courts embrace judicial activism in responding to the interests of environmental movements. It should be noted, however, that the positive role of the judiciary in those cases does not automatically lead to an argument that the judiciary is a natural ally of environmental movements in the region. At least three reservations should be mentioned here. First, the agency of courts is

right to a good and healthy environment. The NGO lawsuit is standing to sue filed by an environmental organisation (as a legal person) to act on behalf of the environment against a party that has caused environmental destruction and pollution.

[61] Decision of Palangkaraya District Court No. 118/Pdt.G/LH/2016/PN Plk. (*Arie Rompas and others* v. *President of Indonesia and others*).

[62] Section 16 of Article II of the 1987 Constitution of the Philippines.

[63] United Nations Development Programme (UNDP), *Environmental Justice: Comparative Experiences in Legal Empowerment* (UNDP, 2014) 15–16.

[64] Parvez Hassan, 'Role of the South in Development of International Environmental Law' (2017) 1 *Chinese Journal of Environmental Law* 133.

[65] The objectives of the Rules are as follows: '(a) To protect and advance the constitutional right of the people to a balanced and healthful ecology; (b) To provide a simplified, speedy and inexpensive procedure for the enforcement of environmental rights and duties recognized under the Constitution, existing laws, rules and regulations, and international agreements; (c) To introduce and adopt innovations and best practices ensuring the effective enforcement of remedies and redress for violation of environmental laws; and (d) To enable the courts to monitor and exact compliance with orders and judgements in environmental cases.'

constrained by the institutional structure of the judiciary. It differs from country to country. It may, in theory, be independent from the executive intervention. However, in practice, especially in environmental cases where the interests of the government or politico-business elites are implicated, the judiciary as a state institution is likely influenced by its relations to the existing power relations. In the Philippines, Dante Gatmaytan-Magno, for instance, argues that the *Minor Oposa* case was indeed a moment to build the reputation of the Supreme Court of the Philippines as 'a proponent of judicial environmental activism', but, afterward, the Court has not always managed 'to live up to its reputation' to produce environmentally sound decisions, especially in matters related to the national interest.[66] Second, overstating the function of courts misses the mark when it comes to the essence of the proceedings. The courts in Indonesia, Thailand, and the Philippines typically only respond to arguments from conflicting parties but remain silent if no dispute arises. As evidenced by those three countries' experience, environmental movements are the central actors that have brought matters before them. In some instances, such as the case of *Metropolitan Manila Development Authority* v. *Concerned Residents of Manila Bay*, they 'appear willing to respond positively to well-crafted arguments that reflect growing public alarm',[67] while in others, they tend to be reactionary. As a result, the ability of courts to play a role in transforming environmental law depends on environmental movements' ability to use law 'tactically and strategically in pursuit of progressive ends'.[68] Third, as evidenced by multiple legal retaliations against environmental defenders, the region's judiciary may likewise become an oppressive state institution against environmental movements. Those experiences reveal a distinct face of the court concerning environmental movements, where the courts have played a role in intimidating and criminalising environmental defenders, and even delegitimising environmental movements through deviance labels, such as criminals or communists (Chapter 5).

Adopting Anti-SLAPP Provisions

Indonesia

Facing backlash is not a new phenomenon for environmental defenders in Indonesia. Legal intimidation towards environmental defenders could also be identified during Suharto's authoritarian regime. In the case of the resort development in Bali by the Bali Nirwana Resort (BNR), owned by a national tycoon, Aburizal Bakrie, three farmers whose land was taken coercively for the resort filed

[66] Gatmaytan-Magno (n 42) 1; in the context of Indonesia, see Agung Wardana, 'Law and the Political Economy of Climate Litigation in Indonesia', (2023) 56 (2) *Verfassung un Recht in Übersee* 351.

[67] Sam Adelman, 'Law in the Climate Crisis: International Environmental Law', in I. R. Wall, F. Middleton, S. Shah & CLAW (eds.), *The Critical Legal Pocketbook* (Counterpress, 2021) 85.

[68] ibid., 83.

a lawsuit against the company. However, the company put a counterclaim against the plaintiffs in the proceeding. The District Court of Tabanan dismissed the plaintiffs' claim in its decision. However, it approved the counterclaim and ordered the plaintiffs to pay compensation of US$35,000 to cover the defendant's legal costs and restore its reputation.[69] In 1998, a SLAPP counterclaim was also filed by the defendants in the Babon River case, where local fishermen filed a lawsuit against several companies that polluted the Babon River, Semarang, Central Java, which had caused losses for the fishermen. In the proceeding, the defendants filed a counterclaim to demand compensation due to damage to their reputation caused by the plaintiffs' claim. However, the District Court of Semarang rejected the counterclaim rationing that 'a party brings an action against another to defend his/her legal rights cannot be characterised in itself as an action which damages the reputation of another, nor as an action contrary to law'.[70]

In the early transitional period towards democratisation, there were several eye-opening incidents concerning an increasingly popular mode of repression through legal actions against environmental defenders. Unlike the previous cases (the BNR case and the Babon River case) where legal intimidation was carried out by the defendants through a counterclaim (*gugatan rekonvensi*) during the court proceeding, in the post-authoritarian era, another model has emerged in which companies become an active agent to attack environmental defenders by reporting them to the police or by filing a lawsuit directly to courts. This first case occurred in 2004 in which the Newmont Nusa Tenggara, a subsidiary of giant US-based Newmont Gold Company, reported Yani Sagaroa, an environmental activist from the Lembaga Olah Hidup, a local NGO in Sumbawa Island, West Nusa Tenggara Province, to the police. Yani Sagaroa was alleged to have committed criminal defamation after releasing a press release to warn local communities about pollution caused by the company's tailings. He was convicted and sentenced to four months in prison by the Sumbawa Besar Civil Court.[71]

Almost the same year, a fishing community in Buyat Bay, North Sulawesi Province, was fighting against another Newmont subsidiary, the Newmont Minahasa Raya, for polluting their means of livelihood.[72] Assisting the community in their struggle, Dr Rignaldo Djamaluddin, a biologist from Sam Ratulangi University and an executive director of a local environmental NGO, was sued by the company for civil defamation after exposing the contamination of mercury in the bay causing environmental problems akin to Minamata. The court found him liable for civil defamation and ruled he pay compensation to the company,

[69] Bali Post, 30–12–1995 cited in Carol Warren, 'Tanah Lot: The Cultural and Environmental Politics of Resort Development in Bali', in P. Hirsch & C Warren (eds.), *The Politics of Environment in Southeast Asia: Resources and Resistance* (Routledge, 1998) 248.

[70] David Nicholson, *Environmental Dispute Resolution in Indonesia* (KITLV Press, 2009) 143.

[71] The Yani Sagaroa case [2006] Supreme Court Decision No. 1212 K/PID/2006.

[72] Down to Earth, 'New Pollution Study Corners Newmont' (*Down to Earth* No. 63, 2004). <www.downtoearth-indonesia.org/story/new-pollution-study-corners-newmont> accessed 2 February 2022.

amounting to US$750,000;[73] if calculated based on his salary as a public university lecturer, it would take him 312 years to pay it off.[74] Newmont's spokesperson, Doug Hock, reportedly stated that the money gained from the lawsuit 'would be donated to communities near Buyat Bay'.[75] The two lawsuits filed by the Newmont subsidiaries demonstrated how the common practice of American companies of intimidating environmental activists through SLAPPs[76] was duplicated in countries where the companies operated, including in Indonesia. This practice has inspired other companies to use it as a more 'elegant' means in dealing with environmental dissent affecting their business.

A close resonance to using the law to threaten environmental defenders following Newmont's legal actions occurred in three other cases in 2008 and 2009. The first case was the lawsuit filed by Riau Andalan Pulp and Paper (RAPP), a subsidiary company of the Singapore-based Asia Pacific Resources International Limited (APRIL), against *Tempo*, an investigative national newspaper, for covering reports on illegal logging connected to the company.[77] The court decided *Tempo* was liable for civil defamation and ordered it to pay IDR 220 million (US$23,400).[78] The second was the Sukolilo case in which nine farmers of Sukolilo village were charged for using a Dutch colonial inherited article of 'hate sowing' (*Haatzai Artikelen*).[79] It was allegedly conducted when they were organising a mass demonstration against the construction of a cement factory by the Semen Gresik within a karst-protected area – the local water source for daily use and irrigation – in Pati district, Central Java.[80] In June 2009, the court convicted and sentenced them to five months in prison. The following case was the Tukijo case, in which a farmer organised six villages to protest against iron sand mining on the southern coast of Kulonprogo, Yogyakarta. The mining was operated by a joint venture between the Jogja Magasa Iron, a local mining company connected to Yogyakarta's royal

[73] Syamsul Huda M. Suhari, 'Rignolda Djamaluddin: Fighting for Fishermen', *The Jakarta Post* (Jakarta, 12 September 2013) <www.thejakartapost.com/news/2013/09/12/rignolda-djamaluddin-fighting-fishermen.html> accessed 2 February 2022.

[74] At that time, according to Government Regulation No. 11 of 2003 concerning the Salary for Public Servants, a lecturer at a public university earned no more than US$200 per month.

[75] Greg Griffin, 'Mining Firm Sues Three Activists', *Denver Post* (Denver, 7 June 2005) <www.denverpost.com/2005/06/07/mining-firm-sues-three-activists/> accessed 29 January 2022.

[76] For further discussion on this, see George W. Pring and Penelope Canan, *SLAPPs: Getting Sued for Speaking Out* (Temple University and Press, 1996).

[77] *RAPP* v. *Tempo Case* [2007] Decision of Civil Court of South Jakarta No. 1089/PDEG/2007/P.N. Jakarta Selatan.

[78] Aloisius A. Ariwibowo, 'Majelis Hakim Menangkan Gugatan RAPP Terhadap Tempo', *Antara News* (Jakarta, 3 Juli 2008) <www.antaranews.com/berita/107850/majelis-hakim-menangkan-gugatan-rapp-terhadap-tempo> accessed 2 February 2022.

[79] It is incorporated in Article 160 of the Criminal Code, which stipulates that '[a]ny person who orally or in writing incites in public to commit a punishable act, a violent action against the public authority or any other disobedience, either to a statutory provision or to an official order issued under a statutory provision, shall be punished by a maximum imprisonment of six years or a minimum fine of three hundred Rupiahs'.

[80] Erwin Dwi Kristianto, *Menyelamatkan Lingkungan Berakhir di Penjara: Kriminalisasi 9 Warga Penolak Pabrik Semen di Sukolilo Pati* (LBH Semarang, 2009).

family, and the China-based Rockcheck Steel Group,[81] aiming to supply around 450,000 tons of iron sand annually to produce steel in Tianjin, China.[82] During a village meeting, Tukijo criticised a village official who supported the mining company, leading to an allegation of committing criminal defamation. The court sentenced him to three months in prison with six months of probation.[83]

The conjuncture (the legal reform on the one side and the use of legal actions against environmental defenders on the other) shaped the debate during the law-making process of the EPM Bill in 2009. Concerning the previous SLAPP cases, representatives of environmental NGOs participating in the bill deliberation strongly advocated the adoption of an anti-SLAPP provision in the bill. Eventually, the bill was adopted as the 2009 EPM Act, which includes Article 66 stipulating that '[a]ny person who fights for the rights to a good and healthy environment should not be charged through criminal proceedings or sued through civil proceedings'. The elucidation of Article 66 clarifies that '[t]he provision is intended to protect victims and/or the reporting parties adopting legal means for environmental pollution and/or damage. The protection is intended to prevent acts of retaliation against the reported parties through criminal and/or civil offences in accordance with the independence of the judiciary body.'

Based on the adoption of the anti-SLAPP provision, several points deserve attention. Conceptually, the constitutional basis of the anti-SLAPP provision in Article 66 of the 2009 EPM Act differs from that of the US anti-SLAPP provisions developed by Pring and Canan. In the US, such provisions are built upon the constitutional right to petition (the Petition Clause). At the same time, since Indonesia does not have such a clause, the provision relies on the right to participate, specifically the procedural aspects of the right to a good and healthy environment.[84] The scope of Indonesia's anti-SLAPP provision is also broader than the original concept used by Pring and Canan, which only includes the use of civil procedures,[85] while in Indonesia, the scope also includes the use of criminal proceedings. Even though actors protected by the anti-SLAPP provision are everyone fighting for the right to a good and healthy environment, this scope is then watered down by the Elucidation of Article 66, which only refers to 'victims and/or the reporting parties', but no definitions of both are provided. The phrase 'the reporting parties' is interpreted as those who make a report on the case of

[81] Arif K. Hermawan, Cahyo P. Edi, Lusia Arumingtyas, Mariyana Rick and Soetana M. Hasibuan, 'Indonesian Farmers Resisting an Iron Mine Run up against a Sultan', *Mongabay* (Jakarta, 28 October 2021) <https://news.mongabay.com/2021/10/indonesian-farmers-resisting-an-iron-mine-run-up-against-a-sultan/> accessed 29 January 2022.

[82] Ahmad Mustaqim, 'Kriminalisasi Petani Pesisir Kulon Progo', in A. Mustaqim, E, Rusdianto, M. Probowo, et.al. (eds.), *Merekam Perjuangan Pembela Lingkungan*, (LBH Pers, 2021) 10.

[83] Human Rights Watch, *Turning Critics into Criminals: The Human Rights Consequences of Criminal Defamation Law in Indonesia* (Human Rights and Watch, 2010) 29.

[84] As stipulated in the Aarhus Convention 1998, the procedural rights here are: (1) access to information, (2) participation in a decision-making process, and (3) access to justice.

[85] George W. Pring and Penelope Canan (n 74) 9.

environmental damage and/or pollution to the state institutions having authority in environmental matters.[86] From this understanding, the reporting parties cannot enforce the law alone (*eigenrichting*). However, they should report environmental issues to the state authority and let the authority do the rest. Hence, this is based on an ideal assumption that the state authority on environmental matters works appropriately to respond to any reports from the public. However, in Indonesia, this is only sometimes the case.

Another issue in the anti-SLAPP provision is related to mechanisms through which victims and/or reporting parties seek to settle environmental conflicts. In this context, the Elucidation of Article 66 uses the phrase 'adopting legal means' (*menempuh cara hukum*), which is open to different interpretations. Such interpretations define which mechanisms deserve protection under the anti-SLAPP provision. A broad interpretation offered by environmental activists and other like-minded legal scholars regards 'legal means' as any means that are 'legal' or not prohibited by existing laws and regulations, which may include demonstrations, consumer boycotts, and other forms of non-violent action. In contrast, a narrow interpretation offered by formalist law enforcement officials, including judges, argues that 'legal means' refers only to the use of legal mechanisms. In this context, they usually refer to the mechanisms provided in the 2009 EPM Act, which stipulates two main mechanisms: (1) outside court mechanisms referring to mediation and arbitration;[87] and (2) inside court mechanisms (litigation) referring to civil, administrative, and criminal proceedings.[88] Accordingly, the anti-SLAPP provision does not protect any conduct other than the two mechanisms mentioned here.

More recently, relevant state agencies have translated the anti-SLAPP provision. In 2013, the Chief Justice of the Supreme Court of Indonesia enacted directive No. 36/KMA/SK/II/2013 concerning the Guidance for the Handling of Environmental Cases. The directive guides how judges should enforce the anti-SLAPP provision by stating that:

> to decide according to Article 66 of Environmental Protection and Management Act [whether or not] a civil lawsuit or a criminal charge is a form of SLAPP [the defendant] may fill a motion stated in the provision, exception or counterclaim (in a civil case) and/or the defence (in a criminal case) and [the motion] shall be decided first in an interim decision.

Since 2019, the Ministry for the Environment and Forestry has been considering issuing a ministerial decree titled 'The Protection of Actions to Ensure the Right to a Good and Healthy Environment'. It is expected to prohibit retaliation through

[86] This interpretation is consistent with the definition of 'the reporting parties' (*pelapor*) provided by the 2013 Prevention and Eradication of Forest Destruction Law, which refers to 'any person who informs alleged, ongoing or recent forest destruction to the authorised official' (Art. 1.19 of the 2009 Indonesian EPM Act).
[87] Articles 84–86 of the 2009 Indonesian Environmental Protection and Management Act.
[88] Articles 87–115 of the 2009 Indonesian Environmental Protection and Management Act.

legal means against individuals, groups of people, and/or environmental organisations working to protect the environment, as well as actions that undermine the community's right to play a role in environmental protection.[89] However, the decree has yet to be issued. Instead, the ministry banned several foreign researchers from conducting studies on biodiversity in the country and issued circular restricting research taking place within conservation areas.[90] This practice appears contradictory to protecting environmental defenders as it affects research activities that collect data and information on biodiversity, which is vital for evidence-based policy advocacy to protect the environment.

Thailand

In Thailand, the continuous political turbulence has informed the dynamics of environmental activism. Following the 2006 military coup, there have been excessive uses of defamation-based laws by the junta and military-backed civil government. The 2007 Computer Crimes Act, which at first was intended to address online fraud and theft,[91] has been weaponised to silence critics of the government and the monarchy. Observing this phenomenon, Streckfuss characterises Thailand as a 'defamation regime' in which defamation-based law has been used to retaliate against opponent groups.[92] As Streckfuss shows in his most recent publication and supported by NGOs' reports, there has been no indication that the use of defamation-based laws is decreasing, indicating that the defamation regime is far from over, regardless of the leadership changes.[93] The legal procedure also contributes to this phenomenon under the Thai criminal justice system, which authorises private parties to bring criminal charges. This has been corporations' most preferred mode of SLAPP, aiming to retaliate against their opponents, including environmental defenders.[94] However, the 1992 ECNEQ has been silent on the increased attacks through legal means against local communities and environmental NGO activists who exercise their rights to participate in environmental matters. In Thailand, unlike

[89] Maysa Zorob, *Defending Defenders: Challenging Malicious Lawsuits in Southeast Asia* (Business and Human Rights Resource Centre, 2020) 13.

[90] Hans N. Jong and Lusia Arumingtyas, 'Fears for Academic Freedom as Indonesia Doubles Down on Scientists' Ban', *Mongabay Indonesia* (Jakarta, 9 December 2022) <https://news.mongabay.com/2022/12/fears-for-academic-freedom-as-indonesia-doubles-down-on-scientists-ban/> accessed 7 July 2023.

[91] Freedom of Expression Documentation Centre, 'The Criminalisation of Freedom of Expression in Thailand', in G. Hariharan (ed.), *Unshackling Expression: A Study on Laws Criminalising Expression Online in Asia* (Global Information Society Watch, 2007) 127.

[92] David Streckfuss, *Truth on Trial in Thailand: Defamation, Treason, and Lese-Majeste* (Routledge, 2011) 6.

[93] David Streckfuss, 'Lese-Majeste within Thailand's Regime of Intimidation', in P. Chachavalpongpun (ed.), *Routledge Handbook of Contemporary Thailand* (Routledge, 2020) 140; Human Rights Lawyers Association, *Recommendations on the Protection of Those Who Exercise Their Rights and Freedom from Strategic Lawsuits against Public Participation* (Human Rights Lawyers Association, 2019).

[94] Lionel Blackman, *Government of Thailand & Chaiwat Limlikhitaksorn v. Wuth Boonlert & Samak Donnapee* (Columbia Law School, 2020) 6.

in the Philippines and Indonesia, although the right to participate is granted in the constitutions (especially the 2007 Constitution) and the 1992 ECNEQ, there is no specific anti-SLAPP provision in the legislation or government regulations.

One attempt to address the defamation problem was undertaken by pursuing an autonomous Office of Attorney General (OAG). This aspiration was stipulated in the 2007 Thai Constitution, which established the autonomy of the Thai OAG in budget, personnel administration, and other activities. The status remains unchanged even though Thailand's Constitution was amended in 2010 and 2017. In this regard, the Public Prosecution Organization and Public Prosecutors Act and the Public Prosecution Official Regulation Act are instrumental for maintaining the integrity of the public prosecutors.[95] Section 21 of the Public Prosecution Institution and Public Prosecutors Act, B.E. 2553 (A.D. 2010) clearly stipulates that

> [t]he public prosecutors are independent in considering and giving orders as to cases and in performing their duties according to the Constitution and laws in an honest and just manner.
>
> Should a public prosecutor find that the institution of a criminal case would not be in the public's interest and would affect the nation's safety and security or an essential benefit of the country, he shall submit the matter to the Attorney General. The Attorney General shall have the power to order that the institution of the case be withheld.

Based on the stipulation, the public prosecutor has 'the power to refer to the opinion to the Attorney General to issue an order of no-prosecution if found that a criminal prosecution has no use to the general public or affects the nation's safety or security or significantly impairs the national interest'.[96] This section, however, has a limited scope of application because it is only applicable to criminal charges that are filed through the public prosecutor's office; thus, it is not applicable for civil cases and criminal defamation that is not filed through the public prosecutor's office.[97] In addition, complaints, including those filed to harass, threaten, or retaliate against human rights activists or others, must be sent only to the Attorney General under Section 21 of the 2010 Public Prosecutor Organ and Public Prosecutors Act. Protection International comments that '[t]his is a lengthy procedure and it's not clear whether adequate resources and support have been provided to the Attorney General's Office to exercise their powers effectively and efficiently'.[98]

[95] Sutthi Sookying, 'Integrity and Independence of Thai Public Prosecutors and Their Roles in Prosecuting Corruption Cases', (2021) Fourteenth Regional Seminar on Good Governance for Southeast Asian Countries. <https://unafei.or.jp/publications/pdf/GG14/24_GG14_CP14_Thailand.pdf> 157.

[96] Government of Thailand. Permanent Mission of Thailand to the United Nations and other International Organizations in Geneva, Thailand's Response to the Joint Communication from HRC Special Procedures No. AL THA 3/2018 dated 10 May 2018, and AL THA 1/2019 dated 30 January 2019. <https://spcommreports.ohchr.org/TMResultsBase/DownLoadFile?gId=34700> accessed 25 April 2024, 6.

[97] Orapin Lilitwisitwong and Thitiphan Pattanamongkol (eds.), *SLAPP: The Public Dreams of Anti-strategic Lawsuit against Public Participation* (Thai Society of Environmental Journalists, 2022) 72.

[98] Protection International, 'Silencing Justice: Battling Systemic SLAPP Attacks on Women and Human Rights Defenders in Thailand', *Protection International* (2023) <www.protectioninternational.org/wp-con

Despite the provision, attacks using criminal defamation have continued. According to data from the Office of the Attorney General, from 2015 to 2018 alone, there were 6,837 defamation cases, with 85 per cent conviction rates.[99] This number does not include defamation cases brought directly to the court by the plaintiff without filing a report to the police and being presented by the public prosecutor to the court. Specifically, on defamation related to public interest, ARTICLE 19, an NGO focusing on the right to freedom of expression, identified fifty-eight defamation cases between 2014 and 2020, with 55 per cent of the defendants being environmental defenders.[100] As a result, during 2016–18, several international organisations expressed concern about the legal attacks on human rights defenders (HRDs) in Thailand, including the CEDAW Committee, especially concerning women HRDs, the Universal Periodic Review with specific recommendation to protect HRDs, and the UN Working Group on Business and Human Rights that recommended Thailand address the attacks on HRDs.[101] Responding to domestic and international pressures, the Government of Thailand claimed to have made progress in protecting freedom of expression. It stated that the Thai Court of Justice has established 'an overarching tool to protect the right to freedom of expression against Strategic Litigation against Public Participation (SLAPP)'.[102] In 2019, the Criminal Procedure Code was amended by introducing Sections 161/1 and 165/2. Section 161/1 of the Criminal Procedure Code stipulates that

> [i]n a case filed by a private complainant, if it appears to the court – or through examination of evidence called at trial – that the complainant has filed the lawsuit in bad faith or distorted facts in order to harass or take undue advantage of a defendant, or to procure any advantage to which the complainant is not rightfully entitled to, the court shall order dismissal of the case, and forbid the complainant to refile such case again. Filling a lawsuit in bad faith, as stated in paragraph one, includes incidents where the complainant intentionally violated a final court's orders or judgment in another case without providing any appropriate reason.

Section 165/2 of the Criminal Procedure Code stipulates that

tent/uploads/2023/09/PIs-report-Battling-Systematic-SLAPP-Attacks-on-Women-and-Human-Rights-Defenders-in-Thailand.pdf> accessed 25 April 2024, 15.

[99] Article 19, *Truth Be Told: Criminal Defamation in Thai Law and the Case for Reform* (Article 19 2021) 13–14.

[100] ibid., 16–17.

[101] Protection International (n 97) 10.

[102] Government of Thailand. Permanent Mission of Thailand to the United Nations, 'Thailand's Policies, Measures and Practices to Prevent, Address, Investigate and Reports on Acts of Intimidation and Reprisals of those Who Seek to Cooperate or Have Cooperated with the UN, its Representatives and Mechanism in the Field of Human Rights', OHCHR (25 March 2019) <www.ohchr.org/sites/default/files/Documents/Issues/Reprisals/GoodPractices/THAILAND.pdf> accessed 7 June 2024, 2; Government of Thailand. Permanent Mission of Thailand to the United Nations and other International Organizations in Geneva, Thailand's Response to the Joint Communication from HRC Special Procedures No. AL THA 3/2018 dated 10 May 2018, and AL THA 1/2019 dated 30 January 2019. <https://spcommreports.ohchr.org/TMResultsBase/DownLoadFile?gId=34700> accessed 25 April 2024, 5–6.

> [i]n the preliminary examination, the defendant may provide a statement of facts or laws that the Court should order no *prima facie* of the case and may stipulate in the statement about a person, document, or materials as supporting evidence on the argument of the facts. In such a case, the Court may summon a person, document, or material as evidence to support the decision as necessary and appropriate. The defendant may examine the court's evidence as allowed by the court.

While the government and some scholars have been optimistic about the amendment,[103] NGO activists and critical scholars remain sceptical that the sections would be effective in preventing SLAPP. They have pointed out several weaknesses of those sections. The code does not provide a legal definition of 'bad faith'. The courts are given the authority to exercise discretion to screen out and dismiss any lawsuit with a bad-faith intention and without any public interest.[104] In other words, the Criminal Procedure Code leaves the decision on what constitutes SLAPP to the court's discretion.[105] The provisions also suffer from ambiguity as they do not specifically address protecting the right to freedom of expression but are generally concerned with defamation. Moreover, they also suffer from the lack of implementing guidance on how to screen SLAPP cases early. The procedural code also does not provide a clear procedure or mechanism for imposing sanctions on parties who have violated Sections 161/1 and 165/2 to disincentivise SLAPP.[106] Empirically, as observed by Protection International, those provisions 'have not proven effective in practice'[107] because they find that 'most applications by Women Human Rights Defenders to invoke Article 161/1 have been denied'.[108] In reality, Thai courts have continued 'to accept charges brought by parties even when, as in the present case, the charges appear unsubstantiated and based on suspect motivation'.[109]

The Philippines

The SLAPP cases are not a recent phenomenon in the Philippines. In 1995, Attorney Antonio Oposa was the target. He was the key figure in the landmark case of *Minors Oposa* who crafted a legal argument to convince the court to accept the legal standing of children and future generations in protecting the environment, which has widened the legal standing to sue for citizens in the Philippine legal system ever since. In a different case, Attorney Oposa, representing a pro bono client, submitted a complaint letter to the Environmental Agency concerning an allegedly illegal activity committed by a hazardous waste generator. In retaliation, he was reported by the generator for committing criminal libel against the generator's reputation.[110]

[103] Kitti Jayangakula, 'State Practice of Asian Countries in International Law: Thailand', (2019) 25 *Asian Yearbook of International Law* 302, 303.

[104] Maysa Zorob (n 88) 13; Lilitwisitwong et al. (n 96).

[105] Blackman (n 29) 6.

[106] Protection International (n 97) 15.

[107] ibid., 11–12.

[108] ibid., 12.

[109] Blackman (n 29) 6.

[110] *People of the Philippines* v. *A Oposa, Crim Case* No. Q 96-64419, Regional Trial Court of Quezon City, Branch 95.

Indeed, this was not the first case in the country. Six years earlier, a powerful logging tycoon, Jose Alvarez, filed a libel lawsuit against Marites Vitug, a Philippino female journalist, and demanded 26 million peso (US$1 million) compensation due to her in-depth investigative report published in the *Far Eastern Economic Review* (coauthored with James Clad) concerning the forest plunder in Palawan and the connection between Alvarez's logging empire and Ramon Mitra, a Palawan Congressman.[111] Even though the courts dismissed the two eye-opening SLAPP cases above, the effects remain. Vitug admits that SLAPP 'can be unnerving and disorienting'[112] and Attorney Oposa states that he may still feel 'the anxiety' after defending the case ever since.[113] Writing in 1998, Oposa suggested that environmental legislation and court procedures should adopt a specific provision related to SLAPP to address its shocking and chilling effects.[114]

Eventually, anti-SLAPP provisions have been adopted in several environment-related legislations. For example, the 1999 Clean Air Act (Republic Act 8749) provides a title of *Suits and Strategic Legal Actions against Public Participation and the Enforcement of This Act*. Section 43 stipulates that

> [w]here a suit is brought against a person who filed an action as provided in Section 41 of this Act, or against any person, institution or government agency that implements this Act, it shall be the duty of the investigating prosecutor or the court, as the case may be, to immediately make a determination not exceeding thirty (30) days whether said legal action has been filed to harass, vex, exert undue pressure or stifle such legal recourse of the person complaining of or enforcing the provisions of this Act. Upon determination thereof, evidence warranting the same, the court shall dismiss the case and award attorney's fees and double damages.

Similarly, the Ecological Solid Waste Management Act (Republic Act No. 9003), especially Section 53, also adopts a similar provision. Moreover, the Republic Act No. 10654, an Act to Prevent, Deter, and Eliminate Illegal, Unreported, and Unregulated Fishing, Amending Republic Act No. 8550 of The Philippine Fisheries Code of 1998, also shares a similar tone in the protection of environmental defenders against SLAPP. Section 139 of the act under the heading of *Strategic Lawsuit against Public Participation (SLAPP) in the Enforcement of This Act* stipulates that

> [a] legal action filed to harass, vex, exert undue pressure, or stifle any legal recourse that any person, institution, or the government has taken or may take in the enforcement of this Code shall be treated as a Strategic Lawsuit Against Public

[111] Rey Abella and Aida Manipon, 'Power from the Forest, Power from the Printed Word', *Foundation for the Philippine Environment* (23 March 2015) <https://fpe.ph/impact_story/power-from-the-forest-power-from-the-printed-word/0> accessed 02 June 2024.

[112] Marites D. Vitug, 'Living with Libel Suits', *Rappler* (Manila, 21 February 2013) <www.rappler.com/voices/thought-leaders/22256-living-with-libel-suits/> accessed 02 June 2024.

[113] Antonio Oposa Jr., 'Setting the Course for Environmental Citizen Suits in the Philippines', (1998) 52 *Lawasia Journal* 52, 73.

[114] ibid., 80.

> Participation (SLAPP). The hearing on the defence of a SLAPP shall be summary in nature, the affirmative defence of a SLAPP shall be resolved within thirty (30) days after the summary hearing. If the court dismisses the action, the court may award damages, attorney's fees, and costs of suit under a counterclaim if such has been filed. The dismissal shall be with prejudice. If the court rejects the defence of a SLAPP, the evidence adduced during the summary hearing shall be treated as evidence of the parties on the merits of the case. The action shall proceed in accordance with the Rules of Court. The Rules of Procedure for Environmental Cases shall govern the procedure in civil, criminal, and special civil actions involving the enforcement or violations of this Code including actions treated as a SLAPP as provided in this section.

Moreover, the 2010 Philippine Supreme Court's Rules of Procedures for Environmental Cases has also included anti-SLAPP provisions. Making the Rules was relatively participative, as the Supreme Court in 2009 organised a Forum on Environmental Justice: Upholding the Right to Balanced and Healthful Ecology to invite diverse stakeholders' feedback and recommendations in addressing and resolving environmental cases.[115] The Rationale for the Rules states that:

> [i]n meeting these objectives, the following guidelines are vital: (1) the Rules must reflect the constitutional and jurisprudential concepts of liberalised standing requirements for plaintiffs in environmental suits; (2) the Rules will facilitate access to courts by providing for litigation tools such as citizen's suits, and anti-SLAPP provisions; (3) the Rules should shape procedural elements of environmental litigation to implement the basic tenets of the precautionary principle; (4) the Rules must provide other innovations deemed necessary for the proper administration of environmental justice.[116]

Unlike Indonesia and Thailand, which do not define SLAPP explicitly in their anti-SLAPP provisions, the Philippines has more elaborate anti-SLAPP provisions. Rule 6 of the Rules of Procedure defines SLAPP as '[a] legal action filed to harass, vex, exert undue pressure or stifle any legal recourse that any person, institution or the government has taken or may take in the enforcement of environmental laws, protection of the environment or assertion of environmental rights shall be treated as a SLAPP and shall be governed by these Rules'.[117] The scope of SLAPP in the Philippines is relatively more comprehensive than the original concept introduced by Pring and Canan[118] in terms of the procedures, which include the use of not only civil procedures but also criminal and administrative procedures to intimidate

[115] Maria Christina Mundin, 'Access to Environmental Justice: A Closer Look at the Rules of Procedure for Environmental Cases', (2011) 55 (4) *Ateneo Law Journal* 1066–1090, 1077; Republic of the Philippines. Supreme Court, 2010, *Rules of Procedure for Environmental Cases* (A.M. No. 09-6-8-SC), 9.

[116] Republic of the Philippines. Supreme Court, 2010, *Rationale to the Rules of Procedure for Environmental Cases, Attachment to the Rules of Procedure for Environmental Cases* (A.M. No. 09-6-8-SC) 66.

[117] ibid., 21.

[118] George W. Pring and Penelope Canan, *SLAPPs: Getting Sued for Speaking Out* (Temple University Press, 1996)

environmental defenders and the subject being retaliated against, which include individual citizens, organisations, and government officials.

Similar to Canada,[119] the basis for anti-SLAPP provisions in the Philippines is '[t]he constitutional rights to freedom of speech, expression, and assembly (and in certain cases, the right to petition the government for a redress of grievances) in relation to the right to a balanced and healthful ecology are affected by a SLAPP'.[120] It connects the right to a balanced and healthful ecology as a substantive right to a set of procedural rights in the form of freedom of speech, expression, and assembly upon which the substantive right can be achieved or protected. In this regard, anti-SLAPP provisions in the Rules can be used to defend against any attempt to prevent or challenge citizens from exercising their rights to freedom of speech, expression, and assembly.[121] To share the burden of proof, the Rules also require the SLAPP filers to show that their suit 'is not a SLAPP' by providing 'evidence in support thereof, within a non-extendible period of five (5) days from receipt of notice that an answer has been filed'.[122] Anti-SLAPP provisions in the Philippines aim to uphold constitutional rights to a balanced and healthful ecology, which are linked to the right to freedom of speech and assembly and the right to petition the government.

In brief, three Southeast Asian countries have enacted provisions to prevent SLAPP cases against environmental defenders due to public and international pressures. In Indonesia, the politico-legal opportunity structure to demand the adoption of an anti-SLAPP provision was opened when a new bill concerning environmental management was discussed in the post-authoritarian era. In Thailand, informed by the common use of criminal defamation for retaliating against HRDs, including environmental defenders, legal reform was pursued to amend specific provisions related to criminal defamation. In the Philippines, learning from SLAPP cases targeting a well-known journalist and a prominent environmental law attorney, several environment-related legislations have adopted anti-SLAPP. From a transnational environmental perspective, the adoption of anti-SLAPP provisions in those countries demonstrates a cross-fertilisation of rules, norms, and mechanisms on how SLAPP, a transnational phenomenon that originated in the US, should be prevented and responded to in the absence of international instruments to address it. Despite such adoption, it is important to test the extent to which the existing anti-SLAPP provisions in the three countries are meaningful to prevent, halt, and challenge the exercise of lawfare against environmental defenders. Chapters 4 and 5 are devoted to examining their efficacy.

[119] Fiona Donson, *Legal Intimidation* (Free Association Press, 2000).

[120] Republic of the Philippines. Supreme Court (n 115) 130.

[121] The Rules state that '[i]n a SLAPP filed against a person involved in the enforcement of environmental laws, protection of the environment, or assertion of environmental rights, the defendant may file an answer interposing as a defence that the case is a SLAPP and shall be supported by documents, affidavits, papers, and other evidence; and, by way of counterclaim, pray for damages, attorney's fees and costs of suit'.

[122] Republic of the Philippines. Supreme Court (n 115) 22.

PART THREE

Strategic Dimensions of HEL

CHAPTER 4

Geographies and Weaponry of Lawfare

This chapter examines hegemonic environmental lawfare (HEL) cases in Indonesia, Thailand, and the Philippines in order to reveal their commonality and differences on how law has been used to intimidate environmental defenders in those countries. For the sake of clarity, 'case' here refers to not only a case law that has been decided by the court but also legal actions through which law is mobilised to attack environmental defenders that have entered the formal legal procedures. Methodologically, I analyse data on cases from the courts' cases directories, NGOs' databases, news outlets, as well as reports from non-governmental and international organisations. In the case of Indonesia, I focus on the attacks against environmental defenders since the enactment of the 2009 Environmental Protection and Management Act, which adopts the anti-SLAPP provision. From 2010 to 2022, there were seventy-five cases involving 204 environmental defenders (at least five of them women) as the target of legal actions, including members of local communities, NGO/student activists, expert witnesses in environment-related cases, and journalists. In the case of Thailand, following the revision of the Criminal Procedure Code, especially Sections 161/1 and 165/2, and the revision of the Public Prosecution Institution and Public Prosecutors Act B.E. 2553, it was found that from 2010 to 2022, there were sixty-two cases of legal action against environmental defenders, with 462 victims (at least 45 of them women) being members of local communities. Meanwhile, in the case of the Philippines, the attacks against environmental defenders, since the adoption of the Supreme Court's Rules of Procedure for Environmental Cases in 2011, were examined. As a result, during 2011–22 it found that there were forty-one cases affecting more than 124 environmental defenders of which at least 51 were women environmental defenders in the Philippines.

Due to limited data, those cases may be far from representative of all lawfare cases in those countries. Nevertheless, they may illustrate how legal actions against environmental defenders are conducted, through which modalities, by whom, and on what outcomes. This chapter interrogates the proximities to its strategic dimensions, namely geography and weaponry.[1] It will start by surveying the geographical dimension of lawfare, followed by explanations of its weaponry referring to legal provisions mobilised for deflecting resources and focus from the core issues in environmental conflicts towards legal battles.

The Geographical Dimension

In the context of lawfare, its geographical dimension refers to the battlefield within which lawfare takes place. Zanin et al. regards this dimension as 'a jurisdictional, administrative or political body which is responsible for applying the law'.[2] Here, jurisdictions encompass subject-matter jurisdictions (criminal, civil, and administrative law) and territorial jurisdictions (legal institutions' geographical scope of competence). The choice of specific jurisdictions in conducting a legal battle will play a decisive role in shaping the outcomes because every jurisdiction is embedded in a specific configuration of powers which in turn facilitates or constrains available resources and alliances to be mobilised by actors involved in conflicts.

Subject-Matter Jurisdictions

Subject-matter jurisdiction relates to the legal procedures mobilised in order to attack environmental defenders. Unlike Pring and Canan's original concept of SLAPP, which limits its use within civil proceedings, the modes of legal actions here are broadened to include civil and criminal proceedings. In Indonesia, from seventy-five cases, the use of the criminal justice system has been the biggest mode of lawfare, representing 93.4 per cent of all modes in the country during 2010–22. Meanwhile, the use of civil proceedings was only 6.6 per cent, but the total compensation demanded by plaintiffs was excessive, reaching 3.56 trillion rupiah (US$247 million) or equivalent to 4.5 per cent of the regional budget of Jakarta, Indonesia's capital city.

The most striking example of criminal lawfare cases in the country is the Budi Pego case. Budi Pego is a farmer and local community organiser defending their forest and mountains in Banyuwangi, East Java, from the Bumi Suksesindo – a gold mining company owned by several Indonesian tycoons, including Sandiaga Uno, the Minister of Tourism. During a demonstration, a banner containing a hammer and sickle (the communist symbol), was raised and the police took photos of it. As

[1] See John L Comaroff and Jean Comaroff, 'Law and Disorder in the Postcolony: An Introduction', in J. Comaroff & J. L. Comaroff (eds.), *Law and Disorder* (University of Chicago Press, 2006) 30.

[2] Cristiano Zanin, Valeska Martins, and Rafael Valim, *Lawfare: Waging War through Law* (Routledge, 2022) 44.

the coordinator of the demonstration, Pego was arrested and accused of spreading the prohibited communist ideology, a very serious crime in Indonesia as communism is considered a threat to the national ideology of Pancasila.[3] However, during the trial the banner was never physically shown before the judges and the public prosecutors only used the photos as evidence. As a result, the Banyuwangi District Court sentenced him to ten months in prison and this decision was upheld by the Surabaya High Court; however, in the appeal in cassation, the Supreme Court increased the sentence to four years due to the serious nature of the crime.[4]

In the Philippines, the modes of lawfare have also been dominated by the use of the criminal justice system, which made up 92.7 per cent of the total cases examined in the country during 2010–22, and the use of civil procedures was only 7.3 per cent. In some instances, environmental defenders have been attacked by a series of legal actions. Jomorito Goaynon, a figure head of Lumad Indigenous communities, which have been in the forefront against encroachment of the ancestral land from large-scale mining operations, for instance, has also been a target of attacks many times. In 2015, he and twenty-nine other Lumad Indigenous peoples were criminally charged for murdering Darlito Dela Mance y Goatnon. A year after that, he was accused of committing a crime against public order by 'convincing' Lumad Indigenous communities to return to their evicted houses.[5] In 2021, he and fifteen other members of Lumad Indigenous communities faced another charge of kidnapping, violence intimidation, and robbery, during 'their involvement in a 2018 attack by the New People's Army (NPA) on a military patrol base in Sigabat town'; however, the charges were dismissed by the Bayugan City Regional Trial Court Branch 7 due to the lack of evidence on their involvement in the attack.[6]

In Thailand, in 2019, the Thai Human Rights Lawyers Association released a report on the situation of human rights defenders in the country and provided

[3] The Five Pillars: (1) Believe in God; (2) Just and Civilised Humanity; (3) the National Unity of Indonesia; (4) Representative Democracy; and (5) Social Justice for All of the People of Indonesia. In fact, communism has been prohibited since the authoritarian regime of Suharto took power through the 1965–66 mass killings of those who were considered as supporters of the Indonesian Communist Party (*Partai Komunis Indonesia*/PKI), leftist intellectuals, and members of radical peasant and feminist movements. For further discussion on this, see John Roosa, *The Pretext of Mass Murder: The September 30th Movement and Suharto's Coup d'Etat in Indonesia* (University of Wisconsin Press, 2006).

[4] In its deliberation, the Supreme Court reasoned that 'communist teachings have been considered to endanger the life of the nation and state because of all aspects of theology, ideology, social, political, and history taught this understanding is very contrary to the teachings of the Indonesian Nation as a state of Democracy and the ideology of Pancasila and in the course of history it turns out that the teachings of communism are very bringing deep suffering. Hence, according to the panel of judges, a more severe punishment is required.' See Banyuwangi District Court's Decision No 559/Pid.B/2017/PN. Byw; Surabaya High Court's Decision No. 174/PID/2018/PT.SBY; Indonesian Supreme Court's Decision No. 1567 K/Pid. Sus/2018.

[5] The case has been put on hold. See Frontline Defenders, 'Judicial Harassment of Indigenous Peoples' Rights Defenders', (*Frontline Defenders*, 2 April 2016) <www.frontlinedefenders.org/en/case/case-history-tina-julieta-tawide-gomez> accessed 18 May 2022.

[6] Jigger Jerusalem, Jane Bautista, and Ryan Rosauro, 'Agusan Court Junks Charge Vs 17 Activists', *Philippine Daily Inquirer* (Manila, 04 December 2011) <https://newsinfo.inquirer.net/1523508/agusan-court-junks-charges-vs-17-activists> accessed 18 May 2022.

recommendations to address this alarming situation. It found that during 1997–2019 there were 212 SLAPP cases targeting human rights defenders, in which criminal procedures had been the most common mode of lawfare against the defenders.[7] The association also observed that, following the coup on 22 May 2014, the military junta utilised the law as a significant tool to stifle people's right to free expression. As a result, the number of instances qualifying as SLAPPs grew after 2014.[8] As the data provided relates to human rights defenders in general, it does not suggest anything specific about environmental defenders.

Specifically on environmental defenders, like in Indonesia and the Philippines, hegemonic environmental lawfare has been pursued through civil and criminal procedures. Statistically, the use of the criminal justice system has outnumbered the civil procedures in which there were 83.8 per cent criminal cases and only 16.2 per cent civil cases, respectively. Observing this phenomenon, Kaewchulkan, a Thai legal scholar, quoted by the Thai Society of Environmental Journalists, notes that the criminal procedure is chosen because it works through state agencies, such as the police department or the public prosecutor office, whereas using civil procedures means that 'the plaintiff will have to file a lawsuit directly in court'.[9] Akin to that of the Philippines, environmental defenders in Thailand tend to face backlash through legal means several times in order to stop their resistance. Surapun Rujichaiyavat, who has been at the forefront for local communities' struggles against the Tungkum mining company in Loei province, Northeast Thailand, for instance, has been slapped at least four times both through criminal and civil procedures, which include criminal defamation, civil defamation, trespassing, as well as disturbing public order.[10]

Territorial Jurisdictions

In Indonesia, the legal actions faced by environmental defenders have occurred in all regions in the archipelago. Java has the highest number of attacks (36 per cent) in the last thirteen years, followed by Sumatera (20 per cent), Sulawesi (18.60 per cent),

[7] Human Rights Lawyers Association, *Recommendations on the Protection of Those Who Exercise Their Rights and Freedom from Strategic Lawsuits against Public Participations* (Human Rights Lawyers Association, 2019) 9.

[8] ibid.

[9] Orapin Lilitwisitwong and Thitiphan Pattanamongkol (eds.), *SLAPP: The Public Dreams of Anti-Strategic Lawsuit against Public Participation* (Thai Society of Environmental Journalists, 2022) 25.

[10] Liberty Asia, *Making the Case for Abolishing Criminal Defamation Laws* (Liberty Asia, 2018) retrieved from <http://freedom.collaborative.prod.s3.amazonaws.com/uploads/20180628_Liberty%20Asia_Defamation%20Paper_final.pdf>; 'Thung Kam Co Ltd. vs Porntip an Anti-Mining Villager', (iLAW Freedom, n.d.) <https://freedom.ilaw.or.th/en/case/632#detail> accessed on 31 January 2023; Maysa Zorob, *Defending Defenders: Challenging Malicious Lawsuits in Southeast Asia* (Business and Human Rights Resource Centre, 2020); Community Resource Centre Foundation, et al., 'Thailand: Stop Judicial Harassment of Human Rights Defenders, A Joint Statement' (online) (*Fortify Rights*, 09 May 2016) <www.fortifyrights.org/tha-inv-2016-05-09/> accessed on 31 January 2023; Fortify Rights, 'Thailand: Protect Right to Peaceful Protest of Environmental Defenders', (Fortify Rights, 13 October 2016) <www.fortifyrights.org/tha-inv-2016-10-13/> accessed on 31 January 2023.

Kalimantan (17.3 per cent), Bali-Nusa Tenggara (5.3 per cent), and Maluku-Papua (2.6 per cent). The cases in Java predominantly occurred in 2017, a moment when President Jokowi's National Strategic Projects undertook the groundbreaking of several infrastructure developments, especially coal power plants, industrial areas, as well as toll roads, concentrated in this most populated region. Consequently, a huge fraction of agricultural land and protected areas has been converted in which local livelihoods were impacted. This has created a sense of disfranchisement among affected communities and environmental NGOs. The *Cahyadi and Carman* case is an example here where local resistance against the Batang Coal Power Plant, developed by the Bhimasena Power Indonesia company, was legally countered by imprisoning Cahyadi and Carman for seven months for committing a physical assault on a company supporter.[11] A similar tactic was also used against Taryani, Taniman, Jauri, and Caryani – local farmers who refused the construction of an Extra High Substation for the Indramayu Coal Power Plant – who were accused of physically assaulting a company official during a demonstration. In fact, in this case, Taryani and others acted because the official strangled and dragged a female protester for several metres. In the proceeding, however, their defence was not taken into consideration whatsoever and they were sentenced to six months in prison.[12]

In fact, the Maluku-Papuan region is Indonesia's last forest frontier in the country. However, over the past two decades, it has been facing threats from a massive expansion of extractive industries, especially mining and plantation, searching for new spaces for capital accumulation.[13] In terms of hegemonic environmental lawfare, the region contributes the least number of cases of attacks against environmental defenders utilising legal means. There are several reasons to explain this. First, due to the state's restrictive policies on West Papua, including those related to press coverage, there was limited available data on legal actions against environmental defenders, specifically. Moreover, environmental issues, particularly in West Papua, are very often submitted under the rubric of the rights to self-determination; as a result, the activists were prosecuted through the crimes of either treason or separatism.[14] Hence, the conflation of those environmental issues and the demand for self-determination in West Papua (which is beyond the scope of

[11] Tommy Apriando, 'Tolak PLTU Batang, Warga Berakhir di Balik Jeruji', *Mongabay Indonesia* (Jakarta, 23 May 2014) <www.mongabay.co.id/2014/05/23/tolak-pltu-batang-warga-berakhir-di-balik-jeruji/> accessed 2 February 2022.

[12] Rahmawati, 'Mereka Yang Dipidana Karena Menolak PLTU Indramayu (1)', *Kompas* (Jakarta, 9 February 2020) <https://pemilu.kompas.com/read/2020/06/08/07370001/mereka-yang-dipidana-karena-menolak-pltu-indramayu-1> accessed 9 February 2022.

[13] Hans N. Jong, 'Plantations and Roads Strip Away Papua's Forests. They're Just Getting Started', *Mongabay Indonesia* (Jakarta, 16 August 2021) https://news.mongabay.com/2021/08/plantations-and-roads-strip-away-papuas-forests-theyre-just-getting-started/ accessed 25 April 2023.

[14] See for instance Jakarta Post, 'Amnesty International Expresses Concern over Criminalization of Papuan Activists', *The Jakarta Post* (Jakarta, 8 May 2015) <www.thejakartapost.com/news/2015/05/08/amnesty-international-expresses-concern-over-criminalization-papuan-activists.html> accessed 9 February 2022.

this chapter) requires more specific attention to provide a more comprehensive understanding.

In the region, HEL cases were related to defending Indigenous communities' livelihoods from encroachment by plantations. In Papua, for instance, a conflict between a Papuan Indigenous community and the Korindo group – a Korea-based palm oil plantation, in Boven Digoel, Papua province – has divided the social cohesion within the community between the supporters and the opponents of the company. In 2020, Petrus Kinggo, an opponent of the company, was reported to the police for stealing a boat that was actually being confiscated for entering the Indigenous territory. In Maluku, Kaleb Yamarua and Stevanus Ahlawan – members of an Indigenous community of Sabuai, East Maluku – took direct action to stop the Sumber Berkat Makmur company from destroying the forest to develop a plantation. Following the protest from Indigenous communities, the owner of the company was charged and found guilty of illegal logging, but the verdict from the court was considered low (two years in prison) compared to the impacts of his company's conduct. In retaliation, the company reported Kaleb Yamarua and Stevanus for damaging the company's property, namely loading trucks, as a result of direct action.[15] In the criminal proceeding, they were found guilty and sentenced to six months in prison with one year probation.[16]

From its geographical contexts, in Thailand, it found that 45 per cent cases occurred in Northeast Thailand, 22.4 per cent in Central Thailand, and 14.6 per cent in Southern Thailand. In addition, 9.8 per cent occurred in Western Thailand, 6.4 per cent Northern Thailand, and 1.7 per cent in Eastern Thailand. The biggest cases occurred in Northeast Thailand, a region that has been regarded as the battleground for environmental defenders, especially against mining industries. In the Cold War period, the region was defined as 'dangerous, irredentist haven for communists'.[17] In this, Thailand's poorest region,[18] the Tungkum mining company has been operating and, as mentioned earlier, has filed at least ten SLAPP cases against the anti-mining group of the Khon Rak Ban Kerd Group (KRBKG).[19] Tegbaru characterises environmental movements in Northeast Thailand, especially in Nong Wai Ngam, as 'local environmentalism' in the sense that it tends to be less formal and 'underwritten by influential and charismatic individuals who draw

[15] Christ Belseran, 'Sabuai Banjir Kala Hutan Hancur, Pengusaha Pembalak Liar Kena Vonis Ringan', *Mongabay Indonesia* (Jakarta, 30 Agustus 2021) <www.mongabay.co.id/2021/08/30/sabuai-banjir-kala-hutan-hancur-pengusaha-pembalak-liar-kena-vonis-ringan> accessed 13 April 2023.

[16] Dataran Hunioma District Court's Decision No. 34/Pid.B/2021/PN Dth; Ambon High Court's Decision No. 12/PID/2022/PT AMB; and Supreme Court's Decision No. 757 K/PID/2022.

[17] Kevin Hewison, 'Black Site: The Cold War and the Shaping of Thailand's Politics', (2020) 50 *Journal of Contemporary Asia* 551, 552.

[18] Fracois Molle, Philippe Floch, Buapun Promphakping and David Blake, 'The "Greening of Isaan": Politics, Ideology and Irrigation Development in the Northeast of Thailand', in F. Molle, T. Foran, & M. Kaekoenen (eds.), *Contested Waterscapes in the Mekong Region: Hydropower, Livelihoods and Governance* (Earthscan, 2009) 255.

[19] Liberty Asia (n 10) 4.

external assistance from their wider networks'.[20] The consequence of this model is that the 'charismatic individuals' become the main targets of attacks by those businesses or activities affected by the movement. This clearly demonstrates how several local figures have been legally intimidated repeatedly in order to prevent them from exercising their activism, including Surapun Rujichaiyavat, as already mentioned.

Following Northeast Thailand, cases in Central Thailand were largely contributed to by Bangkok, where protests or demonstrations against the government's policies and projects very often took place and stricter rules to maintain order in the capital city were applied. Interestingly, those cases taking place in Central Thailand were related to the energy sector. In this context, the *Koontawee Pawan and others* case, for instance, involved Koontawee Pawan and four other members of the local community who were accused of committing public disorder after conducting a street protest at the Phahonyothin Road against a power plant project in Nongsang district, Saraburi province. They were found guilty of causing danger to the public, obstructing the highway, and using loudspeakers without permission; as a result, they received a suspended sentence.[21] In the *Samyong Mookaewkrur* case, Somyong, an energy activist, was accused of committing defamation and computer-related crimes against Sermsak Seesan – the Chief District Officer of Mae Moh District, Lampang – after commenting on the corruption allegation in the development of the power plant that has encroached on reserved forests in the area.[22] The next case is the *M. L. Kornkasiwat* case, in which M. L. Kornkasiwat, director of the Energy Policy Research Centre of Rangsit University, was accused of defamation by the Ministry of Energy after posting a Facebook message stating that Laos's diesel price was lower than that of Thailand.[23]

Furthermore, attacks against environmental defenders also took place in Western Thailand and Northern Thailand regions which were related to forestry issues. They include the *Bong Kloi Indigenous Karen* case, the *Waraporn Utairangsee* case, and the *Wansao Phungam* case. These cases are related to a prolonged conflict between the Karen Indigenous community and the government of Thailand, which regards their village as an encroachment of the Kaeng Krachan National Park. In the *Bong Kloi Indigenous Karen* case, more than eighty members of the Bong Kloi Karen community were forcefully arrested by the police force for returning to their village, and to bail all of their arrested members, the community needed to secure a payment of 60,000 baht (US$1,752) each.[24] The *Waraporn Utairangsee* case was

[20] Amare Tegbaru, 'Local Environmentalism in Northeast Thailand', in A. Kalland & G. Persoon (eds.), *Environmental Movements in Asia* (Routledge, 2013) 173.

[21] 'Assembly against the Construction of Nong Saeng Power Plant – Landfill', (*iLAW Freedom*, n.d.) <https://freedom.ilaw.or.th/en/case/493#basic-information> accessed on 31 January 2023.

[22] 'MaeMoh' (*iLaw Freedom*, n.d.) <https://freedom.ilaw.or.th/en/case/114> accessed on 31 January 2023.

[23] 'Ministry of Energy vs M.L. Kornkasiwat' (*iLAW Freedom*, n.d.) <https://freedom.ilaw.or.th/en/case/629#progress_of_case> accessed on 31 January 2023.

[24] 'Indigenous Karen Villagers Arrested after Returning to Ancestral Land', *Prachatai English* (Bangkok, 6 March 202) <https://prachataienglish.com/node/9104> accessed on 31 January 2023.

concerning a criminal case in which Waraporn, an attorney to the Bang Kloi community, was accused of committing perjury after filing a complaint against Chaiwat Limlikitaksorn – a former superintendent of Kaeng Krachan National Park – for burning members of the community's houses that were regarded as situated within the Kaeng Krachan National Park.[25] In the *Wansao Phungam* case, Wansao Phungam, a woman belonging to the Karen Indigenous community who inherited a piece of land from her parents, was accused of encroaching on the Kaeng Krachan National Park. The Supreme Court of Thailand sentenced her to two years and eight months in prison.[26] Meanwhile, in the Northern Thailand region there was the *Wannueng Yawichaipong* case in which Wannueng Yawichaipong, a Mae Kwak woman villager, was accused of encroaching on the Tham Pha Thai National Park and was sentenced to a year in prison and a fine of 400,000 baht (US$11,682).[27]

In the Philippines, in terms of its territorial jurisdictions, the cases examined in this chapter demonstrate that 48 per cent of them occurred in the Luzon Island group, 45 per cent in the Mindanao Island group, and 7 per cent in the Visayas Island group. In Luzon, the biggest number of cases took place in the National Capital region (13.6 per cent), Cagayan Valley region (9 per cent), and Calabarzon region (9 per cent). However, this does not mean that in the Central Luzon region attacks on environmental defenders were absent. In Tarlac province, Central Luzon, for instance, peasants' struggles against plantations have been notorious, leading to the use of legal intimidation. Florida Sibayan, a survivor of the Hacienda Luisita Massacre[28] and the chairwoman of *Alyansa ng mga Manggagawang Bukid sa Asyenda Luisita* (Ambala), is among those who have been targeted, and has faced dozens of trumped-up cases at both the municipal and regional courts in her struggles for land rights in the province.[29] In 2017, she was charged for breaking fences of the Rizal Commercial Banking Corporation (RCBC) owned by Alfonso Yuchengco, a powerful tycoon, during a mass protest in Tarlac City. The RCBC owns a 128 hectare plot that has been a source of conflict between the company and local farmers. Local farmers regard the plot as an object of land distribution because it is situated within the Luisita Estate, previously owned by the Cojuangco family, a powerful political and economic clan in the

[25] 'Former National Park Head Files Perjury Complaint against Human Rights Lawyer', *Prachatai English* (Bangkok, 3 September 2022) <https://prachatai.com/english/node/9993> accessed on 31 January 2023.

[26] 'Indigenous Woman Sentenced to Jail for Encroachment', *Prachatai English* (Bangkok, 28 July 2022) <https://prachataienglish.com/node/9935> accessed on 31 January 2023.

[27] 'Appeal Court Sentences Lampang Villager to Prison for Encroaching on Forest Land', *Prachatai English* (Bangkok, 17 September 2020) <https://prachataienglish.com/node/8792> accessed on 31 January 2023.

[28] The Hacienda Luisita Massacre is a tragic incident that occurred in November 2004, in Tarlac Province, the Philippines, involving the killing of at least seven farmers and the wounding of many others during a violent dispersal of a peaceful protest by workers and farmers on a sugar plantation owned by the Cojuangco family, one of the most influential families in the country.

[29] Pia Montalban, 'Hacienda Luisita: The Struggle Continues', *Rappler* (Manila, 22 November 2015) <www.rappler.com/moveph/113636-hacienda-luisita-land-reform-florida-sibayan/> accessed 25 May 2022.

country which includes former president Corazon Aquino and her son (former president Benigno Aquino III).[30]

In the Mindanao Island group, the biggest number of cases occurred in the Caraga region (22.7 per cent), followed by the Northern Mindanao (9 per cent) and Soccsksargen regions (9 per cent). In the Soccsksargen region, for example, environmental defenders have not only faced serial attacks through law, but some of them were even killed when all attempts at mobilising legal means could not silence them. The story of Juan Macababbab, an environmental lawyer from the National Union of People's Lawyers in Mindanao (NUPL), is a tragic example. In 2015, an attempt was made to silence him through the civil procedure after Attorney Macababbab assisted a local community against Sumifru Banana plantation.[31] Due to his persistent activism, in September 2021, he was shot by two gunmen in Surrallah, South Cotabato, making his death 'the third member of the NUPL and the 58th lawyer who was gunned down under President Duterte's administration'.[32] From the government's viewpoint, Mindanao Island has been marked by insurgencies from which the extension of martial law to pursue the state's agenda against insurgencies has been justified and in reality intertwined with severe attacks on social movements. Under Duterte, the biggest numbers of killings, including environmental defenders, occurred in Mindanao Island, particularly in Compostela Valley, Davao de Oro province – a mineral-rich province in Davao region – and in 'agribusiness corridors' of Bukidnon province, Northern Mindanao region.

Specifically, the Visayas Island group, from the findings, has been Philippine's Island group with the least number of lawfare cases. In terms of killings of environmental defenders, Visayas is considered a territory where the largest number killings took place under the Duterte regime. In the Visayas Island group, this especially contributed to cases in Negros Oriental province (Central Visayas region) and Negros Occidental province (Western Visayas region).[33] Hence, Negros Oriental and Negros Occidental provinces – together with Davao de Oro province and Bukidnon province in Mindanao – are regarded by Jose Leon Dulce et al. as the most dangerous provinces in the Philippines.[34] If cases occurred in Visayas in last decade, they mostly took place in the Central Visayas region in cases related to the Cordova reclamation project, including *Adelino Sitoy (Mayor of Cordova)* v. *Dante Ramos and others (2012)*. In this case, two lawyers (Dante Ramos and Satiago Ortiz)

[30] Tonette Orejas and Maria A. Sibayan, 2017, 'Hacienda Luisita Activist Detained after Protesters Storm RCBC Compound', *Inquirer* (Manila, 15 November 2017) <https://newsinfo.inquirer.net/945483/philippine-news-updates-hacienda-luisita-alyansa-ng-mga-manggagawang-bukid-sa-asyenda-luisita-corazon-aquino-benigno-aquino-iii> accessed 25 May 2022.

[31] Anne M. D. Umil, 'Another Peoples' Lawyer Killed in Mindanao', *Bulatlat* (Manila, 16 September 2012) <www.bulatlat.com/2021/09/16/another-peoples-lawyer-killed-in-mindanao/> accessed 20 May 2022.

[32] ibid.

[33] Jose Leon A. Dulce, Clemente G. Bautista Jr, Gianina Camille E. Glarino and Karl Daniel A. Begnotea, 'A War of Plunder against Environmental Defenders in the Philippines', (2021) 22 *Policy Matters* 28, 29.

[34] ibid.

and three fishermen (Cirilo Pagobo, Eduardo Quijano, and Alejandro Baguio) were sued by the mayor of Cordova, Adelino Sitoy, after criticising and opposing the reclamation project of Cordova supported by the mayor. In the lawsuit, the mayor demanded 3.3 million peso (US$59,393) compensation for damaging his reputation.[35]

Sectoral Jurisdictions

The nature of a resource-based economy has shaped how legal actions have been used in silencing dissenting voices against extractivist practices. In Indonesia, the highest number of hegemonic environmental lawfare cases during 2010–22 occurred in the forestry and plantation sector, representing 41.4 per cent of the total cases (Figure 4.1). As explained in Chapter 2, as the sector has contributed significantly to the national economy, the Government of Indonesia has a strong incentive to expand this sector even further in order to increase national production. As put by Gellert, palm oil plantations are associated with territorial grabbing, in part, because they require a large plot of monocultural land to be profitable.[36] Consequently, in many parts of Indonesia where the communal rights over Indigenous territories have been strong, the attempt to acquire land for palm oil plantations, as well as logging activities, has created conflicts with local communities.[37] According to the Consortium of Agrarian Reform, in 2020 alone there were 241 conflicts affecting more than 130,000 households across the country, which predominantly occurred within the forestry and plantation sector.[38] On many occasions, such conflicts led to the use of lawfare to settle them, as in the case of Trisno Susilo, a leader of Meratus Indigenous people who was sentenced to four years in prison for illegal forest occupation during his advocacy to defend their forest from the expansion of the Kodeco Timber company in South Kalimantan.[39]

Following the forestry and plantation sector, the mining sector had the next highest, accounting for 24 per cent of total cases. Similar to forestry and plantation, the mining sector is also important to the national economy. In the context of coal mining, for instance, Indonesia is one of the biggest coal-exporting countries, with

[35] Ador Mayol and Norman Mendoza, 'Sitoy Files P3.3M Damage Suit against 3 Fishers, 2 Lawyers', *Inquirer* (Manila, 24 April 2012) <https://newsinfo.inquirer.net/181779/sitoy-files-p3-3m-damage-suit-against-3-fishers-2-lawyers> accessed 8 April 2023; Jessa Agua and Norman Mendoza, 'Lawyer: We Welcome Damage Suit Filed by Cordova Mayor', *Cebu Daily News* (Cebu, 25 April 2012) <https://cebudailynews.wordpress.com/2012/04/25/lawyer-we-welcome-damage-suit-filed-by-cordova-mayor/> accessed 8 April 2023.

[36] Paul K. Gellert, 'Palm Oil Expansion in Indonesia: Land Grabbing as Accumulation by Dispossession', in J. Shefner (ed.), *States and Citizens: Accommodation, Facilitation and Resistance to Globalization* (Emerald Group Publishing Limited, 2015) 79.

[37] ibid, 82.

[38] Ardiansyah Fadli, 'Sepanjang 2020 Konflik Agraria 241 Kasus, Tertinggi Sektor Perkebunan', *Kompas* (Jakarta, 6 January 2021). <www.kompas.com/properti/read/2021/01/06/160000521/sepanjang-2020-konflik-agraria-241-kasus-tertinggi-sektor-perkebunan> accessed 2 February 2022.

[39] *The Trisno Susilo Case* [2017] Decision No.17/Pidsus/2017/PN.BLN.

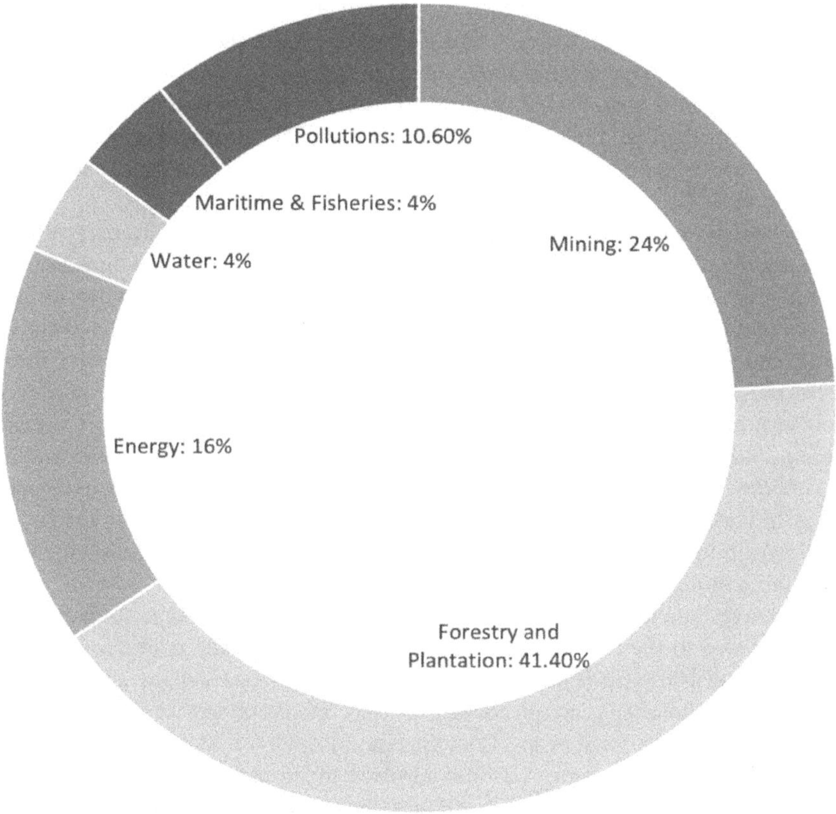

Figure 4.1 Lawfare by sectors in Indonesia.

China, Japan, India, and South Korea as its main markets.[40] Domestically, coal is also the main source of electricity, contributing around 60 per cent of Indonesia's total power capacity.[41] Hence, issues on coal mining are closely related to the energy sector.

In its Enhanced Nationally Determined Contribution (NDC), Indonesia has pledged to reduce emissions by around 31.89 per cent (unconditionally) and 43 per cent with international support.[42] However, the energy policy at the domestic level appears to contradict the pledge in which the Government of Indonesia

[40] Lucky Leonard, 'Indonesia Rajai Pasar Ekspor Batu Bara', *Bisnis.com* (Jakarta, 27 May 2019) <https://ekonomi.bisnis.com/read/20190527/44/927982/indonesia-rajai-pasar-ekspor-batu-bara> accessed 2 February 2022.

[41] Deon Arinaldo and Julius. C. Adiatma, *Dinamika Batu Bara: Menuju Transisi Energi Yang Adil* (Institute for Essential Services Reform, 2019).

[42] Republic of Indonesia, *Enhanced Nationally Determined Contribution* (Ministry for the Environment and Forestry, 2022), 12.

insisted on putting forward a 35,000 MW electricity programme which is dominated by coal-fired power plants.[43] This programme has triggered opposition from NGO activists and local communities where the coal power plants were constructed. Hence, lawfare has been part of the strategy used by the corporations and the state officials for preventing them from exercising their rights to protest and weakening their resistance as in the *Sawin, Sukma and Nanto* case[44] and the *Cahyadi and Carman* case.[45]

The massive construction of coal-fired power plants also has implications for the expansion of the coal mining operations, resulting in the use of the law against anti-mining movements. The Mining Advocacy Network (Jatam) reported that during 2014–20 there were at least seventy-one escalated conflicts between local communities and mining companies located across the archipelago, of which twenty-three were related to coal mining.[46] In East Kalimantan – the biggest coal producer province in the country – at least two lawfare cases occurred in relation to local communities' resistance against coal mining, namely *Jawa Village Communities* v. *Adimitra Baratama Nusantara* and *Multi Guna Farmer's Group* v. *Kaltim Prima Coal.* In both cases, at least seven anti-mining villagers were reported to the police by the Adimitra Baratama Nusantara and the Kaltim Prima Coal, accusing them of disrupting mining activities.[47]

Moreover, both the forestry and plantation sector and the mining sector have been closely related to the politics in the country. Many high-profile politicians and ex-military generals are part of the sectors, either as owners of the company, shareholders, or at least their financial source in political contests. Specifically in the mining industry, they include Luhut Pandjaitan (Coordinating Minister of Maritime Affairs and Investment), whose company was also involved in the *Jawa Village Communities* v. *Adimitra Baratama Nusantara* mentioned above; Prabowo Subianto (Minister of Defense 2019–14, and the President of Indonesia 2024–present); Sandiaga Uno (Minister of Tourism 2020–24); Erick Tohir (Minister of State-Owned Companies 2019–24); and Aburizal Bakrie, the owner of the Kaltim Prima Coal.[48] The intimate

[43] James Guild, 'Jokowi's 35000-Megawatt Dream', *Inside Indonesia* (Canberra, 26 October 2020) <www.insideindonesia.org/jokowi-s-35000-megawatt-dream> accessed 2 February 2022.

[44] Dyaning Pangestika, 'Coal Plant Protesters in Indramayu Face Trial over National Flag Incident', *The Jakarta Post* (Jakarta, 17 October 2018) <www.thejakartapost.com/news/2018/10/17/coal-plant-protesters-in-indramayu-face-trial-over-national-flag-incident.html> accessed 2 February 2022.

[45] Tommy Apriando, 'Tolak PLTU Batang, Warga Berakhir di Balik Jeruji', *Mongabay Indonesia* (Jakarta, 23 May 2014) <www.mongabay.co.id/2014/05/23/tolak-pltu-batang-warga-berakhir-di-balik-jeruji/> accessed 2 February 2022.

[46] Fadiyah Alaidrus, 'Selama Periode Awal Jokowi Ada 71 Konflik Tambang, Kata Jatam', *Tirto* (Jakarta, 6 January 2020) <https://tirto.id/selama-periode-awal-jokowi-ada-71-konflik-tambang-kata-jatam-eqW9> accessed 2 February 2022.

[47] WALHI South Kalimantan, 'Judicial Review UU Minerba Memasuki Masa Sidang di Saat Kriminalisasi Warga yang Makin Masif', (*WALHI Kalsel*, 5 August 2021) <https://walhikalsel.or.id/judicial-review-uu-minerba-memasuki-masa-sidang-di-saat-kriminalisasi-warga-yang-kian-masif> accessed 14 April 2023.

[48] Greenpeace, JATAM, ICW, and Auriga, *Coalruption: Shedding Light on Political Corruption in Indonesia's Coal Mining Sector* (Bersihkan Indonesia, 2018). In this collaborative report, the NGOs reveal several prominent political figures at the national level as having a close connection to the coal mining

relationship between those extractive industries and the politicians has made them politically supported by the national policies. Even during the Covid-19 pandemic, one of the economic measures taken by the government was to relax the taxes and financial obligations of the industries through the revision of the 2009 Mining Act.[49]

With regard to industrial pollution, which accounted for 10.6 per cent, it has been a chronic environmental issue in the country, especially in Java, Indonesia's centre of manufacturing industries. As the most populated region in the country, pollution in Java has created a collective concern among local communities. In many cases, their opposition against pollution has been responded to by intimidating them using criminal proceedings, as in the *Sukoharjo* and the *Pekalongan* cases. The *Sukoharjo* case consists of four separate criminal lawsuits involving seven environmental defenders (members of local communities and student activists) who were fighting against pollution by the Rayon Utama Makmur, a rayon manufacturing company for producing military uniforms, situated in Sukoharjo district, Central Java. Those defenders were charged with two different offences: (1) damaging the company's property during a mass demonstration in which Kelvin Ferdiansyah, Sukemi Edi, Hisbun Payu, Sutarno, and Brillian Yosef Nauval, as the defendants, were sentenced to 2–4.5 years in prison;[50] and (2) the crime of incitement through social media, with defendants Bambang Hesti and Danang Tri Widodo, in which they were sentenced to two and four years in prison, respectively.[51] Meanwhile, the *Pekalongan* case involved local communities struggling against pollution by a garment factory – the Pajitex located close to their areas. Two local residents (Abdul Afif and Kurohman) were charged with damaging the company's property during a protest involving a hundred other residents in demanding the company stop the operation. They were sentenced by the court to two months and ten days in prison.[52]

In Thailand, the largest number of attacks on environmental defenders has been in the mining sector (Figure 4.2). It accounts for 62.9 per cent of the total cases examined in this chapter. After the mining sector, the forestry sector has around 13 per cent, followed by the energy sector (11.3 per cent), infrastructure development projects (8 per cent), environmental policies (3.2 per cent), and the coastal

industry. See also Indonesia Corruption Watch (ICW), *Bisnis Militer Mencari Legitimasi* (Indonesia Corruption Watch, n.d.). In this report, the ICW investigated the relationship between the Indonesian Military Force and the coal mining activity in which it found that the military force has established a commercial body to undertake a coal mining business; Viriya Singgih, 'Profil dan Peta Koneksi Bisnis dan Politik 10 Oligark Batubara Terbesar di Indonesia di Bawah Pemerintahan Jokowi', *Project Multatuli* (Jakarta, 4 February 2022) <https://projectmultatuli.org/profil-peta-koneksi-bisnis-dan-politik-10-oligark-batubara-terbesar-di-indonesia-di-bawah-pemerintahan-jokowi/> accessed 9 February 2022.

[49] Norman Harsono, 'House Approved Revised Mining Law amid Outcry', *The Jakarta Post* (Jakarta, 13 May 2020) <www.thejakartapost.com/news/2020/05/12/house-approves-revised-mining-law-amid-outcry.html> accessed 9 February 2022.

[50] Decision of the District Court of Semarang No. 293/Pid.B/2019/PN.Smg and Decision No.259/Pid/2019/PT.Smg.

[51] Decision the District Court of Semarang No. 244 K/PID.SUS/2019 and Decision No. 252/Pid.Sus/2019/PT.Smg.

[52] Decision the District Court of Pekalongan No. 225/Pid.B/2021/PN.Pkl.

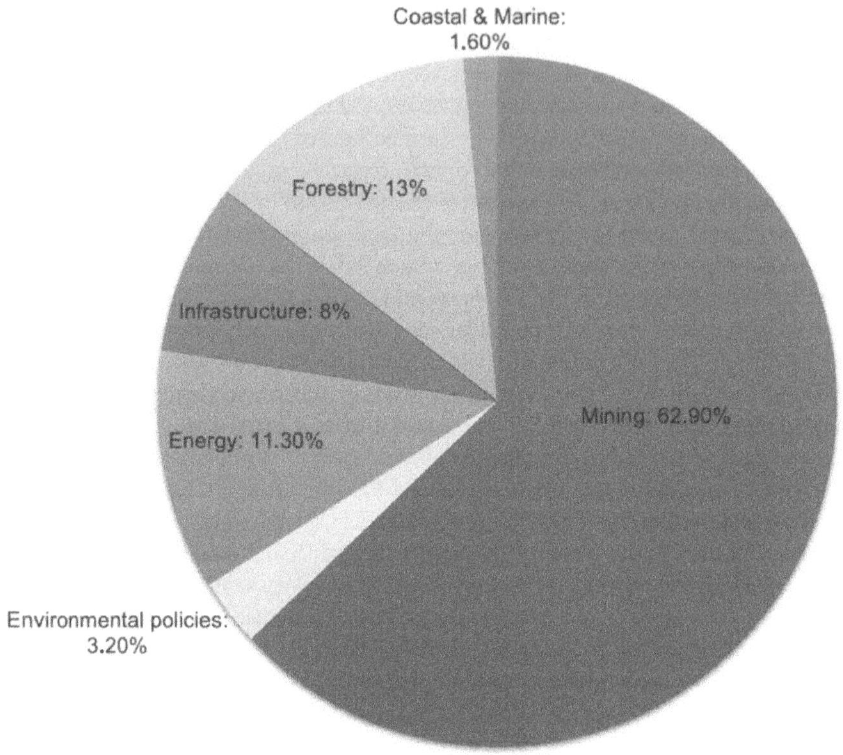

Figure 4.2 Lawfare by sectors in Thailand.

and marine sector (1.6 per cent). Comparable to the Philippines and Indonesia, the mining industry in Thailand also has a close connection to the political and military elites. Besides that, the biggest use of lawfare in the mining sector is by the Tungkum mining company, which, during 2010–17 alone, filed six criminal defamation cases and four civil defamation cases against thirty-three members of the KRBKG and other villagers who have been critical of the company's mining activity, with the total compensation demanded being approximately US$8.93 million.[53]

Furthermore, specifically in the energy sector, besides the *Koontawee Pawan and others* case, the *Samyong Mookaewkrur* case, and the *M.L. Kornkasiwat* case, mentioned earlier, other cases include the *Watcharee Phaoluangthong* v. *the Siam Energy Company* case,[54] the *Saran* case, and the *Prasitchai Noonaun*

[53] Liberty Asia (n 10) 4.

[54] 'Watchree Phaoluangthong: Alternative Energy Campaigner', (iLaw Freedom, n.d.) <https://freedom.ilaw.or.th/en/case/15#detail> accessed on 31 January 2023.

case.[55] In the *Saran* case, for instance, Saran, an admin of the Facebook page 'Take Back Thai Energy', was accused of committing criminal defamation and computer-related crimes after he posted comments on the PTT company accusing it fraudulent practices in causing the rise of energy prices and hiring a third party to intimidate the company's opponents. The Bangkok South Criminal Court found him guilty and sentenced him to nine months in prison; however, the Court of Appeal changed the verdict, suspending the prison sentence and imposing a fine of 30,000 baht (US$8,762).[56]

Like Indonesia, as a country with rich natural resources, extractive industries have also contributed largely to the use of law for intimidating environmental defenders in the Philippines as shown in Figure 4.3. The highest number of attacks occurred in the mining sector (41.5 per cent) and the plantation sector (36.6 per cent), making them the two 'most dangerous sectors' in the country.[57] Within those two sectors also, killings of environmental defenders have taken place, which has led Global Witness to characterise the Philippines as 'the world's deadliest country for defenders'[58] and among 'the most dangerous places to defend land rights or the environment'.[59] As discussed in Chapter 2, the mining industry has played an important role in the economy and it has a long history of being connected to political elites in the country in which many lawmakers and government officials have close ties to mining companies. This has led to concerns about corruption and conflicts of interest, as well as environmental and social impacts on local communities, especially dislocations. Activists and local communities have continued to advocate reforms to the industry, including greater transparency and accountability in the granting of mining concessions.[60] The same treatment also goes to the agribusiness industry, especially plantations, because it is one of the most competitive of the Philippines in the global market. Since the Spanish Colonial era, it has also historically been linked to political elites, so the industry has remained controlled by the Philippines' wealthiest and most powerful elites, which in turn

[55] Prasithchai was reported for committing defamation after criticising the Electricity Generating Authority of Thailand's (EGAT) coal power plant project in Krabi province on his Facebook account. 'Prasithchai: CCA Case for Commenting on Coal Power Plant Project', (iLaw Freedom, n.d.) <https://freedom.ilaw.or.th/en/case/807> accessed on 31 January 2023.

[56] See Bangkok South Criminal Court No: 2637/2557, 4135/2557; 'PTT Company v. Admin of "Take Back Thai Energy" FB Page' (iLaw Freedom, n.d.) <https://freedom.ilaw.or.th/en/case/777> accessed on 31 January 2023.

[57] Wolfram Dressler, 'A Window into the "Everyday" Struggles of Environmental Defenders in Palawan Island, the Philippines', (2021) 22 *Policy Matters* 17, 18–19.

[58] Global Witness, *Enemies of the State? How Governments and Business Silence Land and Environmental Defenders* (Global Witness, 2019a) 17.

[59] Global Witness, *Defending the Philippines: How Broken Promises Are Leaving Land and Environmental Defenders at the Mercy of Business at All Costs* (Global Witness, 2019b) 21.

[60] Jewellord Singh and Alvin Camba, 'Neoliberalism, Resource Governance and the Everyday Politics of Protests in the Philippines', in J. Elias & L. Rethel (eds.), *The Everyday Political Economy of Southeast Asia* (Cambridge University Press, 2016) 51.

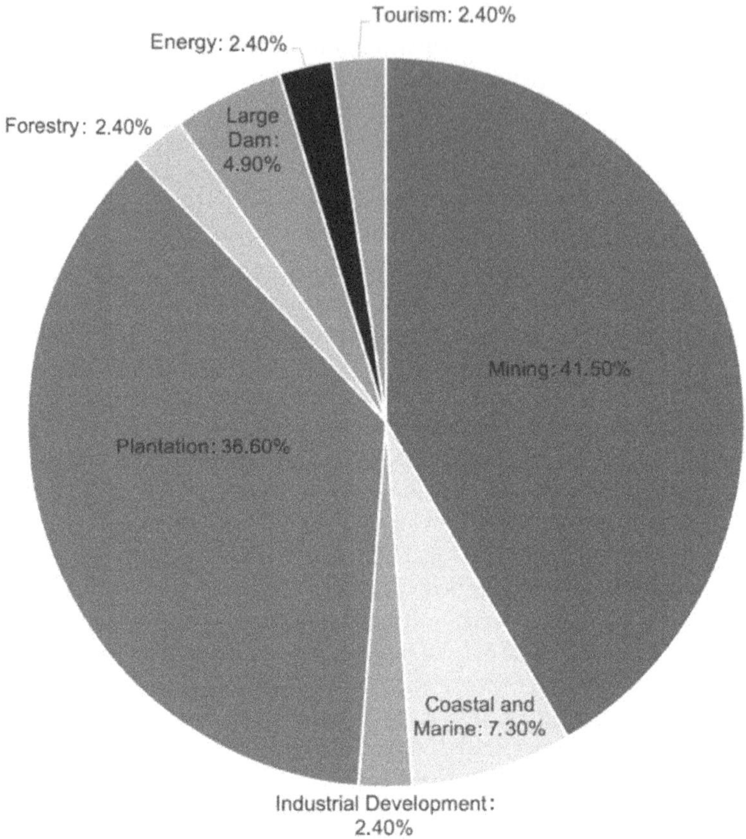

Figure 4.3 Lawfare by sectors in the Philippines.

continues to shape the political landscape in the country. In order to protect those dominant sectors, the government has put pressure on local communities as well as environmental organisations whose work has disrupted their operation.

The Weaponry Dimension

The 'weaponry dimension' of lawfare refers to legal provisions in criminal law, civil law, or administrative law that are mobilised to legally attack environmental defenders. They very often are provisions that may '*contain vague, easily manipulated concepts, allowing for violent precautionary and investigative measures, thus seriously damaging the enemy's image*' (italics original).[61] In Indonesia, weapons in civil law jurisdictions mobilised by the plaintiffs have been the tort law clause as stipulated by Article 1365 of the Indonesian Civil Code, which states that '[e]very unlawful act that causes damage to another person obliges the wrongdoer to compensate for such damage'. They were: (1) *Willy Suhartono* v. *H. Rudy* (2013), involving H. Rudy, who was a local organiser of People's Forum for the Care of Water Spring protesting a hotel development project that might affect a local water spring of Air Gemulo. He submitted complaint letters to government agencies as well as the ombudsman on the issue, but the company's owner filed a tort lawsuit against Rudy for damaging the company's reputation and demanded compensation of 30 billion rupiah (US$2 million);[62] (2) *Bumi Konawe Abadi* v. *Daeng Kadir & Abdul Azis* (2013), in which Daeng Kadir and Abdul Azis, villagers in North Konawe district, Southeast Sulawesi province, were sued by the Bumi Konawe Abadi, a mining company, for conducting public protests by blocking the roads used by the company's trucks in transporting mining deposits. The company accused the blockage of causing financial losses and demanded IDR 8.6 billion (US$579,208) in compensation;[63] (3) *Forum Peduli Lingkungan Pali* v. *PT Pertamina EP Asset 2 Pendopo Adera Field* (2016), involving Forum Peduli Lingkungan Pali, a local environmental group that filed a tort lawsuit against Pertamina, a state-owned oil and gas company, for polluting local rivers. In the proceeding, however, Pertamina filed a counter lawsuit against the plaintiff for damaging the company's reputation and demanded IDR 10 billion (US$673,498) (immaterial) and IDR 100 million (US$6,734) (material) compensation.[64]

Tort law was also mobilised against experts who provided testimony before the courts concerning environmental matters. Here, they were: (1) *Jatim Jaya Perkasa* v. *Bambang Hero Saharjo* (2016). The Jatim Jaya Perkasa, a palm oil company, was charged in a case brought by the Ministry for the Environment and Forestry for committing forest fires within its concession. In the proceeding, Bambang Hero Saharjo, a land and ecosystem professor, provided an expert testimony against the company on the ecological losses caused by the forest fires; based on his calculations, the court ordered the company pay fines of IDR 119.8 billion (US$7.9 million). The company turned to the Cibinong District Court to file a tort lawsuit against Saharjo, claiming that his testimony was inadmissible because he used evidence provided by the Ministry of the Environment and Forestry;[65] and (2) *Nur Alam* v. *Basuki Wasis* (2018). In this case, Nur Alam, a former governor of

[61] Zanin, Martins, and Valim (n 2) 16.

[62] Malang District Court's Decision No. 177/Pdt.G/2013/PN.MLG and the Supreme Court's Decision No. 2263K/Pdt/2015.

[63] Unaaha District Court's Decision No. 16/Pdt.G/2013/PN.Nuh, the Kendari High Court's Decision No. 104/Pdt/2014/PT.KDI, and the Supreme Court's Decision No. 1934K/Pdt/2015.

[64] Muara Enim District Court's Decision No. 17/Pdt.G-LH/2016/PN.Mre; Supreme Court's Decision No. 3304K/PDT/2017.

[65] After a reconciliation process the company finally withdrew the lawsuit. See the Cibinong District Court's Decision No. 223/Pdt.G/2018/PN.CBI.

Southeast Sulawesi, was charged with committing corruption in granting mining permits to a mining company operating in the province. In the proceeding, Basuki Wasis, a senior academic from the Bogor Institute for Agriculture, was appointed by the anti-corruption prosecutors to provide an expert assessment on the impacts of the illegal permit to the ecosystem from which the prosecutors calculated fines in addition to prison charges against the defendant. In retaliation, Nur Alam filed a lawsuit against Wasis based on Article 1365 of the Indonesian Civil Code, claiming that the expert testimony had caused damages and demanding compensation of IDR 1.4 billion (US$94,289) for material losses, and IDR 3 trillion (US$202 million) for immaterial loses.[66]

Similarly, in the Philippines, Article 2217 of the Philippine Civil Code concerning damage has been weaponised against environmental defenders. The article stipulates that '[m]oral damages include physical suffering, mental anguish, fright, serious anxiety, besmirched reputation, wounded feelings, moral shocks, social humiliation, and similar injury. Though incapable of pecuniary computation, moral damages may be recovered if they are the proximate result of the defendant's wrongful act or omission.' This is evidenced in *Resort World Sentosa (RWS)* v. *Earth Island Institute* (2013), in which the Earth Island Institute (EII), an environmental NGO focusing on protecting wildlife, protested trade and captivity of dolphins in the Indo-Pacific region in which in 2012 they found twenty-five dolphins that were imported from Solomon Islands to a Philippine park had been traded to Singapore's Resorts World Sentosa (RWS). The EII and other local environmental organisations filed a lawsuit against the Philippine Department of Agriculture, Bureau of Fisheries and Aquatic Resources, and RWS in the Quezon City Regional Court in order to block the trade. In retaliation for the lawsuit, RWS filed a damage lawsuit against Trixie Conception, director of the EII for Asia, and the institute demanding US$90,000 compensation. The court ordered the institute pay US$15,385 in compensation for 'causing RWS to suffer embarrassment and besmirched reputation'.[67]

Meanwhile, in Thailand, legal actions through the civil proceeding predominantly utilised the civil defamation clause and the civil violation clause as the legal ground. The civil defamation clause is stipulated in Section 423 Thai Civil and Commercial Code, which states that

> [a] person who, contrary to the truth, asserts or circulates as a fact that which is injurious to the reputation or the credit of another or his earnings or prosperity in

[66] Cibinong District Court finally dismissed the lawsuit. Tommy Apriando, 'Pengadilan Cibinong Tolak Gugatan Nur Alam, Basuki Wasis Bebas', *Mongabay Indonesia* (Jakarta, 13 December 2018) <www.mongabay.co.id/2018/12/13/pengadilan-cibinong-tolak-gugatan-nur-alam-basuki-wasis-bebas/> accessed on 9 April 2023.

[67] Mark Palmer, 'Earth Island Philippines Fights SLAPP Suit over Anti-Captivity', (Save Dolphins, 16 October 2019) <https://savedolphins.eii.org/news/earth-island-philippines-fights-slapp-suit-over-anti-captivity> accessed on 09 March 2023; Janvic Mateo, 'Activists to File Charges over Death of Dolphin Shipped to Singapore', (The Philippine Stars, 27 November 2012) <www.philstar.com/headlines/2012/11/27/874565/activists-file-charges-over-death-dolphin-shipped-singapore> accessed on 09 April 2023.

any other manner, shall compensate the other for any damage arising therefrom, even if he does not know of its untruth, provided he ought to know it. A person who makes a communication the untruth of which is unknown to him, does not thereby render himself liable to make compensation, if he or the receiver of the communication has a rightful interest in it.

The civil violation clause is stipulated in Section 420 Thai Civil and Commercial Code, which states that '[a] person, willfully or negligently, unlawfully injures the life, body, health, liberty, property or any right of another person, is said to commit a wrongful act and is bound to make compensation therefore'. Both clauses were weaponised, among others, in: (1) *Watcharee Phaoluangthong* v. *Siam Energy Company.* In this case, Watcharee Phaoluangthong, an environmental activist focusing on clean energy, was sued by the Siam Energy Company Ltd after giving an opinion on the energy policies and the lack of transparency in the concession process and environmental impact assessment (EIA) processes of the company. He was accused of committing defamation and asked for compensation of up to 300 million Thai baht paid to the company;[68] (2) *Peerapol Mining Co. Ltd.* v. *Nine members of Khao Khuha Community Rights Network (KKCRN),* in which the Peerapol Mining Company filed a lawsuit against nine members of the KKCRN for committing civil defamation after they exposed the impacts of the company's mining operation and its non-compliance to the EIA document. The Supreme Court finally dismissed the lawsuit considering that what they did was exercising their rights to protest and to send a petition to the government authorities;[69] and (3) *Tungkum Ltd.* v. *Surapun Rujichaiyavat and Five Others,* in which the companies accused the defendants of damaging their reputation and business operations.[70]

As demonstrated in the section on Subject-Matter Jurisdictions, criminal law has been predominantly used to silence environmental defenders in Indonesia, Thailand, and the Philippines. In Indonesia, the categories of offences used to charge environmental defenders can be seen in Figure 4.4. It shows that crimes against public order have been used at least 21 per cent of the time in twelve years. The highest number of cases utilising the crimes against public order was partly attributed to the use of street demonstration, blockade, and direct action as the popular form of resistance. In this form, it becomes easier for targeted companies and the state officers or even vigilante groups funded by the companies to infiltrate and to provoke the opponent groups to turn to rioting or law breaking. Those forms of resistance have also contributed to a number of environmental activists being charged with the crime of incitement, especially during their oratory speech, as in

[68] See 'Watcharee Phaoluangthong: Alternative Energy Campaigner', (iLAW Freedom, n.d.) <https://freedom.ilaw.or.th/en/case/15#detail> accessed on 31 January 2023.

[69] Maysa Zorob (n 10); Community Resource Centre Foundation (n 10).

[70] The company accused the defendants of damaging the company's business operation and reputation. Liberty Asia (n 10).

Figure 4.4 Criminal weapons in Indonesia.

the *Eva Bande* case[71] and the *Anwar Sadat* case.[72] Moreover, there were three cases in which an act of confiscating companies' equipment, such as chainsaws or boats, was classified as theft by the police, and to be prosecuted through the criminal justice system.[73] In the other cases, halting companies' employers from cutting the forests or conducting their work was considered as an act of crime against personal freedom, according to Article 333 of Indonesia's Criminal Code.[74]

[71] *The Eva Bande Case* [2011] Supreme Court Decision No. 1573 K/PID/2011.

[72] Anwar Sadat is an environmental activist from the Indonesian Forum for the Environment (Friends of the Earth Indonesia/WALHI) who was advocating the rights of local farmers from land grabbing by the PTPN, a state-owned plantation company. A mass demonstration protesting the detention of several members of the local peasant organisations organised by WALHI turned into a clash with the police guards. He was arrested with two other organisers, and, in the proceedings, they were found guilty of incitement and sentenced to five months in prison.

[73] The *Theodorus Tekwan* case demonstrates how Theodorus Tekwan, a member of Lung Isun Indigenous Peoples of Mahakam Ulu, East Kalimantan, was charged with committing theft after confiscating chainsaws used by a logging company's worker to cut the forests within the Indigenous territory. A similar theft case was faced by Riswan, Teki, Embang, Semar, and Efendi Buhing from Kinipan Indigenous Peoples of Central Kalimantan after confiscating chainsaws owned by the Sawit Mandiri Lestari, a palm oil company that attempted to convert their forest for plantation. In Papua, Petrus Kinggo, an Indigenous leader who was actively involved in fighting against the Korindo plantation company, was reported to the police after confiscating a boat entering the Indigenous territory without permission. Following pressure from the Indigenous communities they belong to, the three cases of Theodorus Tekwan and Petrus Kinggo have been put on hold (pending) by the police.

[74] The example of this is the *Tukijo* case: A farmer who was fighting against a sand mining company in Kulonprogo, Yogyakarta, was charged for a crime against personal freedom when he and other villagers

The high use of social media in Indonesia has opened a new space for environmental defenders to conduct campaigns and promote their causes. However, there are many possibilities for being criminally charged due to several contentious provisions in the 2008 Information and Electronic Transaction Act, including online criminal defamation. As a result, 14 per cent have been online criminal defamation cases in the last decade, making it the second route through which environmental defenders were convicted. The *Deddy Febrianto Holo* case is one example among many. Deddy Febrianto Holo is an environmental activist for the Indonesian Forum for the Environment (Friends of the Earth Indonesia/WALHI) who criticised the Head of District of East Sumba, East Nusa Tenggara province, for supporting the Ade Agro Industry, a cotton company. Accordingly, he was sentenced by the court to four months in prison.

Moreover, a relatively high number of prosecutions have occurred using criminal offences stipulated in sectoral laws, especially within the forestry and plantation regime as well as within the mining law regime. In the forestry and plantation law regime, Forestry Law has several criminal provisions on illegal forest occupations,[75] and Plantation Law has a provision to prosecute anyone who is accused of hindering plantation activities. Similarly, Mining Law provides Article 162 to prosecute anyone who is considered to disrupt mining activities.[76] Collectively, crimes in both sectoral regimes were responsible for 19 per cent of the total criminal cases. This includes the *Alas Buluh* case, in which three villagers – Abdullah, Sugiyanto, and Achmad Busiin – were charged with disrupting mining operations after they and 100 other villagers blocked a mining truck that passed through their village daily, causing health issues and environmental harms for the villagers. The District Court of Banyuwangi convicted and sentenced them to three months in prison,[77] but, more recently, in the Supreme Court they were discharged.

A particular area of concern has been the use of crimes against the state's ideology and symbols to intimidate environmental defenders, which made up 5.7 per cent of the total criminal cases. In addition to the *Budi Pego* case concerning the spread of communism discussed in the geographical dimension of lawfare, there were at least four cases related to these crimes. The first one is the *Sawin, Sukma and Nanto* case involving three peasants (Sawin, Sukma, and Nanto) who were charged for committing a crime against the national symbol. During a celebration of the victory of the local communities against the Indramayu Coal Power Plant in their lawsuit, those three peasants raised the national flag around their village, but on one

stopped the company's workers mining. He was sentenced to three years in prison by the Civil Court of Water and the Court of Appeal of Yogyakarta (Civil Court Decision No. 83/Pid.B/2011/PN.Wt and Court of Appeal Decision No.126/Pid.Sus/2011/PTY).

[75] The *Trisno Susilo* case in which Trisno Susilo was charged by Article 50 (3) of the 1999 Forestry Law concerning illegal forest occupation (Decision No. 17/Pidsus/2017/PN.BLN).

[76] Article 162 stipulates that '[e]very person who hinders or interferes with mining activities of a mining permit holder . . . shall be punished with a criminal imprisonment for a maximum of 1 (one) year or a fine of not more than Rp. 100,000,000 (one hundred million rupiah)'.

[77] District Court of Banyuwangi's Decision No.802/Pid.Sus/2020/PN.Byw.

occasion the police officers found that there were several flags waved upside down. Comparably, in the second case, during a demonstration against the reclamation of Benoa Bay, Bali, planned by the Tirta Wahana Bali International (TWBI), a company owned by Tommy Winata, a powerful Indonesian tycoon, protesters from the Balinese Forum against Reclamation (ForBali), including Dharmawijaya and Joniantara, lowered the national flag at the Regional House of People's Representative and raised it up again with ForBali's flag below it. As in the Sawin, Sukma, and Nanto case, Dharmawijaya and Joniantara were also accused of committing a crime against the national symbol by desecrating the national flag.[78] In the third case, Mansur Pasang with three other fishermen in South Sulawesi were accused of desecrating the national currency after defacing money given to them by dredging companies – the Banteng Laut and the Bongkalis International Indonesia, a subsidiary of Dutch-based Royal Bongkalis Westminster – to pay them off in order to stop their rejection of the Makassar New Port development within local fishermen's fishing waters.[79] Putting those together, as evidenced by the *Budi Pego* case, these types of crimes can be seen as the most dangerous weapon utilised by lawfare mongers against environmental defenders not only in terms of their sanctions but also their effectiveness in 'othering' environmental defenders as dangerous, communist, or un-patriotic citizens to justify their punishment.

Regarding the types of criminal offences used to silence environmental defenders, Thailand has a relatively specific feature compared to Indonesia and the Philippines. In Thailand, the dominant offence is criminal defamation, as shown in Figure 4.5. Here, criminal defamation can be based on either Thai Penal Code (Sections 326 and 328) or the 2007 Computer Crimes Act (especially Section 14[80]) if defamation

[78] For a detailed discussion on both cases, see Agung Wardana, 'The Risk of Protecting the Environment: Strategic Litigation against Public Participation (SLAPP) in Post-Authoritarian Indonesia', (2021) 22 *Policy Matters* 44; Agung Wardana, 'Legal Engineering in a Contest over Space in Bali', (2018) 19 *Australian Journal of Asian Law* 1; Agung Wardana, *Contemporary Bali: Contested Space and Governance* (Palgrave Macmillan, 2019).

[79] Basten Gokkon and Wahyu Chandra, 'Indonesian Fishers Opposed on Dredging Project Hit by "Criminalization" Bid', *Mongabay* (Jakarta, 28 August 2020) <https://news.mongabay.com/2020/08/indonesian-fishers-opposed-to-dredging-project-hit-by-criminalization-bid/#:~:text=Indonesian%20fishers%20opposed%20to%20dredging%20project%20hit%20by%20'criminalization'%20bid,-by%20Basten%20Gokkon&text=Police%20have%20arrested%20four%20fishermen,port%20in%20Makassar%2C%20eastern%20Indonesia> accessed 2 February 2022.

[80] Section 14 of the 2007 CCA stipulates: 'Any person who commits any of the following crimes shall be liable to imprisonment for not more than five years, or a fine of not exceeding one hundred thousand baht, or both: (1) dishonestly or deceitfully bringing into a computer system computer data which is distorted or forged, either in whole or in part, or computer data which is false, in such a manner likely to cause injury to the public but not constituting a crime of defamation under the Penal Code; (2) bringing into a computer system computer data which is false, in such a manner likely to cause damage to the public maintenance of national security, public safety, national economic security, or infrastructure for the common good of the Nation, or to cause panic amongst the public; (3) bringing into a computer system computer data which constitutes a crime concerning security of the Kingdom or crime concerning terrorism under the Penal Code; (4) bringing into a computer system whatever computer data with vulgar characteristics, when such computer data is capable of being accessed by the general public; (5) publishing or forwarding computer data, with the knowledge that it is the computer data under (1), (2), (3), or (4).'

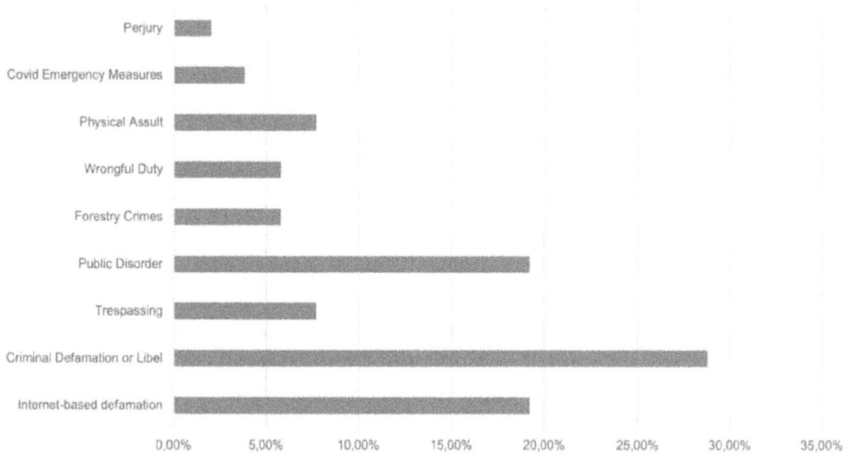

Figure 4.5 Criminal weapons in Thailand.

was committed through information technology. In several cases, such as the *Somluck* case[81] and the *Wirada Saelim & Thai PBS and others* case,[82] both the Penal Code and the Computer Crimes Act were used in combination. As Streckfuss characterised it, criminal defamation is a 'discursive crime' in the sense that it does not aim to prove whether a statement or opinion expressed by an accusant is true; rather, it focuses on establishing evidence of his/her 'intent or motive' to injure another person's reputation.[83] In terms of its proceeding, according to the Code of Criminal Procedure, criminal defamation may be brought to courts either through the public prosecutor or the injured party.[84] Consistent with the finding of Thailand's Human Rights Lawyers Association[85] in the context of lawfare against human rights defenders in general, legal intimidation utilising criminal defamation against environmental defenders is also predominantly pursued through the public

[81] In this case, Somluck Hutanuwart was accused of committing defamation against the Akaara Resources Company, a mining company, after sharing a press conference from the company with a caption stating that '[t]he evil of wicked capitalist is the lack of conscience of nation, religion and monarchy'. The company filed a lawsuit against her based on defamation, insult, and computer-related crimes to the Pichit Provincial Court. Maysa Zorob (n 10).

[82] In this case, ThaiPBS station and its personnel were accused of committing defamation by the Tung Kham mining company after broadcasting a citizen journalism report on the impacts of the mining activities operated by the company in Wangsapung District, Loei Province, to the Criminal Court. In addition, the company also reported Wanpen, a grade 10 student who was the narrator of the report, to the Juvenile Court in Loei. 'Tung Kham Company Sued Youth Journalist and Thai PBS', (*iLAW Freedom*, n.d.) <https://freedom.ilaw.or.th/en/case/706#detail> accessed on 31 January 2023.

[83] David Streckfuss, *Truth on Trial in Thailand: Defamation, Treason, and Lese-Majeste* (Routledge, 2011) 51.

[84] Human Rights Lawyers Association (n 7) 11.

[85] ibid.

prosecutor. Hence, this demonstrates the active role of the state, through the public prosecutor, in intimidating environmental defenders even in criminal defamation.

Following criminal defamation, the second biggest offence used in Thailand relates to public disorder, namely disorderly or unlawful assembly. This especially has taken place after the military coup in May 2014, followed by the enactment of the 2017 Constitution, the 2015 Public Assembly Act, and the Chief of the NCPO's Order No. 3/2558. The 2017 Constitution provides a constitutional basis for restraining the freedom for peaceful assembly 'for the purpose of maintaining security of the State, public safety, public order or good morals, or for protecting the rights or liberties of other persons'.[86] For this purpose, the military government enacted the 2015 Public Assembly Act and the Chief of the NCPO's Order No. 3/2558, which prohibited any unauthorised assembly of more than five persons. As the Act contained 'vague and ambiguous legal terminology', it gave authority to police officers to interpret it in its enforcement, including prohibiting any peaceful assembly, and to criminalise any person for violating the prohibition.[87] This charge, among others, was used against Ponthip Hongchai and six members of an anti-mining community of Khon Rak Ban Kerd (all of them women) for organising a public gathering of 150 persons from six villages in Wang Shapung district, Loei province, in front of a local government office in July 2017 to monitor a meeting which was scheduled to discuss the extension of the Thung Kham Company's gold mining concession to include villagers' agricultural land and forested areas.[88]

The other offences included encroaching on forest areas, Covid-19 emergency measures, and perjury. The punishment of the encroachment on forest areas has been pursued based on Military Government's Order 64/2014. This order has been weaponised, targeting Indigenous communities and ethnic minorities whose land overlaps with protected forest areas, especially from Karen Indigenous communities, who have inhabited forest areas for a very long time.[89] They are regarded as 'forest conservationists' due to their traditional values which see 'their lives as belonging to a holistic "mosaic" of forests, rivers, mountains, land, spiritual beings, people and animals'.[90] As part of the creation of the modern Thai state in which assuming control over forests and their resources was one of the important aspects, the Thai government undertook what Vandergeest calls 'territorial strategies' involving three stages: the first

[86] Article 44 of the 2017 Constitution of the Kingdom of Thailand.

[87] Thai Lawyers for Human Rights, et al., 'Situation of the Freedom of Peaceful Assembly in Thailand: Joint Submission to the UN Human Rights Committee for the Drafting of Its General Comment No. 37 on Article 21 (Right of Peaceful Assembly) of the ICCPR' (*OHCHR*, n.d.) <www.ohchr.org/sites/default/files/Documents/HRBodies/CCPR/GCArticle21/NGO_Thai_Civil_Society_Orgs__.docx>accessed on 31 January 2023.

[88] 'Prosecutor Indicts Isaan Anti-Mine Activists', *Prachatai English* (Bangkok, 26 Juli 2017) <https://prachataienglish.com/node/7293> accessed on 31 January 2023.

[89] Kongpob Areerat, 'Junta's Attempt to "Return Forest" Hurts the Poor', *Prachatai English* (Bangkok, 24 October 2014) <https://prachataienglish.com/node/4441> accessed on 09 February 2023.

[90] Maren Tomforde, 'The Global in the Local: Contested Resource-Use System of the Karen and Hmong in Northern Thailand', [2003] 34 *Journal of Southeast Asian Studies* 347, 353–354.

was undertaken by declaring 'all unoccupied land within the national boundaries' as 'state forest under the jurisdiction of the Royal Forestry Department'; the second stage was pursued by mapping forests 'into reserve and permanent forests, within which clearing and many other uses were prohibited'; and the third stage was through 'functional territorialization' – remapping the forests and other areas in accordance with 'scientific criteria such as slope, soil, type, and watershed classification' as the basis for 'prohibiting and prescribing specific activities in these areas'.[91] As a result, forested areas that have been inhabited by Karen Indigenous communities for centuries were mapped as reserved areas, creating a prolonged conflict between the communities and the Royal Forest Department.

Furthermore, during the Covid-19 pandemic, several environmental defenders were accused of breaching the Covid-19 emergency measures needed to protect public health. In 2021, for instance, thirty-six Chana villagers from the Songkhla province were arrested during a protest camp against the Chana industrial project that would severely affect their livelihood.[92] They were finally released by the police with one condition: 'they must not stage any activity of this kind again'.[93] In 2022, eleven people, including a seventeen-year-old Indigenous Karen girl who participated in a protest on land rights and community rights issues, was charged under the Covid-19 Emergency Decree.[94] Furthermore, the crime of perjury was used against Warapon Utairangsee, a legal attorney for the Bang Kloi Indigenous community. She was intimidated after filing a complaint against Chaiwat Limlikhitaksorn, a former official of Kaeng Krachan National Park, for burning down houses and rice barns owned by the Indigenous community that claimed to be located within the national park. Limlikhitaksorn argued that 'it was perjury because the houses that were burned down were unoccupied and that the burning did not take place' on the dates reported by Warapon.[95]

During legal proceedings, in responding to the plaintiff or public prosecutors' pleadings, like Indonesia and the Philippines, defendants mostly relied on constitutional rights as the legal basis for their work or advocacy. Those rights include the freedom of expression, the right to peaceful assembly and association, as well as the right to a healthy environment. In the *Watson* and the *Tungkum* cases, for instance, Section 4 of the 2014 Constitution[96] was argued as a defence by the defendants who

[91] Peter Vandergeest, 'Mapping Nature: Territorialization of Forest Rights in Thailand', (1996) 9 *Society and Natural Sources: An International Journal* 159, 160–161.

[92] 'Villagers Arrested for Protesting Industrial Zone, Ordered Not to Protest Again', *Prachatai English* (Bangkok, 8 December 2021) <https://prachataienglish.com/node/9597> accessed on 31 January 2023.

[93] ibid.

[94] '11 Activists Charged with Emergency Decree Violations for P-Move Protests', *Prachatai English* (Bangkok, 15 February 2022) <https://prachatai.com/english/node/9697> accessed on 31 January 2023.

[95] 'Former National Park Head Files Perjury Complaint against Human Rights Lawyer', *Prachatai English* (Bangkok, 3 September 2022) <https://prachatai.com/english/node/9993> accessed on 31 January 2023.

[96] Section 4 of the 2014 Constitution stipulates that 'Subject to the provisions of this Constitution, all human dignity, rights, liberties and equality of the people protected by the constitutional convention under a democratic regime of government with the King as the Head of State, and by international obligations bound by Thailand, shall be protected and upheld by this Constitution.'

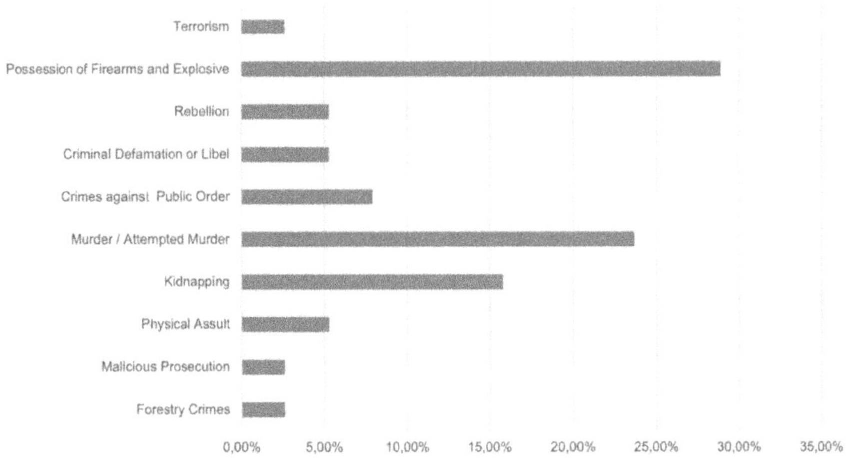

Figure 4.6 Criminal weapons in the Philippines.

were merely exercising their rights to freedom of expression, including the freedom of speech.[97] Particularly when charged with civil or criminal defamation, the defendants should be able to prove that their exercise of freedom of expression is a 'matter of public interest' pursuant to a 2018 court precedent. Accordingly, this gives an authority to judges based on their discretion to determine whether the defendants' claims fulfil the public interest test.[98]

In the Philippines, specifically on the use of criminal procedures to silence environmental defenders, criminal offences have been used dominantly (Figure 4.6). The first offence was the Illegal Possession of Firearms and Explosives, which is stipulated in the Philippine Republic Act (RA) No. 9516, which states that

> [t]he penalty of *reclusion perpetua* shall be imposed upon any person who shall willfully and unlawfully manufacture, assemble, deal in, acquire, dispose, import or possess any explosive or incendiary device, with knowledge of its existence and its explosive or incendiary character, where the explosive or incendiary device is capable of producing destructive effects on contiguous objects or causing injury or death to any person, including but not limited to, hand grenade(s), rifle grenade(s), 'pillbox bomb', 'molotov cocktail bomb', 'fire bomb', and other similar explosive and incendiary devices.

The illegal possession of firearms and explosives contributes up to 29 per cent of the total criminal cases leading to arrest and detention of environmental defenders. They

[97] Maysa Zorob (n 10) 20. [98] ibid, 21.

include the *Roger Gonzales* case[99] and the *Jomorito Goaynon & Irene Ubarde* case.[100] This type of criminal offence is very often a trumped-up charge in which guns or explosives were planted by the military force or state security agencies in the house of targeted environmental defenders before or during a raid. In addition, this crime can only make sense when it is put in a wider context of the state campaign and propaganda to fight against communist insurgency. Here, 'red-tagging' and 'terror-tagging' come into the picture. 'Red-tagging' or 'terror-tagging' is the politics of accusing environmental defenders or organisations of belonging to a rebel, communist, or terrorist group.[101] Jomorito Goaynon, for instance, has been tagged as a 'top leader of the [communist] New People's Army' from which repressions against him have been justified repeatedly.[102] As Cahiles puts it, '[r]ed-tagging is more than just a label. It has been proven to be a death sentence in several instances where activists were killed after being labelled as terrorists [or communists] by the military.'[103]

In other instances, the label of being a communist or terrorist has provided a justification for conducting a house search or issuing an arrest warrant against the labelled defenders. This has been experienced by five environmental defenders in Tacloban, who were suspected of being supporters of the Communist Party of Philippine (New People's Army), and were arrested when, following a series of raids, the authority (police) confiscated pistols, live ammunition, two grenades, and a flag of the New People's Army.[104] The environmental defenders – Franchie Mae Cumpio, Alexander Abinguna, Marielle Domequil, Mira Legion, and Marrisa Cabaljao – were charged under the Comprehensive Firearms and Ammunition Regulation Act (RA 10591).[105] A similar case was also experienced by environmental defenders in Calaca, Batangas. In this *Leovino Julangbayan and others* case, six farmers[106] who had been struggling against plantations owned by a local landlord

[99] Roger Gonzales is a farmer and council member of the *Nagkahiusang Mag-uuma sa Agusan del Sur-Kilusang Magbubukid ng Pilipinas* (NAMASUR-KMP). In February 2018, he was arrested by the Special Weapons and Tactics Team (SWAT) and Provincial Public Safety Battalion accusing him of possessing a caliber .357 gun. The family believed that the gun was planted by the officials during the raid on his house due to his activities in advocating land rights for the local farmers.

[100] Jomorito Goaynon and Irene Ubarde are two peasant leaders belonging to the Kalumbay Lumad Organization who have been involved in struggles against militarisation, mining, and plantation plunder in Northern Mindanao. In January 2018, they were arrested for illegal possession of firearms and explosives. Even though the charge was dismissed due to the lack of substantive merit, Goaynon has remained in detention for other charges, including robbery, kidnapping, and arson.

[101] Jordan Fronda, Marian Grafil and Leon Dulce, *Environmental Defenders in the Time of Covid-19* (Center for Environmental Concerns Philippines, 2020) 22.

[102] Ken Cagula, 'Detained Higaonon Leader among Petitioners vs Anti-Terror Law', *Davao Today* (Davao, 11 August 2020) <https://davaotoday.com/politics/detained-higaonon-leader-among-petitioners-vs-anti-terror-law/> accessed 17 April 2023.

[103] Weng Cahiles, 'Grim Regime: Unceasing Killings Despite the Pandemic', in T. Lopez (ed.), *Reclaiming the Narrative: The Struggles of Environment Defenders in Five Countries in Southeast Asia* (APNED & CEC, 2021) 71.

[104] Fronda, Grafil and Dulce (n 101) 17. [105] Ibid.

[106] Leovino Julongbayan, Virgilio Vidal, Doroteo Bautista, Agaton Bautista, July Julongbayan, and Roilan Tenorio. See Justin Umali, 'Charges vs. 6 Calaca Farmers Dismissed', *Bulatlat* (Manila, 28 July 2020). <www.bulatlat.com/2020/07/28/charges-vs-6-calaca-farmers-dismissed/> accessed 17 April 2023.

were arrested by the SWAT and the Criminal Investigation and Detention Group (CIDG).[107] They were accused of being members of the New People's Army, which provided a ground for their arrest warrants and search of their houses. In the search, the SWAT and CIDG found illegal possession of firearms and explosives. However, the farmers denied they belonged to them and believed the items were planted to charge them through the criminal procedure.[108]

Malicious prosecution has been another weapon in the Philippines as in the *Gloria Estenzo-Ramos* case, involving the Governor of Cebu, Gwendolyn Garcia, against Gloria Estenzo-Ramos, a prominent Cebu environmental lawyer. In 2012, Attorney Gloria Ramos, together with several Cordova fisherfolks, opposed the Cordova Reclamation project by filing a complaint to the ombudsman against Governor Garcia, the Mayor of Cordova, Adelino Sitoy, and other government officials for their failure in protecting the environment of Cordova. However, the complaint was dismissed by the ombudsman, and, in revenge, Governor Garcia filed a criminal charge against Attorney Ramos on the grounds of 'malicious prosecution' stipulated by Section 35 of the 1999 Ombudsman Act (RA 6770).[109] The section states that '[a]ny person who, actuated by malice or gross bad faith, files a completely unwarranted or false complaint against any government official or employee shall be subject to a penalty of one (1) month and one (1) day to six (6) months imprisonment and a fine not exceeding five thousand pesos (P5,000.00)'. However, although Atty. Ramos used the anti-SLAPP provision in the Rules of Procedure in her defence, the case has not been resolved for years. As she puts it, '[y]et it is another case for possible violation of the accused's right to due process of law and a speedy disposition of the case, as well as a period required by the Supreme Court in hearing defense of SLAPP specifically provided under the Rules of Procedure for Environmental Cases and two laws, RA 9003 and RA 8749'.[110]

In brief, from the geographical and weaponry dimensions, the criminal justice system has been predominantly used as a weapon of lawfare in Indonesia, Thailand, and the Philippines. It is preferable because it provides several advantages. First, the use of the criminal justice system may avoid a direct legal battle between corporations and environmental movements because the legal proceeding is taken by the state apparatus, namely law enforcement officials, under the cloak of enforcing criminal law or law and order. Second, unlike in civil proceeding where a corporation as a plaintiff must pay the legal proceeding fees and hire legal

[107] Fronda, Grafil and Dulce (n 101) 16. [108] ibid.

[109] Candeze Mongaya and Manuel Tan, 'Ecology Lawyer Calls Gwen Case a SLAPP', *Cebu Daily News* (Cebu, 16 March 2012) <https://cebudailynews.wordpress.com/2012/03/16/ecology-lawyer-calls-gwen-case-a-slapp/> accessed 17 May 2022.

[110] Gloria Estenzo Ramos, 'The Right to Public Participation in Decision-Making in the Implementation of Fisheries and other Environmental Laws in the Philippines', Green Access Discussion Paper DP-2015–2008 (International Workshop on Participation Principle Indicators under the Environmental Law: Towards Establishing International Collaboration in Pursuit of Environmental Justice, Osaka, March 2005) 20.

attorneys to represent its case, the criminal law is fully 'subsidised' by the state budget; hence, it is cost-efficient from an economic viewpoint. This is not to mention the impacts of the criminal proceeding on environmental defenders in terms of negative labelling that may significantly delegitimise their movements, as shown in Chapter 5.

The dominant use of the criminal justice system also demonstrates the dynamics of 'overcriminalisation' and 'under-criminalisation' in hegemonic environmental lawfare in Southeast Asia. In this view, popular struggles to defend livelihoods and the environment that are very often exercised by environmental defenders as the last resort because of unresponsiveness of the formal institutional channels to address their concerns have been over-criminalised either through the existing criminal offences or through a new formulation of crimes such as the prohibition of peaceful assembly during the Covid-19 pandemic as a tactic; meanwhile, extractive industries that produce social and environmental harms and conflicts to affected communities are under-criminalised.[111] Even during the pandemic, those industries, namely in the mining sector as well as the forestry and plantation sector, that contributed the highest numbers of attacks against environmental defenders have been given incentives by the governments, such as the relaxation of taxes and royalties, and encouraged to expand further in order to boost the slowing economic growth due to Covid-19.[112] Hence, hegemonic environmental lawfare is less about legal merit and more about a political-economic strategy in which the power-holders, the state and corporations whose business-as-usual model of capital accumulation has been disrupted by environmental movements, mobilise the legal system in order to silence the movements as well as to maintain a conducive social order for further expansion.

Whichever jurisdictions and weapons the lawfare mongers use, they share a tactical feature in common. They aim at creating a chilling effect on environmental defenders through excessive demands or overcharges. This has been evidenced by the amount of compensation demanded by the plaintiffs in civil cases, or by the terms in prison, or the amount of fines charged by the public prosecutors in criminal cases. The excessive demands confirm a distinct character of SLAPP cases, as suggested by Pring and Canan, in which they demand unreasonable amounts of compensation from defendants.[113] Even though winning the case is not the primary intention of the lawfare mongers, the excessive demands and overcharges are expected to give a shock therapy to targeted environmental

[111] Valeria Vegh Weis, 'Introduction', in V. Vegh Weis (ed.), *Criminalization of Activism: Historical, Present, and Future Perspectives* (Routledge, 2022) 3–4.

[112] See Agung Wardana, 'The Indonesian Paradox in the Anthropocene', (2022) 24 *Asia Pacific Journal of Environmental Law* 230; Louse M. Simeon, 'Mining Sector to Help Economy Recover', *The Philippine Star* (Manila, 4 January 2021) <www.philstar.com/business/2021/01/04/2067921/mining-sector-help-economy-recover> accessed 25 April 2023.

[113] George W. Pring and Penelope Canan, *SLAPPs: Getting Sued for Speaking Out* (Temple University Press, 1996)

defenders as defendants in lawfare. Thus, in the next chapter, the third dimension of lawfare – externalities – will be examined in order to find out the outcome of hegemonic environmental lawfare in Indonesia, Thailand, and the Philippines, and consequences intended to be borne by environmental movements in general beyond the actual lawfare cases.

CHAPTER 5

Externalities of Lawfare

I talk with communities who pretend to be strong enough to fight the cases [brought against them], but when we talk deeply with them, they are also worried about their cases. They are also worried that they may be shot . . . they may be punished in jail.

– Sor, a Thai public interest lawyer[1]

Geographies and weaponry as the first and second dimensions of hegemonic environmental lawfare have been discussed in previous chapters. They demonstrate how environmental defenders in Indonesia, Thailand, and the Philippines are attacked through legal means, predominantly utilising the criminal justice system, especially in resource-rich or industrial-centred regions. The state has been the dominant actor in intimidating defenders utilising charges of crimes against public order, illegal possessions of arms and explosives, and criminal defamation. In this chapter, lawfare's third strategic dimension, namely externalities, will be discussed to reveal the outcomes of lawfare against environmental defenders and how those outcomes are projected to the wider audience in order to warn the public on what might be the consequences of joining environmental struggles.

Politically, hegemonic environmental lawfare falls within the 'seeing like a state'[2] logic, designed to provide the ability of the state and other powerful groups to understand the complex nature of environmental struggles and control them through simplification using the individualisation tactic and categorisation based on the matrix of legitimate/illegitimate exercise of rights. Individualisation is

[1] Interview with Sor, a public interest lawyer in Thailand, on 9 November 2022.

[2] James C. Scott, *Seeing Like a State: How Certain Schemes to Improve the Human Condition Have Failed, Revised Edition* (Yale University Press, 1999).

undertaken by apportioning responsibility for collective action onto one or more individuals regarded as 'leaders' of the movements. Once leaders are identified, the movement, through its leaders, is subject to control, diversion, and intimidation. Furthermore, as a strategic mode of legal action, hegemonic environmental lawfare aims to create externalities, referring to consequences that go beyond the legal cases that targeted individuals are forced to contend with. These consequences are intended to be borne not only by individuals directly through legal proceedings but also by groups involved in environmental resistance in general. Externalities use at least two interrelated tactics to achieve this purpose: (1) the leadership decapitation tactic and (2) the projecting tactic. Leadership decapitation is a tactical method commonly used in counter-insurgency or counterterrorism measures through which leaders or essential figures within the insurgency or terrorism groups are removed from their group by capturing or murdering them.[3] It has increasingly been used in socio-environmental conflicts, demonstrated by attacks targeting communities' leaders who have been at the forefront of resistance against extractivism.[4] Meanwhile, the projecting tactic aims to control the population so that the maintenance and preservation of the existing social order 'rooted in the "securing" of property, hierarchy, and human-nature exploitation' on which the expansion of extractivism may rely are made possible.[5]

This chapter is structured as follows: the first section is devoted to discussing how the decapitation tactic is employed by state officials and corporations, as a form of externalities of HEL used against environmental defenders in Indonesia, Thailand, and the Philippines. The second section looks at how the externalities are created through the use of the projecting tactic. Here it stresses the significance of hegemonic environmental lawfare as a technology of power used to maintain the status quo in society.

Leadership Decapitation

The Outcomes of the Civil Procedures

In the context of the leadership decapitation tactic, civil and criminal proceedings have been two dominant avenues for intimidating central figures in environmental resistance in Southeast Asia. However, using these procedures as hegemonic environmental lawfare has led to different outcomes. As in the US and Canada, the outcomes of legal actions utilising civil proceedings in Indonesia, Thailand, and the

[3] Patrick Johnson, 'Does Decapitation Work? Assessing the Effectiveness of Leadership Targeting in Counter-insurgency Campaigns', (2012) 26 (4) *International Security* 47.

[4] Andrea Brock and Nathan Stephens-Griffin, 'Policing Environmental Justice', (2021) IDS Bulletin, Online First, https://doi.org/10.19088/1968-2021.130. <https://opendocs.ids.ac.uk/opendocs/handle/20.500.12413/16915> accessed 24 April 2023.

[5] ibid., 3.

Philippines are relatively unsuccessful. In the US, the rate of dismissal is 80 per cent,[6] and in Canada, almost all SLAPP lawsuits are dismissed by the court because they do not have substantive merit.[7] In Indonesia, the rate of dismissal for legal actions utilising civil proceedings is similar to that of Canada, in which, following the adoption of the anti-SLAPP provision in Article 66 of the 2009 Environmental Protection and Management Act, almost all civil lawsuits aimed at intimidating environmental defenders were rejected by the court, even though the defendants did not use the provision in their defence. In the case of Thailand, in relation to the outcomes of the proceedings, the results are more mixed. In the analysis of civil procedure cases, it is found that the court dismissed 40 per cent, while 40 per cent were withdrawn, 10 per cent were approved, and 10 per cent remain pending. In the Philippines, the outcomes of civil proceedings were 66.67 per cent dismissed and 33.33 per cent accepted.

The Outcomes of the Criminal Procedures

In contrast to using civil procedures, the use of the criminal proceedings in these three countries has been comparatively successful in creating chilling effects for environmental defenders through court decisions and/or lengthy legal proceedings. In Indonesia, in only 10 per cent of criminal charges did the court consider the defendants to be 'not guilty' either by acquittal (when the charge is not proven (*vrijspraak*)) or by discharge (when the offence is proven but it is not punishable (*ontslag van alle rechtsvervolging*))[8]. The *Robandi and Others* case should be considered a landmark case in this context. The public prosecutor charged Robandi and five neighbourhood leaders with committing the crime of forgery. They were the head of six neighbourhood units fighting against pollution by Bangka Asindo Agri (BAA), a processing company for tapioca flour situated close to their neighbourhoods. During the Covid-19 pandemic, the company backed by the local government conducted a corporate social responsibility programme that involved distributing food within the village, including the six neighbourhoods. However, Robandi, a neighbourhood head, and five other neighbourhood heads surrounding the company refused to participate in the programme, as they considered it to be the company's strategy to divide villagers, and they decided to resign from their positions. The day after their resignation, they signed an invitation letter to villagers to attend a preparatory meeting for filing a class action lawsuit against the company. They were then reported to the police under the accusation that they were acting as the head of the neighbourhood by signing the letter. However, as they had resigned,

[6] George W. Pring and Penelope Canan, *SLAPPs: Getting Sued for Speaking Out* (Temple University Press, 1996)

[7] Fiona Donson, *Legal Intimidation* (Free Association Press, 2000).

[8] Erik Gritter, 'The Netherlands', in A. Reed & M. Bohlander with N. Wake & E. Smith (eds.), *General Defences in Criminal Law: Domestic and Comparative Perspective* (Ashgate, 2014) 256.

Robandi and the others, including Heti, who was pregnant, were arrested and placed in custody.

In the court, despite using the anti-SLAPP provision in their defence, the District Court of Sungailiat found them guilty of forgery and sentenced them to a month in prison. On appeal, however, the High Court of Bangka Belitung annulled the previous decision and decided to discharge the defendants because they were acting to protect their right to a good and healthy environment.[9] In its deliberation, the court considered that

> the actions of the defendants who affixed the signature and seal of the neighbourhood association on the letter presented by the witness . . . when the defendants had already resigned as the head of the neighbourhood association . . . is an act that has fulfilled the elements of the first and second articles of the indictment of the public prosecutor, but the actions of the defendants were solely to invite participation of the community in the public interest for the effects of pollution in the form of odour caused by the production activities of the BAA company, so the defendants should be released from all criminal charges.

Thus, unlike other criminal proceedings analysed in this book, in which judges used a narrow conception of causality, in the *Robandi and Others* case the judges rely on the legal maxim of *conditio sine qua non* in constructing the causality argument by looking at the broader context within which the offence was committed. In early 2023, defendants in the *Alas Buluh* case, Abdullah, Sugiyanto, and Achmad Busiin, who were sentenced for three months in prison for disrupting mining operations by the district and high courts, eventually in the cassation appeal were acquitted by the Supreme Court based on the anti-SLAPP provision stipulated in Article 66 of the 2009 EPM Law. For some, these decisions were seen as a sign of hope for protecting environmental defenders in Indonesia.[10] Others, however, viewed this as an anomaly within the overriding formalistic mode of legal reasoning used by Indonesian judges in which they tend to treat a SLAPP case as a purely criminal case by isolating it from the socio-environmental conflicts in which they emerge.[11]

In general, the facts show that 62.80 per cent of the criminal charges brought against environmental defenders resulted in guilty convictions for the defendants. Sentences ranged from three months to four years in prison. A more severe punishment was given to defenders who were accused of committing crimes against the state's ideology and symbols (in the *Budi Pego* case) and incitements against the legitimate government (in the *Eva Bande* case[12]), in which defendants in both cases

[9] *Robandi and Others case* [2021] Court of Appeal of Bangka Belitung Decision No.21/PID/2021/PT BBL.

[10] Hans N. Jong, 'Acquittal of Indonesian Villagers Protesting Pollution Marks Rare Win Against SLAPP', Mongabay (2 August 2021). <https://news.mongabay.com/2021/08/acquittal-of-indonesian-villagers-protesting-pollution-marks-rare-win-against-slapp-bangka-asindo-agri/> accessed 6 December 2023.

[11] Agung Wardana, 'The Risk of Protecting the Environment: Strategic Litigation against Public Participation (SLAPP) in Post-Authoritarian Indonesia', (2021) 22 (1) *Policy Matters* 44.

[12] The *Eva Bande* case involved a female agrarian activist from the Consortium of Agrarian Reform advocating for local farmers in Luwuk, Central Sulawesi Province. She was charged under Article 160 of the

were convicted to four years in prison. In 1.40 per cent of the cases, the defendant, a foreign journalist, was deported as he was accused of violating the immigration law in reporting on deforestation and forest fires in Indonesia.[13] Two local environmental defenders died in police custody. They were Hermanus in Central Kalimantan, fighting against the Hamparan Masawit Bangun Persada, a palm oil plantation company,[14] and Muhammad Yusuf, a journalist accused of online criminal defamation after reporting on Multi Sarana Agro Mandiri, a palm oil plantation company owned by a local tycoon, Syamsuddin Arsyad.[15]

In Thailand, the courts found that the 15.4 per cent of defendants charged were guilty, while another 21.2 per cent of cases were withdrawn. Furthermore, 32.7 per cent of cases were dismissed by the courts, notably when the defendants were charged with criminal defamation. In dismissing criminal defamation charges, the courts resorted to the exemption from defamation clauses in the Criminal Code, namely Sections 329 and 330. Section 329 stipulates that an opinion or statement expressed in good faith to protect the public interests shall not be regarded as defamation. In addition, Section 330 stipulates that in a defamation case, if the opinion or statement expressed by the defendant is proven to be true, the defendant shall not be punished.

The utilisation of these sections is well demonstrated in the *Wirada Saelim & Thai PBS and others* case. Here, the court of the first instance in Loei province dismissed the charge of criminal defamation according to Section 329 of the Thai Criminal Code, stating that the defendants were acting and presenting an issue of criticism on the impacts of mining operations by the company in good faith; hence, their conduct should not be considered to constitute defamation.[16] In addition, there is also the case *Government of Thailand & Chaiwat Limlikhitaksorn* v. *Wuth Boonlert & Samak Donnapee* concerning criminal defamation. In this case Chaiwat Limlikhitaksorn, a Superintendent of Kaeng Krachan National Park, brought a private criminal defamation charge against Samak Donnapee, a retired national

Criminal Code with incitement during a mass demonstration against land occupation by the Kurnia Luwuk Sejati, a palm oil plantation company, and its subsidiary, the Berkat Hutan Pusaka (Supreme Court Decision No. 1573 K/PID/2011).

[13] In this case, Philip Jacobson, a journalist of the Mongabay, was accused of violating the Immigration Act by using his business visa to conduct an investigative report on environmental and Indigenous peoples in Central Kalimantan. After being detained for forty-two days, he was finally deported by the Government of Indonesia. Amy Gunai, 'American Environmental Journalist Deported from Indonesia after Prolonged Detention', *Time* (New York, 31 January 2020) <https://time.com/5773581/philip-jacobson-mongabay-indonesia-deported/> accessed 9 February 2022.

[14] Hermanus was suspected of committing a plantation crime on illegal cropping within the company's area. Hans Nicholas Jong, 'Farmer Dies in Custody after Being Charged in Dispute with Palm Oil Firm, Prompting Covid-19 Fears', *Mongabay* (Jakarta, 28 April 2020) <https://news.mongabay.com/2020/04/indigenous-farmer-dies-after-being-charged-with-stealing-from-his-own-land/> accessed 9 February 2022.

[15] Novi Abdi, 'South Kalimantan Journalist Dies While Being Detained on Defamation Charges', *The Jakarta Post* (Jakarta, 12 June 2018) <www.thejakartapost.com/news/2018/06/12/south-kalimantan-journalist-dies-while-being-detained-on-defamation-charges.html> accessed 9 February 2022.

[16] Orapin Lilitwisitwong and Thitiphan Pattanamongkol (eds.), *SLAPP: The Public Dreams of Anti-strategic Lawsuit against Public Participation* (Thai Society of Environmental Journalists, 2022) 34–37.

park officer, and Wuth Boonlert, a human rights advocate for the Karen Indigenous community. In 2016, Samak Donnapee, wrote three posts on his Facebook page on the encroachment of forests, including a resort within a national park owned by Pairote Limlikhitaksorn (a bother of Chiwat Limlikhitaksorn), and one of his posts was shared by Wuth Boonlert. As a response, Chaiwat Limlikhitaksorn claimed that the posts were intended to defame his reputation despite the fact that Samak Donnapee's Facebook posts did not mention his name whatsoever. Eventually, in 2019, the Min Buri Criminal Court (Bangkok) decided to dismiss the charge because it appeared to be in bad faith or politically motivated.[17]

In several cases, the dismissal of defamation cases in the court is based on the fact that the injured parties failed to prove how the defendant's conduct had caused actual harm to them.[18] It can be seen, among others, in *Peerapol Mining Co. Ltd.* v. *Nine members of Khao Khuha Community Rights Network (KKCRN).* Such a failure allowed the defendants to file a counter-lawsuit against the SLAPP filers. During the proceedings in *Peerapol Mining Co. Ltd.* v. *Nine members of Khao Khuha Community Rights Network (KKCRN)*, for instance, a counter-lawsuit was filed by the defendants (members of the KKCRN) against the company. In its decision, the Supreme Court favoured the counter-lawsuit that the defendants were exercising their right to protest. Because the company brought the lawsuit in bad faith, the court ordered it to compensate the defendants for their losses of 60,000 Thai Baht (US$1,700). However, the company has never paid compensation to the defendants.[19]

In the Philippines, 50 per cent of criminal proceeding cases brought against defenders in court found defendants 'not guilty', or they were acquitted. Cases dismissed include the *Leovino Julangbayan and others* case, where the court dismissed charges against defenders during the trial because the search conducted by police was declared invalid due to the lack of 'probable cause for the issuance of search warrants'.[20] Another case of acquittal was in the *Dipio Earth Savers Multipurpose Association* case. Here nine Indigenous peoples of Ifugaos, who were opponents of a large-scale mining project in their village of Barranggay Didipio, were charged with 'illegal forest occupation' under Section 969 of the Presidential Decree 705 of the Revised Forestry Code. After two years of proceedings, the Municipal Trial Court of Kasibu decided that the defendants be acquitted

[17] Lionel Blackman, *Government of Thailand & Chaiwat Limlikhitaksorn v. Wuth Boonlert & Samak Donnapee* (Columbia Law School, 2020).

[18] Maysa Zorob, *Defending Defenders: Challenging Malicious Lawsuits in Southeast Asia* (Business and Human Rights Resource Centre, 2020) 22.

[19] Community Resource Centre Foundation, et al., 'Thailand: Stop Judicial Harassment of Human Rights Defenders, A Joint Statement', *Fortify Rights* (2016) <www.fortifyrights.org/tha-inv-2016-05-09/> accessed 31 January 2023; Maysa Zorob. (n 17) 23.

[20] Jordan Fronda, Marian Grafil and Leon Dulce, *Environmental Defenders in the Time of Covid-19* (Center for Environmental Concerns Philippines, 2020) 16; Justin Umali, 'Charges vs. 6 Calaca Farmers Dismissed', *Bulatlat* (28 July 2020) <www.bulatlat.com/2020/07/28/charges-vs-6-calaca-farmers-dismissed/> accessed 17 April 2023.

of the charge under Rule 19 of the Rules of Procedure for Environmental Cases concerning anti-SLAPP provisions.[21] Similarly, Ronalando Martinez and twenty-nine other Sulamo farmers (twenty-two of them were women) were charged with presenting a grave threat to the company when they struggled against the Riverforest Development Corporation's plans to build an industrial area.[22] The court finally acquitted the defendants after four years of proceedings. Despite the outcome, the chilling effect has remained after the arrest and harassment of the defendants and a long process of proceedings.

Postponing the Proceedings

Another point of concern in the use of criminal procedures in silencing environmental defenders in these three countries is the prolonged process of court proceedings and decisions to put cases on hold (pending). Environmental defenders in Latin America share this concern, referring to it as 'a strategy . . . for . . . maintaining pressure on defendants for as long as possible.'[23] Approximately 22.8 per cent of criminal proceedings against defenders in Indonesia are 'on hold' (pending). In Thailand, it is 30.7 per cent, and in the Philippines 47.4 per cent of the criminal cases against environmental defenders examined remain pending. Commenting on the lengthy process of SLAPP legal proceedings in the Philippines, Rocky Guzman, an environmental law scholar and Deputy Director of the Asian Research Institute for Environmental Law, observes that

> [the legal proceeding] goes on and on, and that should not be the case if we look at the law because . . . SLAPP cases, or environmental cases in general, have a period [of time] when courts should decide. . . . But . . . this does not happen [in reality]. Why? Because there are so many cases in many courts, especially in the provinces, and . . . environmental cases are usually at the bottom [of priority]. Even if they set the prescription and the rules of procedures from the Supreme Court that they should do that within the period, they still do not do it . . . Another factor . . . the courts in the provinces . . . usually have special relationships with government officials. There are allowances given, [or] there may be special accommodation [by the government]. . . . It also happens with prosecutors. . . . They have this allowance from the local government, which has an impact on their impartiality on whether they should file cases or file information for the court, like for criminal cases.[24]

[21] Human Rights Online Philippines, 'SLAPP Suit against Ifugaos in Didipio, Dismissed', *Human Rights Online Philippines* (13 September 2011) <https://hronlineph.com/2011/09/13/press-release-slapp-suit-against-ifugaos-in-didipio-dismissed-lrcksk-org/> accessed 17 April 2023.

[22] Raphael Baladad, 'Land Enclosures versus Historical Occupancy: What Remedy Does Carper Offer', in C. Militante et.al (eds.), *Repormang Agraryo at Pagbabago: Narratives on Agrarian Conflicts, Transitions, and Transformation* (Focus on Global South, 2018), 54–70, 62–63.

[23] Angela Lindt, 'The Dark Side of Judicialization: Criminalizing Mining Protests in Peru', (2023) 58 *Latin America Research Review* 368, 377–378.

[24] Interview with Rocky Guzman, environmental activist and deputy director of the Asian Research Institute for Environmental Law, 29 September 2022.

A high percentage of cases pending (or on hold) is due to bail conditions or not being ready for court proceedings. Slow legal proceedings by courts in these countries were also impacted by the Covid-19 pandemic, where courts could not hear cases due to social distancing and 'lockdown' measures.[25] Some cases went online; however, they tended to be cases with high profile and public attention so were given priority, such as corruption. Postponing criminal proceedings by law enforcement officers is also a tactic in lawfare. This tactic serves at least three objectives. First, pending the proceedings without any time frame for determination may prolong the chilling effect experienced by environmental defenders as they live without any certainty as to how long they will be labelled criminal defendants. Second, pending cases are used as a blackmailing tactic to prevent targeted environmental defenders from continuing their resistance. Third, it aims to disrupt defenders' everyday lives. As Lindt observes,

> these delays often lead to great consternation among defendants because they result in a considerable loss of time and money. For people living on the margins of the state, this loss is often especially severe, which is related to the locality of the law. Courthouses are usually located in urban centers. . . . This results in [high] transportation costs and lost income for those who stayed away from their paid jobs, especially those working in agriculture or the informal sector. . . . Court hearings interrupt everyday life.[26]

The pending tactic above is evidenced by two pending cases in Indonesia. The first is the case of Trisno Susilo, a leader of the Indigenous communities of Meratus, South Kalimantan, who is against the expansion of logging companies' activities within their *adat* territory. In 2011, Trisno and several other community members were arrested by the local police department for allegedly occupying forest areas illegally, pursuant to Articles 50 and 78 of the 1999 Forestry Law. However, due to public pressure, the police released them without notice of halting the proceedings. Six years later, when the conflict between the Meratus Indigenous communities and the companies was escalating, the 2011 case was reopened and Trisna Susilo was re-arrested. This was despite the Constitutional Court declaration in 2014 that Articles 50 and 78 were found to be unconstitutional. The public prosecutor argued that the offence was conducted when the articles were still in effect and that the constitutional court decision was not retrospective.[27] Subsequently, Trisno Susilo was convicted, and the Batulicin District Court sentenced him to four years in prison.

The second is the *Petrus Kinggo* case in Papua. Kinggo, a local Papuan Indigenous leader who has been fighting against the encroachment on indigenous forests by the

[25] Interview with Sor, a public interest lawyer in Thailand, on 9 November 2022.

[26] Angela Lindt (n 22) 378.

[27] Indra Nugraha, 'Bela Masyarakat Meratus Trisno Terjerat Pasal Sudah Dicabut, Apa Kata Para Pakar?' *Mongabay Indonesia* (Jakarta, 13 April 2017) <www.mongabay.co.id/2017/04/13/bela-masyarakat-meratus-trisno-terjerat-pasal-sudah-dicabut-apa-kata-para-pakar/> accessed 2 February 2022.

Korindo plantation company, was accused of stealing a confiscated boat that had entered the Indigenous territory without permission. His case was put on hold by the local police department. Following this, in an unrelated event, four company supporters were searching for Petrus, and because they could not find him, they broke items of property belonging to Petrus's neighbours. The neighbours reported them to the police and the police attempted to conduct a mediation process to settle the case. The police pressured Petrus to ask his neighbours to revoke the report, otherwise the proceedings against him in the case of theft would proceed.[28] Petrus's neighbour eventually revoked the report.

In brief, the leadership decapitation tactic has different consequences for individual environmental defenders. The tactic, especially through imprisonment, may crush dissent but also may become a moment for self-reflection for a targeted leader who may foster his or her resilience to keep fighting once she or he is out of prison.[29] However, those consequences are borne differently depending on the defenders' socio-economic background. Their background can be identified as one of the main differences in the experience of lawfare against environmental defenders in the Global South and the Global North. In the Global North, environmentalism has been characterised as 'full-stomach activism' based on environmental consciousness in which environmental defenders tend to be educated, urban, middle-class activists. Environmental defenders from Extinction Rebellion in the UK or the *Letzte Generation* in Germany, for instance, whose forms of resistance very often employ civil disobedience, are aware of, and even calculate thoroughly, the consequences of their actions, including being criminally charged. Based on their personal capacity and organisational support, including legal services, they may anticipate how to handle the criminal charges against them and how to use the criminal proceeding as a performative action to attract public support for their causes while simultaneously revealing the repressive character of the state against its citizens, which is expected to undermine the state's legitimacy.[30]

In Southeast Asia, in general, environmental defenders who come from rural and lower-class backgrounds suffer more than those defenders whose backgrounds are from urban and middle-class socio-economic positions. Environmental defenders who are farmers or fishermen and the backbone of their families will find hegemonic environmental lawfare frightening both psychologically and economically. Sor, a Thai public interest lawyer who has served as a legal attorney for local communities and activists in many court cases, states that environmental defenders are suffering from the cases brought against them not only psychologically but also economically. She explains that 'they have to spend much money to come to court.

[28] Pusaka, *Laporan Ancaman Kepada Pembela HAM Lingkungan Papua Tahun 2020* (Yayasan Pusaka Bentala Rakyat, 2020) 5–8.

[29] Penny Green and Tony Ward, *State Crime and Civil Activism: On the Dialectics of Repression and Resistance* (Routledge, 2019).

[30] Oscar Berglund and Daniel Schmidt, *Extinction Rebellion and Climate Change Activism: Breaking the Law to Change the World* (Palgrave Macmillan, 2020).

And when they come to the court, they cannot work. Especially with grassroots people because they do not have a salary. They have a daily income so this is very difficult for them also.'[31] According to her estimation, every lawfare case in Thailand will require at least US$3,000 spent by the defendants during the court proceedings for expenses such as transportation, meals, and communication. This amount does not include the costs for the legal attorneys,[32] and the very significant difficulties environmental defenders face in accessing pro bono legal aid especially in remote areas should not be underestimated.

If environmental defenders are then convicted and sentenced to prison, their condition becomes even worse. They will be constantly concerned with their families and communities for whom they care,[33] because in their absence, they cannot feed and look after their families. The reality of prison conditions that convicted environmental defenders face in prisons in these countries can also have significant adverse effects on their physical and mental health. In Thailand, Arnon Nampha, a public interest lawyer who also served as an attorney against the controversial Thai-Malay gas pipeline case in Songkhla,[34] was convicted for violating the *lèse majesté* offence in Article 112 of the Thai Criminal Code and sentenced to four years in prison. In his letter from prison, he writes: 'I ask your permission to write letters to my two children. So that one day, once they grow up enough, they will be able to learn about their father. They will read letters that their father wrote to them while he was in prison. They will learn of my loving and longing and understand why we cannot be together.'[35] He also expresses his gratitude to everyone who helps his family while he is in prison, but also suggests: 'I will be even happier if you look after families of other political prisoners and help them get through this terrible time, too.'[36]

Environmental defenders and their families in Indonesia describe a similar experience. Boby, a fisherman from Pari Island, Indonesia, explained his experience when he was sentenced to seven months in prison after fighting against a resort development project on the island. He admits that it would have been tough for his family during his absence without the support from his community.[37] Great sorrow was also expressed by Nunung, the wife of Danang, who was sentenced to two years in prison for protesting pollution caused by the Rayon Utama Makmur company in his village. Her seven-year-old daughter asked her why her father had not come home for so long. She told her: 'Your father is in prison. But you don't need to be afraid, and you don't need to be ashamed. He is

[31] Interview with Sor, a public interest lawyer in Thailand, on 9 November 2022. [32] ibid.

[33] Angela Lindt (n 22) 377.

[34] For further discussion on the case, see Nopadol Burananuth, 'Conflict of the Thai-Malaysian Gas Pipeline Project', (2014) 8 (9) *International Journal of Information and Communication Engineering* 3175–3178.

[35] Arnon Nampha, *Letters from Prison: Volume 1, translated by Article 122 Project* (Justice in Translation, 2023) 25.

[36] ibid., 14. [37] Interview with Bobi, Pari Island, on 24 November 2023.

here fighting for the people. He is not a bad person. Your father defends the people.'[38] Hence, in a society where social welfare from the state, such as social safety net, education, and health services, are very weak, the risks environmental defenders face of being sent to prison put their families at risk as well. These examples demonstrate how environmental struggles in Southeast Asia bring issues of social class into the spotlight. Being jailed for defending the environment means being absent from daily productive work that environmental defenders need to pay for their children's education, health services, and the costs of everyday living. If defenders are jailed, the only support system available to look after their family is their community. At the same time their communities support them to keep alive their spirit to struggle for justice.

Moreover, prisons are often 'spaces in which the poor quality of food, high mould content in the ambient air and ventilation systems, and extreme heat and cold associated with climate change put the health and well-being of prisoners at risk'.[39] This condition is common in Indonesia, Thailand, and the Philippines, where prisons very often pose life-threatening conditions due to overcrowding and 'a high rate of deaths in custody' due to contagious diseases and harsh conditions.[40] Imprisonment 'produce[s] the logic of environmental injustice'[41] against environmental defenders in which their struggles for environmental justice were punished by sending them to prison – isolated spaces where environmental injustices are normalised. After serving their sentence, their future is also uncertain as their name has been socially maligned and publicly convicted of criminal acts. For environmental defenders in those countries, spending some of their lives in prison was never an intentional choice. Moreover, imprisonment distances an environmental defender from his or her support system that may lead to a feeling of despair because he or she bears the negative consequence of a collective action; in turn, this potentially creates a sense of the unfair distribution of burdens of the resistance, which may shrink trust needed to build a solid movement.[42]

[38] Haris Prabowo, 'Kisah Muram Keluarga Aktivis di Balik Kriminalisasi Limbah PT RUM', *Tirto* (Jakarta, 31 Maret 2020). <https://tirto.id/kisah-muram-keluarga-aktivis-di-balik-kriminalisasi-limbah-pt-rum-eJVD> accessed 6 December 2023.

[39] Erik Kojola and David Pellow, 'New Directions in Environmental Justice Studies: Examining the State and Violence', (2021) 30 *Environmental Politics* 100, 112.

[40] US Department of State, *2021 Country Reports on Human Rights Practice: Indonesia,*www.state.gov/reports/2021-country-reports-on-human-rights-practices/indonesia/> accessed 24 May 3023; Amnesty International, *Thailand: Widespread Abuses in the Administration of Justice* (Amnesty International, 2021) <www.amnesty.org/en/wp-content/uploads/2021/06/asa390032002en.pdf> accessed 24 May 2023, 12; Carlos Conde, 'Injustice and Misery in PH Jails', *Human Rights Watch* (8 March 2016) <www.hrw.org/news/2016/03/08/injustice-and-misery-ph-jails#:~:text=Many%20detention%20centers%20in%20the,ill%2Dtreatment%20are%20also%20common> Accessed 24 May 2023.

[41] Kojola and Pellow (n 38) 112.

[42] See Melissa Venegas and Karolien van Teijlingen, 'The Gendered Criminalization of Land Defenders in Ecuador', in M. Menton & P. Billon (eds.), *Environmental Defenders: Deadly Struggles for Life and Territory* (Earthscan, 2021) 81.

Creating Externalities

As previously established, hegemonic environmental lawfare is not employed merely to silence targeted environmental defenders through legal means. More importantly, it is about how individual cases may be used as a proxy to manage environmental resistance. In this regard, attempts to discipline resistance and the public are fundamental and those are pursued through projecting consequences that may be borne by those who exercise their resistance outside boundaries designated by the state. Hegemonic environmental lawfare (HEL) serves as a technique to 'enable capitalist states to oscillate between the imposition of naked repression and popular consent-building for the repressive function of the state'.[43] In other words, when direct repression may lead to the questioning of state legitimacy and provoke broader oppositional movements, both state and private powerholders resort to lawfare as a cunning means for suppressing dissenting voices in the name of enforcing the rule of law. For this purpose, HEL can be effective in neutralising environmental resistance because it involves methods that shape the conditions where resistance appears to be challenging, including the deflection and the politics of othering, the control of civil society, and the reproduction of the atmosphere of violence.

Deflecting Socio-environmental Conflicts

Hegemonic environmental lawfare deployed as a technology of power is never aimed at resolving socio-environmental conflicts. Rather HEL is exercised to deflect attention away from the underlying social structures and relationships that underpin social conflicts. In the context of SLAPP, Pring and Canan identify three motives for engaging in SLAPP lawsuits which have the effect of deflecting: conflict transformation, forum transformation, and issue transformation.[44] In conflict transformation, SLAPP aims to deflect attention away from the root causes of socio-environmental conflicts, for instance environmental destruction or pollution, by engaging in a semantic game around the interpretation of law and facts. Issue transformation is related to the motive underlying a SLAPP action, which is designed to divert community issues and concerns over environmental pollution and/or destruction into a legal case, for instance, of defamation or libel. Meanwhile, forum transformation is an attempt to shift the forum for expressing environmental concerns from the public sphere into a legal proceeding conducted in the court.

Taking these deflection motives together, courts as a 'juridical field' provide an indirect and effective means for intimidating environmental movements. This is

[43] Ignas Bernant and David Whyte, 'Criminalization as Strategy of Power: The Case of Catalunya 2017–2020', in V. Vegh Weis (ed.), *Criminalization of Activism: Historical, Present, and Future Perspectives* (Routledge, 2022) 141.

[44] Pring and Canan (n 5).

made possible by the court procedure and rulings or decisions. In the context of the legal procedure, echoing Bourdieu, the court 'operates like a *neutral space* that *neutralizes* the stakes in any conflict through the de-realization and distancing implicit in the conversion of a direct struggle between parties into a dialogue between mediators'.[45] In this regard, a double exclusion occurs for environmental defenders who are turned into defendants: first, before the court, only those who are licensed or have a legal standing to speak are allowed to express their opinion; second, a conversation between licensed parties should be translated into a legal-technical language that ordinary people barely understand. Hence, the defendants should be accompanied by a legal attorney acting as their legal broker to translate and articulate their concerns into legal language. Finding affordable and accessible legal attorneys has become another bottleneck for environmental defenders from remote areas in the region. Furthermore, court decisions should be 'accepted as impartial because they have been defined according to the formal and logically coherent rules of a doctrine perceived as independent of the immediate antagonism'.[46] Consequently, if environmental defenders serving as defendants in a SLAPP case do not accept a court decision, they should still play according to the rules of the game by appealing to a higher court, which consequently may prolong the chilling effects.

As SLAPP is a form of HEL, these deflective motives may also be attributed to HEL. However, HEL goes beyond the three motives because in Southeast Asia lawfare against environmental resistance predominantly relies on the criminal justice system, demonstrating that the role of the state institutions has been apparent. This is evidenced by the overcriminalisation of environmental activism through 'primary criminalisation' and 'secondary criminalisation'. In the former, certain behaviours that do not correspond to social norms are considered criminal offences under the law, even though they may not constitute harmful elements, such as demonstrations and consumer boycotts. In the latter, selective enforcement is commissioned by (1) 'law enforcement profiling' (whether a criminal act brought to the criminal justice system is influenced by the profile of its perpetrator. A wrongdoing committed by a lower class or perceived to be powerless person is more likely to be prosecuted than that a person from powerful elite social classes); (2) discretion of law enforcement officers (which cases are prosecuted, how facts are interpreted, and which articles are applied in their charges lie solely within the discretion of law enforcement officers); and (3) 'differential penalization' (although cases involving a similar criminal offence are prosecuted, there may be a disparity in the verdicts when considering the nature and context of the cases).[47]

[45] Pierre Bourdieu, 'The Force of Law: Toward a Sociology of the Juridical Field', (1987) 38 *The Hastings Law Journal* 805, 830.

[46] ibid.

[47] Valeria Vegh Weis, 'Introduction' in V. Vegh Weis (ed.), *Criminalization of Activism: Historical, Present, and Future Perspectives* (Routledge, 2022) 2–3.

Due to their struggles that often pose a threat to the status quo, environmental defenders are more vulnerable to prosecution or receiving harsher punishment. Indeed, as Claudelice Santos, a Brazilian female environmental defender, observed, '[b]ehind every act of violence' against environmental defenders 'are organized interests with capital and political strength. Whoever crosses their path, whoever is "getting in the way" of these groups' goals, will be "excluded from society".'[48] This has been made possible by negative labelling of environmental movements by the state or corporations through the mass media as the 'enemy of the state', 'anti-development', 'barrier to progress', or even as 'communists' or 'terrorists', a topic that brings us to the tactic of 'othering' environmental defenders.

'Othering' Environmental Movements

As already discussed, Pring and Canan emphasise three motives of SLAPP: conflict transformation, issue transformation, and forum transformation. However, they overlook that using the law as a strategy for silencing environmental defenders is also directed at transforming their subjectivities. Hence, this may be termed 'subjectivity transformation' in which the personal identity of environmental defenders is reconstructed through a new set of identities characterised as deviant by the public. Hirsch and Lazarus-Black argue that '[t]he productivity of the law ... yields new subjectivities and thereby refigures relations of power. The making of subjectivity through law is a particular intimate locus for the operation of hegemony and resistance.'[49] The motive of transforming subjectivities of environmental defenders is crucial for boundary-making between 'good us' versus the 'dangerous them' by giving a demonised category to justify punishment in the name of maintaining law and order or security.[50] As observed by Mireanu, this identity maker 'functions perfectly for the state, because it harvests legitimacy beyond the confines of democratic political nuances'.[51] Here, targeted environmental defenders, through the legal proceedings, are transformed into 'thieves', 'criminals', or 'provocateurs', and this is not to mention that once they are criminally convicted and finish their term in prison, carrying the label of being an ex-prisoner is unavoidable. Consequently, this may inhibit their social acceptance in society.

As the individual defender is a proxy of the environmental struggle in which he or she is involved, the subjectivity transformation is generalised and projected upon the struggle itself. In this regard, hegemonic environmental lawfare is not only

[48] Claudelice Santos, 'Conflicts in the Amazon: The Assassination of Zé Claudio and Maria', in M. Menton & P. Billon (eds.), *Environmental Defenders: Deadly Struggles for Life and Territory* (Earthscan, 2021) 15.

[49] Susan F. Hirsch and Mindie Lazarus-Black, 'Introduction/Performance and Paradox: Exploring Law's Role in Hegemony and Resistance', in M. Lazarus-Black & S. Hirsch (eds.), *Contested States: Law, Hegemony and Resistance* (Routledge, 2012) 13.

[50] Manuel Mireanu, 'The Criminalisation of Environmental Activism in Europe', (2014) LIX (2) *Studia UBB Sociologia* 87, 89.

[51] ibid., 102.

a direct attack on individual defenders but also serves as a technique of 'othering' environmental struggles. In doing so, environmental movements are pictured 'as a threat to a peaceful, law-abiding society'.[52] They are portrayed as 'anti-development radicals, foreign-funded activists, land squatters, or poachers. Often racialized when involving Indigenous peoples and historically marginalized populations, these representations form the basis of symbolic violence that characterizes processes of exclusion and criminalization, as well as direct forms of violence.'[53] It is not exclusively a Global South phenomenon because it also has been increasingly apparent in the Global North. In Germany, Letzte Generation, a radical environmental group, has been declared a criminal organisation.[54] Similarly, the UK's Extinction Rebellion has been characterised as a threat to internal security[55] and, even long before, the US's Earth Liberation Front and Animal Liberation Front have been labelled as domestic terrorist organisations.[56] In Romania, the state uses 'the trope of "eco-anarchism" as a fear monger' aiming 'to move the discussion from the political level to one in which any repressive measure can be justified publicly as "national defence" against extremists'.[57] Not only facing demonising labels, in Italy, No Tav activists were, in fact, charged with committing terrorism.[58] In Canada, Indigenous communities' struggles against Alberta Tar Sands are described as eco-terrorist.[59] In this context, Bernant and Whyte elaborate that

> [t]he process of criminalization has always facilitated the production of a range of different 'suitable enemies' ... whether they are enemies of the socio-economic order or enemies of the liberal political order. What unites the criminalization of more overtly political movements and the criminalization used against "street" crime is that both seek a process of de-politicization. Criminalization as a strategy, no matter its target, always looks to remove political and social content from the acts or types of behavior (that) are criminalized. That is, de-politicizing through criminalization is a tactical state move to displace conflict from the political to the legal

[52] Ignas Bernant and David Whyte, 'Criminalization as Strategy of Power: The Case of Catalunya 2017–2020', in V. Vegh Weis (ed.), *Criminalization of Activism: Historical, Present, and Future Perspectives* (Routledge, 2022) 141–142.

[53] Philippe Le Billon and Mary Menton, 'Introduction', in M. Menton & P. Billon (eds.), *Environmental Defenders: Deadly Struggles for Life and Territory* (Earthscan, 2021) 4.

[54] Kate Connolly, 'German Police Stage Nationwide Raids against Climate Activists', *The Guardian* (London, 24 May 2023). <www.theguardian.com/world/2023/may/24/german-police-stage-nationwide-raids-against-climate-activists> accessed 6 December 2023.

[55] Berglund and Schmidt (n 29).

[56] Stefan Leader and Peter Probst, 'The Earth Liberation Front and Environmental Terrorism', (2003) 15 (4) *Terrorism and Political Violence* 37–58.

[57] Mireanu (n 49) 93.

[58] Anna Di Ronco and Xenia Chiaramonte, 'Harm to Knowledge: Criminalising Environmental Movements Speaking Up Against Megaprojects', in B. Pali, M. Forsyth, & F. Tepper (eds.), *The Palgrave Handbook of Environmental Restorative Justice* (Palgrave Macmillan, 2022) 421–448.

[59] Anna Zalik, 'Protest-as-Violence in Oil Fields: The Contested Representation of Profiteering in Two Extractive Sites', in S. Feldman, C. Geisler, & G. Menon (eds.), *Accumulating Insecurity: Violence and Dispossession in the Making of Everyday Life* (University of Georgia Press, 2011) 261–284.

> arena. Doing so always reduces any immediate crisis of the social order (the riot, the protest, the strike) to the level of a threat to *law and order*.[60]

As environmental movements threaten the state and elites, they are often associated with certain categories of 'common enemies' of the state leftover from the Cold War and, more recently, by the post-9/11 security measures: communism and terrorism. Indeed, the 'communist' label or red-tagging has also been influential in delegitimising environmental movements in Thailand, Indonesia, and the Philippines because it provides an underpinning of political legitimacy for state repression. In Thailand, for instance, the use of a logo akin to a hammer and sickle by a Thai student movement, Free People, more recently, sparked controversies because it offers a 'pretext to delegitimise the protest movement [in general] as "communist"'.[61] In Indonesia, after Budi Pego was convicted of spreading communism, the anti-mining movement of Tumpang Pitu Mountain in which he was involved has 'faced pressures from religious-nationalist groups led by the NU [Nahdlatul Ulama], which have acted to safeguard the state from communist ideology and have framed the anti-mining movements as a communist-affiliated group'.[62] Similarly, in the Philippines, Lia Mai Torres, the coordinator of the Asia Pacific Network of Environmental Defenders, mentions, '[s]o, one of the biggest threats to us now . . . is what we called "red-tagging", or calling individuals or groups as terrorists, communists, rebels, and that is usually their justification for arrest or killing'.[63] In a similar vein, Rocky Guzman, a Filipino environmental activist, observes that '[t]here has been a communist insurgency in the Philippines, and the government lumped environmental defenders as [being] part of the insurgencies. So . . . environmental defenders got a bad wrap, especially those who are really fighting with the communities.'[64]

This form of othering has been instrumental in delegitimising environmental movements and distancing them from the public. Lia Mai Torres admits that reg-tagging has had a destructive effect for environmental movements in the Philippines. In 2019, the Centre for Environmental Concern, the Philippines, mobilised public donations for families affected by Covid-19, but the government accused the fundraising of being used for funding terrorist organisations or communist insurgencies. She observes that this accusation 'has a great effect on the partners we are working with since they might say that these partners are also

[60] Bernant and Whyte (n 51) 141.

[61] Sebastian Strangio, 'In Thailand, a Political Movement's Choice of Logo Prompts Controversy'. *The Diplomat* (9 December 2020). <https://thediplomat.com/2020/12/in-thailand-a-political-movements-choice-of-logo-prompts-controversy/> accessed 6 December 2023.

[62] Farid A. Alkatiri and Amir S. Kiwang, 'The Roles of Religious Organizations in the Decline of the Anti-Mining Movement in Banyuwangi, East Java', (2023) 179 (5) *Bijdragen Tot De Taal-, Land- En Volkenkunde* 31.

[63] Interview with Lia Mai Torres, the Coordinator of the Asia Pacific Network of Environmental Defenders (APNED) based in Manila, the Philippines, 12 April 2022.

[64] Interview with Rocky Guzman, environmental activist and deputy director of the Asian Research Institute for Environmental Law, 29 September 2022.

related to the terrorist organisation and also affect the support we get from international funding agencies'.[65] Moreover, through hegemonic environmental lawfare, court decisions are pursued to provide an official rubber stamp or to formalise negative labels given to environmental defenders. Lindt argues that '[t]he possibility of receiving a conviction from judicial authorities meant that activists' protests are at risk of being publicly discredited and officially declared inadmissible'.[66] In Indonesia, the accusation that communists have infiltrated environmental movements was formalised with the Supreme Court decision in the case of Budi Pego, a local community organiser against mining operations, who was charged and convicted of spreading Marxism–Leninism/communism. The case illustrates 'how judicial proceedings manifest and consolidate hegemonic positions within a society, which directly impact the political struggles of social movements'.[67]

This experience demonstrates how the state suppresses any potential opposition, redirecting it to more equivocal forms.[68] Accordingly, environmental movements become subjects of policing in which control, scrutiny, and repression against them are justified by the public to maintain law and social order. By othering environmental defenders and their movements, the broader society may reproduce and reinforce negative images attached to them and perpetuated through hegemonic environmental lawfare. Thus, the public, who should in fact be the direct constituents of the environmental movements, instead wish to avoid being associated with the movements, which in turn influences the dynamics within the civil society sphere.

Furthermore, the externalities of hegemonic lawfare are significantly gendered. As shown by Venegas and van Teijlingen in resistance against mining in the Ecuadorian Amazon, men and women are affected differently by attacks against environmental defenders.[69] Similarly, in Southeast Asia, HEL is not only a psychological matter related to its chilling effect but also places an economic burden on individual defenders and their families. If their husbands are in prison, women and children suffer the most. This condition places additional burdens on women to make a living as well as to supply additional nutrition for their husbands in prison, because insufficient food remains a chronic problem in prisons in developing countries. Where women themselves are targeted as environmental defenders, they face more severe consequences than their male counterparts. Protection International observes that

> [a]side from interfering in the practical needs of the family, their frequent absences can result in women being accused of 'neglecting their duties.' The social stigma

[65] Interview with Lia Mai Torres, the Coordinator of the Asia Pacific Network of Environmental Defenders (APNED) based in Manila, the Philippines, 12 April 2022.

[66] Lindt (n 22) 377. [67] ibid.

[68] Edward Aspinall, *Opposing Suharto: Compromise, Resistance, and Regime Change in Indonesia* (Stanford University Press, 2005) 3.

[69] Melissa Venegas and Karolien van Teijlingen, 'The Gendered Criminalization of Land Defenders in Ecuador', in M. Menton & P. Billon (eds.), *Environmental Defenders: Deadly Struggles for Life and Territory* (Earthscan, 2021), 80.

> suffered by women judged to be failing to take care of their family is very serious, especially in rural communities. The additional economic burdens of childcare, travel and legal support increases women's stress and hardship.[70]

Thus, women environmental defenders are among the most vulnerable actors in environmental movements. Their work in securing the care of their families may be undermined as they must dedicate time to defending their case, including travel preparations for often long journeys to attend law enforcement offices and court hearings.

Governing Civil Society

Civil society as a contested space may become a source of resistance against the hegemonic power, and this is precisely why the state and private actors aim to control it.[71] Following Gramsci, Rodan argues that 'civil society is necessarily a relationship between dominant and dominated classes' through which the dominant class attempts to achieve ideological hegemony by exercising its leadership politically, morally, and intellectually, including by establishing a particular view of the world and shaping the interests of the dominated classes.[72] As a contested space, civil society is also used as a centre of gravity through which the rule of law, democracy, and civic freedom are measured. Maintaining a seemingly autonomous sphere in civil society is essential for maintaining a government's political legitimacy. Hence, social conflicts taking place within this sphere should be managed intelligently to demonstrate the responsiveness of the state to societal demands and to prevent them from transforming into political forces that may disrupt the status quo but, at the same time, preserve the notion of autonomy and civil freedom.

To achieve this, the dominant class utilises four modes of participation (MoP) referring to 'institutional arrangements and accompanying ideological rationales defining the permissible limits to who can politically participate, and how and on what basis to manage societal conflicts'.[73] They are: (1) 'Civil Society Expression', the creation of independent forms of collective action that enjoy the highest degree of relative autonomy from state control; (2) 'Individualised Expression', a mode where individuals may express their freedom with a relatively high degree of autonomy from state regulatory control; (3) 'Societal Incorporation', an institutional model of participation within the state or in the state structure that is sponsored by the state to 'provide avenues through which groups may influence public policy, yet on terms set by officials'; and (4) 'Administrative Incorporation',

[70] Protection International, 'Silencing Justice: Battling Systemic SLAPP Attacks on Women and Human Rights Defenders in Thailand', *Protection International* (2023) <www.protectioninternational.org/wp-content/uploads/2023/09/PIs-report-Battling-Systematic-SLAPP-Attacks-on-Women-and-Human-Rights-Defenders-in-Thailand.pdf> accessed 25 April 2024, 5.

[71] Penny Green and Tony Ward, *State Crime and Civil Activism: On the Dialectics of Repression and Resistance* (Routledge, 2019).

[72] Garry Rodan, *Civil Society in Southeast Asia* (Cambridge University Press, 2022) 13.

[73] ibid., 14.

an institutional model of participation aiming at steering individuals, including through 'public grievance, consultation, and feedback mechanisms of state bureaucracies' where 'conflicts are translated into issues about the refinement and implementation of government policy'.[74] Conceptually, SLAPP, as a subset of HEL, is an instrument to prevent participation in environmental matters. Thus, it does not fall within Rodan's MoP framework, but it demonstrates similar objectives in managing social conflicts and shaping civil society to achieve ideological hegemony. As Lindt puts it, '[t]he criminalization of social protest is a form of governing dissent groups that oppose large-scale extractive projects'.[75]

Practically, resorting to courts through hegemonic environmental lawfare is also done to influence the sphere of civil society and subordinate groups such that they align with the interests of the dominant social class. This can be undertaken by shaping the preferences of civil society organisations in exercising their agenda and in engaging with the state and the market. As White observes, environmental activists that rely on the use of conciliatory tactics or engagement, such as closed-door cooperation or lobbying, are less likely to be attacked by the state and corporations than those that utilise confrontational tactics, such as mass mobilisation, trespass, or eco-sabotage.[76] In this context, it is necessary to draw a boundary and differentiate between 'civilised' (good) and 'uncivilised' (bad) environmental activists. Delmas, referencing to *Walker* v. *Birmingham* (1963) in the US, perceives that '[c]ivility is equated with law-abidance and deference'.[77] She continues:

> The powerful often use calls for civility to control and silence activists, to cast a negative light on their activities and prejudice the public against them. Calls for civility ignore and obscure the differentials of power – the fact that it is easy for those in power, and harder for entrenched minorities, to speak and be listened to and therefore to be civil. The former have ready access to the public sphere, while the latter not only lack such access but are also vulnerable to discrimination, prejudice, and epistemic injustice which consists of doing wrong to people in their capacity as knowers, for instance by failing to really listen to them or by deflecting the credibility or sincerity of their testimony.[78]

Delmas's observation demonstrates how 'civility' is weaponised by the powerful group. The power to define who is 'civilised' or 'uncivilised' lies in the hands of elite powerholders to redirect the ways in which conflicts should be resolved. In this context, the 'civilised' activists are those who utilise the conciliatory tactics, or Rodan's third and fourth MoP to pursue their interests, while 'uncivilised' environmental activists are those who use confrontational tactics or mobilise the first

[74] ibid., 14–15. [75] Lindt (n 22) 370.

[76] Rob White, 'Environmental Activism and Resistance to State-Corporate Crime', in E. Stanley & J. McCulloch (eds.), *State Crime and Resistance* (Routledge, 2013) 128–140.

[77] Candice Delmas, *A Duty to Resist: When Disobedience Should be Uncivil* (Oxford University Press, 2018) 32.

[78] ibid., 34.

and second modes, but once they pose threats to the powerholders, the control of those modes is exercised through the use of lawfare. When the boundaries between legality and illegality appear to be blurred, uncivilised environmental activists may also resort to stretching the boundaries of existing laws[79] by committing petty crimes, including forgery or blockades, confiscating companies' equipment, or civil disobedience, to attract public attention to the socio-environmental conflicts or environmental injustices they face. By punishing 'uncivilised' environmental dissent, powerholders seek to set the frame within which 'civilised' environmental dissent should operate without fear of being criminalised or sanctioned.

In its attempt at 'civilising' civil society, HEL in Southeast Asia has produced jurisprudence that shapes legal theories and practices in the region. One notable jurisprudence in this regard is related to the doctrine of liability, especially in the development of new models of criminal liability. At least two models have emerged here, namely association-based liability and negligent protest liability. First, association-based liability or crime by association refers to individuals who may be criminally liable if they are associated with a group considered to be a state-declared criminal or 'uncivilised' civil society group. Second, in 'negligent protest' liability, protest leaders are held accountable for the repercussions of any disruptive and illicit activities committed at public events. Zick argues that the negligent protest liability 'authorizes holding leaders accountable for the violence, even those *opposed* to the protest on the theory that such violence was "foreseeable."'.[80] The second model of criminal liability is also observed by Di Ronco and Chiaramonte in Italy in how the public prosecutor charged fifty-three defendants who were accused of resisting and committing violence against the police. They elaborate that

> [g]iven the difficulty of proving who resisted the police, the public prosecutor decided to accuse all those who were present during the two-day protest of complicity in the crime (concorso). The first-instance judges supported this thesis and clarified that demonstrators who see a protest turning violent should leave it, otherwise they would become accomplices in the violent crimes committed by others.[81]

The Indonesian court in the *Budi Pego* case also applied the negligent protest model of criminal liability. In this case, the panel of judges imposed an expanded interpretation in constructing criminal liability against the defendant, Budi Pego. During the trial there was no evidence presented that Budi Pego made the banner

[79] White (n 75) 128–140.

[80] Timothy Zick, 'The Costs of Dissent: Protest and Civil Liabilities', (2021) 89 *The George Washington Law Review* 233, 273.

[81] Anna Di Ronco and Xenia Chiaramonte, 'Harm to Knowledge: Criminalising Environmental Movements Speaking up Against Megaprojects', in B. Pali, M. Forsyth, & F. Tepper (eds.), *The Palgrave Handbook of Environmental Restorative Justice* (Palgrave Macmillan, 2022) 433.

containing the hammer-sickle logo and this fact was referred to directly in the court's decision. This concurs with that statement of the Banyuwangi District Court judge:

> that there is no other evidence submitted by the Public Prosecutor that supports or proves that the banner containing the hammer and sickle image was made by the Defendant or any of the participants of the demonstration. Indeed, the public prosecutor's indictment that a banner with a hammer and sickle image was made at the defendant's house was not proven.[82]

However, Budi Pego was found criminally culpable in his position as the field coordinator of the demonstration, as he did not cancel the demonstration nor prevent the banners from being put up. The basis for this argument is Article 12(1) of Law No. 9 of 1998 concerning the Freedom of Expression in Public, which stipulates that 'the person in charge of the activity ... shall be responsible for ensuring that the activity is carried out in a safe, orderly and peaceful manner'. However, the article does not state that the person in charge of the activity is criminally liable if a criminal offence occurs during the action but is committed by other persons. In the deliberation, the court rationale was that: '[c]onsidering, that even though it could not be proven that the making of the banner with the hammer and sickle was done at the Defendant's house, when the rally was held there was an image of a hammer and sickle on the banner that was unfurled during the rally'.[83] It continues, 'the Defendant's responsibility as the leader of the rally on 4 April 2015, should have [been to] immediately stop or prohibit the unfurling of the banner because it was an unlawful act'.[84] Due to his failure to take this responsibility, Budi Pego was convicted for spreading Marxism–Leninism/communism and sentenced to four years in prison. Echoing Zick, such a decision that uses the argument of negligent protest liability 'not only ignores protest realities but also turns fundamental free speech and assembly principles on their head by basing liability on the foreseeability of disruption'.[85]

Furthermore, there has been a growing concern about the use of administrative measures for regulating or restraining civil society. In Indonesia, for instance, the legal basis for restrictive control over environmental NGOs was made possible after revising the Mass Organisations Act 2017, which enables the government's banning of mass organisations if they are considered to be against the state ideology and the public order.[86] The Hizbut Tahrir Indonesia, a radical Islamic mass organisation, was the first organisation to be banned. In the future, there will be possibilities to undertake similar moves that target organisations expressing dissent against the government, including environmental NGOs. One indication of this was several

[82] Decision of the District Court of Banyuwangi No. 559/Pid.B/2017/PN.Byw, 54. [83] ibid., 54.
[84] ibid., 55. [85] Zick (n 79) 273.
[86] Agustinus Beo Da Costa, 'Indonesia Passes Law to Ban Organizations Deemed against Its Ideology', *Reuters* (London, 24 October 2017) <www.reuters.com/article/us-indonesia-islamists-idUSKBN1CT1JZ> accessed 9 February 2022.

public statements from high-ranking state officials after Greenpeace Indonesia criticised flawed data used by President Jokowi during the COP 26 UN Climate Change Conference in Glasgow concerning deforestation. The Coordinating Ministry of Maritime and Investment, Luhut Pandjaitan, then made a statement regarding the need to audit environmental NGOs in Indonesia by stating that '[t]hose NGOs will be audited, so they will not spread wrong information; I say [that] we will audit [them], [because] it is not good if you give flawed news'.[87] The spokesperson for the Coordinating Ministry followed by saying that 'the public also has the right to obtain information regarding the sources and uses of NGO funds', especially those organisations funded by foreign parties.[88] However, how the government will proceed with this administrative form of legal action against environmental movements remains to be seen.

Similar tendencies have occurred in the Philippines. Here, civil society organisations may be targeted for administrative measures by the government due to 'suspicious' financial transactions. The Aminahan National Federation of Peasant Women, a Mindanao grassroots organisation advocating for agrarian reform and the rights of rural women, for instance, suffered after its bank account was frozen by the Anti-Money Laundering Council, accusing it of funding activities carried out by the Communist Party of the Philippines and the New People's Army.[89] Eventually, the Manila Regional Trial Court lifted the freeze order considering that 'no specific allegation or even a single transaction' demonstrated 'being used for terror financing'.[90]

Moreover, the use of *persona non-grata* (an unwelcome person) may affect the work of Filipino environmental movements. In Palawan, the Palawan NGO Network Inc. (PNNI) has organised para-enforcers, a group of citizens who enforce environmental law against violations in the region, including by confiscating chain-saws from illegal loggers. It follows Philippine's environmental law that allows citizens to participate in the enforcement. Business actors whose interests have been impacted by the work of PNNI's para-enforcers retaliated against them. As a result, at least twelve of its para-enforcers have been murdered since 2001.[91] In 2019, Attorney Robert Chan campaigned against the government's policy to divide

[87] 'Tuduh Sebarkan Berita Tidak Benar, Luhut Akan Audit LSM-LSM', *CNN Indonesia* (Jakarta, 12 November 2021) <www.cnnindonesia.com/nasional/20211112161252-20-720384/tuduh-sebarkan-berita-tak-benar-luhut-akan-audit-lsm-lsm> accessed 2 February 2022.

[88] Caesar Akbar and Resseno Aji Nugroho, 'Luhut Pandjaitan's Spokesman Talks of NGO Audit Plan', *Tempo* (Jakarta, 15 November 2021) <https://en.tempo.co/read/1528635/luhut-pandjaitans-spokesman-talks-of-ngo-audit-plan> accessed 2 February 2022.

[89] Anne M. Umil, 'Peasant Women's Group Decries AMLC's Freezing of Its Bank Accounts', *Bulatlat* (Manila, 10 June 2021). <www.bulatlat.com/2021/06/10/peasant-womens-group-decry-amlcs-freezing-of-its-bank-accounts/> accessed 6 December 2023.

[90] Dominic Gutoman, 'Court Finds No Evidence Women's Group Bank Account Is Used for Terror Financing', *Medium* (Manila, 7 April 2022). <https://nicorev.medium.com/court-finds-no-evidence-womens-group-bank-account-is-used-for-terror-financing-bulatlat-f6d9114e2c40> accessed 6 December 2022.

[91] Nick Aspinwall, 'Threats, Raids, and Murders Stalk Filipino Environment Activists', *Aljazeera* (16 December 2019). <www.aljazeera.com/news/2019/12/6/threats-raids-and-murders-stalk-filipino-environment-activists> accessed 6 December 2023.

Palawan Island into three provinces, which is considered to have detrimental effects on the ecosystem and biodiversity of the fragile Palawan Island.[92] In retaliation, the Government of Palawan declared a resolution of '*persona non grata*' against Attorney Chan, the chairperson of the PNNI.[93] Despite the declaration of Attorney Robert Chan as *persona non grata* based on a resolution, it has effectively prevented him from entering Palawan. The declaration of *persona non-grata* to Attorney Chen 'is political … [It] physiologically matters because once you are declared as "*persona non-grata*", you are concerned with your security in that area.'[94] Consequently, this impacts the advocacy work of the PNNI, including direct action used in fighting against the destruction of Palawan's ecosystem. Hence, a declaration of *persona non grata* against environmental defenders should be seen as part of the administrative machinery of local governments used not only to prevent and to constrain the work of targeted environmental defenders but also to discipline environmental groups by setting acceptable boundaries within which environmental defenders or environmental groups should advocate their causes in a given administrative territory.

Attacks against environmental defenders have become normalised due to the rampant impunity, which is made possible within the 'atmosphere of violence'. It refers to 'the creation of climates of fear and oppression, to violence against the bodies, minds, and territories of defenders' and has been perpetuated by the media with a growing use of information technologies.[95] Zanin et al. explain that the role of the media in lawfare is to provide 'administration by deception' that is mobilised exactly to create 'an environment supposedly legitimizing such persecution by projecting a presumption of guilt on the given enemy … in order to: (i) convict without evidence, or (ii) encourage public opinion to demand a conviction'.[96] This administration becomes influential in demonising environmental movements

[92] Keith A. Fabro, 'Palawan Gov't Declares Environmental Lawyer Persona Non-Grata', *Rappler* (Manila, 23 January 2021). <www.rappler.com/nation/environmental-lawyer-declared-persona-non-grata-palawan/ > accessed 6 December 2023.

[93] Indeed, under the Philippine governmental system, a local government may issue a declaration of '*persona non-grata*' (an unwelcome person) through an ordinance or a resolution. The difference between the two is explained in *Municipality of Paranque* v. *Realty Corporation* (G.R. No. 127820, 20 July 1998), which states that: 'We are not convinced by petitioner's instance that the terms of "resolution" and "ordinance" are synonymous. A municipal ordinance is different from a resolution. An ordinance is a law, but a resolution is merely a declaration of the sentiment or opinion of a lawmaking body on a specific matter. An ordinance possesses a general and permanent character, but a resolution is temporary. Additionally, the two are enacted differently – a third reading is necessary for an ordinance, but not for a resolution, unless decided otherwise by a majority of all the Sanggunian members.' *Municipality of Paranque* v. *Realty Corporation* (G.R. No. 127820, 20 July 1998) cited in Department of the Interior and Local Government's Legal Opinion No. 30 S. 2020. <www.dilg.gov.ph/PDF_File/issuances/legal_opinions/dilg-legalopinions-2020226_5de785aea2.pdf> accessed on 25 May 2022.

[94] Interview with Garthie Mayo Anda, an environmental attorney in the Philippines, 21 October 2022.

[95] Mery Menton, Grettel Navas, and Philippe Le Billon, 'Atmosphere of Violence: On Defenders' Intersecting Experiences of Violence', in M. Menton & P. Billon (eds.), *Environmental Defenders: Deadly Struggles for Life and Territory* (Earthscan, 2021) 51.

[96] Cristiano Zanin, Valeska Martins, and Rafael Valim, *Lawfare: Waging War through Law* (Routledge, 2022), 27–28.

because of the structural asymmetries drawn upon to influence the media and public opinion. In the context of the Philippines, Rocky Guzman observes that 'with social media, the attacks on activists in general [orchestrated] by the Duterte regime, have gotten worse ... [P]eople have become vocal against activists in general.'[97] Similarly, in Indonesia and Thailand, environmental movements were subject to smear campaigns and stigmatisation by accusing them of being 'foreign agents', 'enemies of the state', 'unpatriotic', and so forth.[98] In this 'atmosphere of violence', such negative characterisations may lead to convictions and even violent attacks against defenders that are deemed permissible under the claim of maintaining social order.

To conclude, as a form of strategic legal action, HEL is not only deployed to attack targeted defenders individually, but more importantly, it also aims to create projecting externalities. These externalities refer to the consequences intended to be borne by environmental movements in general beyond the actual lawfare cases as a tactic to maintain the social order that is conducive to capital accumulation through extractive activities. For this purpose, the externalities of HEL involve deflection motives, a technique of othering environmental movements, an attempt to shape civil society dynamics, and the reproduction of the atmosphere of violence. This understanding contradicts Böhm's characterisation of 'criminalisation' as merely an expression of physical violence.[99] This chapter has demonstrated that HEL in all its forms, including criminalisation, encompasses Galtung's three expressions of violence: the physical violence suffered by targeted defenders, structural violence exercised against people involved in environmental struggles, and cultural violence projected towards the general population to secure legitimacy for the use of physical and structural violence against those it is considered hinder the state's agenda of the pursuit of economic growth. The HEL launched by the powerholders to maintain the status quo should not be assumed to be internalised passively by environmental defenders. As demonstrated in the following chapter, they have attempted to challenge such silencing strategies through legal mobilisation and beyond.

[97] Interview with Rocky Guzman, environmental activist and deputy director of the Asian Research Institute for Environmental Law, 29 September 2022.

[98] Amnesty International, *Silencing Voices, Suppressing Criticism: The Decline in Indonesia's Civil Liberties* (Amnesty International Indonesia, 2022) 31; 'Thailand's NGO Law: Uprooting Foreign Influence or Gagging Government Critics?' *Thai PBS* (Bangkok, 21 April 2021). <www.thaipbsworld.com/thailands-ngo-law-uprooting-foreign-influence-or-gagging-govt-critics/> accessed 7 December 2023.

[99] Maria Laura Böhm, *The Crime of Maldevelopment: Economic Deregulation and Violence in the Global South*, (Routledge, 2019) 154.

CHAPTER 6

Resistance against Lawfare

As elaborated in the previous chapters, HEL, through which law has been mobilised by the powerful to intimidate and punish environmental defenders, is part of a hegemonic project of the alliance of powerful groups to maintain the status quo. To understand HEL, it is insufficient to only examine its geographies, weaponry, and externalities. Focusing solely on these three strategic dimensions may lead to an assumption that HEL is a one-directional process and that environmental movements have passively internalised lawfare's externalities. Echoing Scott, however, a hegemonic project is never achieved as an absolute stage because it always opens possibilities for resistance.[1] Hence, resistance or fightback should be understood as a fourth dimension of lawfare. This dimension is overlooked by Zenin et al., a position which may risk slipping into affirming the hegemony of powerholders in 'creating a sense of powerlessness, undermining people's confidence to act'.[2] Environmental lawfare as a hegemonic project will always invite counter-hegemonic acts in various ways and by some people, especially those affected directly by the state's policy or state-backed development projects. This chapter examines how environmental movements in Southeast Asia challenge, contest, halt, and prevent HEL. Here, resistance to HEL involves people in processes of exercising social agency in opposing the use of law or legal means to attack environmental defenders. This exercise of agency simultaneously involves communicating messages to the public on the unjust nature of HEL to transform the existing conditions through which HEL emerges.

The first section of the chapter discusses rights-based legal mobilisations as the most common form of resistance to HEL that is exercised by environmental

[1] James C. Scott, *Domination and the Arts of Resistance: Hidden Transcripts* (Yale University Press, 1990).

[2] Elizabeth Stanley and Jude McCulloch, 'Resistance to State Crime', in E. Stanley & J. McCulloch (eds.), *State Crime and Resistance* (Routledge, 2013) 2.

movements, a phenomenon not exclusive to Southeast Asia. It examines the mobilisation of human rights claims to build arguments that challenge lawfare in litigation and legal reform at domestic, regional, and international levels. The second section discusses rights-based mobilisations in Southeast Asia to demonstrate their limitations in resisting lawfare in the region. It shows how existing rights-based legal mobilisation approaches used in resisting HEL in Southeast Asia are insufficient or thus far ineffective in protecting its environmental defenders. Inspired by the 'duty-turn' in resistance studies, the third section of the chapter proposes an alternative approach of duty-based legal mobilisation. This approach conceptualises the obligation to defend the environment as a justificatory defence in resisting lawfare. It discusses how rights claims can be transformed (and thus codified, interpreted, classified) as an exercise of duty to defend the environment which can be used as a legal defence in criminal litigation. It will be argued that the duty-based approach may incorporate an eco-defence argument – defending the environment as a form of private defence and self-defence – that should be regarded as a justificatory defence in criminal law in which wrongful acts committed by the defenders in their struggles to protect their livelihood and the environment can be omitted on the grounds of legal doctrines concerning private defence and self-defence.

Rights-Based Resistance

As discussed in Chapter 1, legal attacks on environmental defenders are predominantly understood through the framework of SLAPP as a threat to a legitimate exercise of rights. Pring and Canan clearly understand attacks utilising legal means as a strategy to prevent the exercise of the right to petition as guaranteed by the US Constitution,[3] while Donson and others examine them in connection to the right to freedom of expression.[4] As legal actions against environmental defenders are framed as a violation of human rights, the ways such actions are resisted are also predominantly framed within the human rights lens. Here, human rights have become 'the key theatres of battle and conflict' to claim the protection of environmental defenders in exercising their rights.[5] Accordingly, resistance to hegemonic environmental lawfare is grounded on the language of rights by mobilising human

[3] George W. Pring dan Penelope Canan, *SLAPPs: Getting Sued for Speaking Out* (Temple University Press, 1996).

[4] Fiona Donson, *Legal Intimidation* (Free Association Press, 2000); Byron Sheldrick, *Blocking Public Participation: The Use of Strategic Litigation to Silence Political Expression* (Wilfrid Laurier University Press, 2014); Nikhil Dutta, *SLAPPs in the Global South: Features and Policy Responses* (International Centre for Not Profit Law, 2020); Thalia Anthony, 'Quantum of Strategic Litigation – Quashing Public Participation', (2009) 14 (2) *Australian Journal of Human Rights* 1.

[5] Makau Mutua, *Human Rights Standards: Hegemony, Law, and Politics* (State University of New York Press, 2016) 2.

rights norms and standards both in litigation and in advocacy for policy and legal reform to protect environmental defenders at the domestic, regional, or international levels.

Mobilising Rights in Litigation

In legal proceedings, when defenders are criminally charged or civilly sued in relation to their environmental defence actions, their arguments predominantly are based on the notion of rights in their various national context-specific formulations. In Indonesia, for instance, environmental defenders argue when defending against SLAPP cases that they were exercising their rights to a good and healthy environment as stipulated by the 1945 Indonesian Constitution and the 2009 Environmental Protection and Management Law; accordingly, they should be given protection from any attempts to prosecute them in exercising their rights. Similarly, in the Philippines, defenders mobilise the 1987 constitutional provision on the right of the people to a balanced and healthy ecology in accord with the rhythm and harmony of nature as well as the Philippine Supreme Court's Rules of Procedures for Environmental Cases, especially Rule 6 concerning anti-SLAPP provisions. In Thailand, as defamation is the biggest weapon employed in HEL, defendants turn to the exemption from defamation clauses in the Criminal Code, namely Section 329[6] and Section 330,[7] arguing for the freedom of expression. As discussed in the previous chapter, however, the outcomes of the rights-based legal mobilisation before the courts are mixed. In some cases, judges accepted their defence, but in other cases, arguments based on human rights did not exempt them from their alleged criminal offences, as shown by the *Sukoharjo* case in Indonesia, where the judges reasoned that the right to a good and healthy environment should be pursued through legal means instead of by breaking the law.[8]

Furthermore, the experience of Indonesia, Thailand, and the Philippines reveals how the courts interpret and apply the existing anti-SLAPP provisions in those countries. In this regard, there are at least three responses or counters to the provisions. First, the courts ignore the anti-SLAPP provisions in the case. This is demonstrated in cases considered to be serious crimes related to the integrity of the national ideology, symbols, or state institutions. In Indonesia's *Budi Pego* case, the false accusations of communist affiliations which remain illegal in Indonesia outweighed the defence that Budi Pego was exercising his right to protest against the

[6] Section 329 stipulates that '[w]hoever expresses an opinion or statement in good faith: (1) for the sake of righteousness, protecting himself, protecting his interests; (2) as an official acting in the capacity of the person (3) to give a fair comment about a person or something that is the nature of the people would do; (4) to report the news with fairness, expedite open action in court. Thus, at that meeting, there was no defamation.'

[7] Section 330 stipulates that 'in the case of defamation, if the accused that the allegation of defamation is true, they are not punished, but they are forbidden to prove if the accusation of defamation is personal, and the verdict will not benefit the public'.

[8] The *Sukoharjo* Case (2019) Decision No. 293/Pid.B/2019/PN.Smg and Decision No.259/Pid/2019/PT.Smg.

threat of gold mining activities in East Java that had caused damage to the forests and local livelihoods.[9]

Second, the courts may refer to anti-SLAPP provisions in building their legal deliberations regardless of the defendants' use in the defence. In the *Kampol Case* in Thailand, Kampol, an environmental activist who was charged with criminal defamation for criticising Phayom Rattanamanee, a researcher who developed an artificial reef made of coal's bottom ash, was acquitted from the charge by the Nakhon Sri Thammarat Provincial Court based on Section 329 of Thai Criminal Code.[10] The section stipulates that no offence of criminal defamation has been committed if a person 'expresses an opinion or statement in good faith' as part of the right to freedom of expression. Similarly, with a relatively comprehensive provision on anti-SLAPP in the Philippine Supreme Court's Rules of Procedure judges referred to the provision in adjudicating SLAPP cases in the country, resulting in a relatively high number of cases that are acquitted, albeit after a prolonged legal proceeding.

Third, in the absence of clear and comprehensive anti-SLAPP provisions in countries like Indonesia and Thailand, courts may be instrumental in providing legal interpretation of the existing provisions. Here, the *Robandi et al.* case in Indonesia provides a germane illustration of how courts interpret Article 66 of the 2009 EPM Act, which only stipulates that '[a]ny person who fights for the rights to a good and healthy environment should not be charged through criminal proceedings or sued through civil proceedings'. The Supreme Court's Decision No. 36 of 2013 concerning the Guidance for the Handling of Environmental Cases only mandated that in a criminal case indicated to be SLAPP, 'the defendant shall file a motion to be decided by the panel of judges in its provisional decision'. However, it is unclear how the panel should examine the motion to implement Article 66 of the EPM Act. In its deliberation, even though the judicial panel in this case affirmed that Robandi and others were acting to protect the right to a good and healthy environment, as argued by their legal attorneys, it decided that, instead of being acquitted, the defendants were to be 'discharged' from the prosecutor's allegations. Conceptually, this means that they were proven to have committed the acts as charged by the public prosecutor in the indictment, but their actions did not constitute a criminal offence. The panel accepted that their acts were legally justified, so the unlawful nature of their actions was omitted. As a landmark case, the court has made a jurisprudence that wrongful acts in pursuing the right to a good and healthy environment can be justified within the Indonesian criminal justice system. In their decision however, the court does not provide any further

[9] The *Budi Pego* case (2018) Banyuwangi District Court's Decision No 559/Pid.B/2017/PN. Byw; Surabaya High Court's Decision No. 174/PID/2018/PT.SBY; Indonesian Supreme Court's Decision No. 1567 K/Pid.Sus/2018.

[10] Nakhon Sri Thammarat Provincial Court No: 3846/2557 on 29–10–2014. 'Kampol: Defamation to a Coal's Ashes Researcher', *iLAW Freedom* (online)<https://freedom.ilaw.or.th/en/case/705> accessed on 31 January 2023.

standard for applying the justificatory defence in SLAPP cases, a theme discussed in the next section.

Mobilising Rights in Legal Reform

Even though SLAPP may open an opportunity to expose injustice suffered by environmental defenders and to mobilise public support for their cause, mobilising rights in defending a case in a strategically motivated legal battle is not without costs. As Sheldrick put it, '[i]n general, it is always preferable to avoid litigation costs in favour of ongoing political expression and action. It is for this reason that the regulation and limitation of SLAPPs is so very critical to fostering and protecting political debate and engagement.'[11] Resisting the use of law for silencing defenders cannot solely take place during litigation despite the trend that the chances of winning the case are relatively high. The chilling effect must be prevented promptly; hence, it is always better without going through a resource-intensive, prolonged legal proceeding. This is why struggles to pursue legal reform in enacting and continuously improving the existing anti-SLAPP legal instruments are proposed by many legal scholars and activists.[12]

The question is what constitutes a practical anti-SLAPP legal framework at the domestic level. Influenced by rational choice theory, Sheldrick suggests that a practical framework needs 'to address the underlying reasons for SLAPPs and create a different set of incentives structures than normally exists in the judicial system'.[13] He includes several features, including protecting the defendant from economic and financial burdens from litigation. The SLAPP filers must bear these burdens, and if necessary, economic disincentives should be made possible, such as in the form of a costs award or to fund the defendant's defence, so that the filers may calculate the cost and benefit before filing a SLAPP lawsuit.[14] Moreover, mechanisms should be in place to reduce the chilling effects and resolve the lawsuit promptly and efficiently. This is important to 'send a clear signal that political participation is an important value and that individuals and groups will not be penalised for engaging in lawful political activities'.[15] However, this suggestion only makes sense in the Global North, especially the US and Canada, where the dominant actor who pursues legal actions against environmental defenders is a private actor, especially a corporation, in which the standard cost and benefit analysis is embedded in their practices and projections. As demonstrated in Chapter 4, in Southeast Asia the state is the dominant actor attempting to silence environmental defenders. Adjudicating cases against those who are deemed to be criminals is part of their regimen in maintaining law and order as well as the public interest (whatever the state defines it), and the state budget funds this regimen; hence, a decision whether to resort to lawfare cannot be understood simply by the cost

[11] Sheldrick (n 4) 139. [12] See, for instance, Sheldrick (n 4); Anthony (n 4) 1–38.
[13] Sheldrick (n 4) 90. [14] ibid., 92. [15] ibid., 91.

and benefit analysis because it also involves different considerations, including ideological ones. Thus, a different framework is required here to reflect different challenges faced by environmental movement activists in Southeast Asia to respond to the legal actions that target them.

In Indonesia, given the vague nature of Article 66 of the 2009 EPM Act, environmental non-governmental organisations have been advocating for enacting more operative regulations in law enforcement bodies. State legal institutions have been targeted, rather than pursuing a revision of the 2009 EPM Act or enacting a special bill on the protection of environmental defenders, primarily due to the difficulties of navigating the national parliaments in which the majority (55 per cent) of its members are from the corporate business sector,[16] whose interests in national resource extraction can be compromised by any attempts to improve environmental safeguards and protection for environmental defenders. For instance, the Indonesian Center for Environmental Law and the Partnership for Governance Reform (*Kemitraan*) chose to lobby the Office of the Attorney General and assist the Supreme Court in issuing an internal procedure for handling environmental cases, including SLAPP lawsuits. They have established relationships with those institutions in providing technical assistance and capacity building for public prosecutors and judges, including training in the certification of environmental judges since the early 2000s.

As a result, the Attorney General's Office and the Supreme Court have issued important measures in line with public demands. In October 2022, the Attorney General's Guidance No. 8 of 2022 on the Handling of Criminal Cases concerning Environmental Protection and Management Matters was enacted. It provides a list of conducts that constitute an act to defend the right to a good and healthy environment that will be protected under the anti-SLAPP provision.[17] For this purpose, the public prosecutor, in studying and examining the results of the investigation, ensures formal completeness and material completeness, primarily related to (a) the causal relationship between reports and complaints of criminal offences and the conduct of the suspect in fighting for the right to a good and healthy environment; (b) the qualifications of the suspect, including as an environmental activist, environmental organisation, victim affected by environmental

[16] Tsarina Maharani and Krisiandi, 'Riset Marepus Corner: 5–6 dari 10 Orang Anggota DPR Pengusaha', *Kompas* (23 October 2020). <https://nasional.kompas.com/read/2020/10/23/19162181/riset-marepus-corner-5-6-dari-10-orang-anggota-dpr-pengusaha> accessed 16 January 2024.

[17] The act of fighting for the right to a good and healthy environment can be done, among others, by (a) submitting proposals in the context of protection and sound environmental management, (b) submitting objections, complaints, or grievances related to environmental pollution and/or destruction; (c) reporting of alleged criminal offences, filing of administrative or civil lawsuits, or other legal proceedings relating to the protection and management of the environment; (d) expression of opinion in public; (e) submission of testimony or statement in court and/or; (f) communication to ministries/institutions related to the right to a healthy and good environment, orally or in writing, either directly or by electronic means. Those actions are carried out lawfully and in good faith in the context of fulfilling access to information, access to participation, and access to justice in fulfilling the right to a good and healthy environment.

pollution, and/or destruction, journalist, and/or Indigenous community; (c) the motive of the defendant; (d) the presence or absence of unlawfulness and guilt; and (e) the presence or absence of justification and excuse. Based on the research conducted in the investigation, if the public prosecutor believes that the suspect's conduct in fighting for the right to a good and healthy environment is lawful and in good faith, the suspect cannot be prosecuted criminally. Akin to the anti-SLAPP provision concerning criminal defamation in Thailand, the public prosecutor in Indonesia is also instructed to drop the case.

In addition, the Supreme Court has enacted a new regulation concerning guidance on the handling of environmental defender cases. The 2023 Supreme Court's Regulation on the Guidance for the Handling of Environmental Cases replaces the 2013 Supreme Court's Guidance by elaborating on several important matters not addressed in the previous guidance, including SLAPP matters. The scope of actions in pursuing the rights to a good and healthy environment that are protected by the anti-SLAPP provision are: (1) providing suggestions or refusal on policies and projects in environmental matters; (2) complaining, whistleblowing, and reporting violations of environmental law; (3) giving opinions, witnesses, and expertise before the courts; (4) presenting opinion in the public sphere, press, social media, demonstration, and other forums; and (4) communicating to the state or government institutions related to the rights to a good and healthy environment.[18] Moreover, once a case is identified as SLAPP, the court must make a provisional decision to stop it promptly. Taking the Attorney General's Guidance and the 2023 Supreme Court's Regulation together, however, the efficacy of both instruments in resisting HEL in the country remains to be seen.

Following the persistent attacks on environmental defenders in the Philippines, civil society groups agreed to establish the first Filipino alliance of environmental defenders in 2018. The Environmental Defenders Congress comprises rural activists, Indigenous peoples, women's rights activists, environmental NGO activists, scholars, and professionals.[19] Like in Thailand, where NGO activists have taken a scale-jumping strategy to put the country under the international community's spotlight concerning violations of human rights, Filipino activists have employed a similar strategy to pursue reform from above through the UN Human Rights bodies, using their reporting mechanisms and special rapporteur appointments. In 2014, Victoria Tauli-Corpuz, a Filipina Indigenous Kankana-ey Igorot of the Cordillera Region, was appointed by the United Nations Human Rights Council (UNHRC) as the UN Special Rapporteur on the Rights of Indigenous Peoples. However, due to her critical voice on the conditions of Indigenous peoples of the Philippines under the Duterte regime, she was placed on a 'terrorist' list to be

[18] Article 48 para (3) of Indonesian Supreme Court's Regulation No. 1 of 2023 concerning the Procedures to Handle Environmental Cases.

[19] Weng Cahiles, 'Grim Regime: Unceasing Killings Despite the Pandemic', in T. Lopez (ed.), *Reclaiming the Narrative: The Struggles of Environment Defenders in Five Countries in Southeast Asia* (APNED & CEC, 2021) 74.

targeted for retaliation,[20] which triggered international concerns. In response, Resolution 41/2 by the UNHRC was adopted in July 2019 to express 'deep concern about allegations of threats, intimidation and personal attacks directed against special procedure mandate holders, including the Special Rapporteur on the Rights of Indigenous Peoples'.[21]

In addition, the resolution also mandates the High Commissioner for Human Rights (OHCHR) to conduct 'a comprehensive written report on the situation of human rights in the Philippines'.[22] In its report, the OHCHR notes that there have been 'pervasive attacks – online and offline – against human rights defenders over many years. For decades, red-tagging – labelling individuals and groups as communists or terrorists – has been a persistent and powerful threat to civil liberties and freedom of expression.'[23] Specifically concerning environmental defenders, it observes that they 'feature prominently among the documented killings of human rights defenders' with 'widespread impunity for such killings'.[24] The report provides recommendations, including those directed towards the protection of civil space, stating: '[e]nsure that the rights to freedom of expression, association and peaceful assembly are respected and protected; drop politically motivated charges against human rights defenders ... and others, and take legal measures to ensure their protection'.[25]

Domestically, in response to the findings, progressive lawmakers initiated a political move in December 2020 to propose an Environmental Defence Bill/ EDB (House Bill 817). The EBD aims to 'strengthen the protection of the environment from further destruction as well as protect the human rights of environmental defenders from any form of violence, threats, and harassment'.[26] Substantively, the bill adopts the principle of state responsibility for any violations against environmental defenders 'until credible evidence is presented to prove that non-government forces have committed it' and the presumption of validity in which '[a]ny complaint about environmental and human rights violations is presumed to be valid unless proven otherwise'.[27] It urges the government to undertake all necessary precautions to ensure that no environmental defender is subjected to threats, violence, harassment, discrimination, or other arbitrary measures for lawfully exercising their rights as an environmental defender.[28] Those measures include providing an annual allocation to support financially disadvantaged defenders and members of marginalised communities who intend to file a lawsuit to defend their

[20] Rina Chandran, 'Worried for Safety, Says U.N. Special Rapporteur on Philippine "Hit List",' *Reuters* (10 March 2018). <www.reuters.com/article/us-philippines-rights-un/worried-for-safety-says-u-n-special-rapporteur-on-philippine-hit-list-idUSKCN1GM0HO/?edition-redirect=uk> accessed 17 January 2024.

[21] UNGA Resolution A/HRC/RES/41/2 on 17 July 2019. [22] ibid.

[23] Report of the UN High Commissioner for Human Rights on the Situation of Human Rights in the Philippines A/HRC/44/22 on 29 June 2020, para 49, 10.

[24] ibid., 14. [25] ibid., 18.

[26] Center for Environmental Concerns – Philippines, *A Primer on the Environmental Defense Bill (House Bill 8170)* (CEC-Philippines, 2021) 2.

[27] ibid., 3. [28] ibid., 4.

environmental rights from violation, as well as an incentive for lawyers who provide free legal services to environmental defenders.[29]

Historically, the EDB is the second bill proposed by environmental movements to protect environmental defenders. Before the EDB, an anti-SLAPP bill was proposed to Congress in 2011 but has yet to be adopted. Due to the lack of regard paid by the political establishment to issues concerning the protection of environmental defenders, the EDB will likely follow the fate of the 2011 Anti-SLAPP Bill. As Lia Mai Torres puts it:

> [I]f we look at the composition of the congressmen, we will see that many of them also have an interest in resource extraction. . . . So it is hard to expect anything from them if they, themselves, would be in trouble once these bills are passed. So, we see that every time, more priority bills are railroaded, for example, the anti-terror law, even though we have been filing bills for several years already and nothing has happened.[30]

Her observation is valid because a meaningful political transformation has yet to occur in Congress. Rocky Guzman also expresses a similar observation that the bills are perceived to hold a left-leaning political agenda. The Duterte regime's ability to demonise left-wing politics in the public led to progressive groups' inability to mobilise a significant base of political constituents. Thus, the bills receive little support from citizens.[31] So far, there has been plodding progress, if not stagnancy, in advocating changes or reform concerning protecting environmental defenders within the domestic legal system. Here environmental movements may pursue scale-jumping strategies which are perceived as a better framework for protecting environmental defenders beyond the domestic scale.

Mobilising Rights beyond the Domestic Sphere

The HEL, especially in the form of SLAPP, is not a unique phenomenon that occurs only in Southeast Asia. Instead, it is a transnational phenomenon that can be observed to occur in many parts of the world, both in the Global South and the Global North. Amnesty International reports that SLAPP suits are increasingly understood to be a severe threat to the rights of freedom of expression and peaceful assembly in Europe. In 2022, for example, in the case of Sunčica Kovačevic and Sara Tuševljak, two young environmental activists from Bosnia and Herzegovina face defamation charges due to their protest against a Belgian-owned hydropower company on the Kasindolska river.[32] In 2023 in the UK, Stephen Gingell, a climate

[29] ibid., 6.

[30] Interview with Lia Mai Torres, the Coordinator of the APNED based in Manila, the Philippines, 12 April 2022.

[31] Interview with Rocky Guzman, environmental activist and deputy director of the Asian Research Institute for Environmental Law, 29 September 2022.

[32] Amnesty International, 'Bosnia and Herzegovina: Young Environmental Activists Face Baseless Defamation Charges from Belgian-Owned Hydropower Company in Bosnia', *Amnesty International* (20 October 2022). <www.amnesty.org/en/latest/news/2022/10/bosnia-and-herzegovina-young-environ

activist from Just Stop Oil, was sentenced to six months in prison by the Manchester Magistrate Court for violating the 2023 Public Order Act.[33] In South Africa, attacks on environmental defenders utilising legal means is 'a serious emerging threat to public interest litigation generally, and more particularly in environmental litigation, yet environmental protection heavily relies on the activities of public interest environmental organisations'.[34] In Latin America and the Caribbean, environmental movements have faced a shrinking of political space, where we witness a growing rate of criminalisation of environmental defenders with charges, including crimes against public order or public safety, abduction, disobedience against authority, riots, and disruption of public transport.[35]

Therefore, due to the failure of the national legal system in addressing HEL and protecting environmental defenders, environmental movements have pursued a scale-jumping strategy to present the issues in forums beyond national jurisdictions. Moreover, this strategy is pursued considering that states' behaviour at the domestic level may also be shaped by global power relations, such as serving the interests of multi- or transnational corporations.[36] As shown in Chapters 2 and 3, environmental conflicts that deploy HEL in Southeast Asia have been primarily shaped by the pursuit of new frontiers to expand natural resource extraction to supply the demand of the global resource market. For this reason, struggles against HEL should also be scaled beyond national boundaries. For this purpose, environmental movements mobilise legal, political, and institutional resources available at the regional and international levels to advocate for legal frameworks that provide better protection against HEL.

Several international and regional organisations have expressed their concerns about increasing attacks on environmental defenders across the globe. In 2017, the UN Special Rapporteur on Human Rights Defenders, John Knox, conducted a study to analyse the situation of environmental defenders. He observed three factors contributing to 'the acute and growing vulnerability' of environmental defenders: (1) increasing demand for natural resource extraction and exploitation; (2) groups that are affected by the increasing demand being politically and legally weak; and (3) a culture of impunity caused by 'weak and corrupt legal institutions'.[37] The report makes several recommendations to the states that are the duty-bearer in the context of human rights, which include: (1) emphasising the key requirements that

mental-activists-face-baseless-defamation-charges-from-belgian-owned-hydropower-company-in-bosnia/> accessed 18 December 2023.

[33] Damien Gayle, 'Just Stop Oil Activist Jailed for Six Months for Taking Part in Slow March', *The Guardian* (15 December 2023). <www.theguardian.com/environment/2023/dec/15/just-stop-oil-activist-is-first-to-be-jailed-under-new-uk-protest-law> accessed 18 December 2023.

[34] Tumai Murombo and Heinrich Valentine, 'SLAPP Suits: An Emerging Obstacle to Public Interest Environmental Litigation in South Africa', (2011) 27 *SAJHR* 81, 107.

[35] Angela Lindt, 'The Dark Side of Judicialization: Criminalizing Mining Protests in Peru', (2023) 58 *Latin America Research Review* 368, 373.

[36] Stanley and McColloch (n 2) 7.

[37] John Knox, *Environmental Human Rights Defenders* (Universal Rights Group, 2017) 10.

the state has to meet in ensuring an environment that is safe and enables defenders to exercise their rights; (2) adopting a constitutional provision on the right to a good and healthy environment to 'provide a stronger backbone to [environmental defenders'] domestic advocacy'; (3) complying with obligations enshrined in human rights instruments, including the rights relating to the environment and the rights of Indigenous peoples and marginalised communities; (4) reducing 'barriers to standing in environmental cases and consider instituting environmental courts, and they should facilitate training of judges on the relationship of human rights and the environment'.[38]

Welcoming the UN Special Rapporteur on Human Rights Defenders, the General Assembly issued Resolution A/HRC/RES/40/11 (2019) concerning recognising the contribution of environmental human rights defenders to the enjoyment of human rights, environmental protection, and sustainable development. It recognises 'the positive, important and legitimate role played by human rights defenders in the promotion and protection of human rights as they relate to the enjoyment of a safe, clean, healthy and sustainable environment' and expresses deep concern with their risk.[39] Accordingly, the resolution

> urges all states to take all measures necessary to ensure the rights, protection and safety of all persons, including environmental human rights defenders, who exercise, inter alia, the right to freedom of opinion, expression, peaceful assembly and association, online and offline, which are essential for the promotion and protection of human rights and the protection and conservation of the environment.[40]

In addition, the UN General Assembly has adopted Resolution A/76/L.75 concerning the human right to a clean, healthy, and sustainable environment. In this resolution, the role of environmental defenders 'in safeguarding the environment' is also recognised.[41]

In its report, the UN Special Rapporteur also recommends that regional organisations and communities adopt legal frameworks to protect environmental defenders in their regions. Regional treaties are expected for countries that 'lack effective national legal systems' in protecting environmental defenders and, at the same time, 'filling the current vacuum in international law'.[42] In the European region, for instance, Article 3 (8) of the Aarhus Convention stipulates that '[e]ach Party shall

[38] ibid., 21–22.

[39] UNGA, 'Resolution A/HRC/RES/40/11 Concerning Recognising the Contribution of Environmental Human Rights Defenders to the Enjoyment of Human Rights, Environmental Protection and Sustainable Development', United Nations Digital Library (21 March 2019) <https://digitallibrary.un.org/record/3804641>, 2.

[40] ibid., 3.

[41] UNGA, 'The Human Right to a Clean, Healthy and Sustainable Environment', United Nations Digital Library (26 July 2022). <https://digitallibrary.un.org/record/3982508?ln=en>, 3.

[42] Ian Grant, 'Protecting the Defenders: Exploring the Role of Global Corporations and Treaties', (2020) *E-International Relations*. <www.e-ir.info/2020/07/08/protecting-the-defenders-exploring-the-role-of-global-corporations-and-treaties/> accessed 22 July 2023, 4.

ensure that persons exercising their rights in conformity with the provisions of this Convention shall not be penalised, persecuted or harassed in any way for their involvement'. However, threats to environmental defenders remain a persistent feature in environmental activism in the region as reported in AC/WGP-24/Inf.16 concerning information note on the situation regarding Environmental Defenders in Parties to the Aarhus Convention from 2017 to date. As a response, in 2021, the United Nations Economic Commission for Europe (UNECE) issued a Rapid Response Mechanism which decided that 'all Parties shall ensure that penalisation, persecution, harassment and other forms of retaliation against environmental defenders are promptly brought to an end that Parties shall take effective measures to eliminate these inclusions, including . . . to bring justice those responsible'. Under this mechanism, an independent Special Rapporteur on environmental defenders has been established and appointed to undertake protective measures for environmental defenders who experience or are under imminent threat of persecution, penalisation, or harassment. The measures provided can be 'immediate' in an emergency circumstance or 'ongoing' in a condition under investigation by the Special Rapporteur.[43]

In addition, the European Union has adopted EU Directive 2019/1937 concerning the protection of whistleblowers, including in environmental matters. It is regarded as 'an important legal development' due to its comprehensiveness 'both in its material and personal scope of application'.[44] Specifically in environmental matters, Paragraph 10 regulates that 'the introduction of such protection is necessary to ensure effective enforcement of the Union environmental acquis, the breaches of which can cause harm to the public interest with possible spillover impacts across national borders'. It also includes a provision to protect whistleblowing from retaliation, including from SLAPP lawsuits. Paragraph 88, for instance, stipulates that '[w]here retaliation occurs undeterred and unpunished, it has a chilling effect on potential whistleblowers. A clear legal prohibition of retaliation would have an important dissuasive effect and would be further strengthened by provisions for personal liability and penalties for the perpetrators of retaliation.'[45] For this purpose, the Directive employs the standard of shifting the burden of proof in which the plaintiffs should prove that their lawsuit does not constitute a retaliation against the defendant,[46] and provides legal remedies and compensation

[43] Teresa Weber, 'Are Climate Activists Protected by the Aarhus Convention? A Note on Article 3(8) Aarhus Convention and the New Rapid Response Mechanism for Environmental Defenders', (2022) 31 (1) *Review of European, Comparative, & International Environmental Law* 67, 75.

[44] Vigjilenca Abazi, 'The European Union Whistleblower Directive: A "Game Changer" for Whistleblowing Protection?' (2020) 49 (4) *Industrial Law Journal* 640, 646.

[45] Directive (EU) 2019/1937 of the European Parliament and of the Council of 23 October 2019 on the Protection of Persons who Report Breaches of Union La. <https://eur-lex.europa.eu/legal-content/EN/TXT/PDF/?uri=CELEX:32019L1937>, L 305/30.

[46] Para 93 EU Directive 2019/1937 stipulates that 'once the reporting person demonstrates prima facie that he or she reported breaches of made a public disclosure in accordance with this Directive and suffered a detriment, the burden of proof should shift to the person who took the detrimental action, who should then

for defendants.[47] To have an effect, the EU Directive urges member states to adopt measures to prevent and deter the use of legal action to intimidate and silence whistleblowers.

Latin American and Caribbean countries have issued a Regional Agreement on Access to Information, Public Participation and Justice in Environmental Matters in Latin America and the Caribbean (Escazu Agreement). Taking the three pillars provided by the Aarhus Convention as inspiration, the Escazu Agreement adopted in 2018 moves beyond the convention by taking the current threats towards environmental defenders as one of its central focuses. The preamble recognises 'the important work of the public and human rights defenders in environmental matters for strengthening democracy, accessing rights and sustainable development and their fundamental contributions in this regard'. Furthermore, Article 9 stipulates explicitly about environmental defenders, stressing the responsibility of the state party to ensure 'a safe and enabling environment' for environmental defenders so that they may be able 'to act free from threat, restriction and insecurity', to undertake 'adequate and effective measures to recognise, protect and promote' their rights, including 'the right to life, personal integrity, freedom of opinion and expression, peaceful assembly and association', and to undertake 'appropriate, effective and timely measures to prevent, investigate and punish attacks, threats or intimidations' against them. It has been in force since April 2021 after being ratified by eleven state parties. As a new regional treaty, it is too early to evaluate its effectiveness, and it remains to be seen how it is mobilised by environmental movements to protect the defenders in exercising their rights and struggles against environmental injustices in the region.

The Problems of Rights in Southeast Asia

Responding to increasing attacks on environmental defenders and to prevent further attacks, European states, as well as states in the Latin American and Caribbean regions, have taken preventive measures, including enacting new agreements and strengthening existing regional treaties to address the issues. Environmental defenders in Southeast Asia have pursued similar strategies to bring attacks on environmental to regional and international forums as environmental defenders in the region have been continuously under attack despite existing

be required to demonstrate that the action taken was not linked in any way to the reporting or the public disclosure'. See Vigjilenca Abazi, 'The European Union Whistleblower Directive: A "Game Changer" for Whistleblowing Protection?' (2020) 49 (4) *Industrial Law Journal* 640, 649.

[47] Para 94 of E.U. Directive 2019/1937 stipulates that '[t]he appropriate remedy could take the form of actions for reinstatement, for instance, in the event of dismissal, transfer or demotion, or of withholding of training or promotion, or for restoration of a cancelled permit, licence or contract; compensation for actual and future financial losses, for example for lost past wages, but also for future loss of income, costs linked to a change of occupation; and compensation for other economic damage, such as legal expenses and costs of medical treatment, and for intangible damage such as pain and suffering'.

anti-SLAPP provisions in domestic legal jurisdictions. The establishment of the Asia Pacific Network of Environmental Defenders (APNED) has been as a response to the persistent threats faced by environmental defenders in the region and to develop coordinated strategies for tackling the threats in a wider geographical jurisdiction. Lia Mai Torres, the coordinator of the APNED, explains that the APNED was formed in 2018 'with the need of many organisations for a way to connect and to support each other with regards to environmental issues and with the growing concern of environmental defenders'.[48]

The APNED, together with other environmental and human rights organisations in the region (Fortify, Asian Institute for Environmental Law/AIEL, Forum Asia, and others), have been voicing and advocating for better protection of environmental defenders at regional and international levels. Currently, under the auspices of the UNEP Southeast Asia, the ASEAN Intergovernmental Commission on Human Rights and the Economic and Social Commission for Asia and the Pacific have held several coordinating meetings and conferences to understand the conditions of environmental defenders in the region and have been commissioned and attempted to pursue a regional framework concerning the protection of environmental defenders. Rocky Guzman argues that for this regional framework to be effective, it needs not only to include essential tools for environmental defenders, such as how to exercise the right to information, participation in decision-making, and access to effective remedies, but also to include 'a more enabling environment for environmental defenders to operate and for them to enjoy the full enjoyment of environmental rights'.[49] Meanwhile, as the framework is being processed, they have issued a series of toolkits to provide better equipment and resources that environmental defenders in the region need to prevent and address threats, including SLAPP lawsuits.[50]

Unlike those in the European region and the Latin America and Caribbean region, the rights-based legal mobilisation in pursing better protection in the Southeast Asian region appears to be challenging for environmental defenders and their supporting organisations. Institutionally, ASEAN's Asian Ways is an essential constraint to any attempt to take necessary measures to address the current situation of environmental defenders. Despite the enactment of the ASEAN Human Rights Declaration, as Gerthie Mayo Anda, a senior public interest lawyer and law professor in the Philippines, says, 'it is still rhetorical. It is still in writing. . . . When discussing human rights at the regional level, you also deal with sovereignty. . . . At the ASEAN level, we have had difficulties getting concrete political positions.'[51]

[48] Interview with Lia Mai Torres, the Coordinator of the APNED based in Manila, the Philippines, 12 April 2022.

[49] Interview with Rocky Guzman, environmental activist and deputy director of the Asian Research Institute for Environmental Law, 29 September 2022.

[50] APNED, *Environmental Human Rights Defenders Toolkits* (APNED, 2022) <https://apned.net/wp-content/uploads/2022/12/EHRD-Toolkit_full.pdf> accessed 12 June 2024.

[51] Interview with Gerthie Mayo Anda, a public interest lawyer and law professor at Palawan State University, the Philippines, 21 October 2022.

Putanee Kangkan, a prominent Thai human rights activist, also shares this concern, stating that 'ASEAN is mainly decided for business engagement rather than [wider social] engagement, such as human rights. . . . So, I do not see ASEAN as the good mechanism . . . for [resolving] issues like human rights.'[52] Indeed, this concern is particularly valid given that ASEAN was established in 1967 as an attempt to maintain regional security against communism and to foster economic cooperation.

Attacks on environmental defenders tend to be framed as primarily a legal and competency issue. For instance, the Business and Human Rights Resource Centre emphasises the lack or absence of anti-SLAPP legal frameworks as the main problem perpetuating the abuse of the judicial system to exhaust defenders' resources with impunity.[53] The effectiveness of legal intimidation against environmental defenders is also attributed to judges' lack of knowledge and skills in hearing SLAPP cases. Hence, it advocates that

> [i]n order to effectively fight SLAPPs – both in Southeast Asia and globally – we need robust legal frameworks and policies that prevent companies from filing SLAPPs in the first place and allow courts to identify, call out and dismiss them as soon as they are filed. To make this happen, governments, businesses, and investors, alongside defenders and civil society (and the lawyers who defend them), need to act decisively to protect civic freedom and human rights defenders.[54]

However, it is only partly true that the lack of or absence of legal frameworks have contributed to the growing attacks against environmental defenders utilising legal means. There are limited legal tools for defendants, and especially judges, to assess whether a case is a SLAPP case or not; and without such criteria and tools, the decision on legal motions is primarily based on the personal assessment of the judges. In this context, judges' visions of the world (ideology) may play a decisive role in their decision.[55] This can be seen in the tendency of judges to consider SLAPP cases in isolation from the specific socio-environmental conflicts in which they arise. This failure to see SLAPP cases in the context of the environmental conflicts in which they emerge makes judges see those cases as purely criminal or civil and decide on them using traditional legal reasoning. As a result, without examining the broader context of the cases, environmental defenders are very likely to be positioned as the punishable party by court decisions. Nevertheless, it should not be assumed that once an anti-SLAPP legal framework is in place, SLAPP cases will be automatically resolved. As long as the political-economic structure from which the exercise of law to defend the status quo in the first place remains intact, hegemonic lawfare will continue to be mobilised to contain environmental struggles.

[52] Interview with Putanee Kangkun, an activist of Fortify Rights Thailand and a victim of SLAPP, 31 October 2022.

[53] Maysa Zorob, *Defending Defenders: Challenging Malicious Lawsuits in Southeast Asia* (Business and Human Rights Resource Centre, 2020) 24–25.

[54] ibid., 25.

[55] Duncan Kennedy, *A Critique of Adjudication* (Harvard University Press, 1997).

In the face of this reality, rights-based legal mobilisation has been a dominant form of resistance against HEL. It has several notable strengths both at ideological and practical levels. Discursively, the language of rights represents a strong claim that cannot be separated from a duty borne by the state to respect, promote, and fulfil those rights. By claiming that defending an environment is an exercise of the right to a good, healthy, and sustainable environment, the duty-bearer, the state, must ensure such an exercise is protected from retaliation. Practically, advocating the protection of environmental defenders utilising the language of rights also provides a similar frame of legal judgment across different scales (local, national, regional, and international).[56] Once the protection of environmental defenders is included in human rights texts or norms, it becomes a moral and legal code upon which a state's behaviour is assessed and judged by its citizens and the international community. This is because human rights has become a lingua franca understood by activists, governments, and international organisations. Moreover, using rights in legal mobilisations resisting HEL may bring together both environmentalists and human rights activists into the same camp. Historically, there is a tension between these two modes of activism when they have different causes that in some cases may be in opposition to each other. There have been occasions where environmentalists advocate the protection of the environment, yet their advocacy may affect the enjoyment of human rights for communities that depend on resources or ecosystem services provided by the environment.[57] Framing environmental issues as human rights issues brings them together to advocate a shared cause and objective. Similarly, in the context of HEL, by framing people who defend livelihoods and the environment as exercising environmental rights, any attacks on them will bring attention to environmental and human rights activists, leading to collaborative responses to defend the defenders.

Despite such strengths, the rights-based legal mobilisation in resisting HEL also presents several weaknesses. Laura Böhm observes that although human rights are 'intrinsic to the human being and in theory do not require prior recognition, in practice they have required normative documents to recognise them and provide them with a protective framework'.[58] Here, the recognition and protection of human rights relies on the state's power to establish such a framework. If the public and international pressures to establish the framework to protect environmental defenders in the region are too strong and the risks of non-action are too high, states in the region may design such a framework without sacrificing the states' paramount interests in a carbon- and resource-intensive economic growth model. This

[56] Michael Anderson, 'Human Rights Approaches to Environmental Protection: An Overview', in A. Boyle & M. Anderson (eds.), *Human Rights Approaches to Environmental Protection* (Oxford University Press, 1996) 22.

[57] See, for instance, James Fairhead, Mellisa Leach and Ian Scoones, 'Green Grabbing: A New Appropriation of Nature', (2012) 39 (2) *The Journal of Peasant Studies* 237.

[58] Maria Laura Böhm, *The Crime of Maldevelopment: Economic Deregulation and Violence in the Global South* (Routledge, 2019) 52.

condition is particularly evident in Southeast Asia when the dominant actor who takes legal actions against environmental defenders is the state itself, that is, the institution that should have the obligation to protect these same defenders.

In Southeast Asia, the state is the most prominent and powerful agent of economic development, utilising its coercive and ideological apparatuses to ensure economic growth at all costs. Even with a legal protective framework, this does not guarantee 'a better position regarding the possibilities of compliance' with the framework because different state actors and institutions can act in contradictory or even oppositional ways to the framework that may be considered as a barrier to their business as usual practices.[59] In other words, the existence of the framework for protecting environmental defenders does not automatically neutralise threats experienced by environmental movements on the ground. On several occasions, the courts used the framework to dismiss HEL in their decisions, but this comes with a cost where defenders who have been turned into defendants in those cases struggle during a prolonged legal proceeding; hence, the chilling and transformative effects of HEL remain. Echoing Stanley and McCulloch, mobilising state institutions to resist lawfare 'can simultaneously confirm the institutional basis of the state and reinforce the parameters of "the law", as well as dominant ideologies that states are "good", protective and democratic'.[60]

In addition, since the concept of human rights encompasses many different types of rights, a set of rights may also be confronted by another set of rights. This tendency may lead towards an antinomy of 'right against right'. As Marx put it, '[b]etween equal rights, force decides',[61] for instance the right to development advanced by the state to favour capital investments in the extraction of natural resources may conflict with the right to freedom of expression claimed by environmental defenders in exposing and refusing such extractive activities. In this regard, the former likely prevails at the expense of the latter in the hands of the state as the authorised agent who has the final say. As evidenced by Chua in the context of the gay rights movement in Singapore, 'rights, particularly civil-political rights, are being traded off for the socially constructed goods of social stability and economic "progress" that help to reaffirm and maintain existing political hegemony'.[62] Indeed, repressing civil and political rights to maintain political and social stability and pursue the right to development (narrowly defined as economic growth) is not a feature unique to Singapore. This tendency is commonly experienced in Southeast Asia in general. The notion of civil and political rights remains a sensitive issue within ASEAN states. It leaves these issues to be dealt with as domestic matters cloaked in the doctrine of state sovereignty, which is applied through the principle

[59] ibid. [60] Stanley and McColloch (n 2), 48.

[61] Karl Marx, *Capital Volume I* (Penguin, 1976) 344.

[62] Lynette J. Chua, *Mobilising Gay Singapore: Rights and Resistance in an Authoritarian State* (Temple University Press, 2014) 159.

of non-interference.[63] As demonstrated in the case of Rohingya, where the Rohingya ethnic group has been systematically persecuted by the state of Myanmar, for instance, even gross violations of human rights could not be addressed collectively by ASEAN as a regional institution. More problematic again are human rights violations against environmental defenders that are not regarded as gross violations of human rights as these are unlikely to be of institutionalised concern to ASEAN states. In other words, if a gross violation of human rights could be implicitly condoned by ASEAN states, demands to protect the rights of environmental defenders are more likely to be disregarded by state authorities in the region.

The experience in Europe has also demonstrated the problem of rights-based resistance. This is evidenced in at least two cases, *Drieman and Others* v. *Norway* (2000) and *Chernega and Others* v. *Ukraine* (2019), held in the European Court of Human Rights, which is regarded internationally as the human rights courts champion. The former case concerned several Greenpeace activists who were arrested and fined for conducting a direct action against a Norwegian whaling ship in order to stop its operation. The Court was silent on whether such a mode of action was protected under Article 11 of the European Human Rights Convention on freedom of assembly and association. It reasoned that '[f]orcing the whaling ship to abandon its lawful activity' could not be considered as an action that would 'enjoy the same privileged protection under the Convention as political speech or debate on questions of public interest or peaceful manifestation of opinions on such matters'.[64] The latter case concerned measures taken by the Ukraine police to arrest and convict protesters for disobeying a police order during their obstructive demonstration against a road construction project. In its deliberation, the Court recalled that 'an interference with the right to freedom of peaceful assembly gives rise to a breach of Article 11, unless it can be shown that it was "prescribed by law", pursued one of the more legitimate aims as defined in paragraph 2 of that Article, and was "necessary in a democratic society"'.[65] As the action was obstructive, the measure by the authority to remove the protesters from the construction site was 'proportionate to the legitimate aim pursued'.[66] Accordingly, the Court found no violation of Article 11 of the Convention. If this *ratio decidendi* is applied in the context of SLAPP cases, it is likely that principled 'criminal' acts committed by environmental defenders do not fall within the scope of justifiable means of public participation; hence, those acts are not protected under anti-SLAPP legal instruments.

[63] Article 2 of the 1976 Treaty of Amity and Cooperation in Southeast Asia stipulates that '[i]n their relations with one another, the High Contracting Parties shall be guided by the following fundamental principles': Among others, '(a) mutual respect for the independence, sovereignty, equality, territorial integrity and national identity of all nations'; '(b) the right of every State to lead its national existence free from external interference, subversion or coercion'; and '(c) non-interference in the internal affairs of one another'.

[64] Council of Europe, *Guide to the Case-Law of the European Court of Human Rights* (Council of Europe/European Court of Human Rights, 2022) 65–66.

[65] *Chernega and Others v. Ukraine (2019),* para 231, 54.

[66] ibid., para 259, 61.

Duty-Based Resistance

The 'rights turn' in environmental politics is not a new phenomenon; indeed the proliferation of 'rights' talk in the post–World War II era has influenced this.[67] Moyn, as cited by Burdon, argues that at that time, human rights instruments were attractive to 'counter more radical demands made by the anti-colonial movement and international communism'.[68] Burdon further states that '[h]uman rights rose to prominence because they did not require a commitment to sharing power, a redistribution of wealth or a radical restructuring of society'.[69] In environmental matters, Boyd argues that an explicit constitutional provision on the rights to a good and healthy environment will provide a legal resource to be mobilised by social actors in demanding state responsibility. More than 140 countries have embraced environmental constitutionalism, in which the guarantee of environmental rights is expressed explicitly or implicitly in their constitutions.[70] However, environmental conflicts are far from decreasing, and ecological boundaries have continuously encroached even on systemic and planetary scales, leading to the Anthropocene.[71] Thus, the rights turn is not a panacea; that is, it is clearly not an adequate cure to transform the existing structure of capital accumulation from which environmental conflicts are its inherent consequences. As has been discussed, one set of rights can be outweighed by another, depending on who is in a position to define the result. In a structurally asymmetrical condition, elites have the power to decide, often at the expense of marginal social groups and the environment.

Here, a new proposal must be offered. Inspired by the 'duty-turn' in resistance studies, this section elaborates on why turning to duty or obligation in resisting HEL is illuminating. Delmas has argued that resistance is no longer a right but a duty in the face of structural injustice. For her, structural injustice occurs when the capacities of some people are hindered, while others benefit from the existing systems, which involves 'the interplay of law, social institutions, cultural understandings, and practices'.[72] She states, '[t]here is . . . a moral duty to obey the law in legitimating states – a duty grounded in widely accepted normative principles', and 'these same principles can justify and even require resistance in the face of injustice'.[73] Rather than advocating for rights as a basis of resistance, Burdon advances the concept of 'the priority of obligations' as a legal concept may 'displace the hegemony of rights'.[74] This is because a 'duty' or 'obligation' contains 'a deep ethical claim based on their necessity for human flourishing and communal life'.[75] Feminist

[67] Peter Burdon, *The Anthropocene: New Trajectories in Law* (Routledge, 2023). [68] ibid., 52
[69] ibid.
[70] James May and Erin Daly, *Global Environmental Constitutionalism* (Cambridge University Press, 2015)
[71] Will Steffen, Paul Crutzen and John McNeill, 'The Anthropocene: Are Humans Now Overwhelming the Great Force of Nature?' (2007) 38 *AMBIO: A Journal of the Human Environment* 614, 618.
[72] Candice Delmas, *A Duty to Resist: When Disobedience Should Be Uncivil* (Oxford University Press, 2018) 13–14.
[73] ibid., 48. [74] Burdon (n 67) 56. [75] ibid., 58–59.

Environmental Ethics has advanced the standpoint that every relationship will always give rise to a duty to its agent, which is the moral and legal basis for maintaining and nurturing the relationship.[76] Under unjust structural conditions, people should not 'be bound to obey the law in a society fraught with pervasive, grave injustice, even if that society provides some important public goods such as security and order'.[77] To state it bluntly, resistance is a duty in a society where the environment and people's means of survival are continuously destroyed in the pursuit of profit and economic growth, causing environmental and ecological injustices. An ethics of care requires people to resist such disregard because the environment is the source of life and livelihoods from which their survival is dependent.

Defending the Environment as a Legal Defence

After discussing the weaknesses of rights claims in resisting HEL and the need to develop duty-based resistance, the question remains of how to conceptualise the notion of obligation in the context of defending environmental defenders. To address this question, it is essential to begin with legal duties that protect the environment. In Thailand, for instance, chapter 3 Section 69 of the Thai Constitution stipulates: 'Every person shall have a duty to … conserve natural resources and the environment.' In Indonesia, such duties are stipulated by Article 67 of the 2009 EPM Act, which states that '[e]veryone is obliged to maintain the preservation of environmental functions and control pollution and/or damage to the environment'.

As an illustration, the *Robandi et al.* case (Indonesia) can be revisited. In its reasoning, the panel of judges stated that the defendants were proven to have committed the acts as charged by the public prosecutor. However, their actions did not constitute a criminal offence. Despite the progressive nature of this decision to protect environmental defenders from being silenced, the panel of judges did not provide a specific explanation of what grounds of defence the judges' verdict was built upon. In criminal law, there are two grounds of defence: excusatory and justificatory. The doctrine of the excusatory defence concerns an argument to eliminate 'guilt' for an unlawful act, which renders the position of the defendant as one where they cannot be convicted. Meanwhile, the justificatory defence is concerned with a self-defence argument that removes the unlawfulness of criminal conduct, which, in the Indonesian Criminal Code, is defined in four categories: (1) a conduct committed under duress;[78] (2) a conduct committed in defence of

[76] Kathryn Norlock, 'Ethics of Care', in J. B. Callicott & R. Frodeman (eds.), *Encyclopedia of Environmental Ethics and Philosophy* (Gale Cengage Learning, 2009) 399.

[77] Delmas (n 72) 111.

[78] Article 48 of the Indonesian Criminal Code stipulates that '[a]ny person commits an act under the influence of duress shall not be punished'.

necessity;[79] (3) a conduct in the execution of a statutory obligation;[80] and (4) a conduct in the execution of an official order.[81] Accordingly, the panel in the *Robandi et al.* case situated the conduct of defending the environment to be understood as a justificatory defence based on the statutory obligation stipulated by Article 67 of the 2009 EPM Act.[82] This deliberation is significant for developing a legal doctrine based on the duty to defend the environment in context of the current global environmental crisis predicament in which social-ecological relationships are built upon the moral and legal duties to ensure the planet's survival and its living beings – a notion that cannot be understood solely within an anthropocentric human rights framework.

Consequentialist and Eco-defence Arguments

Forms of conduct or expression utilised in defending the environment are often used to decide whether such forms are legitimate and deserve protection. In contrast to the standard narrow view that defending the environment should be carried out through legal or lawful means, it should be advocated that unlawful means may also be regarded as a legitimate form of struggle for the environment. However, the question remains of how to draw the boundaries for whether unlawful conduct to defend the environment is justified and, as a result, should not be punished. Minimally, there are two modes of argument to address this question. The first is the consequentialist argument. Anti-SLAPP provisions in Indonesia currently apply this argument. The Indonesian Attorney General's Guidance acknowledges that fighting for the right to a good and healthy environment may be carried out through lawful and unlawful means. Similarly, the Indonesian Supreme Court's Regulation also provides for the possibility to struggle to defend the environment by utilising means beyond the lawful scope provided by the regulation. In this context, a person engaged in unlawful conduct to defend the environment can be discharged from punishment if it meets the criteria of proper justification, which are (a) there is no alternative or other choice of action other than unlawful action, and (b) it is done to protect a greater legal interest for the benefit of the wider community.[83] Accordingly, the anti-SLAPP provision may be applied to protect environmental

[79] Article 49 para (1) of the Indonesian Criminal Code stipulates that '[a]ny person who is compelled to perform an act in defence by an unlawful attack or threatened attack, against himself or another person; against honour (*eerbaarheid*) or property of himself or another person, shall not be punished'.

[80] Article 50 of the Indonesian Criminal Code stipulates '[a]ny person commits an act to implement a statutory provision, shall not be punished'.

[81] Article 51 para (1) of the Indonesian Criminal Code stipulates that '[a]ny person commits an act in execution of an official order given by the competent authority, shall not be punished'.

[82] Article 67 of Environmental Protection and Management Law stipulates: '[e]very person is obliged to maintain the preservation of environmental functions and control pollution and/or damage to the environment'.

[83] Section VI para (7) of the 2022 Attorney General's Guidance on Handling Criminal Cases in Environmental Protection and Management; Article 48 para (4) of Indonesian Supreme Court's Regulation No. 1 of 2023 concerning the Procedures to Handle Environmental Cases.

defenders in using unlawful means, provided that the conduct meets the requirements of necessity (no alternative) and consequentialism (serving the greater good).

Specifically concerning the consequentialist argument, although it may provide the opportunity for environmental defenders to avoid being criminally charged in litigation, it is problematic both at the conceptual and practical levels. Conceptually, the consequentialist argument does not adequately reflect the character and substance of the claims of environmental movements in Southeast Asia, which have been characterised by 'environmentalism of the poor'[84] as 'a response to threats on livelihood'[85]. In this regard, their relations to the environment are not solely defined by an instrumental value from which the environment is merely natural resources to be used and managed, from which it can easily be subject to a cost–benefit analysis. Take the nature of land, for example. In Southeast Asia, land remains an imperfect commodity. Many people's relationships to land and other natural resources, especially Indigenous communities, are very often complex, involving rich symbolic meanings, including a sense of responsibility that connects the past, present, and future generations. This reality often underpins the emergence of sharp social conflicts when land is appropriated by the state or corporations, regardless of whether financial compensation may be paid.[86] In this condition, people's decisions are not the outcome of some form of cost–benefit analysis, rather their defence of their land and the environment is intrinsically bound to defending their livelihoods on which their survival depends. In these contexts, people rarely frame their struggles as fighting for the greater good but rather as a struggle for survival.[87]

In addition, using a consequentialist argument as a legal defence in a criminal case may have broader practical implications. As already mentioned, consequentialist logic assumes that social actors' conduct and actions are to serve the greatest happiness of the greatest numbers. In the context of Indonesia, for instance, a consequentialist argument was used by the Supreme Court to increase the sentence of environmental activist Budi Pego from ten months to four years. This decision was based on the accusation of the crime of spreading communism, which is considered a grave threat to the national ideology of Pancasila that holds the nation together. In Thailand and the Philippines, consequentialist logic has also been used to justify repression against those who are regarded as anti-monarchy or communist, respectively. Simply put, akin to human rights discourse, a consequentialist argument can quickly counter a consequentialist argument; ultimately, the powerholders decide which argument will prevail. Furthermore,

[84] Joan Martinez-Alier, *The Environmentalism of the Poor: A Study of Ecological Conflicts and Valuation* (Edward Elgar, 2002).

[85] Philip Hirsch and Carol Warren, 'Introduction: Through the Environmental Looking Glass: The Politics of Resources and Resistance in Southeast Asia', in P. Hirsch & C. Warren (eds.), *The Politics of Environment in Southeast Asia: Resources and Resistance* (Routledge, 1998) 10.

[86] Rebecca Mackelburg and Agung Wardana, 'The Political Economy of Land Acquisition for Development in the Public Interest: The Case of Indonesia', (2024) 137 *Land Use Policy* 1.

[87] See *Robandi and Others case* [2021] Court of Appeal of Bangka Belitung Decision No.21/PID/2021/PT BBL.

requiring defendants' motive to be in line with a consequentialist argument as a defence in litigation would mean putting more burden on them to justify to what extent their conduct will contribute to the general interests of the wider community. This is indeed a herculean work because the burden of proof of the standard of necessity and consequentialism is on environmental defenders' shoulders, as stipulated by Article 48 para (4) of the Indonesia Supreme Court's Regulation.[88]

Instead of being based on a consequentialist argument, the unlawful conduct in defending the environment is better justified by what Turner terms the 'eco-defence' argument.[89] This argument follows the notion of self-defence against intruders put by Abbey, the author of *the Monkey Wrench Gang*, who argues:

> If a stranger batters your door down with an axe, threatens your family and yourself with deadly weapons, and proceeds to loot your home of whatever he wants, he is committing what is universally recognised – by law and morality – as a crime. In such a situation, the householder has the right and obligations to defend himself, his family, and his property by whatever means necessary. This right and this obligation is universally recognised [sic], justified, and even praised by all civilised human communities. Self-defence against attack is one of the basic laws not only of human society but of life itself, not only of human life but of all life.[90]

Turner further develops the statement to defend the use of eco-sabotage carried out by Earth First! in the US on self-defence grounds. He states: '[a]ccording to the ordinary understanding of self-defence, we are entitled to defend (at most) ourselves, other persons, and our property against attack'.[91] Contextualising the eco-defence argument as a legal defence in hegemonic environmental lawfare requires some adjustment from Turner's concept, which is developed in the context of resorting to unlawful means, namely ecotage, by environmental activists to defend wilderness in the US. Hence, the actor here is environmental activists, and the object is wilderness in which he or she does not have a connection based on a sense of life necessities or direct dependencies to the environmental features being defended. In criminal law, this notion of private defence falls within the category of 'defence of another' – 'the application of force by a third party against one who attacks another person, in order to protect the life of the person attacked, his body or liberty'.[92] Meanwhile, in Southeast Asia, the defenders can be environmental

[88] Article 48 para (4) of Indonesian Supreme Court's Regulation No. 1 of 2023 concerning the Procedures to Handle Environmental Cases stipulates that '[t]he struggle to realise the right to a good and healthy environment as referred to in paragraph (1), paragraph (2), and paragraph (3) is carried out in accordance with applicable law unless it can be proven that: (a) there is no other alternative or choice of action other than the actions that have been carried out; and (b) the action is carried out in protecting the greater legal interests for the benefit of the wider community'.

[89] Derek Turner, 'Monkeywrenching, Perverse Incentives and Ecodefence', (2006) 15 (2) *Environmental Values* 213.

[90] Edward Abbey, 'Foward!' in D. Foreman & B. Haywood (eds.), *Ecodefense: A Field Guide to Monkeywrenching, 3rd Ed.* (Abbzug Press, 1993) 3.

[91] Turner (n 89) 222.

[92] Boaz Sangero, *Self Defence in Criminal Law* (Hart, 2006) 1.

activists concerned with biodiversity, as Philippine activists of the Earth Island Institute exercised in their struggles to protect dolphins being traded to the Resort World Sentosa.[93] As shown in previous chapters, environmental defenders in Southeast Asia are predominantly members of affected communities whose lives depend on the environment being encroached upon for development projects or extractive industries. Thus, in Southeast Asia, the eco-defence argument in resisting HEL encompasses not only the category of 'defence of another' as exercised by the Earth Island Institute but also the category of 'self-defence', which refers to 'the application of force by the person attacked against the aggressor in order to protect his own life, body or liberty'.[94]

The eco-defence argument here is grounded on two fundamental propositions. First, the environment is a means of livelihood. In other words, it is home to local communities and ecosystems upon which their necessities of life depend. Second, external forces, be they the state or corporations, are attackers who intrude on the local environment. They are encroaching on local livelihoods and ecosystems. Therefore, local communities are entitled to take measures to defend their livelihoods and ecosystems from encroachment by the attackers. Defending their necessities of life should be seen as a defence mechanism against intruders. One may argue that the state, as the political organisation representing the public interests, can utilise resources within its territory to pursue general welfare under the public trust doctrine. This liberal conception of the state is unattainable in Southeast Asia, where the state's claim for development in the public interest or national security very often benefits the powerful economic elites closely linked to the state officials.[95] Hence, in countries deeply captured by the interests of politico-business elites, the state's claim to act in the public interest, including in natural resource allocation or conservation, needs to be assessed critically to reveal the winners and losers. Eco-defence exercised by environmental defenders against the state's or corporation's encroachment should also be seen as a communicative action questioning the legitimacy of the state and corporations.

Others would argue that the eco-defence argument may lead to the abuse of law to justify conduct in bad faith. A wrongdoer can hide behind the cloak of the eco-defence argument to escape criminal liability. Indeed, this concern is valid. However, as an exception to the criminality of the act, the eco-defence argument also needs to be assessed based on two requirements: necessity and proportionality. The necessity requirement means unlawful conduct committed to defend the environment is out of necessity. Here, such necessity has two principal requirements: immediacy (the conduct committed due to immediate or foreseeable existential threat to their lives) and the duty to retreat (before committing the conduct,

[93] See the *Resort World Sentosa (RWS) v. Earth Island Institute (2013).*

[94] Sangero (n 92) 1.

[95] Mackelburg and Wardana (n 86), 1–9; Prachatai, 'Thongchai Winichakul: We Live under "Royalist Rule of Law"', Pratachai English (7 June 2024). <https://prachataienglish.com/node/10970> accessed 10 June 2024; Global Witness, *Defending the Philippines* (Global Witness, 2019).

defenders have exhausted appropriate means to express their dissent). Moreover, the requirement of proportionality refers to the standard that the harm caused by the conduct claimed to be self-defence should not be disproportionate to the harm avoided.[96] Unlike the consequentialist argument, which stresses the result of an act of self-defence, which should serve the greatest interests of society, the eco-defence argument emphasises the act of defence itself, aiming to prevent severe social and environmental harm.[97] In addition, echoing Sangaro in criminal law in general, unlawful acts of eco-defence should also not be assessed without considering the power dynamics between actors involved in environmental conflicts.[98] In this, it is essential to understand that the resort to unlawful acts of self-defence committed by environmental defenders is shaped by the structural constraints caused by imbalanced power relations and the ineffectiveness of formal politics (including political representation) and legal mechanisms in addressing people's grievances. Martin Luther King Jr., in the context of civil rights movements in the US, famously states: '[c]ertain conditions continue to exist in our society, which must be condemned as vigorously as we condemn riots. But in the final analysis, a riot is the language of the unheard.'[99] By saying this, it does not mean justifying unlawful conduct in making dissenting voices heard, but it deserves serious consideration of why aggrieved people turn to law-breaking actions.

To conclude, rights-based resistance against HEL in the form of anti-SLAPP provisions has been ineffective in Southeast Asia. Moving beyond the national legal systems, strategies of scale-jumping have been pursued by environmental movements in the region to demand that international and regional organisations, especially ASEAN, undertake necessary measures for strengthening the protection of environmental defenders in the region, including from the exercise of HEL by the state and corporations. However, such strategies have yet to produce positive outcomes. Arguing this does not mean that I deny the importance of pursuing regional and international legal frameworks for protecting environmental defenders. These matters should be approached with caution and moderation considering what such frameworks can offer to effectively protect environmental defenders within the context of given configurations of power and political-economic structures that remain intact in the region. As Rocky Guzman cautiously states, 'given the hesitancy of ASEAN to push for effective investigation of human rights and environmental defenders' abuses, we should not lose hope, but we should not also expect too much'.[100] In such a condition, a new approach is required to provide more weapons for resisting HEL. Another possibility worth pursuing is to develop duty-based resistance against HEL under the rubric of the eco-defence argument.

[96] Sangaro (n 92) 174. [97] ibid., 174. [98] ibid., 149.

[99] Cited in Ken Jackson, '"A Riot Is the Language of the Unheard": What Dr Martin Luther King Jr Said and Why It Applies Today' (Urbancny.com, 30 May 2020) <www.urbancny.com/a-riot-is-the-language-of-the-unheard-what-did-dr-king-said-and-why-it-applies-today/> accessed 2 February 2022.

[100] Interview with Rocky Guzman, environmental activist and deputy director of the Asian Research Institute for Environmental Law, 29 September 2022.

In this regard, unlawful acts taken to defend the environment are justifiable if they meet the necessity and proportionality requirements in order to be regarded as a form of justificatory defence in HEL through the criminal justice system.

Furthermore, Granit observes that the root causes of attacks on environmental defenders are 'complex and range from [a] lack of adequate governance, insecurity, inconsistent legal systems, and lack of accountability'.[101] One significant cause that is very often disregarded is the political-economic structure of the countries in relation to global market forces. Due to the structural asymmetry, the consequences of environmental extraction and exploitation are unevenly distributed within society, but they are distributed following class, race, gender, and other lines of social stratification that exist in the society.[102] Sheldrick demonstrates, in the case of Canada, that the effort to pursue reform in advocating anti-SLAPP legal instruments has faced difficulties 'in overcoming entrenched [interests] around access to courts, and . . . in overcoming opposition from those interests that are most likely to seek recourse to SLAPPs as a political strategy', namely corporate lobbyists and politicians.[103] In the context of the developing countries of Southeast Asia, Rocky Guzman states that HEL is a product of 'the percussiveness of corruption, the partnership of those who are in [political] power . . . with corporations or industries . . . [which] harm the environment [and destroy local livelihoods] . . . Because it is a structural issue, it requires a system change and a change in how the government works.'[104] Hence, demanding change either through rights-based or duty-based resistance against HEL requires continued struggles to dismantle the existing structures from which the attacks on environmental defenders are exercised in the first place. These struggles are not only about winning and losing because even in the case of losing, these struggles may also still have a successful dimension, by influencing, mitigating, constraining, and postponing activities or policies that may lead to environmental and social harm.[105]

[101] Ian Granit, 'Protecting the Defenders: Exploring the Role of Global Corporations and Treaties' (2020) E-International Relations. <www.e-ir.info/2020/07/08/protecting-the-defenders-exploring-the-role-of-global-corporations-and-treaties/> accessed 22 July 2023, at 4.

[102] See Jorge E. Hardoy, Diana Mitlin, and David Satterthwaite, *Environmental Problems in Third World Cities* (Earthscan, 1992) 102.

[103] Sheldrick (n 4) 103–120.

[104] Interview with Rocky Guzman, environmental activist and deputy director of the Asian Research Institute for Environmental Law, 29 September 2022.

[105] Stanley and McColloch (n 2).

Conclusion

This book has demonstrated how powerful actors mobilise law and legal institutions to contain environmental conflicts in Indonesia, Thailand, and the Philippines. The experience of those countries shares several notable features that shape the increasingly common strategy of those actors to resort to law to retaliate against environmental struggles. Those countries have undergone periods of colonisation either directly (Indonesia and the Philippines) or indirectly (Thailand). These colonial experiences have left significant legacies for the postcolonial eras, including their societal, economic, legal, and governance structures. In the context of land governance, for instance, the Hacienda system as a Spanish colonial legacy in the Philippines, the *domain verklaring* declaration as a Dutch colonial legacy in Indonesia, and forest colonisation in Thailand for supplying global demand in timber products have been a decisive factor leading to socio-environmental conflicts in the countries ever since. In the postcolonial context, the countries have been marked by political upheaval where authoritarian regimes use their authority and resources to expand extractive sectors, such as mining, forestry, and plantation, prioritising their alliances to maintain loyalty. This has led to the concentration of wealth and power in the hands of few politico-business elites which have continued to shape the political dynamics in the countries in the post-authoritarian eras.

Moreover, the three countries have also comparably undergone economic transformation under capitalist development which heavily relies on resource-based extraction. The resource-intensive development model to pursue economic growth has been a persistent economic feature in those countries. They seem to agree that the lack of infrastructure has been the bottleneck that prevents foreign investments in the countries. Hence, the contemporary governments in those countries have made infrastructure development one of the key development strategies for creating jobs and pursuing economic growth. Jokowi's 'Work,

Work, Work' slogan in Indonesia,[1] Prayut's vision of Thailand 4.0,[2] and Duterte's 'Build, Build, Build' tagline in the Philippines[3] are paramount examples of how the three countries prioritise business-friendly development policies and practices at the expense of protecting local livelihoods and environmental sustainability. Consequently, environmental issues as the inherent consequences of capitalist development have been alarming. Thailand, for instance, is characterised by the UNDP as a country going 'from being one of the most resource-abundant areas of the planet' into 'resource constrained over the space of one generation'.[4] Similarly, Indonesia is among the world's ten biggest greenhouse gas emitters, caused primarily by deforestation, forest degradation, and land use changes, especially for palm oil production.[5] The Philippines is regarded as 'one of the most severely deforested tropical countries' and the 'fourth in the world's top ten most threatened forest hotspots'.[6] According to the World Risk Report, those three countries are among the world's twenty-five highest-risk and most vulnerable countries. The Philippines is even ranked first, and Indonesia is second, whereas Thailand is ranked twenty-third, with the highest risk from disaster and exposure to global environmental changes.[7]

The rapid environmental changes and their effect on local communities have led to the rise of environmental movements concerned about economic transformation's impacts on people's livelihoods and the environment. This indicates what Karl Polanyi calls 'double movement',[8] in which the transformation towards market capitalism has been confronted by social forces whose interests and visions of the world are implicated. Unlike the Global North, where environmental movements are often seen as an expression of the urban middle class's concern for quality of life,[9] such movements in Southeast Asia might be seen as 'a response to threats on livelihood, notably those of the poor'.[10] In the region, environmental movements

[1] Rendi Witular, 'Jokowi: It's All Work from Now on', *The Jakarta Post* (Jakarta, 20 October 2014). <www.thejakartapost.com/news/2014/10/20/jokowi-its-all-work-now.html> accessed 30 April 2024.

[2] Thailand Board of Investment, 'Thailand 4.0 Means Opportunity Thailand', (2017) 27 (1) *Thailand Investment Review* 1–12. <www.boi.go.th/upload/content/TIR_Jan_32824.pdf> accessed 30 April 2024.

[3] Ferdinand Patinio, '"Build, Build, Build": Paving the Way to Progress', *Philippine News Agency* (Manila, 23 July 2021) <www.pna.gov.ph/articles/1147990> accessed 30 April 2024.

[4] UNDP, *Thailand Development Report: Sufficiency Economy and Human Development* (UNDP, 2017) 24.

[5] J. Friedrich, M. Ge, and A. Pickens, 'Shows Changes in the World's Top 10 Emitters', (*World Resources Institute*, 2 March 2023) <www.wri.org/insights/interactive-chart-shows-changes-worlds-top-10-emitters> accessed 3 July 2023.

[6] Yves Boquet, *The Philippine Archipelago* (Springer, 2017) 798.

[7] Ilona Frege, Vanessa Bliecke, Denis Djikzeul, et.al, *World Risk Report 2023* (Bündnis Entwicklung Hilft, 2023) 54.

[8] Karl Polanyi, *The Great Transformation: The Political and Economic Origins of Our Time* (Beacon Press, 2001 [1944]).

[9] See Hein-Anton van der Heijden, 'Political Opportunity Structure and the Institutionalisation of the Environmental Movement', (1997) 6 *Environmental Politics* 25, 26.

[10] Philip. Hirsch and Carol Warren, 'Introduction: Through the Environmental Looking Glass: The Politics of Resources and Resistance in Southeast Asia', in P. Hirsch and C. Warren (eds.), *The Politics of Environment in Southeast Asia: Resources and Resistance* (Routledge, 1998) 10.

heavily focus on defending the environment and local livelihoods from the encroachment of resource extraction and state-backed development projects. Their struggles also question 'the political systems that govern these resources that organise and extract capital and the associated uneven distribution of environmental harms'.[11] Hence, Indonesia, Thailand, and the Philippines demonstrate a comparable model of 'environmentalism of the poor', which has grown out of 'ecological distribution conflicts caused by economic growth and social inequalities'.[12]

To address environmental problems caused by rapid industrialisation and economic development, the countries developed their domestic environmental policies and laws. Indeed, modern environmental law in the three countries has evolved since the 1972 Stockholm Declaration, which indicates a move from a piecemeal approach towards a comprehensive approach to the environment. It should be noted, however, that environmental movements have contributed to the progress of the development of environmental law in those countries. Like their counterparts in the UK,[13] despite the hostile legal-political economic structure, environmental movements in Southeast Asia do not passively wait for their interests to be accommodated by the state. However, they persistently struggle to push the normative boundaries of law to respond to the rapidly changing environment caused by development and to widen access to environmental justice. Through strategic litigation, they attempt to make the state and corporations accountable and liable for environmental protection, leading to several landmark cases. In the Philippines, the *Minor Oposan* v. *Factoran* (1993) case was among the world's first jurisprudence that recognised the future generation's legal standing to sue in environmental matters. In Indonesia, the *WALHI* v. *Inti Indorayon* (1989) case changed the legal landscape in the country by giving an environmental NGO legal standing before the court as the guardian of the environment. In Thailand, the *Map Ta Phut* case (2009) has been a crucial example of how environmental activists turn to the court to block an industrial activity that may harm the environment.

However, this 'legal mobilisation by the powerless' through strategic litigation has been countered by 'legal mobilisation by the powerful'[14] through which corporations and state officials whose interests are affected by environmental struggles resort to courts to contain the struggles. Corporations have increasingly turned to courts to retaliate against their opponent groups in the post-authoritarian eras which have brought the waves of democratisation, human rights, and the rule of law into the public discourse. As a result, corporations could no longer rely on mobilising the state

[11] Eli Elinof and Vanessa Lamb, 'Environmental Politics in Thailand: Pasts, Presents, and Futures', in P. Chachavalpongpun (ed.), *Routledge Handbook of Contemporary Thailand* (Routledge, 2020), 379–393, 379.

[12] Joan Martinez-Alier, *The Environmentalism of the Poor: A Study of Ecological Conflicts and Valuation* (Edward Elgar, 2002) 14.

[13] Lisa Vanhala, 'Legal Opportunity Structures and the Paradox of Legal Mobilisation by the Environmental Movement in the UK', (2012) 46 (3) *Law and Society Review* 523.

[14] Michael McCann, 'Litigation and Legal Mobilisation', in K. Whittington, R. Kelemen, & G. Caldeira (eds.), *The Oxford Handbook of Law and Politics* (Oxford University Press, 2008) 534.

apparatuses, namely the military force, to repress environmental struggles utilising direct violence. In Indonesia, for instance, after the fall of Suharto's authoritarian regime, it did not seem to be a coincidence that the US model of corporate practices in filing lawsuits against activists was transplanted into Indonesia's business legal practice. This is evidenced by the fact that the first two SLAPP lawsuits in Indonesia were brought almost simultaneously by two subsidiary companies of the Newmont Corporation, a giant US gold company, respectively the Newmont Minahasa operated in South Sulawesi and the Newmont Nusa Tenggara operated in West Nusa Tenggara. In 2015, Newmont's affiliated company in Peru, Minera Yanacocha, also used a similar strategy to retaliate against environmental defenders who fought against its Conga Mining Project.[15] Thus, resorting to law and legal institutions appears to be the company's habitus when dealing with opponent groups.

The increasing tendency of corporations operating in post-authoritarian states to use legal actions to retaliate against environmental defenders cannot be separated from the increasingly popular discourse of the rule of law. Here, the rule of law should be seen as an ideological underpinning because it may 'display an independence from gross manipulation [of power]' and 'pretends to reconcile the interests of all degrees of men'.[16] Thus, mobilising law strategically may complement the reliance on the use of coercive measures once deploying those measures is no longer possible in a given context due to being increasingly condemned by the public in the era of democratisation and human rights. The persistent reliance on direct violence may lead to a crisis of legitimacy both for the corporation and the state and, in turn, may radicalise the populace. Indeed, the rule of law provides the right to access an effective remedy by utilising legal mechanisms to demand compensation if a private actor suffers losses, including reputation damage, caused by another private actor's conduct. Echoing Thompson, the powerful groups 'were content to be subject of the rule of law only because this law was serviceable and afforded to their hegemony the rhetoric of legitimacy'.[17] For the company's advocates, filing a lawsuit is an attempt to represent themselves respecting and complying with the rule of law which directs conflicting rights (the right to an effective remedy versus the right to freedom of expression) to be resolved by legal means, especially the courts.

In brief, historical junctures have shaped the political-economic trajectories in those countries and provide the structural contexts through which environmental movements have emerged as responses to political and economic transformation. These movements are far from monolithic as they have diverse characteristics in terms of organisational forms or tactics and strategies of resistance[18] influenced by

[15] Lady Nancy Jaramillo and María Leoni, *SLAPPs in Latin America: Strategic Lawsuits against Public Participation in the Context of Business and Human Rights* (Business & Human Rights Resource Center, 2022) 9.

[16] Edward P. Thompson, *Whigs and Hunters: The Origin of the Black Act* (Breviary Stuff Publications, 2013 [1975]) 205–210.

[17] ibid.

[18] Hirsch and Warren (n 10), 1; Paul Jobin, Ming-sho Ho and Hsin-Huang M. Hsiao, 'Environmental Movements and Politics of the Asian Anthropocene: An Introduction', in P. Jobin, M. Ho and H. M. Hsiao

the legal and political opportunity structure where they are operated. More importantly, the structural conditions have shaped strategies for responding to environmental struggles by the state and non-state actors whose interests are affected by the struggles, including resorting to law and legal institutions.

SLAPP and anti-SLAPP Provisions

Environmental law in the region has been shaped by social conflicts over the environment and has become a strategic terrain through which different interests over the environment and natural resources are fought for. In this regard, to manage those conflicts, the law is mobilised as a resource by powerful actors filing lawsuits against opponent groups to silence, intimidate, and punish their struggles. An important aspect of the lawsuits is 'the unequal relations of power and status'.[19] Moreover, they shift the conflicts that are deeply rooted in the political-economic structure into the legal sphere as a strategy of deflecting them from the root cause. Following several cases concerning the attacks against environmental defenders and the pressure of reforming environmental law, Indonesia, Thailand, and the Philippines have responded through legal measures. In Indonesia, an anti-SLAPP provision has been adopted in Article 66 of the 2009 Environmental Protection and Management Act. In the Philippines, a similar provision has also been incorporated in the Clean Water Act, the Ecological Solid Waste Management Act, as well as the Republic Act No. 10654 on Act to Prevent, Deter and Eliminate Illegal, Unreported and Unregulated Fishing, Amending Republic Act No. 8550 of the 1998 Philippine Fisheries Code. The judiciaries in both countries have also responded to the SLAPP phenomenon by issuing the Philippine Supreme Court's Rules of Procedures for Environmental Cases in the Philippines and the Indonesian Supreme Court's Chief Justice Directive No. 36 of 2013 concerning the Guidance to the Handling of Environmental Cases (later replaced by the 2023 Indonesian Supreme Court's Regulation), which both include anti-SLAPP provisions. In Thailand, preventing SLAPP has been pursued through the 2010 revision of the Public Prosecution Institution and Public Prosecutors Act BE 2553 (AD 2010), followed by revising the Criminal Procedure Code. Despite such adoption, the attacks on environmental defenders utilising legal actions have been a persistent challenge faced by environmental movements in the countries.

Indeed, enacting anti-SLAPP provisions does not necessarily lead to a decrease in the use of law to silence environmental defenders. By stating this, I do not mean to disregard the existence of those provisions. However, I devote this book to

(eds.), *Environmental Movements and Politics of the Asian Anthropocene* (ISEAS, 2021) 1; Arne Kalland and Gerard Persoon, 'An Anthropological Perspective on Environmental Movements', in A. Kalland and G. Persoon (eds.), *Environmental Movements in Asia* (Routledge, 2013) 1.

[19] Orapin Lilitwisitwong and Thitiphan Pattanamongkol (eds.), *SLAPP: The Public Dreams of Anti Strategic Lawsuit Against Public Participation* (Thai Society of Environmental Journalists, 2022) 14.

understanding why those provisions aiming to protect environmental defenders have little effect on the ground. Here, by taking the experience of Southeast Asia, I argue that the outcome of anti-SLAPP provisions is contributed by the inadequacy of SLAPP, a conceptual framework that originated in the Global North, to capture the dynamics of legal mobilisation by the powerful to silence, intimidate, and punish environmental defenders in the Global South. This inadequacy is due to at least two points: first, it perceives environmental conflicts from which the use of law to retaliate against dissent groups' struggles results from a conflict of rights. Accordingly, those struggles are seen as an exercise of rights, especially the right to petition, the right to participate in environmental matters, or the right to freedom of expression; second, it conceives the state from a liberal perspective as a neutral institution that seeks to balance diverse and competing interests in society, including the interests over the environment and natural resources.

Both conceptions are problematic in Southeast Asia. The narrative of human rights has rarely been considered a serious matter in the region where suppression of such rights tends to be part of the routinised exercise of state power in pursuing the public interest defined in economic development and growth terms. In this regard, the Rohingya crisis in Myanmar has been notable evidence of the failure of Southeast Asian countries to respond collectively to a gross violation of human rights in the region, utilising the ASEAN's principle of non-intervention.[20] If gross human rights violations do not receive an adequate response, it is doubtful that ASEAN will do any better in responding to civil rights violations, such as the right to freedom of expression and association, which are easier to sweep under the carpet. Furthermore, as the duty bearer in the human rights context, the state is far from a neutral agent. Instead, as discussed in Chapter 4, the state is the dominant actor that exercises legal attacks on environmental dissent. Accordingly, expecting the state to take its duty to protect environmental defenders from being legally retaliated against when exercising their rights appears to be wishful thinking. Based on this premise, the book offers a fresh framework to understand the phenomenon comprehensively termed 'hegemonic environmental lawfare' (HEL).

Hegemonic Environmental Lawfare

Chapter 1 examines different conceptions used to understand legal retaliation against environmental defenders. Those diverse understandings can be situated within two main streams: the liberal and critical streams. To date, the liberal stream tends to appeal to legal scholars because it fits nicely with rights-based perspectives in perceiving environmental conflicts. This is evidenced by the use of the term 'SLAPP' as the official legal concept by many countries, regional institutions, and

[20] Mathew Davies, 'The Perils of Incoherence: ASEAN, Myanmar and the Avoidable Failures of Human Rights Socialization', (2012) 34 (1) *Contemporary Southeast Asia* 1.

international communities to capture the resort to law in preventing the exercise of the procedural elements of the rights to a clean, healthy, and sustainable environment (R2E), specifically the right to public participation in environmental matters. As legal attacks on environmental defenders are seen from the rights-based perspective, responses to them are also pursued through strengthening environmental rights, namely their procedural elements. Meanwhile, the critical stream situates legal attacks within the broader political-economic structure as part of the state and corporation's strategy to pursue their interests against environmental movements that are regarded as barriers. However, to date, the critical stream utilising the concept of 'criminalisation' stresses exclusively the coercive elements of the law represented by the criminal justice system. As a result, the hegemonic element of the attacks through legal means is overlooked.

This book works within the critical stream by introducing HEL as a political strategy by resorting to law and legal institutions to pursue strategic objectives. Legal actions directed towards environmental defenders in the Global South should be situated in a broader context of using law for political ends. In this regard, HEL, regardless of its form, such as SLAPP, criminalisation/penalisation, or legal intimidation, is 'a species of political displacement' taking place within the domain of 'hegemonic lawfare' as the use of law and legal institutions as a weapon exercised by the powerholders in order to maintain their hegemony. It should be noted that the exercise of HEL is not designated as a conflict resolution mechanism through which environmental conflicts are resolved directly. Instead, it is a technology of power to govern environmental conflicts, which encompasses interests, resources, procedures, ideologies, and strategies to deflect environmental conflicts from their root cause so that environmental struggles lose their capacity to resist. Its consequences are projected beyond environmental defenders directly involved in the conflicts towards the general populace, from which the legitimacy of legal actions against defenders are harvested and general consent is mobilised. Thus, this framework understands that legal mobilisation to attack environmental defenders 'does not happen in isolation' but is 'part of a spectrum or playbook of escalating tactics deployed by corporations and their allies to divide communities, distract leaders, and weaken social movements'.[21]

Moreover, the use of HEL should be seen as an attempt by those in power to find a more subtle way to control environmental movements while minimising the risk of losing legitimacy. The dominant view is that legal measures against environmentalists, such as SLAPP and criminalisation, abuse legal processes that have arisen in an untrustworthy state of the rule of law. In contrast to this view, the book presents these moves as a result of the neoliberal rule of law which encompasses two paradoxical tendencies: on the one hand, the law and legal institutions

[21] Nina Lakhani, Damien Gayle, and Matthew Taylor, 'How Criminalisation is Being Used to Silence Climate Activists across the World', *The Guardian* (12 October 2023) <www.theguardian.com/environment/2023/oct/12/how-criminalisation-is-being-used-to-silence-climate-activists-across-the-world> accessed 12 April 2024.

are presented as independent, with judicial decision-making based on due process and a legal technocracy that strives for logical coherence; on the other hand, they are instrumentalised to create a conducive climate for investments and the market economy to flourish. For this purpose, the rule of law, through its doctrine of equality before the law, provides a fiction of an equal chance for actors to win a case brought before the court because the legal system runs on the internally coherent logic and due process of law. Accordingly, whatever decision resulting from the legal proceeding should be respected by the disputing actors and challenges to it can only be carried out through designated mechanisms within the system.

In countries where structural asymmetries such as unequal power and resource relations and unequal access to justice exist between social actors, the rule of law becomes an ideological basis for HEL to combat environmental struggles that disrupt capital accumulation and economic growth. The HEL is a consequence of neoliberal legal reform through which law and legal institutions are aligned to the interests of business enterprises to accumulate profit. It also aims 'to silence out and discourage those who would like to imagine and practise alternatives to the existing economic system'.[22] In other words, HEL should not be seen as merely a legal mobilisation by the powerful elites to intimidate, silence, or punish environmental defenders; its strategic impacts are projected towards the populace.

Putting legal attacks within the 'hegemonic lawfare' frame makes it possible to reveal its strategic dimensions: geography, weaponry, externalities, and resistance. The geography of HEL refers to the battlefield within which lawfare takes place, which may encompass three forms of jurisdiction: (1) subject-matter jurisdictions, that is, the legal procedures mobilised to silence, intimidate, or attack environmental defenders; (2) territorial jurisdictions (legal institutions' geographical scope of competence); and (3) sectoral jurisdictions, referring to the economic sectors in which HEL is commonly exercised. Data on legal action cases against environmental defenders during 2010–22 in Indonesia, Thailand, and the Philippines reveals that the liberal stream's argument that adopting anti-SLAPP provisions would prevent SLAPP cases should be treated cautiously in Southeast Asia. This argument is only partly valid because defending a case utilising the anti-SLAPP provisions tends to be applied only limitedly by the court in civil proceedings. This is because the civil proceeding provides more freedom for the judges to apply the anti-SLAPP provision, and it is also under less pressure than a criminal case since the disputing parties are private actors in which the judges may distance themselves from the interests of the parties.

It should be noted that the criminal justice system in the region seems preferable for the powerful groups to retaliate against environmental defenders. Throughout the history, '[t]he criminal law', as Hay characterised, has been 'critically important

[22] Manuel Mireanu, 'The Criminalisation of Environmental Activism in Europe', (2014) LIX (2) *Studia UBB Sociologia* 87, 102.

in maintaining bonds of obedience and deference, in legitimizing the status quo, in constantly recreating the structure of authority which arose from property and in turn protected its interest'.[23] In the context of HEL, besides providing an opportunity to avoid a direct legal battle against environmental defenders under the cloak of enforcing criminal law, corporations find the criminal proceeding to be more cost-efficient because it runs on the state budget, unlike the civil procedure in which the plaintiff should bear the cost of the legal proceeding and hiring legal representatives. It should be noted that the criminal justice system has been the primary jurisdiction mobilised by powerful actors in silencing environmental movements in the regions. In Thailand, for instance, corresponding to Strekfuss's characterisation of the country as a 'defamation regime',[24] the findings presented in Chapter 4 show how defamation has served as the biggest weapon to retaliate against environmental defenders. In Indonesia and the Philippines, criminal offences used to punish environmental defenders dominantly fall within the crimes against public orders, the crimes against the state ideology and symbols, and the incitements against the legitimate government. In the Philippines, besides the criminal justice system, administrative law measures, such as freezing bank accounts and the declaration of 'persona non grata', have increasingly been exercised by the state officials that affect the work of environmental organisations and activists on the ground. In criminal proceedings, however, anti-SLAPP provisions appear less effective because judges tend to isolate the intimidating cases from the primary issue, environmental conflicts. Hence, the outcomes of HEL pursued through the criminal justice system have been largely mixed.

Two dominant sectors that resort to HEL are the mining sector and the forestry and plantation sector; both are closely associated with the countries' powerful politico-business elites. As Kojola and Pellow put it: '[m]ining is a form of ecological violence – literally tearing apart the earth – that creates environmental injustices as the often-working class, rural, and Indigenous residents and workers are exposed to toxic pollution and the instabilities of boom-and-bust resource economies'.[25] Thus, extractive industries, including mining and plantation, accumulate their wealth not only through extracting labour and cheap resources in their production but also through taming or retaliating against resistance from those who disrupt their operations. In addition to those two dominant sectors, the energy and tourism industries have also contributed a comparable number of HEL cases in the region.

[23] Douglas Hay, 'Property, Authority, and the Criminal Law', in D. Hay, P. Linebaug, J. G. Rule, E. P. Thompson and C. Winslow, *Albion's Fatal Tree: Crime and Society in Eighteenth-Century England* (Pantheon Books, 1975) 25.

[24] David Streckfuss, *Truth on Trial in Thailand: Defamation, Treason, and Lese-Majeste* (Routledge, 2011) 5.

[25] Erik Kojola and David Pellow, 'New Directions in Environmental Justice Studies: Examining the State and Violence', (2021) 30 *Environmental Politics* 100, 110.

In contrast to the Global North, where the legal battle occurs between two non-state actors – corporations versus environmental activists – in Southeast Asia, and the Global South in general, attacks through criminal law demonstrate the active role of state officials and agencies. This tendency is evidenced by the legal provisions or criminal offences mobilised as a weapon to retaliate against environmental defenders. They are crimes against public order and the state's ideology/symbols. In contrast to complaint-based offences (*klachtdelicten*) which require an aggrieved party to submit a complaint to law enforcement officers and the proceedings are undertaken based on the aggrieved party's consent, the crimes against public order, state ideology, and symbols, as well as incitement against the government are designated as ordinary offences (*gewone delicten*) which require no complaint. Technically, they can be reported anonymously, so the suspects do not know who made the report. In addition, these categories of crimes provide the monopoly of legal interpretation to law enforcement officers on what constitutes public order, a threat against the state ideology or symbols, and a threat against the legitimate government, and the authority to decide whether cases involving these crimes will be put forward for a trial.

Furthermore, the externality of HEL refers to consequences that are intended to be imposed, targeted not only by individual defenders but also by groups involved in environmental resistance collectively. As a form of strategic legal action, HEL aims to create projecting externalities, referring to the consequences that seek to be borne by environmental movements beyond the actual legal cases. From the experience of Southeast Asia, through legal actions, environmental defenders have been turned into 'the other', such as criminals, communists, or terrorists. This form of othering is effective in delegitimising environmental movements and keeping them at bay because the public is frightened to be associated with communists or terrorists.

Resistance to HEL points out acts or events through which it is challenged, contested, halted, and prevented by environmental movements. As counterarguments, environmental defenders who were defendants in lawfare cases have used the constitutional provisions, especially related to the rights of freedom of expression, opinion, and peaceful assembly, to protect themselves against the charges. In addition, they have used the anti-SLAPP provisions to demonstrate that the charges against them were SLAPP and that their struggles were an exercise of their rights to a good and healthy environment. However, the outcomes of this mobilisation of those provisions are relatively uncertain. Even though several criminal cases found that the defendants were acquitted, they had to go through a time- and resource-intensive legal proceeding. Many cases have been suspended or postponed, which represents another tactic to prolong the chilling effects and hold the defendant hostage to make them surrender or at least soften their resistance, otherwise the legal case will proceed.

As pointed out by the political geography literature, scales may serve as a terrain through which resources are accessed, and alliances are built in social conflicts; social forces that find difficulty in confronting their rival in a particular geographical scale may utilise a scale-jumping strategy to different scales available. Similarly, considering the ineffectiveness of domestic anti-SLAPP provisions, Southeast Asian environmental movements build alliances and networks beyond their localities, including by advocating protective measures at the regional and international levels. At the regional level, Latin America and the Caribbean countries have provided regional safeguards to environmental defenders by enacting the Escazu Agreement on Access to Information, Public Participation and Justice in Environmental Matters.[26] In addition, European countries have taken measures to protect environmental defenders, such as the enactment of EU Directive 2019/1937 concerning the protection of whistleblowers[27] and establishing a Rapid Response Mechanism, including appointing a Special Rapporteur on Environmental Defenders under the 1998 Aarhus Convention.[28] In the Southeast Asian region, environmental and human rights groups, under the auspices of the UNEP Southeast Asia and the ASEAN Intergovernmental Commission on Human Rights, have been preparing the Declaration on Environmental Rights, including anti-SLAPP measures.[29]

To date, however, responses against HEL remain predominantly human rights-based, even though mounting evidence shows that this approach narrative has been ineffective in the region. This condition opens new opportunities to craft different strategies. Inspired by the 'duty-turn' in resistance studies,[30] as demonstrated in Chapter 6, the book proposes duty-based legal mobilisation by conceptualising the obligation to defend the environment as a justificatory defence in HEL cases. This duty-based legal mobilisation contends that environmental struggles in the time of systemic environmental injustices and the environmental crisis should be viewed as collective moral and legal duties. Here, instead of arguing based on human rights, HEL is challenged by an eco-defence argument based on two simple propositions. First, the environment supports life. In other words, it serves as a livelihood for local communities and the habitat for the local ecosystems. Second, externally powerful entities, be they the state or corporations, that invade the local environment are aggressors because they disrupt livelihood ecosystems

[26] Kendrick Foster, 'Protecting Latin America's Environmental Defenders: The Fight for the Escazú Agreement', (2021) 42 (3) *Harvard International Review* 22.

[27] Vigjilenca Abazi, 'The European Union Whistleblower Directive: A "Game Changer" for Whistleblowing Protection?' (2020) 49 (4) *Industrial Law Journal* 640.

[28] Teresa Weber, 'Are Climate Activists Protected by the Aarhus Convention? A Note on Article 3(8) Aarhus Convention and the New Rapid Response Mechanism for Environmental Defenders', (2023) 32 (1) *Review of European, Comparative & International Environmental Law* 67.

[29] Liang Lei, 'As ASEAN Environmental Rights Draft Takes Shapes, Advocates Fear Weakened Safeguards', Eco-Business (Singapore, 28 March 2024) <www.eco-business.com/news/as-asean-environmental-rights-draft-takes-shape-advocates-fear-weakened-safeguards/#:~:text=The%20Asean%20draft%20text%2C%20stemming,right%20to%20protect%20such%20conditions> accessed 20 April 2024.

[30] Candice Delmas, *A Duty to Resist: When Disobedience Should be Uncivil* (Oxford University Press, 2018); Kimberly Brownlee, *Conscience and Conviction: The Case for Civil Disobedience* (Oxford University Press, 2012).

essential to local survival.[31] Accordingly, protecting their livelihoods and ecosystems from outside intrusion should be seen as a local defence strategy against encroachment or intrusion into the environment and their means of survival.

Implications to the Literature

In an edited book entitled *Law, Capitalism and Power in Asia*, Jayasuriya examines empirically the relationship between law and capitalist development in the East Asian region, utilising social conflict theory.[32] He points out that the causal link between the legal system and economic development seems to be dubious and argues that 'high levels of economic performance bear little or no relation to the development of a credible legal system'; however, for him, capitalism in the region is 'a kind of "political capitalism" characterised by networks of non-market relationships operating horizontally between economic agendas, and vertically between economic agents and state actors'.[33] Rather than facilitating the sphere of markets directly, for example through instruments that provide calculability and predictability for economic actors, as assumed by Law and Development scholars, the law tends to be mobilised by the state and powerholders to shape the spheres of the state and society. In this regard, Jayasuriya observes that 'the law is a substitute for politics. . . . Legality would underpin the actions of the government and provide the basis for bureaucratic procedures . . . [L]aw [is] both an instrument of state-building as well as a useful instrument of legitimation.'[34] This observation provides an important insight for elaborating the different roles of law in capitalist development. Although it is not considered to have a decisive role in directly stimulating economic activities, the law remains an essential institution for maintaining the social order, a condition required for the market economy to flourish. This includes how law is mobilised to contain social conflicts related to the environment in the form of hegemonic lawfare, as this book has demonstrated.

Furthermore, locating SLAPP and legal intimidation in a broader framework of 'lawfare' makes it possible for researchers to understand legal actions against environmental defenders more comprehensively. This is because the framework of HEL brings together Pring and Canan's original conception of SLAPP and critical criminologists' framework of criminalisation to examine legal mobilisation directed towards intimidating, silencing, retaliating against, and punishing environmental dissents. Here, the legal attacks are not solely launched by private actors (corporations

[31] Derek Turner, 'Monkeywrenching, Perverse Incentives and Ecodefence', (2006) 15 (2) *Environmental Values* 213.

[32] Kaniskha Jayasuriya (ed.), *Law, Capitalism and Power in Asia: The Rule of Law and Legal Institutions* (Routledge, 1999).

[33] Kaniskha Jayasuriya, 'Introduction', in K. Jayasuriya (ed.), *Law, Capitalism and Power in Asia: The Rule of Law and Legal Institutions* (Routledge, 1999) 6.

[34] ibid., 14.

or their associated actors) against other private actors (environmental activists or organisations) in environmental conflicts,[35] but, as the experiences of Southeast Asia and many Global South countries have shown, the state actively exercises those attacks. In Southeast Asia, the Asia Pacific Network of Environmental and the Center for Environmental Concerns Philippines state that '[t]he government which was supposed to protect its citizens has become a tool to protect profit-making interests. Therefore, impunity persists, and the attacks continue.'[36] Whatever the outcomes of the proceeding are, in any criminal punishment, as Foucault puts it, 'there must always be a portion that belongs to the prince [the state]'.[37] This is because the criminal justice system is defined by state agencies, which are responsible for criminalising conduct at the primary or secondary levels and running the penitentiary facilities.

Moreover, from the lens of HEL, researchers may moderate the expectation in what contexts anti-SLAPP provisions can have a positive effect in safeguarding environmental defenders and in what contexts those provisions are ineffective. To date, there has been a dominant optimistic view which embraces that enacting anti-SLAPP legal frameworks within the domestic legal system is foundational in preventing SLAPP.[38] This may be partly true if the state and its legal institutions work correctly, as assumed by liberal pluralist scholars for whom the state is a neutral agent whose duty is to strike a balance between conflicting rights within society. In the Global South, however, this assumption is not the case, and there, the state is, in fact, not reluctant to step in by repressing environmental struggles once the state-backed development agendas in the pursuit of economic growth are interfered with by those struggles. As noted by Katharina Pistor, the success or failure of an elected government no longer lies in the ability to distribute wealth and increase human development, but instead in the ability to maintain or even increase economic growth.[39] Thus, pursuing economic growth is part of the state agenda to maintain its political legitimacy.

This is not to mention countries which state institutions have been dominated by the interests of politico-business elites, such as Indonesia, Thailand, and the Philippines. The economic growth rate becomes not only the political legitimacy

[35] George W. Pring dan Penelope Canan, *SLAPPs: Getting Sued for Speaking Out* (Temple University Press, 1996); Fiona Donson, *Legal Intimidation* (Free Association Press, 2000); Thalia Anthony, 'Quantum of Strategic Litigation: Quashing Public Participation', (2009) 14 (2) *Australian Journal of Human Rights* 1; Nikhil Dutta, *SLAPP in the Global South: Features and Policy Responses* (International Center for Not-For-Profit Law, 2020); Byron Sheldrick, *Blocking Public Participation: The Use of Strategic Litigation to Silence Political Expression* (Wilfrid Laurier University Press, 2014).

[36] Asia Pacific Network of Environmental Defenders & Center for Environmental Concerns – Philippines, *Reclaiming the Narrative: The Struggles of Environmental Defenders in Five Countries in Southeast Asia* (Center for Environmental Concerns – Philippines, 2021) 105.

[37] Michael Foucault, *Discipline and Punish: The Birth of the Prison*, translated by Alan Sheridan (Vintage Books, 1995 [1977]) 48.

[38] Anthony (n 34); Sheldrick (n 33).

[39] Katharina Pistor, *The Code of Capital: How the Law Creates Wealth and Inequality* (Princeton University Press, 2019) 20.

for the elected government but also the veil of the continuous capital accumulation process for the business elites. Based on this assumption, any attempt to disrupt investment would be seen as a threat to the state in achieving the growth target; hence, it should be prevented or even sanctioned because it potentially leads to political failure for the elected government and economic failure for the business elites. By problematising the notion of the state and its legal embodiment, HEL will moderate or qualify our expectation that having anti-SLAPP provisions within an existing political-economic structure may have little effect when it comes to cases related to the extractive industries from which the continuation of the structure is relied upon.

Using the law to attack environmental defenders should be seen as strategic litigation by the alliance of powerful actors that serves two objectives: coercive and hegemonic functions. The coercive function aims at directly intimidating or even punishing targeted environmental defenders who are considered responsible for constraining and disrupting investment for extracting natural resources, infrastructure projects, or other commercial activities. The hegemonic function refers to creating externalities borne by environmental movements and the public. Through this function, the state sends a warning that they may face similar repression if they participate in the movements. The use of crimes against the public order and the state ideology and symbols also aims at creating a negative image of targeted environmental defenders and environmental movements in general, showing the public that environmental movements are built on selfish interests at the expense of the public interests, for example protecting land from being acquired for infrastructure projects that are claimed to benefit the general welfare. The conviction for crimes against the state ideology and symbols would portray environmental movements as potentially subversive groups seeking to topple the legitimate government and change the official state ideology. In some countries, such as the US, environmental groups (Earth First! or the Animal Liberation Front) have been targeted as internal terrorist groups,[40] and in the UK, Extinction Rebellion is regarded as an 'anarchist' group, a label that has nothing to do with the Anarchist ideology and movements, which aims to 'delegitimise them as enemies of social order' to justify state repression.[41]

In non-communist Southeast Asia, the fear of communism remains a standard narrative mobilised by the state. By labelling environmental defenders and environmental movements as communists, the state actor attempted to demonstrate to the public that although it has been prohibited, communism is still alive, and nowadays, it has infiltrated environmental movements. Expectedly, people will be suspicious of

[40] Adam Federman, 'Revealed: How the FBI Targeted Environmental Activists in Domestic Terror Investigation', *The Guardian* (London, 24 September 2019) <www.theguardian.com/us-news/2019/sep/23/revealed-how-the-fbi-targeted-environmental-activists-in-domestic-terror-investigations> accessed 3 February 2022.

[41] Oscar Berglund and Daniel Schmidt, *Extinction Rebellion and Climate Change Activism: Breaking the Law to Change the World* (Palgrave Macmillan, 2020) 10.

environmental movements and distance themselves from the movement if they do not want to be associated with communism.[42] This proves how the legacy of the Cold War has remained strong in the region and currently is strategically mobilised to discredit environmental movements. The politics of 'othering' environmental defenders and movements is a hegemonic element of HEL in containing environmental conflicts. This subjectivity transformation should be regarded as the fourth motive of legal actions against environmental defenders, besides the conflict transformation (transforming environmental conflicts into a legal dispute); the forum transformation (transforming the public forum to express an environmental dissent into an exclusive forum of the judiciary); and the issue transformation (transforming issues related to environmental injustices into a legal issue of defamation, tort, and others).[43]

Furthermore, the experience of Southeast Asia shows the limitation of the liberal stream, which conceives legal actions against environmental defenders as an attack on public participation. It implies that complex and rich motives of environmental struggles that are often related to the question of existence are reduced to exercising the right to petition or freedom of expression. Here, citizens are assumed to be autonomous agents who have equal access to shaping public policies through public participation when the government's policies or projects affect their interests. In unequal societies, social inequalities have led to asymmetric access to public participation. Due to the strong discourse on public participation, many states in the region have used it as a new technology for legitimacy but at the same time as a politics of exclusion by defining 'who can participate, how, and on what particular questions and issues at stake are contested and/or tightly controlled matters'.[44] Often, affected communities may be invited to a public consultation process. In a tokenistic forum, their attendance is needed to justify the claim of a 'participatory' decision-making process, but their concerns are disregarded from being considered. On other occasions, social groups identified as potential opponents to a proposed project are excluded from participating by not inviting them. Due to the lack of adequate formal mechanisms to express their grievances, they resort to other means, such as public pressure, demonstrations, and street protests, to make their voices heard. In highly escalated environmental conflicts, damaging and burning property owned by companies like fences or excavators should be seen as a consequence of the inabilities of the existing institutions (including political representation) and legal mechanisms to address people's grievances.

[42] Agung Wardana, 'The Risk of Protecting the Environment: Strategic Litigation against Public Participation (SLAPP) in Post-Authoritarian Indonesia', (2021) 22 *Policy Matters* 44; Global Witness, *Enemies of the State? How Governments and Business Silence Land and Environmental Defenders* (Global Witness, 2019) 7.

[43] Pring and Canan (n 33).

[44] Gary Rodan, *Participation without Democracy: Containing Conflict in Southeast Asia* (Cornell University Press, 2018) 3.

From the lens of HEL, empirical findings in Southeast Asia presented in the book pose a challenge to the foundation of SLAPP and anti-SLAPP frameworks. Given that the liberal stream regards legal actions on environmental defenders as an attack on the exercise of public participation, it has a narrow scope of what constitutes a legitimate exercise of public participation that deserves protection. In Australia, for instance, according to the 2008 Protection of Public Participation Act, the anti-SLAPP legislation, public participation does not include conduct that 'causes, or is reasonably likely to cause, physical injury or damage to property'.[45] As elaborated in the previous chapters, there are three events or moments where HEL is exercised: intentionally law-breaking acts of resistance (principled wrongdoings), trumped-up crimes, and acts of self-defence. Accordingly, disruptive forms of protests and eco-sabotage (as intentionally law-breaking acts of resistance) and acts of self-defence are not protected under the Australian anti-SLAPP framework. Moreover, anti-SLAPP frameworks in many countries rely on the rational choice to disincentive the exercise of SLAPP. In the Californian anti-SLAPP framework, for instance, providing mechanisms for environmental defenders to SLAPP back to demand financial compensation and the litigation cost is believed to prevent corporations from filing a SLAPP lawsuit against defenders considering its financial risk.[46] This rational choice perspective in the anti-SLAPP framework will only be effective if SLAPPs are filed by private actors, namely corporations, who calculate whether to resort to SLAPP based on the cost–benefit analysis. However, as attacks on environmental defenders in the Global South are mainly through the criminal justice system, the cost–benefit analysis is not applicable because the system runs on the state budget.

The Future Research Agenda

Indeed, this book has several limitations that may turn into insights for pursuing future research on HEL. As the arguments of the book are derived from the experiences of three Southeast Asian countries, generalisation needs to be treated cautiously. This may invite possibilities to test the central premise of the book in different jurisdictions beyond Southeast Asia to enrich current literature on transnational environmental law by taking the experiences and scholarship of the Global South as the focus. This is because, to date, the theme of SLAPP, not to mention HEL, is underexplored in the Transnational Environmental Law (TEL) scholarship. The book provides a new research agenda for transnational environmental law scholars to reveal the universality of this phenomenon and expose the inadequate responses of both the domestic legal system and international environmental law to address this alarming concern.

[45] Section 7 of Australia's 2008 Protection of Public Participation Act.

[46] Sheldrick (n 33).

In this context, HEL, borrowing Carlarne and Farber's words in the context of climate adaptation, should also be seen as 'a challenge that lies firmly within the realm of transnational environmental law'[47] for at least five reasons. First, HEL encompasses a transnational legal practice originated in the practice of SLAPP in the US spreading across the Global North and the Global South. Second, this practice cannot be neatly situated within public/private law dichotomies. It can be exercised through a private dispute involving two private parties, as conceived originally by the concept of SLAPP, and through the criminal law where environmental defenders are charged for committing criminal offences. Third, due to the absence of a global legal regime in protecting environmental defenders, environmental movements have advocated the incorporation of anti-SLAPP provisions in the domestic environmental law regime by adjusting US anti-SLAPP models as the benchmark. As a result, models of anti-SLAPP provisions differ from country to country in terms of not only their constitutional rights basis but also their scopes of applications. Thailand, for instance, focuses on qualifying the most common legal provision weaponised to attack environmental defenders in the country, which is criminal defamation. In terms of scope, Indonesia decides to confine the scope of the application of anti-SLAPP provision within the criminal and civil jurisdiction, while the Philippines widens the jurisdictional scope to include not only the criminal justice system and the civil procedure but also the administrative law procedure.

Moreover, attacks on environmental defenders utilising legal means should be approached through an interdisciplinary perspective to provide a comprehensive understanding. This is because it encompasses different legal fields of law beyond the traditional boundaries of environmental law, including constitutional law, criminal law, civil law, administrative law, and international law. This is not to mention the need to engage with other scholarship, namely criminology and political ecology, to illuminate studies on this phenomenon. Finally, the mode of resistance through regional coalition-building strategies has also demonstrated a transnational nature. In Southeast Asia, this can be seen by establishing the Asia Pacific Network on Environmental Defenders (APNED) as a transnational NGO to advocate for regional legal frameworks for the protection of environmental defenders once the domestic framework appears inadequate. In this regard, coalitions of environmental NGOs and Southeast Asia-based UN bodies have been working to establish regional frameworks to be imposed upon ASEAN member states, albeit the outcomes of this advocacy remain uncertain.

Moreover, Chapter 5 on externalities touches upon the gendered impacts of HEL to demonstrate how the consequences of HEL are experienced differently by environmental defenders and their families following the gendered lines that intersect with class, race, caste, and geographical relations. In this regard, it shows

[47] Cinnamon Carlarne and Daniel Farber, 'Law beyond Borders: Transnational Responses to Global Environmental Issues', (2012) 1 (1) *Transnational Environmental Law* 13, 20.

how women environmental defenders suffer differently from HEL both culturally and materially due to their vulnerable position in a patriarchal society. If male environmental defenders are convicted, this puts more burden on their wives to be responsible not only for providing a living for the family but also for ensuring their husband's well-being in prison. Nevertheless, the book does not manage to analyse systematically the gendered impacts of HEL in Southeast Asia because it is beyond the scope of this book. Therefore, this matter will be a promising research agenda to be pursued in the future by scholars interested in HEL. For this purpose, it may ask questions about how the existing political-economic structure in the Global South constrains and advances the agency of women environmental defenders in defending their environment and livelihoods and how their struggles are affected by the exercise of HEL by the state and corporations. This research agenda will enrich the literature and provide more comprehensive pictures of the increasing use of law to intimidate environmental defenders so that measures or strategies to resist it can be more effectively crafted.

INDEX

For EU product safety concerns, contact us at Calle de José Abascal, 56–1°, 28003 Madrid, Spain or eugpsr@cambridge.org.

www.ingramcontent.com/pod-product-compliance
Ingram Content Group UK Ltd.
Pitfield, Milton Keynes, MK11 3LW, UK
UKHW020811270926
475880UK00019B/197
* 9 7 8 1 0 0 9 6 7 6 6 4 9 *